To Joe:

The most loyal, generous law
student and R A I have ever had
the pleasure to know. You're a gem!

Mike Green

Bendectin and Birth Defects

Bendectin and Birth Defects

The Challenges of Mass Toxic Substances Litigation

Michael D. Green

University of Pennsylvania Press

Philadelphia

Library of Congress Cataloging-in-Publication Data

Green, Michael D., 1950–
    Bendectin and birth defects : the challenges of mass toxic
substances litigation / Michael D. Green.
        p.   cm.
    Includes bibliographical references and index.
    ISBN 0-8122-3257-7 (alk. paper)
    1. Products liability—Drugs—United States. 2. Toxic torts—
United States. 3. Complex litigation—United States.
4. Bendectin—Toxicology. 5. Abnormalities, Human. I. Title.
KF1297.D7G74 1996
346.7303'8—dc20   95-42306
[347.30638]   CIP

To my children,
ABBY, BRETT, and ROSS
for whom I am endlessly grateful

Contents

Preface

When Bendectin litigation first emerged, with allegations that it caused birth defects, I was a young law professor who was teaching—and learning—products liability law. I took notice of the litigation as well because a dear friend had suffered from severe morning sickness during her first pregnancy, and I knew that she had used Bendectin to help quell her nausea and vomiting. The emerging concerns about birth defects posed a quandary for me as to whether I should alert my friend about these developments during her next pregnancy. I chose the uncourageous path, consoling myself that I really didn't know whether there was any truth to the claims.

Later, in the mid-1980s, while working on a Products Liability casebook, I was reading Bendectin cases that reached conflicting outcomes, which further piqued my curiosity. How could these cases be resolved differently? What was the situation with regard to the evidence of Bendectin's connection with birth defects? The early stages of asbestos litigation had been characterized by similar differing results, and I decided that it might be interesting to investigate Bendectin litigation. I was lucky enough to have a job that permitted me to do so. Around that time, Peter Schuck published his splendid account of the Agent Orange litigation and that book served as a model for my effort. Schuck's work stands as a standard for an increasing number of in depth chronicles of prominent case congregations.

The difficulty with a case study such as this one is the extent to which that data point can usefully be extrapolated to understand the larger system or landscape from which the information is derived. Anecdotes are often misused, and the challenge of a case study such as this is to separate the useful from the spurious, the enlightening from the misleading, the sample from the idiosyncratic. While I'm not sure that I've succeeded in that effort, I have become persuaded of its importance as I've examined various phases of the Bendectin litigation. I leave it to the reader to examine critically my judgments on when to generalize and when not to do so.

This is a book about real cases, involving real lawyers, plaintiffs, and a pharmaceutical company. While the account is necessarily truncated, it attempts to detail and understand the people, motivations, and incentives that were in operation, against the backdrop of the civil justice system, tort law, and the sciences so critical to understanding the causes of disease. Among other goals, I hope the effort will provide data and information for others to examine and analyze in trying to understand how the law can best respond to the challenges posed by these combinations of modern technology and scientific uncertainty. Peter Schuck's book about the Agent Orange litigation furnished a wealth of information to those interested in mass toxic substances cases; I hope this book will make a similar contribution for those who continue to study the peculiar problems of these cases.

There are a number of dilemmas in writing an academic account of a major piece of modern litigation. One of the most difficult was to write this book so that it would be accessible to a variety of audiences, including interested non-lawyers, yet still provide insights and lessons for those familiar with the toxic substances litigation area. I may not have successfully walked the tightrope in the view of each reader, but I hope I've been able to provide enough for each to satisfy most who are willing to invest their time in this book.

Those familiar with tort law and its historical development will probably want to skip the initial portion of chapter 2. The latter portion of chapter 2 describes the emergence of mass toxic substances cases over the past several decades and will be familiar to some. Similarly, chapter 4, which describes the Food and Drug Administration and its regulation of prescription drugs, will not provide anything new to anyone conversant with that process. By contrast, chapter 15 attempts a rigorous legal examination of the trend to aggregate cases in mass torts and to tease out the implications of the experience with Bendectin litigation for that trend; non-lawyers may find modestly inaccessible that chapter and portions of chapter 17, which detail and analyze the courts' efforts to come to grips with the evidentiary threshold required of plaintiffs to demonstrate that the toxic agent they accuse caused their injuries. Thus, I hope that the core of this book will be accessible and useful to all, but some readers may find that omitting a chapter or two will facilitate the former goal, yet not compromise the latter.

Acknowledgments

This book would not have been possible without the assistance of a number of participants in the Bendectin litigation. Many at Marion Merrell Dow Inc., including W. Glenn Forrester, Alfred Schretter, and John Chewning, have patiently answered my many questions. Becky Young has tirelessly and with good humor responded to my requests for information and documents, even when I have requested the proverbial needle in a haystack. Frank Woodside, who represented Merrell in many of the Bendectin cases, has graciously responded to my inquiries. Richard Nolan and Doug Peters also willingly shared their experiences in the MER/29 and Bendectin cases, respectively, with me.

Many of the lawyers representing plaintiffs have literally opened their offices and files to me. Barry Nace, George Kokus, and Tom Bleakley all indulged my eccentric curiosity and permitted me to root through their files and make copies of documents that have been enormously helpful in understanding the motivations and conflicts that existed among the lawyers who represented plaintiffs, and especially the schism between the individualists and the aggregationists. Nace, Kokus, Bleakley and Arthur Tifford, Allen Eaton, James Butler, and Stanley Chesley spent many hours with me attempting to educate me about the Bendectin litigation, though I suspect that they, as well as those associated with Merrell, will feel that they were not entirely successful in their educational endeavors. Betty Mekdeci, the first Bendectin plaintiff, will no doubt share that view; nevertheless she provided me with invaluable insights into how the Bendectin litigation began and its early course of events.

Two judges who presided over Bendectin trials, Judge Thomas Jackson and Judge Carl Rubin, agreed to talk with me about the cases they tried and were far more candid about their views than I had any right to expect. Judge Rubin kindly paved the way for me to spend one of the most fascinating weekends of my life, in room 912 of the federal building in Cincinnati, a musty storage room. There I pored through six file cabinets containing the court documents in the consolidated Bendectin case over which Judge Rubin presided.

I have also been fortunate to have the benefit of discussions with many others who have contributed to the evolution of my thinking about the legal issues in Bendectin. Many have read and provided me with invaluable comments and criticism about various portions of earlier drafts of this book. If memory serves me, and it may not, those individuals include Ed Bell, Bert Black, Troyen Brennan, Bonnie Brier, Arthur Bryant, Trudy Burns, Marion Finkel, Marc Galanter, Steven Garber, Joe Gastwirth, Clay Gillette, Norman Gorin, Jim Hanson, Jim Henderson, Walter Hoffman, David Jung, David Kaye, Louis Lasagna, Leo Levin, David Levine, Rick Marcus, Mike Martin, Rick Matasar, Richard Merrill, James Morrison, Chris Mueller, Jennifer Niebyl, Paul Rheingold, Michael Saks, Bill Schultz, Craig Spangenberg, Shanna Swan, Harvey Teff, Roger Transgrud, Neil Vidmar, William Vodra, Carl Weiner, and Peter Wolf. Participants in a workshop at the University of London provided helpful comments. Two anonymous reviewers for the University of Pennsylvania Press supplied valuable suggestions for improving this book. Peter Schuck provided wise guidance and periodic moral support for this endeavor.

Several journalists who covered various aspects of the Bendectin litigation shared their thoughts and their coverage with me. They are Norman Gorin of *60 Minutes*, Ben Kaufman of the *Cincinnati Enquirer*, Davin Light of the *Orlando Sentinel Star*, and David Wright of the *National Enquirer*.

My greatest debt is to Joe Sanders, of the University of Houston, who shares my fascination with the Bendectin litigation. Over the years I have spent countless intriguing and insightful hours with him sharing ideas, theories, and details about various aspects of the litigation. He has unselfishly shared his work with me, and I count the strong friendship that we developed as one of the unexpected pleasures of this book. I could not have asked for a more constructive and critical reviewer of an earlier draft of this book than he provided. His thoughts, analysis, and research are so deeply imbedded in the fabric of this book that citation alone is wholly inadequate to reflect his contribution. In a few areas, he failed to persuade me of the errors of my ways; I remain responsible for the mistakes that remain.

I was also the beneficiary of outstanding research assistance from Brian Boysaw, Mark Schroeder, Michelle Busse, Jennifer Staley, Scott Lund, and Lyn Potts. Ted Olt's contributions to this book go beyond that of a research assistant. He has tirelessly tracked down arcane medical, public health, and legal materials, assisted me in analyzing them, and carefully reviewed the manuscript with an appreciation for the importance of rigor and precision that will make him a superb lawyer. My able secretary, Diana DeWalle, has uncomplainingly typed, retyped, formatted, and reformatted numerous drafts of this book with her customary attention to detail and correction of my errors. My Dean, N. William Hines, found the means to provide research support and release time to enable me to undertake and complete this work.

Finally, I would like to thank my wife, Carol, who has supported me at every turn, sacrificed to provide me the freedom to work on this project, and remained my best friend throughout. I cannot express the depth of my gratitude to her with words.

Chapter 1
A Birth Defect Child Is Born

David Mekdeci was born on March 22, 1975. As was immediately evident to those in the delivery room, including his mother, he was one of the approximately five percent of babies born with a birth defect. David's right forearm was shortened, he was missing two fingers from his right hand, he had limited use of two other fingers, and his hand was malformed. Missing pectoral muscles in his chest left him with diminished ability to move his right arm and a concave chest that appeared deformed. Later in his life, concerns were raised about a congenital heart defect.[1]

David was born to an unexceptional middle-class family in Orlando, Florida. His father, Michael, was a guidance counselor in the Orlando school system, and his mother, Betty, then 33 years old, was a free-lance copywriter and producer of television commercials. The Mekdecis had one other child, Christy, born three and a half years earlier, whose birth had been uneventful.

David Mekdeci's conception had been carefully planned, in part because Betty Mekdeci had previously had a miscarriage. The Mekdecis had decided that three years was the optimal spacing between children, and in the early summer of 1974, Betty Mekdeci, consistent with her compulsive tendencies, began charting her basal temperature to hone in on the date of ovulation. She became pregnant shortly thereafter, early in July 1974.

Shortly after becoming pregnant, Betty Mekdeci began suffering from morning sickness, a common affliction for pregnant women. Although the morning sickness was limited to nausea, it was severe, continual, and left her, as she later described it, feeling seasick. After having her pregnancy confirmed and arranging an appointment with a new obstetrician,

Mrs. Mekdeci called the obstetrician's office, explained that she had her first appointment in two weeks, reported on her morning sickness, and inquired if there was anything that could be done to alleviate her discomfort. The nurse with whom she spoke told her that a prescription would be telephoned to her pharmacist, and on August 1, 1974 Betty Mekdeci joined millions of other pregnant women and took her first two Bendectin pills. Although she substituted dramamine for two days because she felt that the Bendectin was not alleviating her morning sickness, she returned to Bendectin and continued to take it into November, when her nausea subsided.

In addition to morning sickness, Betty Mekdeci suffered a number of other common illnesses during her pregnancy. Aggressive about seeking medical care, she was prescribed Actifed (an antihistamine and decongestant) for hay fever allergies, Hemocyte, an iron supplement, Erythromycin (an antibiotic) for a cold, Mycostatin and Mycolog, two topical drugs, for vaginal itching, and Penbritin (a type of penicillin) and Azo Gantrisin (an antifungal agent) for cystitis (a bladder infection). She also purchased an over-the-counter vitamin supplement, Natabec, which she began taking when she realized that she was pregnant. Prescriptions for a number of other drugs were written for her during this period, but not taken.

Among the emotions and reactions by parents of a child born with birth defects is the urge to understand why. As George Kokus, the Mekdecis' lawyer, told a jury four years later, "Michael asked why; Betty asked why. God's will? Was it genetic or was it caused by something in the environment, either in the air or ingested? The answer to that question led to us being here today." [2]

The pursuit of that question consumed Betty Mekdeci for several years after David's birth. Betty Mekdeci is an unusual individual: imbued with a strong intellect and an equal confidence in it, and an intense and spirited persona. Outspoken and candid, her skeptical nature was refined by her experience while employed in the advertising industry. Her voice resonates with a tinge of a southern accent that evidences her Tennessee rearing in a conservative Republican family.

The inquiry into the source of David's birth defects led naturally to the question of the etiologic role of the drugs that Betty Mekdeci had taken during pregnancy. Betty Mekdeci was among those shocked and horrified when the revelation of the tragic consequences of thalidomide were revealed a decade earlier. She recalled the most severely deformed children, some born without limbs or with flipper-like limbs. The latter condition was known as phocomelia, drawn from the Greek "phoke," meaning seal and "melia," meaning limbs. David Mekdeci's hospital record identified his birth defect—incorrectly—as phocomelia.

The day before David's fifth birthday, March 21, 1980, a jury in federal court in Orlando awarded Michael and Betty Mekdeci $20,000 in their lawsuit against Merrell National Laboratories, the manufacturer of the Bendectin that Betty Mekdeci had taken during her pregnancy.[3] Thus began Bendectin litigation, which involved several thousand claims by children with birth defects and their families. After over fifteen years in courthouses throughout the United States, Bendectin litigation is just coming to a close.

Notes

1. The account of David Mekdeci's birth, his family, and the drugs that Betty Mekdeci took during her pregnancy is drawn from Depositions and Trial Testimony of Elizabeth Mekdeci, Mekdeci v. Merrell National Laboratories, No. 77-255-Orl-Civ-Y (M.D. Fla. Jan. 12, Jan. 18, and Apr. 12, 1978, July 3, 1979, and Feb. 5–6, 1980), which together comprise 960 transcribed pages and the documentary exhibits thereto; Interview with Elizabeth Mekdeci (Dec. 28, 1989).

2. Transcript of Trial at Vol. 4, p. 5, Mekdeci v. Merrell National Laboratories (M.D. Fla. Jan. 24, 1980).

3. The jury awarded nothing to David, an inconsistency that signaled a compromise verdict by the jury, which had been deadlocked for a week. *See* chapter 6.

Chapter 2
Locating Bendectin Within the Mass Toxic Landscape

Introduction

The lawsuit that the Mekdecis brought against Merrell was a tort action, although it fell within a subspecies of tort known as products liability. Products liability addresses the obligations of manufacturers of products when consumers suffer personal injury. Tort law is more general, covering suits for wrongful injury that do not arise from a contract between the parties. Over the past three decades, products liability has evolved and grown to the point where it plays a major role in the civil liability arena. Within products liability, *Mekdeci v. Merrell National Laboratories* was a toxic substance case—different from most products liability cases because the injuries involved were not sudden and traumatically induced, but rather the result of slowly developing disease or developmental anomaly. The boundaries of tort law are wide and fuzzy, but plainly encompass accidental injuries such as David Mekdeci suffered. When a person suffers personal injury or property damage at the hands of another and there is no contract between them governing their respective rights, tort law provides the governing body of rules that determines who will be responsible for the loss.[1] A wide variety of actions, activities, and harms fall within this legal universe: automobile accidents, professional malpractice, defamation, assault and battery, environmentally induced personal injury, and fraud. At times tort and criminal law may overlap: a wrong may be privately remedied in a civil suit and prosecuted by a representative of the state in a criminal action.

Five essential elements must be present for a plaintiff to establish a prima facie (legally supportable) tort claim that is submissible to a jury. The first two require the plaintiff to show that the defendant has a legally enforceable duty to the plaintiff and through its conduct breached that duty. In addition, the plaintiff must prove three additional elements: 1) that he or she suffered some cognizable injury; and that the defendant's breach of duty was the 2) factual and 3) legal cause of that injury. Thus five elements—duty, breach of duty, factual and legal cause, and injury—are necessary conditions for a plaintiff to succeed in a tort suit. Affirmative defenses that relieve the defendant from liability also exist; two of the most prominent in tort suits have been contributory negligence by the plaintiff[2] and the statute of limitations, which bars suits that are brought after a specified period has elapsed.

The Development and Goals of Tort Law

Although the basic elements of a tort claim have remained constant, the tort system of several centuries ago would be quite unfamiliar to us today. Indeed, tort did not emerge as a separate body of law until the nineteenth century, and was no more than "a twig on the great tree of law"[3] until the twentieth century. Personal injury lawsuits played virtually no role in a society in which agriculture and land played dominant roles. Interactions between strangers were uncommon and the engines that fueled industrialization (and wreaked their havoc on those unfortunates who got in the way) were yet to be developed. Society was no better off healthwise, indeed it was considerably worse off, but the causes of death, illness, and injury were largely the result of natural sources rather than human-developed technology and societal interactions. Strict liability—imposed when the defendant's conduct "caused" the plaintiff's injury—was largely the liability rule applied to those activities and harms that the courts recognized in tort, a considerably limited class of cases.

The mid-nineteenth century was heavily influenced by the emergence of the railroad, surely one of the most important technological developments in the history of the human race. As the number of incidents causing injury grew and the scope of injuries that the courts recognized expanded, movement toward a fault-based rule of law developed. "[T]he modern negligence principle in tort law seems to have been an intellectual response to the increased number of accidents involving persons who had no preexisting relationship with one another—'stranger' cases."[4] Some historians have hypothesized that the movement away from strict liability in the late nineteenth century was for the purpose of aiding the development of fledgling industry.[5] Enterprise liability developments in the latter half of the twentieth century provide a sharp counterpoint to the pro-industry explanation of tort law at the turn-of-the-century period.

The tort law that was being developed during this period was judge-made "common law." Cases determining the appropriate standard of liability, or adopting a rule that a plaintiff could not recover if her fault also contributed to the injury, the "fellow-servant" rule that barred an employee from recovering from his employer where the injury was due to the fault of a coemployee, and the assumption of risk defense that barred recovery when a person voluntarily encountered a known risk were all crafted by judges acting in the common law tradition. It is worth observing that this early period was largely characterized by rules of tort law that left the loss with the injured party. Mark Twain, with his incisive version of sarcasm, captured this state of affairs in the novel *The Gilded Age* that he wrote with Charles Warner. A horrible steamboat disaster kills over twenty people, with over a hundred missing or injured. An investigation is mounted to find who is to blame, but the outcome is the same everyone had been accustomed to "all the days of our lives—'NOBODY TO BLAME.' " [6]

By the early twentieth century, fault—expressed as negligence—had captured the day. American courts resisted the British movement toward pockets of strict liability and adopted a duty standard that required a plaintiff to prove negligence—a failure to exercise reasonable care—on the part of the defendant in order to recover damages. At the same time, some areas were identified for special treatment. In the workplace, there was dissatisfaction with the fate of the injured worker in obtaining compensation through the tort system because of the fellow-servant rule and the assumption-of-risk defense. This concern resulted in the passage of workers' compensation statutes that provided a guaranteed payment for all those injured in the workplace, but at a diminished level from the damages afforded by the common law tort system. Thus the workers' compensation system provided a no-fault system, designed to serve a compensatory function for injured workers, that obviated the need to inquire into the employer's breach of duty or fault-based affirmative defenses.

After Upton Sinclair's exposé of the meat industry in *The Jungle*, federal law was enacted in 1906 to oversee the purity of foodstuffs and drugs sold to the public. By contrast with tort law, which indirectly provides incentives for safety by imposing liability ex post, regulatory provisions attempt to facilitate this goal in a more direct way. For over fifty years, the Food and Drug Administration (FDA) has required drug manufacturers to prove the safety of their drugs before they can be marketed. Similar agencies were established later in the twentieth century to regulate risk and safety in a variety of other areas of commercial activity, including the Consumer Product Safety Commission, the Environmental Protection Agency, the Federal Aviation Administration, and the National Highway and Transportation Safety Agency. These regulatory agencies, like worker's compensation, serve one of several tort goals—

the control of risk—in a more direct fashion than the liability incentives provided by tort law.

Thus the tort system is but one of many societal mechanisms for coping with accidental injury by providing compensation to its victims, incentives for those who create risk to reduce it to an optimal level, and a means to allocate the losses to the appropriate spheres of activity.[7] The mix of systems in existence in the United States is not universal: New Zealand adopted a universal compensation scheme (financed by general tax revenues) for all injury victims, and most European countries rely on a more aggressive system of regulation in conjunction with strong social welfare programs rather than on the tort system. One of the most controversial issues of the current tort system is the extent to which the tort system should defer to regulatory determinations when the latter has made a conscious choice about the appropriate level of safety.[8]

Aside from tort law as an instrument for compensation, providing incentives for safety, and loss allocation, it serves a retributive justice function, one that rather than being instrumental (serving to foster some other purpose) is an end in itself. This view of tort law, which is often characterized as "corrective justice," focuses simply on the two parties involved in the incident and inquires whether wrongdoing on the part of the injurer requires that she repay the victim for the invasion of the injured party's rights occasioned by the wrongdoer's acts. Related to this corrective justice perspective is the tort system providing an aggrieved victim a civilized and fair forum in which to pursue his grievance and seek recompense rather than resorting to more primitive and violent means.

This intuitive and philosophical ground for tort law often stands in sharp counterpoint to the instrumental vision set forth previously, but nevertheless continues to play a role in contemporary tort law. Thus tort law can maximize incentives for safety in industrial machinery accidents by imposing the loss on the manufacturers of the machines. Those manufacturers—profit-making entities that plan and respond to their (legal) environment—should rationally take all cost-effective steps to improve the safety of their machines, by adding additional guards, providing fail-safe mechanisms to prevent unintended cycling, and similar steps. Of course, the likelihood of injury is a function not simply of the safety investment by the manufacturer, but also of the prudence of the operator. Yet tort law will have little or no influence on the behavior of individual victims; machine operators take precautions because of the fear of the consequences of an accident: the loss of a limb, pain, disability, etc. Yet, if the accident is the result of foolish or imprudent behavior by the operator, corrective justice would mandate that at least some of the loss be borne by her. Thus, while instrumentalism might call for imposing the entire loss on the manufacturer, corrective justice may conflict with that assessment. Although the instrumental school of tort law is in the ascendancy, it would be a mistake to ignore the continuing influence of corrective justice on the current tort system. Tort law continues to reflect contemporary notions of blameworthiness and rough justice, regardless of the theoretical instrumental models employed, if for no other reason than the leavening influence of the jury on tort law.

The Intellectual Foundations and Doctrinal Development of Products Liability

One of the key developments that set the stage for the modern development of products liability law was the overturning of the rule that limited a manufacturer's obligations to those persons who had directly purchased the product from the seller. Judges had imposed this "privity of contract" requirement in the nineteenth century after recoiling at the virtually unlimited liability to which manufacturers would be exposed if anyone harmed by their stagecoach wheels collapsing or their coffee urns exploding were permitted to sue.

The privity of contract requirement insulated most manufacturers from suit by consumers where intermediate distributors existed. When the privity requirement was swept away in a seminal decision by Judge Cardozo in *MacPherson v. Buick Motor Co.*,[9] in 1916, the potential liability of product manufacturers was greatly expanded. With *MacPherson*, the framework for the development of modern products liability law began. Henceforth manufacturers would owe a duty of due care to all who might foreseeably be harmed by the use of the product.[10]

The change in tort law during the second half of the twentieth century has been even more revolutionary. Strict products liability and its theoretical enterprise liability underpinnings dramatically reconceptualized the tort landscape. Developments in other tort areas—medical malpractice, for instance—considerably eased the burdens on injured claimants attempting to recover for their losses. The eased burdens made successful prosecution easier, thereby attracting more claimants. Juries became comfortable awarding six and seven figure verdicts to plaintiffs with serious injuries. Punitive damages became an important weapon in the personal injury lawyer's arsenal.

It would be a mistake to attribute this development to any one source—a number of threads were operating that contributed to this reformation. In the larger political and social realm, the New Deal and the rise of the welfare state contributed to the idea of shifting responsibility for risk from individuals to the government and larger social institutions. Stoicism and suffering were out; government and law had a far more activist role to play in fostering the collective welfare, especially for those with special needs.[11]

In the legal academy, the writings of a small coterie provided the intellectual foundations.[12] Fleming James of Yale Law School emphasized and championed risk distribution as a goal of the tort system; the enterprise responsible for personal injuries should compensate injured individuals, thereby providing a form of social insurance. Professor George Priest credits Friedrich Kessler, a German-trained lawyer who taught at Yale for thirty years, with the contribution that free markets, specifically ones with unequal bargaining power, pose a dangerous threat to democracy. That idea led to a powerful distrust for freedom of contract, an important ingredient in the hegemony of tort law in the products liability field, where consumers are in a contractual relationship with those supplying goods. By contrast, in most tort cases the parties are strangers, and no opportunity exists for a contractual allocation of risks in advance. As currently formulated, strict products liability imposes obligations on manufacturers independent of, and more demanding than, any express agreement between buyer and seller and does not permit the manufacturer to obtain a waiver of tort liability from the individual consumer.

While a small group of academics were thinking and writing about the expansion of tort liability, one of their fellow intellectual travelers who was a justice on the California Supreme Court and former faculty member at the Berkeley Law School, Roger Traynor, began a crusade for imposing strict liability on manufacturers in 1944. In a now-famous concurring opinion, Traynor articulated the risk spreading rationale that would influence many courts and scholars over the next quarter century:

> Those who suffer injury from defective products are unprepared to meet its consequences. The cost of an injury and the loss of time or health may be an overwhelming misfortune to the person injured, and a needless one, for the risk of injury can be insured by the manufacturer and distributed among the public as a cost of doing business. It is to the public interest to discourage the marketing of products having defects that are a menace to the public. If such products nevertheless find their way into the market it is to the public interest to place the responsibility for whatever injury they may cause upon the manufacturer, who, even if he is not negligent in the manufacture of the product, is responsible for its reaching the market. However intermittently such injuries may occur and however haphazardly they may strike, the risk of their occurrence is a constant risk and a general one. Against such a risk there should be general and constant protection and the manufacturer is best situated to afford such protection.[13]

Traynor, however, was unable at the time to persuade any of his fellow Justices on the California Supreme Court to adopt this change. Nevertheless, his clarion call would influence incremental changes through the 1950s in extending strict liability to foodstuffs and other products, such as perfume, that were used in intimate contact with the body.

The early 1960s were the years of most dramatic doctrinal changes in the courts. In 1960, in *Henningsen v. Bloomfield Motors, Inc.*, the New Jersey Supreme Court echoed Justice Traynor's ideas and held that a car manufacturer could be liable for injuries caused by a defect in the car, without proof of negligence, and despite a contractual disclaimer of any implied warranty and a written limitation that excluded liability for personal injury. The court wrote:

> [T]he burden of losses consequent upon use of defective articles is borne by those who are in a position to either control the danger or make an equitable distribution of the losses when they do occur. . . .
>
> • • •
>
> Accordingly, we hold that under modern marketing conditions, when a manufacturer puts a new automobile in the stream of trade and promotes its purchase by the public, an implied warranty that it is reasonably suitable for use as such accompanies it into the hands of the ultimate purchaser.[14]

The *Henningsen* decision was grounded in contract law—through the vehicle of adopting an implied warranty that the seller could not disclaim. That mandate, which is virtually indistinguishable from the legally imposed obligations of tort law, is a far cry from the consensual notions that underlie contract law. Thus, although the agreement between the parties excluded liabilities, the court imposed an obligation on the manufacturer that could not be bargained around. And so it was only a short step for tort law to impose a similar obligation.

The same year as *Henningsen*, William Prosser, then the Dean of the University of California at Berkeley Law School and one of the leading commentators of the day on tort law, wrote an important article entitled *The Assault upon the Citadel (Strict Liability to the Consumer)*. He catalogued the developments removing barriers to imposing liability on manufacturers, thereby expanding the scope of seller's liability, and outlining a strict tort liability action for consumers who are injured due to a defect in a product.[15] Prosser added to the risk distribution ground three additional arguments on behalf of a strict tort liability regime: 1) contemporary public sentiment valued highly the protection of human health and safety; the law should reflect the polity in providing protection from dangers in products; 2) modern advertising and marketing techniques created an impression that products were both fit and safe for use by consumers purchasing them; and 3) contract and warranty law, which might otherwise impose the same result as strict tort liability, were fraught with technical aspects that might frustrate the goal or make it unnecessarily expensive to achieve.[16]

In 1963 Justice Traynor finally persuaded a majority of his colleagues on the California Supreme Court to impose strict tort liability on the manufacturer of a Shopsmith, which could be used as a variety of power tools. While the purchaser's husband was using the Shopsmith as a lathe, set screws that were inadequate to hold the wood stock in place gave way and the wood flew out of the machine, hit the plaintiff in the head, and caused serious injuries.

Rejecting both contract law and fault-based tort notions, which the defendant argued should govern its liability, Justice Traynor wrote:

A manufacturer is strictly liable in tort when an article he places on the market, knowing that it is to be used without inspection for defects, proves to have a defect that causes injury to a human being.
　　　　•　•　•
The purpose of such liability is to insure that the costs of injuries resulting from defective products are borne by the manufacturers that put such products on the market rather than by the injured persons who are powerless to protect themselves.[17]

In the following year, 1964, the influential American Law Institute adopted section 402A of the second Restatement of Torts. Not surprisingly, with Prosser as the reporter for the Restatement, section 402A reflected the strict tort provision outlined by him in his 1960 *Assault upon the Citadel* article. The revolution was complete: by 1966, Prosser could publish an article entitled *The Fall of the Citadel (Strict Liability to the Consumer)*,[18] in which he catalogued (if a bit inflatedly and overenthusiastically) the courts that had adopted strict products liability.

The remainder of the 1960s and much of the 1970s saw widespread acceptance of expanded manufacturer liability.[19] During this period, many jurisdictions enlarged the areas to which this new strict liability applied. As with virtually all tort law, products liability is a creature of state common law. This means that each state judiciary has the power to shape its own law, creating the possibility of variations and inconsistency. It also means that judges and courts, rather than legislatures, are the primary institution making this law.

But the widespread acceptance of strict liability did not end the lawmaking process. The concept of a "defect"—a requirement that distinguishes strict liability from absolute liability (i.e., all harm caused by the product)—would require fleshing out. The courts of most states struggled to give content to the defect element of strict tort liability. Decisions distinguished three different kinds of "defects": manufacturing flaws, design, and warning defects. A manufacturing flaw is a defect that is unintended by the manufacturer. These defects represent a failure of the quality control process. Relatively rare, manufacturing flaws provide no conceptual difficulties and liability is imposed unqualifiedly if there is proof the product's deviation from the norm caused injury. By contrast, a design defect is a claim that the product should have been constructed in a different, and safer, manner than that chosen by the manufacturer. Failure-to-warn claims assert that the seller provided inadequate information about risks or safe use of the product. Since the manufacturer almost always has superior knowledge of product-related risks, the warning obligation has played a major role in products liability cases over the past quarter century. Its comparative ease for plaintiffs— it does not require as extensive reliance on experts as design defects claims—has contributed to its vogue among plaintiffs' lawyers.

The obligation of a manufacturer to provide information about adverse side effects plays the dominant role in the drug liability field. Drugs can only rarely be designed to be safer, and the courts have not been sympathetic to the claim that an alternative drug or vaccine employed for the same therapeutic purpose but which poses less danger makes the former drug defective and subjects the manufacturer to liability.[20]

The obligation to warn of dangers in the pharmaceutical context is a derivative of the concept of informed consent. Individuals should be afforded full information about the benefits and risks of a medical procedure or treatment and as autonomous human beings make the choice about whether to undergo the procedure. Thus the legal obligation of a drug manufacturer is to inform of all risks that a reasonable person would desire to know about in making an informed decision whether to use the drug. Of course, the prescription decision is made by a physician, by design in consultation with the patient. Thus the obligation is to inform the physician of these risks. The predominant rule is that the manufacturer is only obligated to warn of dangers of which it has knowledge or should have knowledge (an "objective" standard). However, as an entity that operates in a specialized field, it should take appropriate steps (both in its own research and in remaining informed about others' research) to be informed of the forefront of scientific knowledge.

There are a number of subtleties and nuances to the warning obligations,[21] but they would play almost no role in Bendectin litigation. Similarly, alternative legal theories for recovery often asserted, such as negligence, breach of implied warranty, recklessness, and fraud, did not affect the crux of the liability issues in Bendectin litigation. The essential products liability issues in the cases that emerged would be whether Bendectin caused teratogenic effects in the offspring of women who took it (causation) and if so, whether the manufacturer had failed in its obligation to warn of the teratogenic effects.

Perhaps as important as the doctrinal developments in the tort revolution has been a shift in societal attitudes about the acceptability of risk, control of risk, and responsibility for risk, which help explain at least some of the expansion of liability[22] and upward movement in tort damages over the past several decades. This phenomenon, difficult to document or describe in its precise contours, is exemplified by the $125 million jury verdict for punitive damages (and $3 million in compensatory damages) in the Ford Pinto case in 1978 in California.[23] Public concern about the invisible dangers of toxic substances is particularly acute.[24] At least in part this is the result of the lack of choice in confronting most of the imperceptible risks of exposure to toxic substances. The effect of increased affluence on social attitudes about and responses to risk, safety, and health is evidenced in other spheres as well. The 1960s and 1970s saw a major expansion of governmental regulatory programs in the occupational, consumer, and environmental safety spheres[25] that very much parallel the increasing prominence of tort law on the contemporary legal scene.

Toxic Substances and Tort Law

To locate the Mekdecis' suit (and Bendectin litigation more generally) on the products liability map requires mention of the emergence of toxic substances litigation. Again, technological advances fueled this development: first with the emergence of the asbestos industry in the late nineteenth century to provide asbestos insulating materials for the engines, machinery, and ships of the industrial revolution. This "miracle mineral," as *Scientific American* proclaimed it in a cover story in 1881, would later cause an enormous toll of debilitating respiratory disease, cancer, and death among hundreds of thousands of victims. Later the chemical, pharmaceutical, and medical device industries produced Agent Orange, DES, the Dalkon Shield IUD, and other lesser known agents that cause (or are alleged to cause) insidious disease rather than the skull fracture suffered by Mr. Greenman when his Shopsmith failed.

Some scattered toxic substances litigation had taken place before asbestos litigation burst onto the scene in the 1970s and rapidly expanded. Several smoking victims brought suit against cigarette manufacturers in the late 1950s and early 1960s, but were singularly unsuccessful. Plaintiffs who believed that benzene had caused their leukemia also sued, again without any notable success. The anti-cholesterol drug MER/29 produced several hundred lawsuits in the 1960s.[26]

The first mass toxic substances litigation involved asbestos and had its genesis with an important decision by the Fifth Circuit Court of Appeals in 1973, which upheld the first asbestos plaintiff's jury award—a modest $60,000 verdict for the widow of a deceased insulation worker.[27] Judge John Minor Wisdom wrote a lengthy opinion that provided a roadmap of many of the legal issues that would arise for future asbestos plaintiffs. Significantly, Judge Wisdom made it plain that manufacturers had a legal obligation to conduct adequate research into the risks posed by their products, a proposition courts had not embraced a generation earlier.[28] Because of the widespread use of asbestos (thousands of marine, industrial, and home products from brake linings to ceiling tile to textiles to lamp sockets incorporated it) and its toxicity, within ten years over twenty thousand asbestos plaintiffs[29] had brought suit and twenty years later over a hundred thousand cases had emerged.[30]

Both the Agent Orange and the Dalkon Shield litigation involved huge numbers of potential claimants, but neither one proliferated as asbestos did. Agent Orange litigation by Vietnam veterans exposed to herbicides containing small amounts of dioxin was confined to a class action consisting of 600,000 veterans and their families. The case took on the role of a metaphor for the treatment of Vietnam veterans after the war, a role that made the lawsuit enormously emotional and consequently even more difficult to resolve than the numerous knotty liability and causation issues might have dictated. The defendants had produced Agent Orange for the government, which itself was shielded from tort liability to the veterans,[31] in its wartime effort, and defendants claimed they should share the government's immunity. Because the veterans in the class came from all fifty states, fifty different state laws might have been employed in resolving the class liability claims against defendants. Various state statutes of limitations would have to be interpreted and applied, with the possibility of tolling (extending the time frame in which to bring suit) during the period before a veteran knew he suffered from injury. Finally, causation was exceedingly problematical for a variety of reasons: 1) there was no way to distinguish the Agent Orange manufactured by each defendant, yet the dioxin contamination varied by an order of magnitude among them; 2) scanty information existed about most veterans' exposure to Agent Orange while serving in Vietnam and the extent of any exposure; and 3) the scientific evidence on Agent Orange's capacity to cause any or all of the variety of maladies asserted by the members of the class ranged from solid (in one case) to flimsy to absent. Yet the legal and factual issues that made the case virtually unmanageable never fully saw the light of day in a courtroom because of the class-wide settlement of $180 million that Judge Jack Weinstein, one of the preeminent federal trial judges, crafted in 1984 through his determined efforts.[32]

The Dalkon Shield litigation, which also involved hundreds of thousands of claimants from among the 2.2 million women who had the Shield implanted, was largely resolved in a single bankruptcy proceeding. Individual cases had been litigated since 1974 against The A.H. Robins Pharmaceutical Company, but by the 1980s evidence of corporate wrongdoing and fraud had emerged that led to a bevy of punitive damages awards that threatened the financial viability of the company. Robins entered bankruptcy court voluntarily in 1985, and a plan to permit injured women to choose an administrative compensation scheme instead of litigation was implemented in 1989.[33]

Both the asbestos and the Dalkon Shield cases were initiated by individual plaintiff's attorneys taking on, in David and Goliath fashion, major companies or industries with enormous financial resources to resist the poorly financed, understandably ignorant plaintiff's attorneys. The civil discovery process, which provides access to documents controled by the opponent and allows oral examination of witnesses under oath, was their best hope of obtaining information that would reveal whether their clients had meritorious claims and, if so, provide the evidence to enable their clients to prevail. The persistence of a few attorneys, motivated by the potential for future clients if the early cases were successful, and the fortuity that a few of the early claims were successful, thereby providing financing for future cases, enabled the attorneys to expand their efforts at discovering additional information from the defendants that would strengthen the plaintiffs' cases. In asbestos litigation, plaintiffs' lawyers obtained more and more memoranda, correspondence, scientific studies, and testimony of industry officials that demonstrated the industry's awareness of the hazards of asbestos and their acts to suppress that information. The pattern of corporate misbehavior revealed in the Dalkon Shield IUD cases so influenced juries that multi-million dollar punitive damages became routine once the evidence was finally discovered in Robins's files and brought into court.[34]

The drug DES (diethystilbesterol) was prescribed for pregnant women to improve the chances of a healthy delivery. A generation later physicians found that it caused adenosis (abnormal gland development) and vaginal adenocarcinoma (a form of cancer) in the female offspring of women who took the drug. Genitourinary defects have been found in male offspring, and recently suits have been filed alleging that third generation offspring were harmed by the DES taken by their grandmothers. Since the 1970s, several thousand DES victims have sued dozens of pharmaceutical companies in suits scattered across the country.[35]

In addition to the mass victim toxic substances cases, numerous cases have been brought involving a single individual, small group, or modestly larger coterie of alleged victims of toxic substances. Sometimes this results from the occupational exposure of an employee, sometimes it results from the exposure of a neighborhood to radiation or the escape of hazardous waste from a site at which it had been disposed.[36] Many of these cases are not products liability cases, because the seller of the product is not involved, but they nevertheless have at their core a similarity with the products liability toxic substances cases catalogued above—insidious disease that may be the result of exposure to a chemical agent.

Any attempt to organize and categorize has its limitations: categories are not inherent qualities of nature, but human attempts to systemize and impose order on information so as to be able to examine, analyze, and make sense of what would otherwise be masses of disaggregated facts. The utility of categorization and generalization should not obscure its limitations: often there are important differences among those items grouped together; one must always guard against over- and undergeneralization in the organizational process. With that caveat, there are a number of common threads to the toxic substances cases outlined above. Moreover, there is every reason to believe that society and the legal system will face toxic substances cases in the future and that many of the lessons learned from existing cases can be put to productive use in those future ones.

The one defining characteristic of toxic substances cases is the existence of insidious disease—slowly developing disease or personal injury that often cannot be detected until it manifests itself in the form of a cancer, neurotoxic effect, birth defect, or other organic disease. Concomitant with insidious disease are lengthy latency periods from exposure to the agent until disease manifestation that vary from months to many decades. Some asbestotic diseases have latency periods as long as fifty years. While many known teratogens have latency periods in the range of several months (because the delivery mechanism is transfer from mother to fetus during gestation), many congenital defects are not evident at birth and may not be clinically diagnosable for several years.

Long latency periods and poor understanding of the pathological mechanisms by which insidious disease develops make identifying causal relationships a difficult, lengthy, complex, accretive, contentious, and uncertain enterprise. Those difficulties and uncertainties of determining causation are the single largest challenge (and second defining characteristic) that toxic substances litigation poses for the legal system. Existing methodologic limitations make identification possible only for toxins that have a relatively strong effect, which enables that effect to be distinguished from background (unknown) causes of the same disease.[37] Yet, because of the legal requirement that the defendant's conduct or product cause the plaintiff's injury, this issue is one that the tort system cannot avoid. Because of the need for scientific expertise in resolving these causal questions, expert witnesses in a variety of scientific disciplines, both clinical and research, are pervasive in toxic substances litigation. Expert witnesses in theory provide the science that assists the jury in resolving a case, but pose the difficulty of accommodating the very different cultures of law and science, especially in the clash between the law's adversary system and science's open and unbiased inquiry. Chapter 3 elaborates on the science of determining the causes of insidious diseases, its limitations, and applications in the courtroom.

A third important characteristic is that many toxic agents are sufficiently pervasive that large numbers of individuals are exposed, often spanning wide temporal and geographical ranges. As a result, litigation may involve large numbers of potential plaintiffs scattered over many jurisdictions (though often disproportionately) and spread out over years or decades. Asbestos is the largest and most prominent example of this dispersed mass tort litigation. The litigation has imposed such enormous demands on the judiciary that Judge Edward Becker of the United States Court of Appeals for the Third Circuit characterized it, with some hyperbole, as "the most serious crisis the federal court system has faced in its history." [38] Chapter 15 considers efforts to use a variety of aggregative procedures to facilitate resolution of mass toxic litigations.

Another characteristic of mass toxics is that they threaten major impact on some of the largest and most successful financial entities of twentieth-century America. Johns-Manville was a building products company ranked 181 in the Fortune 500 of industrial corporations when asbestos litigation forced it into bankruptcy court.[39] Several other major companies that manufactured asbestos followed Johns-Manville into bankruptcy court. The A.H. Robins Company was a major pharmaceutical company with over a half billion dollars of sales in the early 1980s when the Dalkon Shield litigation came to a head. Modern tort law thus plays an important role for corporate management, insurers, shareholders, and the attorneys hired to defend them, as well as the alleged victims. The days of routine tort actions with modest stakes over an automobile accident have been overshadowed by the major social dislocations implicated by mass torts.

Bendectin fits squarely in the category of toxic substances litigation, although like each of the other toxic substances it has its own characteristics, metaphors, and story. Surely the uncertainties and difficulties of ascertaining Bendectin's teratogenicity and the time frame in which that occurred exemplify the causal difficulties that bedevil toxic substances litigation. And that is so even though the latency period for most birth defects is much less than other prominent toxics. Bendectin litigation has been modest in terms of the number of cases filed—approximately 2,000 overall—although it had the potential to become much larger, with millions of pregnant women exposed to Bendectin and tens of thousands of children born with birth defects every year. Like other mass toxics, attempts were made to streamline the litigation by consolidating a large number of cases and resolving them together in an innovative trial procedure.

Bendectin litigation raises a number of important and perplexing questions about the legal system's ability to resolve mass toxic substances cases consistent with the traditional concept of adversarial litigation. In this model, the contending parties, represented by their lawyer-agents, are the central focus. The parties control the course of their case. The use of contingent fee arrangements in tort cases creates some tensions in this model, as attorneys acquire a stake in the litigation. The incentives created by the potential for future claims in mass tort litigation create even greater discord for this model. That lesson became evident in the course of the Mekdecis' case against Merrell. Even greater strains on the traditional model are revealed in the consolidated Bendectin case in Cincinnati, the controversy over which continues to reverberate with each emergence of a new mass tort, the latest of which is the breast implant litigation.

These mass tort cases raise disquieting questions for those familiar (and comfortable) with the traditional model. Should mass tort litigation transform the familiar model to one that is lawyer-centered? The faceless and too-numerous claimants become inventory. In this paradigm shift, an entrepreneurial attorney provides financing for the litigation, arranges for necessary legal services, controls the course of the case, and receives significant compensation (in the form of an attorney's fee) for providing these services. The outcome is often a global resolution to be apportioned among the faceless and sometimes unidentified claimants. And even if this entrepreneurial model is unattractive as an ideal, is it nevertheless a second-best solution when huge numbers of claims do not, as a practical matter, permit individual resolution?

The Tort Crisis

The growth of tort law in tandem with the industrialization of society and technological development is no coincidence and provides important insights into the contemporary tort system. While industrialization and technology have improved society's well being immeasurably, they have, at the same time, transferred many risks from natural causes to human controlled causes. Those inherent risks of nature were of little interest to the tort system, but transferring risks to human and technological control creates numerous opportunities for errors to occur and harm to result. Kidney dialysis machines prolonged the lives of many with kidney disease, but at the same time created opportunities for machine or human error that could cause significant harm.[40] Similarly some cavemen probably died of lung cancer caused by radon, but today with the technology to measure it and construction techniques to ameliorate it, contractors are being sued for failure to take adequate precautions against radon. Thus, paradoxically, while Aaron Wildavsky has argued with a great deal of force and significant empirical support that material improvement in society enhances safety,[41] the shift of risks to human control has fueled significant growth in the tort system.

By the mid-1980s, criticism of the tort system had become rife. The expansion of liability, overlitigiousness by Americans, the spiraling awards of compensatory damages by juries, the vast increase in punitive damage awards, and the uncertainty about where it all would end was widely perceived as a crisis. Liability insurance premiums dramatically increased and insurance became unavailable at any price in a few niches. Concern was expressed about overdeterrence: useful technology and innovation would not be developed or brought to market because of liability concerns. According to this account, American industry's competitiveness in the international marketplace was also compromised by the heavy tort tax imposed on it. The crisis and critique were general to the tort system, but had particularly saliency in the products liability and environmental liability contexts.

Many commentators disagreed with several aspects of the crisis account, its causes, and its consequences. Those commentators pointed out the lack of data to support many of the claims. Nevertheless, the crisis movement had a significant impact.[42] Many became persuaded that the tort system had become a heavy and expensive drag on economic development. A number of state legislatures enacted tort reform legislation, and a decade-old and flagging attempt to enact a federal products liability statute was given added credence and energy.

Toxic substances litigation provided much of the fodder for the critique of the tort system. A frequently cited statistic to demonstrate overlitigiousness in the midst of the torts crisis is that the number of products liability cases filed between 1974 and 1985 increased over 700 percent.[43] But by 1985 asbestos filings made up 31 percent of the products liability filings in federal court. The General Accounting Office also published a study concluding that non-toxic substances products liability filings grew by only 104 percent for the 1976–1986 decade. Litigation involving asbestos, and to a lesser extent the Dalkon Shield and Bendectin, accounted for over 60 percent of the growth in filings during that decade.[44]

Thus, the emergence and growth of toxic substances litigation illustrates nicely the half-full, half-empty controversy over the incidence of claiming by Americans. In relative terms the incidence has increased sig-

nificantly over time, especially in several specific areas like products liability and environmental harms. But in absolute terms, the incidence of
claiming is well below the incidence of injurious events that might justify
a claim.[45] The emergence of the harms caused by toxic substances both
vastly increased the number of persons with a new form of claim and the
overall incidence of events that might result in claiming.

Two other specific aspects of dissatisfaction with the tort system require mention. One is the widespread view that the expert witness system
is seriously flawed. Judge Jack Weinstein has often articulated this concern, which many others have echoed:

[A]n expert can be found to testify to the truth of almost any factual theory, no
matter how frivolous, thus validating the case sufficiently to avoid summary judgment and forcing the matter to trial. At the trial itself, an expert's testimony can
be used to obfuscate what would otherwise be a simple case. The most tenuous
factual bases are sufficient to produce firm opinions to a high degree of "medical
(or other expert) probability" or even of "certainty." Juries and judges can be,
and sometimes are, misled by the expert-for-hire.[46]

A federal government task force that investigated the sources of the
tort crisis concurred:

It has become all too common for "experts" or "studies" on the fringes of or
even well beyond the outer parameters [sic] of mainstream scientific or medical
views to be presented to juries as valid evidence from which conclusions may be
drawn. The use of such invalid scientific evidence (commonly referred to as
"junk science") has resulted in findings of causation which simply cannot be
justified or understood from the standpoint of the current state of credible scientific and medical knowledge.[47]

The final aspect of the contemporary critique is that the system is biased in favor of plaintiffs, whom sympathetic jurors favor. Part of this
criticism is that juries are not up to the task of understanding and evaluating the evidence in a complex case; part is that even if they do understand the evidence they systemically prefer providing compensation to
an injured and sympathetic victim to rendering a verdict for a manufacturer, even one who is not legally responsible. Even judges are subject to
a pro-plaintiff bias, according to Justice Richard Neely of the West Virginia Supreme Court, who wrote a provocative book[48] about the ills of
the products liability system. Neely argues that state court judges cannot
be relied on to correct the biases of juries because judges routinely favor in-state plaintiffs over out-of-state manufacturers. These forces, Justice Neely claims, have created a massive "off-line, wealth-redistribution
system."[49]

These attacks on the tort system are particularly salient to Bendectin
litigation: perhaps the defining and unique characteristic of Bendectin

is the criticism it has generated of plaintiffs and their attorneys, who, it is asserted, avariciously pursued a drug for which there was no evidence of its teratogenicity, employed "experts" who practiced "junk science," and ultimately drove a beneficial drug off the market because of the costs imposed on the manufacturer in successfully defending itself. The secondary villains in this indictment are the legal system for permitting such claims to be pursued and to proliferate and the jury system for its bias and employment of laypersons who are asked to resolve highly complex and technical scientific matters.

Peter Huber, the most strident critic of the tort system, has adopted Bendectin as his personal favorite to illustrate the ills he believes are extant. In his 1988 book, *Liability: The Legal Revolution and Its Consequences,* Bendectin litigation receives comment and criticism no less than five times. In a more recent book, *Galileo's Revenge: Junk Science in the Courtroom* (1991), Huber devotes an entire chapter entitled "Nausea" (and a variety of other derisive references) to Bendectin litigation. Another book that Huber co-edited unsurprisingly contains a chapter devoted to Bendectin.[50]

Huber denounces the plaintiffs' lawyers and experts who pursued Bendectin litigation. He freely employs terms such as "antics," "surpassing greed," "tortogen," "zealotry," and "fraud." In the end, Huber suggests that greed and hysteria by plaintiffs' lawyers and their quack experts have exacerbated the effects of morning sickness and may be causing an increase in birth defects. Even the *New York Times,* which had earlier published accounts sympathetic to Betty Mekdeci and her efforts, joined in the chorus of criticism when a $120 million settlement of Bendectin claims was announced: "With Bendectin . . . the law has made a devastation and called it a settlement."[51]

Bendectin litigation and its lessons are more complicated than these critics recognize or acknowledge. While one can confidently state that Bendectin is not the second coming of thalidomide, assessing toxicity is a complicated, difficult, and time-consuming process that often leaves varying degrees of residual doubt: even today, no serious observer would guarantee that it, like many other drugs, does not have weak effects undetectable by current scientific methods. This, as Kenneth Boulding wrote, represents "irreducible uncertainty," with which society must cope.[52] Moreover, at the time Bendectin litigation began in 1977, the record on its toxicity was quite thin, leaving much room for suspicion and inference. Even Bendectin's withdrawal from the market involves more than its simple removal because of litigation costs: as questions about its safety were raised, demand for the drug dropped, and Merrell responded by raising prices, which continued the declining spiral of demand. In the end, after a number of missteps and far too much cost, the legal system deserves credit: it has essentially separated Bendectin from asbestos and the Dalkon Shield and ruled correctly.

This is not to suggest that there is no fault to be found or no lessons for improving the legal system that might be derived from Bendectin. Some juries were plainly swayed by sympathy and the opportunity to engage in a little wealth redistribution. Some juries had their eyes directed away from the ball by trial structures and strategies that failed to focus on the most important evidence. Plaintiffs' attorneys continued to pursue Merrell after epidemiological studies began to proliferate, impelled by the huge investment they had made, a psychological conviction borne of playing the role of an advocate, and the lure of a few early favorable Bendectin verdicts. The legal system surely can do a better job of obtaining and presenting the scientific expertise that it needs to resolve toxic substances cases, although increased education in the sciences comprising human toxicology and statistical methods or large expenditures for scientific advisory boards, who will themselves have to be educated in the relevant legal standards, may be required to make a marked difference.

To examine seriously the critique and to understand the context in which Bendectin litigation developed requires an appreciation of the science of determining the cause (etiology) of insidious disease, the subject of the next chapter.

Notes

1. For an in-depth and sensitive account of the scope, role, policies, and rules of tort law in modern society, *see* MARSHALL S. SHAPO, A.B.A., THE SPECIAL COMMITTEE ON THE TORT LIABILITY SYSTEM, TOWARDS A JURISPRUDENCE OF INJURY: THE CONTINUING CREATION OF A SYSTEM OF SUBSTANTIVE JUSTICE IN AMERICAN TORT LAW (Chicago: ABA, 1984).

2. Freedom from contributory negligence historically was an element of the plaintiff's prima facie case. During the twentieth century, as courts became dissatisfied with its harsh effects, many ameliorated the impact by shifting to the defendant the burden of proving plaintiff's contributory negligence.

3. LAWRENCE M. FRIEDMAN, A HISTORY OF AMERICAN LAW 467 (New York: Simon & Schuster, 2d ed. 1985).

4. G. EDWARD WHITE, TORT LAW IN AMERICA: AN INTELLECTUAL HISTORY 16 (New York: Oxford University Press, 1980).

5. The most prominent advocates of the "subsidy theory" include FRIEDMAN, *supra* note 3, at 467–87, and MORTON HORWITZ, THE TRANSFORMATION OF AMERICAN LAW, 1780–1860, at 85 (Cambridge, MA: Harvard University Press, 1977). That account is disputed in Gary T. Schwartz, *Tort Law and the Economy in Nineteenth-Century America: A Reinterpretation*, 90 YALE L.J. 1717 (1981).

6. MARK TWAIN & CHARLES D. WARNER, THE GILDED AGE 29 (New York: Trident Press, 1964) (1873).

7. AMERICAN LAW INSTITUTE REPORTERS' STUDY, ENTERPRISE LIABILITY FOR PERSONAL INJURY 55–251 (Philadelphia: American Law Institute, 1991).

8. *See, e.g.*, James Krier & Clayton Gillette, *Risk, Courts, and Agencies*, 138 U. PA. L. REV. 1027 (1990).

9. 111 N.E. 1050 (N.Y. 1916).

10. *See* William Prosser, *The Assault upon the Citadel (Strict Liability to the Consumer)*, 69 YALE L.J. 1099, 1100–03 (1960).

11. *See* Robert Rabin, *Tort Law in Transition: Tracing the Patterns of Sociolegal Change*, 23 VAL. U. L. REV. 1, 22–24 (1988).

12. For a thorough account of these developments, *see* George L. Priest, *The Invention of Enterprise Liability: A Critical History of the Intellectual Foundations of Modern Tort Law*, 14 J. LEGAL STUD. 461 (1985).

13. Escola v. Coca Cola Bottling Co., 150 P.2d 436, 441 (Cal. 1944) (Traynor, J., concurring).

14. Henningsen v. Bloomfield Motors, Inc., 161 A.2d 69, 81–84 (N.J. 1960).

15. Prosser, *supra* note 10, at 1100–03.

16. *Id.* at 1122–24.

17. Greenman v. Yuba Power Prods., Inc., 377 P.2d 897, 900–901 (Cal. 1963).

18. William Prosser, *The Fall of the Citadel (Strict Liability to the Consumer)*, 50 MINN. L. REV. 791 (1950).

19. Priest, *supra* note 12, at 518.

20. *See, e.g.*, Johnson v. American Cyanamid Co., 718 P.2d 1318 (Kan. 1986); RESTATEMENT (SECOND) OF TORTS § 402A cmt. k (1965).

21. *See* Dix W. Noel, *Products Defective Because of Inadequate Directions or Warnings*, 23 SW. L.J. 256 (1969).

22. George L. Priest, *Products Liability Law and the Accident Rate*, in LIABILITY: PERSPECTIVES AND POLICY 202–6 (Robert E. Litan & Clifford Winston eds., Washington, DC: Brookings Institution, 1988).

23. Grimshaw v. Ford Motor Co., 174 Cal. Rptr. 348 (1981). The $125 million award was reduced by the court to $3.5 million.

24. *See* MARY DOUGLAS & AARON WILDAVSKY, RISK AND CULTURE: AN ESSAY ON THE SELECTION OF TECHNICAL AND ENVIRONMENTAL DANGERS 128 (Berkeley: University of California Press, 1982); Kai Ericson, *Toxic Reckoning: Business Faces a New Kind of Fear*, 90 HARV. BUS. REV. 118 (1990).

25. ROBERT LITAN & WILLIAM NORDHAUS, REFORMING FEDERAL REGULATION 34–58 (New Haven, CT: Yale University Press, 1983); Robert Rabin, *Federal Regulation in Historical Perspective*, 38 STAN. L. REV. 1189, 1284–86 (1986).

26. On the early smoking cases, *see* Richard A. Wegman, *Cigarettes and Health— A Legal Analysis*, 51 CORNELL L.Q. 678 (1966); Robert A. Rabin, *A Sociolegal History of the Tobacco Tort Litigation*, 44 STAN. L. REV. 853 (1992). On benzene, *see* Miller v. National Cabinet Co., 168 N.E.2d 811 (N.Y. 1960). The MER/29 litigation is covered in chapter 5. For a description of the mass tort litigations (including traumatic injury cases) over the past 30 years, *see* Deborah R. Hensler & Mark A. Peterson, *Understanding Mass Personal Injury Litigation: A Socio-Legal Analysis*, 59 BROOK. L. REV. 961 (1993).

27. Borel v. Fibreboard Paper Products Corp., 493 F.2d 1076 (5th Cir. 1973), *cert. denied*, 419 U.S. 869 (1974).

28. *See* Rabin, *supra* note 26, at 861.

29. JAMES S. KAKALIK ET AL., COSTS OF ASBESTOS LITIGATION 12 (Santa Monica, CA: Rand, 1983).

30. For a somewhat tendentious account of the behavior of the asbestos industry and litigation against it, *see* PAUL BRODEUR, OUTRAGEOUS MISCONDUCT: THE ASBESTOS INDUSTRY ON TRIAL (New York: Pantheon Books, 1985). For a discus-

sion of the numerous legal issues involved, *see* THOMAS E. WILLGING, TRENDS IN ASBESTOS LITIGATION (Washington, DC: Federal Judicial Center, 1987).

31. In Feres v. United States, 340 U.S. 135 (1950), the Supreme Court held that members of the military injured in the course of their service could not sue the government for damages.

32. For a thorough and insightful account of the Agent Orange litigation, *see* PETER H. SCHUCK, AGENT ORANGE ON TRIAL: MASS TOXIC DISASTERS IN THE COURTS (Cambridge, MA: Belknap Press of Harvard University Press, enlarged ed. 1987).

33. On the Dalkon Shield litigation, *see* RONALD J. BACIGAL, THE LIMITS OF LITIGATION: THE DALKON SHIELD CONTROVERSY (Durham, NC: Carolina Academic Press, 1990); MORTON MINTZ, AT ANY COST: CORPORATE GREED, WOMEN, AND THE DALKON SHIELD (New York: Pantheon Books, 1985); SUSAN PERRY & JAMES L. DAWSON, NIGHTMARE: WOMEN AND THE DALKON SHIELD (New York: Macmillan, 1985); RICHARD B. SOBOL, BENDING THE LAW: THE STORY OF THE DALKON SHIELD BANKRUPTCY (Chicago: University of Chicago Press, 1991).

34. The early stages of litigation in asbestos and the Dalkon Shield litigation are addressed in BRODEUR, *supra* note 30 and BACIGAL, *supra* note 33, respectively.

35. Grover v. Eli Lilly & Co., 591 N.E.2d 696 (Ohio 1992); Smith v. Eli Lilly Co., 560 N.E.2d 324 (Ill. 1990); *see* ROBERTA J. APFEL & SUSAN M. FISHER, TO DO NO HARM: DES AND THE DILEMMAS OF MODERN MEDICINE (New Haven, CT: Yale University Press, 1984).

36. *See, e.g.*, Anderson v. W.R. Grace & Co., 628 F. Supp. 1219 (D. Mass. 1986) (suit on behalf of leukemia victims who allegedly contracted their disease due to contaminated groundwater).

37. For an account of the lengthy history of the identification of asbestos as a carcinogen, *see* Michael D. Green, *The Inability of Offensive Collateral Estoppel to Fulfill Its Promise: An Examination of Estoppel in Asbestos Litigation*, 70 IOWA L. REV. 141, 155–59 (1984).

38. *3d Circuit Hears Three Hours of Arguments on School Class Action Appeals*, Asbestos Litig. Rep. (Andrews) 11,480, 11,481 (Jan. 17, 1986).

39. Barnaby Feder, *Manville Submits Bankruptcy Filing to Halt Lawsuits*, N.Y. TIMES, Aug. 27, 1982, at A1.

40. Mark F. Grady, *Why are People Negligent? Technology, Nondurable Precautions, and the Medical Malpractice Explosion*, 82 NW. U. L. REV. 293 (1988).

41. Aaron Wildavsky, *Richer is Safer*, 60 PUBLIC INTEREST 23 (Summer 1980); AARON WILDAVSKY, SEARCHING FOR SAFETY (New Brunswick, NJ: Transaction Books, 1988).

42. A substantial body of literature analyzed the crisis: for a discussion of the liability insurance crisis, *see* Kenneth S. Abraham, *Making Sense of the Liability Insurance Crisis*, 48 OHIO ST. L.J. 399 (1987); on the state tort law reform process, *see* Joseph Sanders & Craig Joyce, *"Off to the Races": The 1980s Tort Crisis and the Law Reform Process*, 27 HOUS. L. REV. 207 (1990); on the effects of products liability on industry, *see* THE LIABILITY MAZE: THE IMPACT OF LIABILITY LAW ON SAFETY AND INNOVATION (Peter Huber & Robert Litan eds., Washington, DC: Brookings Institution, 1991); on overclaiming by Americans, *see* Michael J. Saks, *Do We Know Anything About the Behavior of the Tort Litigation System—and Why Not?*, 140 U. PA. L. REV. 1147 (1992).

43. *See* U.S. ATT'Y GEN., REPORT OF THE TORT POLICY WORKING GROUP ON THE CAUSES, EXTENT, AND POLICY IMPLICATIONS OF THE CURRENT CRISIS IN IN-

SURANCE AVAILABILITY AND AFFORDABILITY 45 (Feb. 1986); PETER W. HUBER ET AL., LEGAL SYSTEM ASSAULT ON THE ECONOMY 2 (Washington, DC: National Legal Center for the Public Interest, 1986).

44. Marc Galanter, *The Day After the Litigation Explosion*, 46 MD. L. REV. 3, 21– 25 (1986). GENERAL ACCOUNTING OFFICE, BRIEFING REPORT TO THE CHAIRMAN, SUBCOMMITTEE ON COMMERCE, CONSUMER PROTECTION AND COMPETITIVENESS, COMMITTEE ON ENERGY AND COMMERCE, HOUSE OF REPRESENTATIVES: PRODUCTS LIABILITY, EXTENT OF "LITIGATION EXPLOSION" IN FEDERAL COURTS QUESTIONED 2–3, 20–28 (1988). The GAO estimates understate the role of toxics in the growth of products claims; the GAO limited its toxic category to asbestos, Dalkon Shield, and Bendectin cases, which excludes DES, chemical, and other assorted toxic cases.

45. Marc Galanter, *Reading the Landscape of Dispute: What We Know and Don't Know About Our Allegedly Contentious and Litigious Society*, 31 U.C.L.A. L. REV. 4 (1983).

46. Jack B. Weinstein, *Improving Expert Testimony*, 20 U. RICH. L. REV. 482 (1986); *see also* Michael D. Green, *Expert Witnesses and Sufficiency of Evidence in Toxic Substances Litigation: The Legacy of Agent Orange and Bendectin Litigation*, 86 NW. U. L. REV. 643, 669–71 (1992) (cataloguing criticisms of expert witnesses).

47. U.S. ATT'Y GEN., *supra* note 43, at 35.

48. RICHARD NEELY, THE PRODUCT LIABILITY MESS: HOW BUSINESS CAN BE RESCUED FROM THE POLITICS OF STATE COURTS (New York: Free Press, 1988).

49. *Id.* at 2.

50. PHANTOM RISK: SCIENTIFIC INFERENCE AND THE LAW (Kenneth R. Foster et al. eds., Cambridge, MA: MIT Press, 1993).

51. *Morning Sickness, Legal Miscarriage*, N.Y. TIMES, July 30, 1984, at A20.

52. Kenneth Boulding, *Irreducible Uncertainties*, SOCIETY, Nov. / Dec. 1982, at 15; *see also* Joseph Sanders, *From Science to Evidence: The Testimony on Causation in the Bendectin Cases*, 46 STAN. L. REV. 1, 9 (1993).

Chapter 3
The Science of Determining Toxic Causation

The definition of causation has engendered considerable philosophical, scientific, and legal debate and controversy. A workable model of causation, one that is commonly employed in a variety of fields, conceives of causal elements as necessary links in a chain that lead to the outcome. Any link that, if removed, would eliminate the occurrence of the outcome can be said to be a cause of the outcome. Thus there are many causes of any given phenomenon: fire requires fuel, oxygen, and an ignition source at a minimum; all are a cause of the fire. Of course, certain causes are of greater (or lesser) interest to the legal system—generally the actions of those accused of having acted in a legally substandard manner. In the toxic substances context, there are a number of distinct aspects to the question of whether a defendant's deficient conduct caused the plaintiff's injury; the most problematic is whether the toxic substance for which the defendant is responsible caused the plaintiff's disease.

Ideally, to demonstrate that a given agent was a necessary link in the causal chain[1] that led to an individual's disease, one would trace each of the steps in the biology of the development of the disease, including the essential role played by the agent.[2] To state this ideal is to recognize its futility, at least given the current state of scientific affairs.[3] As one federal Court of Appeals sardonically observed, "What scientists know about the causes of cancer is how limited is their knowledge."[4] Because the pathological mechanisms of most diseases are understood marginally at best, other devices are necessary to attempt causal attributions. In the absence of direct evidence, scientific methods that permit causal inference—generalizations from observed phenomena—are employed. Those methods result in bifurcating the causal inquiry: the general causation question addresses the capacity of the agent to cause a given disease; the specific causation aspect inquires whether the agent was a necessary element in the plaintiff's disease. This bifurcation is necessitated by the scientific tools available to make toxic causation assessments.

The general methodology used by scientists is inductive: they proceed by generalizing or making predictions from empirical observation. David Hume criticized this methodology, arguing that a scientific prediction of causation could never be proved conclusively true because there is always the possibility that the observations relied on were coincidental rather than causal. Thus a conclusion from observation that lower temperature is a cause of snow might be merely a result of extraordinary coincidence that would be disproved by a snowstorm in Florida in August.

From Hume's criticism emerged the idea that, while induction never could conclusively prove a proposition, it could falsify one. Thus, based on the framework provided by Karl Popper, knowledge is gained by attempting to disprove or falsify a hypothesis based on empirical investigation.[5] Scientific methodology today is based on generating hypotheses and testing them to see whether they can be falsified.[6] Theoretically, therefore, hypotheses are not affirmatively proved, only falsified.[7] Of course, if a hypothesis repeatedly withstands falsification, one may tend to accept it, even if conditionally, as true.

In the science of toxicology, there are five different types of evidence that may contribute to an inference of causation: epidemiology, animal toxicology, in vitro testing, chemical structural analysis, and case reports. In addition, some limited information may be available based on what is known about the mechanisms by which the disease develops—the field of molecular biology—but this evidence is almost always incomplete and of limited utility in causal assessments. The most desirable evidence is epidemiological, because it can be better generalized to those outside the studied group, supporting inferences about the effect of an agent in causing disease in humans.

Epidemiology is the study of the causes of disease in humans as inferred from observation of humans.[8] Epidemiological studies are conducted on groups of individuals, a sample, to isolate and determine the effect of a given agent or factor on the incidence of disease in the population as a whole. These studies entail a comparison of the incidence of disease in a population exposed to the agent with the incidence of disease in an otherwise similar, but unexposed, population. When epidemiologists study agents that are thought of as toxins—cigarettes, asbestos, drugs, and chemicals—the results of their study may be helpful to the legal system in assessing causation.

The Types of Epidemiological Studies

An epidemiological investigation begins with the "null hypothesis"—the hypothesis that the agent under study has no effect in causing the disease being studied.[9] Disproving the null hypothesis does not prove conclusively that such a causal role exists, for it may be sheer coincidence or methodological errors that explain the results observed.[10] Despite this epistemological quandary, where the epidemiological results are consistent with extant biologic knowledge, pragmatism justifies making reasonable assessments of causation.[11]

There are many different types of epidemiological study, but the gold standard is a controlled experimental study in which the participants are randomly separated, each group exposed either to an agent or a placebo in precise dose, and evaluated for the incidence of the effect under study (the dependent variable) by researchers and participants unaware of the exposure status of the participants. This methodology is known as a clinical trial. Researchers, often clinical physicians with the assistance of biostatisticians, employ it when evaluating new drugs for efficacy and safety while the drug is under consideration for FDA approval.

The crucial information that emerges from an epidemiological study is the ratio of the rates of disease in the exposed versus the unexposed populations. This proportion is known as a relative risk or risk ratio and may be expressed algebraically as

$$RR = \frac{I_e}{I_c} ,$$

where RR is the relative risk, I_e is the incidence of disease in the exposed population, and I_c is the incidence of the disease in the unexposed population. The higher the relative risk, the stronger or more powerful is the association between the agent and the disease. A relative risk of one means that exposure to the agent has no association with the disease— the incidence of disease in the exposed and the unexposed groups is the same.

As long as there are background rates of the disease, that is, causal chains of the disease in which the agent is not a necessary element, epidemiology cannot provide direct evidence of whether the disease in any given individual was caused by exposure to the agent or not.[12] At best, epidemiology assesses the likelihood that the agent caused a specific individual's disease.[13] By way of example, lung cancer exists in the population of those unexposed to cigarette smoke.[14] Thus there are causal mechanisms that do not require cigarette smoke for the occurrence of lung cancer. Let us assume for the sake of this illustration that the relative risk of lung cancer for some level of cigarette smoking is 11. For any given smoker who suffers from lung cancer, all other factors being equal, the most that can be inferred from the epidemiological evidence is that it is 10/11 or .91 probable that smoking was the cause of lung cancer in the examined individual.[15]

The randomized, double-blind, placebo-controlled experiment described above obviously cannot be ethically performed when there is a suspicion that the agent is toxic. Thus, ethical proscriptions require epidemiologists to conduct observational studies (known as cohort studies), rather than experimental studies, of those individuals who voluntarily (or sometimes unknowingly) expose themselves to the full gamut of potentially harmful substances—cigarettes, fatty diets, alcohol, and the like. Those who expose themselves are treated as the exposed cohort and a control group is fashioned from others with similar characteristics (except for exposure to the agent). Many cohort studies are prospective or "follow-up" studies, in which the control and cohort groups are followed over time to assess the incidence of disease that occurs in each group.

A number of potential drawbacks exist in employing cohort studies. First, researchers sometimes use general population data for the control cohort; where risks are widespread, reliance on general population data creates a danger of misclassification error. In addition, cohort studies can be expensive; some large cohort follow-up studies cost in excess of $100 million.[16] Finally, where the incidence of disease is low, cohort studies are often infeasible because their insensitivity (inability to detect an effect even though one exists) is unlikely to justify the expense involved.

An alternative to the cohort study is the case-control study, which affords the advantage of requiring fewer subjects to evaluate whether an association exists. Case-control studies have the advantage of being more powerful and therefore are particularly helpful where the studied disease is rare. Rather than using exposure as the independent variable, epidemiologists use the existence of the disease as the independent variable and use as their "cases" those with the studied disease. Controls are selected from among those without the disease. Valid selection of controls is critical to the validity of case-control studies and requires that the controls be chosen independent of their exposure to the agent.[17] Thus, the "cases" might consist of all patients of a group medical practice diagnosed with acute lymphoblastic leukemia (ALL). The "controls" would be all patients of the group practice without ALL, but who, if they had it, would have been included in the cases. By determining the number of cases and controls who were exposed and unexposed to the agent in question and comparing exposure rates among the exposed with and without the disease rates, an odds ratio that is similar to the relative risk when disease incidence is small can be calculated.[18] Because case-control studies begin with those having the disease, smaller sample sizes can be used to determine if an association exists.[19]

A major disadvantage of case-control studies is that they, unlike cohort studies, are usually limited to investigating one disease. Additionally, in the hands of unskilled investigators, these studies are particularly susceptible to biases.

Epidemiological Error: The Sources of Methodological Mistake

Both cohort and case-control studies are susceptible to a variety of errors—termed "biases"[20]—that may affect the validity of the studies' results. These "systematic errors" (as distinguished from sampling errors, discussed below) may result from a variety of sources. One epidemiologist has catalogued dozens of systematic biases that may create inaccuracies in a study.[21] For purposes of understanding the scientific evidence and the controversy over it in Bendectin litigation, it is not necessary to address all of these biases, but it is helpful to sketch out the nature of the problem and explain a few of the major ones.

Selection bias occurs when the exposed group is selected in a way that makes it more or less susceptible to disease for reasons independent of exposure. Thus, a study of occupational exposure to an agent on causing premature death that uses those not employed as a control group may suffer from selection bias because those who work are generally healthier than those who do not work.

Diagnostic bias or ascertainment error may occur when the disease in question is not accurately determined. For example, discovery of the role of asbestos in causing mesothelioma was hampered when researchers relied on death certificates to determine the incidence of mesothelioma. Because mesothelioma is a rare disease that resembles other forms of cancer, it was frequently misdiagnosed.[22] Similarly, some birth defects may not be found if hospital birth records are relied upon because the defect may not manifest itself until after discharge from the hospital. Diagnostic bias also may occur in case-control studies when the unexposed subjects are less likely to have their disease detected because of diminished medical screening. Furthermore, this bias occurs when researchers fail to define the disease or effect being investigated at an appropriate level of specificity. For example, if all cancers are the designated effect and the agent only causes one specific type of cancer, the study's results will understate the true effect of the agent.

A third source of error is in measurement of exposure. Using Bendectin as an example, in a study of limb reduction defects, researchers might define exposure as the mother taking Bendectin during the first trimester of pregnancy. But the period of organogenesis (forming of the limbs) lasts only two weeks; this is the only time period during which a drug can affect limb development. By diluting the exposed cohort, the study will understate any effect that may exist.[23]

Recall bias—the tendency of those who are in a study to recall incorrectly whether they were exposed to the agent being studied—is a significant source of error in those studies in which exposure is determined by the subject's recollection. Non-differential recall bias occurs when both cases and controls are equally inaccurate in their recollection of exposure. This problem will tend to bias toward the null effect. Differential recall bias, which generally involves the "cases" (i.e., those with the disease) recalling exposure at a higher rate than the controls, are the two primary types of recall bias.[24] Differential recall bias usually tends to exaggerate the true effect.[25]

The existence of unaccounted for confounders, although not technically a bias, nevertheless can produce associations that are not causal. A confounder is an extraneous factor that is independently associated with a higher or lower disease rate but is differentially present in the exposed cohort. Again, Bendectin provides an example: one epidemiological study found an increased incidence of pyloric stenosis—an obstruction in the stomach that prevents food from passing into the small intestine—in the offspring of mothers who took Bendectin. If morning sickness itself is associated with a higher incidence of pyloric stenosis and differentially associated with the exposed group (more women taking Bendectin have morning sickness than do those that do not take Bendectin), morning sickness is a confounder that will tend to exaggerate the association between Bendectin and pyloric stenosis. Confounders can either exaggerate or diminish the true effect if unaccounted for by the researcher.[26]

Random Sampling Error and Statistical Significance

In addition to systematic error, random sampling error may skew the results of an epidemiological study. Sampling error occurs in epidemiology because multiple examinations of limited samples will vary because of random occurrences. When a finite sample is examined, the results may err (i.e., not reflect the true relationship) because of chance. This is the same random chance that may result in a fair coin coming up heads seven times out of ten. Statistical analysis provides a means for assessing the plausibility that the result of any given study reflects a true association or random chance.

One common way to express the concept of statistical significance is through a p value. The p value for a study expresses the probability that the association of the magnitude found, or an even greater degree, would have been found *if the null hypothesis of no association is true*; that is, the p value expresses the likelihood that one would erroneously conclude that there is a real effect based on the data obtained, because of random sampling error. To avoid this false positive error, scientists in a wide variety of fields ordinarily use the convention that no conclusion will be drawn from a study unless p is less than .05, which means that the effect found would occur by random chance only 5 times out of 100. Ordinarily, a study is said to be statistically significant only when p is less than .05.[27]

The concept of statistical significance is illustrated in the curve in Figure 1. The shaded portion of the area under the curve (with the entire area under the curve taken at unity) to the right of point a, represents the probability that a relative risk equal to or greater than S would be found in a study even though there is no effect. Any result that is far enough to the right that no more than .05 of the area under the curve is to the right of the result is deemed statistically significant.

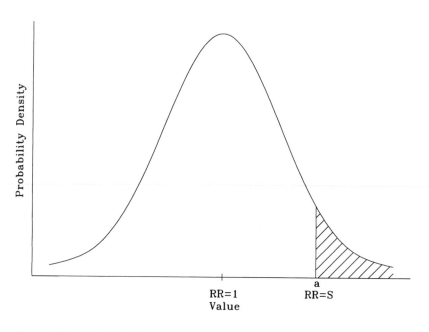

Figure 1. Statistical significance.

The concept of statistical significance played an important role in the Bendectin litigation and has emerged as a key issue in toxic substances litigation generally. Merrell consistently insisted, before both juries and judges, that unless an epidemiological study found an association that was statistically significant, it could not serve as proof of causation. Merrell had mixed success in this effort. After describing Merrell's successes in this regard, chapter 17 contains a discussion of the appropriate role for statistical significance in toxic substances cases.

Causal Inference

Because of systematic biases, random sampling error, confounding, and imprecise measurement of variables, an association that emerges from an epidemiological study may still not be due to a true causal relationship. Making a causal inference requires further analysis based on informed judgment by a scientist familiar with the disease and what is known about the etiologic mechanisms associated with it.

Making that assessment requires consideration beyond the association found and involves informed judgment that cannot be conveniently quantified. A sine qua none for a causal inference is that the effect occur after exposure. This requirement is definitional: packed in our understanding of cause is a chronological dimension that requires the effect to follow the cause, at least until time runs backward.[28] In addition to timing, epidemiologists consider: 1) the strength of the effect (the magnitude of the relative risk); 2) consistency of results in distinct studies; 3) specificity of the effect—that is, that the agent causes a single or specific diseases rather than multiple ones; 4) a dose-response relationship between exposure and effect; and 5) biological plausibility, based on what is known about the mechanisms of the agent and disease.

The Limits of Epidemiology

Finally, a basic difficulty with epidemiology, especially cohort studies, is its inability to discover small increases of risk above a background rate.[29] If the toxic effect is powerful, epidemiology may be unnecessary. For example, thalidomide caused birth defects in an estimated 50 percent of the children whose mothers took the drug, against a background rate of fewer than one in a thousand similar birth defects. With a relative risk upwards of 500, no epidemiological study was necessary to demonstrate thalidomide's teratogenicity, once its role was appreciated. But if the agent has only a small or modest effect, it will go undetected in a cohort study unless a massive number of subjects are included. The power of cohort studies in this situation is quite low.

This sensitivity limitation is illustrated by the National Regulatory Commission's analysis of an epidemiological study's power to detect a hypothesized increase of 200 cancers in a population of 100,000 exposed to low-level radiation. Because the hypothesized relative risk was 1.01, (i.e., a background cancer rate of 20,000 per 100,000), to establish that relative risk with a significance level of .05 would require control and cohort populations of 700,000 persons each.[30] However, while this limitation on epidemiology has important implications for the regulatory process, its impact on private tort litigation is attenuated because very low relative risks would not support a finding of causation by a preponderance of the evidence.

The above discussion is not intended to catalog all of the potential systematic errors in epidemiology, nor to imply that epidemiology is trivial in making causal assessments, nor even to suggest that a study with one or more of these biases has no probative value. Rather, the point is that the value of any given set of epidemiological studies in making causal inferences requires a careful consideration, assessment, and accounting for possible systematic biases and random sampling errors.[31]

Animal Studies

In Vivo Studies

Beyond epidemiology, live animal studies are frequently employed by toxicologists.[32] Animal studies have a number of advantages over epidemiological studies. First, animal studies are experimental rather than observational, enabling the researcher to better control the study and reduce the likelihood of biases affecting the results. Thus the dose for the exposed cohort can be carefully calibrated. Second, the environment of all animals can be made uniform, therefore eliminating the possibility that other differences will be responsible for the outcome. Third, large doses can be given to animals to determine whether the agent being tested has an effect of the sort being investigated. Therefore, even if epidemiological studies are too insensitive to detect a toxic effect, an animal study with much higher doses will reveal a higher incidence of disease in the exposed cohort if there is a dose-response relationship. Fourth, many animal species reproduce readily and have short life cycles, thereby reducing the time required to conduct an experimental study.[33] Mice, hamsters, and rats particularly fit this criterion. Interestingly, rats have another quality that makes them attractive for toxicological study: they do not have a mechanism for vomiting, which means that high doses of an agent administered orally will not be rejected. Fifth, the animals can be sacrificed after a study is completed and the implicated tissue microscopically examined to provide additional information about the existence of disease and the pathological mechanisms by which it develops and proceeds.

However, there are two significant disadvantages of animal studies. First, because of interspecies variation (in size, life span, metabolism, and other significant, but unknown, factors), the causal inference from an animal study to a similar effect in the human population is much more tenuous than with epidemiological studies.[34] This problem is referred to as external validity—the ability to generalize the results of a study of a given population to a different group. Second, different animal species provide better surrogates depending on the agent being tested, its method of ingestion, and pathogenic effects; often the better surrogates are less feasible species for laboratory experiments.

Dr. Bernard Weinstein of the School of Public Health at Columbia University has summarized current knowledge regarding the validity of extrapolating rodent bioassays to humans:

[V]irtually all of the specific chemicals known to be carcinogenic in humans are also positive in the rodent bioassays, and sometimes even at comparable dose and with similar organ specificity. Furthermore, the rodent bioassays have frequently revealed carcinogens that were subsequently found to cause cancer in humans. It is true that there are also a large number of chemicals that are carcinogenic in rodents that are not known to cause cancer in humans, but most of these have not been adequately evaluated in humans, because of their recent discovery or the relative insensitivity of epidemiological studies.[35]

In the area of teratogens, the FDA has found that negative animal studies have some validity in assessing human teratogenicity. Among 38 known human teratogens, 37 produced an effect in at least one animal species and 27 produced an effect in more than one species. The converse is not as accurate. Of 165 agents believed not to be teratogenic in humans, 41 percent were found to have an effect in at least one animal species and only 28 percent were negative in all species. However, monkeys were a relatively good human predictor, as 80 percent of the human nonteratogens elicited a similar lack of effect in monkeys.[36] One of the keys to valid animal toxicology is the selection of an appropriate animal species given the agent being studied, the toxic effect suspected, and the similarities in pathogenesis in humans and the animal species.

The dose-response relationship discussed by Dr. Weinstein creates additional difficulties in extrapolating the results of an animal study to the human population. Animal studies are planned by first determining the maximum tolerated dose (MTD), the dose at which toxic effects other than those being studied occur. Study animals then are exposed to a dose just below the MTD, thereby increasing researchers' ability to identify and measure any potential association. But if the dose to which the animals are exposed is many multiples or orders of magnitude of a typical human dose, difficult questions are raised about the shape of the dose-response curve,[37] as well as whether there is a threshold below which there is no effect.[38]

Beyond the dose response, extrapolating or "scaling" an equivalent dose in humans involves projections for which there is no confirmation or unanimity.[39] The Environmental Protection Agency, for example, summarized the difficulties of using animal studies for assessing human carcinogens:

There are major uncertainties in extrapolating both from animals to humans and from high to low doses. There are important species differences in uptake, metabolism, and organ distribution of carcinogens, as well as species and strain differences in target-site susceptibility.[40]

Despite these difficulties, most toxicologists believe that animal studies do have a role in predicting human toxicity.[41] They clearly assist in understanding the mechanisms by which disease develops, and they are the primary tool for risk assessment for regulatory purposes. Their probity in proving causation in individual toxic substances cases, however, is considerably more controversial, as discussed in chapter 17.

In Vitro Studies

Three additional measures of toxicity exist, but their value is even more variable and difficult to assess than epidemiological and toxicological studies. First, a variety of short term or in vitro tests have been designed to identify various types of toxins. These studies have the advantage of being quite inexpensive to perform.[42] In vitro studies are conducted in the laboratory, and examine the biochemical effects of agents on DNA, cells, bacteria, organs, or even embryos. For example, the test employed for cancer examines mutagenesis (a genetic mutation) in the reproduction of test cells and assumes that mutagenesis is a proxy for carcinogenesis. In vitro teratogenic testing involves transplantation of animal fetal cells, organs, or embryos into a medium where they are subjected to agents of interest to study the effects on the transplanted tissues. Performing the tests on embryos is most difficult because they survive and continue to grow the least time outside of the womb. The primary benefit from these tests is not the identification of teratogens but studying the biological mechanisms of known teratogens. Because these studies are performed on animals, they have all of the difficulties previously identified with interspecies variation and dose response relationships.[43] In addition, the mediating metabolic or bioactivation influence of the mother and placenta are absent in these tests, which results in yet another layer of uncertainty with regard to extrapolation to humans. Moreover, the technique is more useful for studying some forms of teratogenic effects, such as malformations, than it is for studying others, such as neurotoxic effects.[44]

The difficulty with these forms of testing is the validity of generalizing the results of in vitro testing to animals or humans. Some researchers have found a correspondence between demonstrated in vivo effects in animals and in vitro testing in limb buds. Estimates are that short time tests of carcinogenicity correlate with the results of in vivo animal tests only 50 to 70 percent of the time.[45] However, data on the correlation between in vitro tests and effects on man are considerably more sketchy than they are for the in vivo animal test to humans.[46]

Additional Measures of Toxicity

Toxicologists also use similarities in the molecular structures of agents to assess toxicity. If an agent with a known toxic effect has a structure similar to that of another agent, there is some reason to believe that the second agent will have similar effects.[47] Yet even a single change in the molecular structure may result in vastly different effects in humans.

Adverse case reports are another source of evidence bearing on causation. Medical journals frequently report on adverse reactions, and the FDA maintains a registry of drug experience reports that document instances of individuals who have suffered adverse effects after ingesting a drug. Case reports are troublesome to evaluate because they may be purely coincidental, rather than reflecting any causal mechanism, especially where the adverse outcome is a common one. Yet case reports are sometimes validated by subsequent epidemiological study.[48] Occasionally, when the effect of the agent is powerful enough, scientists will tentatively accept case reports as sufficient to establish a causal relation.[49]

There plainly is a hierarchy to these different forms of toxic effect evidence. Epidemiology is at the top, and structural similarity, in vitro testing, and case reports are at the bottom.[50] Yet any one of these forms of evidence may have some utility in attempting to ascertain whether a causal connection exists. To be sure, though, the saliency of the less desirable tests is dependent on the availability and quality of the more authoritative types of scientific studies.

Notes

1. I use the term "causal chain" to reflect the model of causation first developed by Hume and Mill, adapted to the legal context by Hart and Honore, and recently expounded on by Richard Wright. This model views as a "cause" of an event any necessary element of a set (or causal chain) that is sufficient to result in the outcome. *See* H.L.A. HART & ANTHONY HONORE, CAUSATION IN THE LAW (New York: Clarendon Press, 2d ed. 1985); Richard W. Wright, *Causation in Tort Law*, 73 CALIF. L. REV. 1735 (1985); *see also* KENNETH J. ROTHMAN, MODERN EPIDEMIOLOGY 13 (Boston: Little, Brown, 1986) (epidemiologist articulating a necessary element of a sufficient set as model for causation). In most cases, the familiar "but for" test is equivalent to the causal chain concept set forth above.

2. The text deals generally with toxic agents, which would include carcinogens, teratogens, neurotoxins, and other agents that cause a variety of diseases. Because cancer claims 500,000 lives per year in the United States and because of the psychology of the "dread disease," it tends to be emphasized in research and in discussions of toxic causation.

There are variations in the researchers' methods involving different types of disease, largely because of the different biological mechanisms involved in conditions such as cancer and birth defects.

3. Those who believe in stochastic phenomenology would contend that science will never provide these answers because some events are purely probabilistic as opposed to deterministic. The determinists simply define all probabilistic events as ones that involve factors that existing science cannot understand or explain. Einstein's famous statement, "God does not play dice [with the universe]," reveals him as a confirmed determinist. *See* JAMES GLEICK, CHAOS: MAKING A NEW SCIENCE 251 (New York: Viking, 1987).

4. Environmental Defense Fund v. Environmental Protection Agency, 598 F.2d 62, 89 (D.C. Cir. 1978); *see also* Office of Science and Technology Policy, *Chemical Carcinogens: A Review of Science and Its Associated Principles*, 50 Fed Reg. 10,372, 10,379 (1985) ("We still lack an in depth understanding of the mechanisms and stages of cancer induction and expression").

5. KARL R. POPPER, THE LOGIC OF SCIENTIFIC DISCOVERY (New York: Harper & Row, 1965).

6. *See* David L. Faigman, *To Have or Have Not: Assessing the Value of Social Science to the Law as Science and Policy*, 38 EMORY L.J. 1005, 1015–17 (1989).

7. Interdisciplinary Panel on Carcinogenicity, *Criteria for Evidence of Chemical Carcinogenicity*, 225 SCI. 682, 683 (1984).

8. Philip Cole, *The Evolving Case-Control Study*, 32 J. CHRON. DIS. 15 (1979).

9. DONALD F. AUSTIN & S. BENSON WERNER, EPIDEMIOLOGY FOR THE HEALTH SCIENCES 61 (Springfield, IL: C.C. Thomes, 1982).

10. Making the leap from an association to a causal relationship between an agent and disease requires a considered assessment of criteria identified at text accompanying note 28. *See also* Donald W. Large & Preston Michie, *Proving that the Strength of the British Navy Depends on the Number of Old Maids in England: A Comparison of Scientific Proof with Legal Proof*, 11 ENVTL. L. 557 (1981).

11.

All scientific work is incomplete—whether it be observational or experimental. All scientific work is liable to be upset or modified by advancing knowledge. That does not confer upon us a freedom to ignore the knowledge that we already have or to postpone the action that it appears to demand at a given time.

Sir Austin Bradford Hill, *The Environment and Disease: Association or Causation*, 58 Proc. R. Soc. Med. 295 (1965).

12. There are some diseases that do not occur without exposure to a given toxic agent; this phenomenon is equivalent to a relative risk of infinity and has been characterized as a "signature disease" because the existence of the disease necessarily implies the causal role of the agent. *See* Kenneth S. Abraham & Richard M. Merrill, *Scientific Uncertainty in the Courts*, Issues Sci. & Tech., Winter 1986, at 93, 101.

13. For an explanation of the shift from the frequentist statistical approach of the epidemiologist to the assessment of the likelihood of causation in an individual case, *see* David H. Kaye, *Apples and Oranges: Confidence Coefficients and the Burden of Persuasion*, 73 Cornell L. Rev. 54, 54–62 (1987); Note, *Causation in Toxic Torts: Burdens of Proof, Standards of Persuasion, and Statistical Evidence*, 96 Yale L.J. 376, 390 (1986).

14. Even this simple example includes a potential bias of the sort explained below. If we separate the population into those who smoke cigarettes as the exposed group and those who do not smoke as the unexposed group, exposure measurement bias will exist because some of the members of the "unexposed" group will be exposed to passive smoke. This bias, as well as almost all exposure classification biases, will result in an underestimation of the relative risk of smoking in causing lung cancer. *See* Rothman, *supra* note 1, at 86–87.

15. This uncertainty is sometimes described as the problem of the indeterminate plaintiff. *See In re* Agent Orange Prods. Liab. Litig., 597 F. Supp. 740, 833–35 (E.D.N.Y. 1984), *aff'd*, 818 F.2d 145 (2d Cir. 1987); Michael Dore, *A Commentary on the Use of Epidemiological Evidence in Demonstrating Cause-in-Fact*, 7 Harv. Envtl. L. Rev. 429 (1983); Richard Delgado, *Beyond* Sindell: *Relaxation of Cause-in-Fact Rules for Indeterminate Plaintiffs*, 70 Calif. L. Rev. 881 (1982); David Rosenberg, *The Causal Connection in Mass Exposure Cases: A Public Law Vision of the Tort System*, 97 Harv. L. Rev. 849 (1984); Bert Black & David E. Lilienfeld, *Epidemiological Proof in Toxic Tort Litigation*, 52 Fordham L. Rev. 732, 782–83 (1984).

The astute reader will note that the text refers to a relative risk of 11 at some level of smoking. For most toxic substances (teratogens are the major exception), the strength of the effect is a function of the dose, which is the magnitude of exposure multiplied by the time of exposure. However, there is much controversy over the appropriate model to use to extrapolate the dose-response curve from a given finding at a known dose. *See infra* text accompanying notes 37–41.

16. Rothman, *supra* note 1, at 60.

17. *See* Linda A. Bailey et al., *Reference Guide on Epidemiology*, in Federal Judicial Center, Reference Manual on Scientific Evidence 121, 136–37 (1994).

18. *See* Joseph Gastwirth, Statistical Reasoning in Law and Public Policy 286–92 (Boston: Academic Press, 1988).

19. *See* Joseph L. Fleiss, *Confidence Intervals for the Odds Ratio in Case-Control Studies: The State of the Art*, 32 J. Chron. Dis. 69 (1979); Rothman, *supra* note 1, at 62–69.

20. "Bias" has a different meaning in this context than it does in the legal realm. Bias in scientific investigation includes any phenomenon that tends to produce results that deviate from the truth other than random sampling error.

EDMOND A. MURPHY, THE LOGIC OF MEDICINE 239–62 (Baltimore: John Hopkins University Press, 1976).

21. David L. Sackett, *Bias in Analytic Research,* 32 J. CHRON. DIS. 51 (1979).

22. Michael D. Green, *The Paradox of Statutes of Limitations in Toxic Substances Litigation,* 76 CALIF. L. REV. 965, 976 n.49 (1988). Unless diagnostic bias is differential across the exposed, nonexposed axis, it normally will not bias the results, since the errors will occur in both populations. The difficulty occurred with asbestos because mesothelioma is a signature disease, only associated with asbestos exposure. Moreover, differential diagnostic error may occur, for example, where a physician is predisposed to diagnose a patient as suffering from a given disease where the patient has been exposed to an agent suspected of causing that disease.

23. Thomas W. McDonald et al., *Exogenous Estrogen and Endometrial Carcinoma: Case-Control and Incidence Study,* 127 AM. J. OBSTET. GYN. 572 (1977) (demonstrating how changes in definition of exposure can produce relative risk outcomes ranging from .9 to 5.1).

24. *See* Martha M. Werler et al., *Reporting Accuracy Among Mothers of Malformed and Non Malformed Infants,* 129 AM. J. EPIDEM. 415 (1989).

25. Steven S. Coughlin, *Recall Bias in Epidemiologic Studies,* 43 J. CLIN. EPIDEMIOL. 87 (1990).

26. N.E. Day, *Statistical Considerations, in* INTERPRETATION OF NEGATIVE EPIDEMIOLOGICAL EVIDENCE OF CARCINOGENICITY 14 (N.J. Wald & R. Doll eds., New York: Oxford University Press, 1985).

27. *See generally* DAVID FREEDMAN ET AL., STATISTICS 493 (New York: Norton, 2d ed. 1991).

28. *See* STEPHEN HAWKING, A BRIEF HISTORY OF TIME 15–34 (London: Bantam Books, 1988).

29. *See* Day, *supra* note 26, at 13; The Environmental Protection Agency—Carcinogen Guidelines, 51 Fed. Reg. 33,992, 33,995–96 (1986).

30. Junius McElveen & Pamela Eddy, *Cancer and Toxic Substances: The Problem of Causation and the Use of Epidemiology,* 33 CLEV. ST. L. REV. 29, 40–41 (1984).

31. The difficulties of conducting epidemiological studies account for the finding that conflicting results were obtained for some 100 cause-effect relationships that were the subject of epidemiological study. Alvan R. Feinstein, *Scientific Standards in Epidemiologic Studies of the Menace of Daily Life,* 242 SCI. 1257, 1257 (1988).

32. For a more detailed overview of animal studies, *see* Jack L. Landau & Hugh O'Riordan, *Of Mice and Men: The Admissibility of Animal Studies to Prove Causation in Toxic Torts,* 25 IDAHO L. REV. 521, 532–49 (1988).

33. MICHAEL A. KAMRIN, TOXICOLOGY: A PRIMER ON TOXICOLOGY PRINCIPLES AND APPLICATIONS 54 (Chelsea, MI: Lewis Publishers, 1988); Ernest Hodgson, *Measurement of Toxicity, in* MODERN TOXICOLOGY (Ernest Hodgson & Patricia Levi eds., New York: Elsevier, 1987).

34. *See* Lorenzo Tomatis, *The Predictive Value of Rodent Carcinogenicity Tests in the Evaluation of Human Risks,* 19 ANN. REV. PHARMACOLOGY & TOXICOLOGY 511 (1979); William J. Visek, *Issues and Current Applications of Interspecies Extrapolation of Carcinogenic Potency as a Component of Risk Assessment,* 77 ENVTL. HEALTH PERSP. 49 (1988); Thomas J. Slaga, *Interspecies Comparisons of Tissue DNA Damage, Repair, Fixation and Replication,* 77 ENVTL. HEALTH PERSP. 73 (1988) (reviewing literature on interspecies variation).

35. I. Bernard Weinstein, *Mitogenesis is Only One Factor in Carcinogenesis*, 251 SCI. 387, 388 (1991) (footnotes omitted); David P. Rall, *Carcinogens and Human Health*, 251 SCI. 10 (1991) (of 34 known chemical carcinogens in humans, 31 also have been shown to be carcinogenic in animals, with the other three not yet adequately studied); INTERNATIONAL AGENCY FOR RESEARCH ON CANCER, MONOGRAPHS ON THE EVALUATION OF CARCINOGENIC RISKS TO HUMANS (Lyon, France: International Agency for Research on Cancer, Vols. 1–42, Supp. 7 1988); Lorenzo Tomatis et al., *Human Carcinogens So Far Identified*, 80 JPN. J. CANCER RES. 795 (1989); Bruce C. Allen et al., *Correlation Between Carcinogenic Potency of Chemicals in Animals and Humans*, 8 RISK ANALYSIS 531 (1988).

36. IAN C.T. NISBET & NATHAN J. KARCH, CHEMICAL HAZARDS TO HUMAN REPRODUCTION 98–106 (Park Ridge, NJ: Noyes Data, 1983); *see also* EDWARD J. CALABRESE, PRINCIPLES OF ANIMAL EXTRAPOLATION 237–38 (New York: Wiley, 1983); Gary P. Carlson, *Factors Modifying Toxicity*, *in* TOXIC SUBSTANCES AND HUMAN RISK: PRINCIPLES OF DATA INTERPRETATION 47 (Robert G. Tardiff & Joseph V. Rodricks eds., New York: Plenum Press, 1987).

One difficulty with the comparisons is that for reasons explained at *supra* text accompanying notes 29–30, one almost never can be certain that a given agent does not have a weak effect on human beings.

37. A variety of models exist, the most popular of which is a linear model, in which a proportional effect is hypothesized at reduced doses. It may be that different models are appropriate for different toxins or even for any given effect of a toxin. *See* FRANK B. CROSS, ENVIRONMENTALLY INDUCED CANCER AND THE LAW: RISKS, REGULATION, AND VICTIM COMPENSATION 54–57 (New York: Quorum Books, 1989); Troyen A. Brennan, *Causal Chains and Statistical Links: The Role of Scientific Uncertainty in Hazardous Substance Litigation*, 73 CORNELL L. REV. 469, 505–06 & nn. 194–96 (1988).

Controversy over the shape of the dose-response curve has recently developed because of the use of near toxic doses of the agent. Several scientists have posited that the near toxic doses of the agent induce greater cell proliferation in response to the toxic wounding and that cell proliferation increases the risk of cancer. Thus, the high doses would overstate the risks because lower doses would not involve the same toxicity-induced cancer mechanism. *See* Bruce N. Ames & Lois S. Gold, *Too Many Rodent Carcinogens: Mitogenesis Increases Mutagenesis*, 249 SCI. 970 (1990). Ames and Gold are not without their critics. *See, e.g.*, Jean Marx, *Animal Carcinogen Testing Challenged*, 250 SCI. 743 (1990).

38. *See* Irving Selikoff, U.S. DEP'T OF LABOR, DISABILITY COMPENSATION FOR ASBESTOS-INDUCED DISEASE IN THE UNITED STATES 182–220 (1981) (study by Irving Selikoff); Paul Kotin, *Dose-Response Relationships and Threshold Concepts*, 271 ANNALS N.Y. ACAD. SCI. 22 (1976); Panel, *Based on Available Data Can We Project an Acceptable Standard for Industrial Use of Asbestos?*, 330 ANNALS N.Y. ACAD. SCI. 205 (1979).

Dr. Bernard Weinstein of the Columbia University School of Public Health testified before Congress:

[A]lthough the response to various types of carcinogens is likely to be dose dependent, I know of no evidence that clearly establishes a threshold level for any carcinogen. Furthermore, even if this were established in a given experimental system, it would be difficult to predict with confidence the threshold level in a heterogenous human population.

Hearings on Control of Carcinogens in the Environment Before the Subcommittee on Commerce, Transportation, and Tourism of the House Committee on Energy and Commerce, 98th Cong., 1st Sess., at 16 (1983).

Moreover, development of evidence relating to the threshold effect is exceedingly unlikely because of the insensitivity of epidemiology and animal toxicology to very small or weak effects. *Cf.* Arnold L. Brown, *The Meaning of Risk Assessment,* 37 ONCOLOGY 302, 303 (1980) ("no empirical approach is available to demonstrate a threshold").

For a topology of the various models that have been proposed to extrapolate the risks at low doses, see Troyan A. Brennan & Robert F. Carter, *Legal and Scientific Probability of Causation of Cancer and Other Environmental Disease in Individuals,* 10 J. HEALTH POL., POL. & LAW 33, 43–44 (1985).

39. Michael D. Hogan & David G. Hoel, *Extrapolation to Man, in* PRINCIPLES AND METHODS OF TOXICOLOGY 711–18 (A. Wallace Hayes ed., New York: Raven Press, 1982).

40. EPA, Final Guidelines for Carcinogenic Risk Assessment, 51 Fed. Reg. 33,992, 33,997 (Sept. 24, 1986). *See also* Howard Latin, *Good Science, Bad Regulation and Toxic Risk Assessment,* 5 YALE J. REG. 89 (1988).

41. NATIONAL RESEARCH COUNCIL, NATIONAL ACADEMY OF SCIENCES, RISK ASSESSMENT IN THE FEDERAL GOVERNMENT: MANAGING THE PROCESS 22 (1983) (animal studies "have . . . proved to be reliable indicators of carcinogenic properties"). *But see* Gio Batta Gori, *The Regulation of Carcinogenic Hazards,* 257 SCI. 208 (1980) (questioning whether results of animal tests have any validity in predicting human effects).

42. *See* O.P. Flint, *An In Vitro Test for Teratogens Using Cultures of Rat Embryo Cells,* in IN VITRO METHODS IN TOXICOLOGY 356 (C.R. Atterwill & C.E. Steele eds., New York: Cambridge University Press, 1987).

43. Some researchers hypothesize, with some experimental support, that virtually any chemical agent will be toxic to in vitro cells at a sufficiently high dosage, but that no effect will occur at some threshold dose. Ruth Clayton & Ahment Zamir, *The Use of Cell Culture Methods for Exploring Teratogenic Susceptibility, in* DEVELOPMENTAL TOXICOLOGY 59, 69–71 (Keith Snell ed., New York: Praeger, 1982). This thesis simply transforms the threshold limit debate to the in vitro context.

44. A.J. Dewar, *Neurotoxicity Testing—With Particular Reference to Biochemical Methods in* TESTING FOR TOXICITY 199, 214 (J. W. Gorrod ed., London: Taylor & Francis, 1981).

45. Interdisciplinary Panel on Carcinogenicity, *Criteria for Evidence of Chemical Carcinogenicity,* 225 SCI. 682, 684 (Aug. 17, 1984).

46. Nigel Brown & Sergio Fabro, *The In Vitro Approach to Teratogenicity Testing, in* DEVELOPMENTAL TOXICOLOGY 31, 50 (Keith Snell ed., New York: Praeger, 1982).

47. Umberto Saffoti, *Identification and Definition of Chemical Carcinogens: Review of Criteria and Research Needs,* 6 J. TOXICOL. ENVTL. HEALTH 1043 (1980).

48. Robert W. Miller, *Striped Neckties and Other Etiologic Observations, in* CHEMICAL AND RADIATION HAZARDS TO CHILDREN 126 (L. Finberg ed., Columbus, OH: Ross Laboratories, 1982). Benzene's effect in enhancing the risk of leukemia was first identified through case reports and subsequently confirmed by epidemiological study. JOSEPH V. RODRICKS ET AL., ELEMENTS OF TOXICOLOGY AND CHEMICAL RISK ASSESSMENT 11 (Washington, DC: Environ, 1986).

49. That was the course of events with thalidomide, which caused a dramatic increase in the incidence of limb reduction defects among the offspring of women who took the drug while pregnant. Dr. Widuken Lenz of Germany and Dr. William McBride of Australia are credited with discovering thalidomide's teratogenic effects based on the observations and investigations of cases of limb defects that were occurring at a horrifying rate. *See* HENNING SJÖSTRÖM & ROBERT NILSSON, THALIDOMIDE AND THE POWER OF THE DRUG COMPANIES 97–111 (Harmondsworth: Penguin, 1972).

50. *See* JOSEPH SANDERS, BENDECTIN ON TRIAL (Ann Arbor: University of Michigan Press, forthcoming 1996).

Chapter 4
The Food and Drug Administration

A number of the peculiar characteristics of Bendectin litigation were identified in chapter 2. An important influence on Bendectin litigation is that the drug is a product of an industry that, along perhaps with commercial airline travel, is the most heavily regulated with regard to safety in the United States. Federal drug regulation, which dates back to the Pure Food and Drug Act of 1906, and the Food and Drug Administration, which was created in 1927 to carry out the regulatory mandate of the Act, sets Bendectin apart from asbestos, the Dalkon Shield,[1] and Agent Orange, to mention several of the other most prominent mass toxic litigations. This scrutiny by a governmental agency and its scientists provides a strong case for leaving safety concerns about drugs to FDA experts as opposed to the lay juries on which the common law system relies. Moreover, the presence of FDA oversight of Bendectin had a multifaceted impact on the course of Bendectin litigation.

Any attempt to describe the FDA must confront the fact that it is not a static entity; significant changes occur in response to political, social, medical, and scientific developments. The AIDS scourge and efforts to find drug treatments and vaccines for it has had a significant impact—some knowledgeable observers characterize it as a "revolution"—on the FDA and its new drug regulatory policies.[2] The growth of managed care in the delivery of health care has changed many traditional pharmaceutical marketing practices. Changes in the executive branch of the federal government and attitudes about regulation affect the operation, staffing, and funding of the FDA. Because the purpose of this chapter is to provide an understanding of the FDA and its role in the Bendectin litigation, the (not entirely exclusive) focus is on the FDA during the period from the late 1950s through the early 1980s, when Bendectin was regulated by the FDA, rather than the FDA of today. The question of the role of tort law in augmenting regulation of pharmaceuticals (or vice versa, as some might prefer) is deferred to chapter 18.

The theory justifying regulatory oversight of the pharmaceutical industry is straight forward. Both physicians and consumers lack adequate information of the benefits and risks of drugs, especially new ones. This informational inadequacy is thought to justify governmental intervention to prevent market failure. The high costs for consumers and their agents of obtaining information and of errors (in their impact on health and safety) make drugs a peculiarly appropriate subject for regulatory oversight.[3]

The tension between facilitating new and useful pharmaceutical technology and preventing the tragedies that have pockmarked the drug industry during its history informs competing perspectives of the FDA. It also provides an important backdrop to Bendectin litigation, products liability law, and public policy. Estimates are that it costs in excess of $200 million and takes 12 years to develop a pharmaceutical and obtain regulatory approval for it.[4] Some observers view this as an immense barrier to the introduction of new and useful drugs in the United States. This barrier discourages research and development in the pharmaceutical industry, thereby reducing the flow of promising new ideas.[5] A competing vision postulates industry "capture" of the regulatory agency. The FDA acts as a tool of the pharmaceutical industry and is insufficiently sensitive to consumer concerns.[6] The truth, as is so often the case, is more complicated than either of these competing paradigms.

The FDA's regulation of drugs is the highest profile aspect of its work, has engendered the most criticism, and is the area of concern for Bendectin litigation. But the broad scope and huge magnitude of the agency's regulatory authority deserve mention. The FDA has regulatory authority over $700 billion of retail purchases, which amounts to 25 cents of every dollar spent by consumers.[7] Inevitably, when errors are made or problems surface within the FDA's bailiwick, they occur in high profile areas of public and political interest, which often subjects the FDA to intense scrutiny and scapegoat status.

The beginning of governmental regulation of drugs goes back almost a century, and reveals the stimulus necessary to create a major governmental regulatory scheme. Drug regulation has always been a creature of major catastrophes or exposés.[8] Often the only means to move a legislature, for which inaction is far easier and safer politically than affirmative activity, from the status quo is for public opinion to coalesce because of a prominent, gripping, or tragic event that captures and molds public opinions. Thus in 1906 the Pure Food and Drug Act was enacted in response to the disclosure of inflated health claims for quack medications by the crusading Dr. Harvey Wiley, then the head of the

Bureau of Chemistry in the U.S. Department of Agriculture, and the exposé of the unsanitary practices of the meat industry by Upton Sinclair in *The Jungle.*[9] The 1906 Act was of limited scope in regulating drugs—its focus was on preventing misbranded and adulterated drugs from reaching the market, and it had no provision for pre-marketing approval of new drugs. While some unsafe drugs might be misbranded and subject to regulation under the 1906 Act, safety alone remained unregulated.[10]

The next major legislative incursion into the pharmaceutical arena was a direct response to the sulfanilamide tragedy of 1937. Sulfanilamide was a popular antibiotic that the Massengill Company marketed in liquid form. Unfortunately, the solvent that Massengill employed was quite toxic, and 107 persons, including many children, were killed before the drug was removed from the market. Despite the danger posed by the drug, the FDA's only authority to intervene under the existing law was because the drug was misbranded as an elixir. The term "elixir" required that the drug contain alcohol, which Massengill's liquid sulfanilamide did not.[11]

The Food, Drug, and Cosmetic Act of 1938 (the Act) resulted in the FDA adopting a regulation that began the prescription system for many drugs, thereby placing physicians rather than consumers in the decision making role.[12] Physicians, however, like consumers before them, remain dependent on the pharmaceutical industry for information about the therapeutic benefits, as well as the risks, of prescription drugs. The 1938 Act added for the first time a consumer protection goal to the informational (and thereby market enhancing) function of the 1906 Act.[13]

To further the protective concerns, the 1938 Act required a drug manufacturer to file a new drug application (NDA) with the FDA before marketing a new drug. The NDA required the manufacturer to provide evidence of the safety of the new drug, established by appropriate testing, which would then be reviewed by the FDA. Safety testing was to be conducted by the manufacturer, not the FDA. Unless the FDA objected, the NDA became effective sixty days after it was submitted, and the manufacturer could then proceed to market the drug. Thus, the system was one of pre-marketing notification, rather than affirmative approval by the FDA. Bendectin (whose NDA became effective in 1956), and its components, were considered by the FDA under the 1938 Act.

The ethical drug industry (prescription pharmaceuticals) grew in the ensuing decades as scientists became better able to discover and develop chemical formulations that provided clinical benefits to patients. By the 1960s, over 90 percent of the 200 most popular drugs had been introduced after the 1938 Act.[14] During this period, the industry enjoyed large growth, made substantial profits, and developed into a powerful political organization, one that quickly recognized the enormous sway that Congressional and regulatory activity had over the fortunes of the industry.

In 1958, Senator Estes Kefauver, then the Chair of the Senate Subcommittee on Antitrust and Monopoly, began a Congressional investigation of the pharmaceutical industry. Kefauver initiated the investigation primarily because of concerns about the high cost of drugs and the higher than average profits of the pharmaceutical industry. The safety and efficacy of drugs was of minor concern at the initiation of the investigation, but gradually concerns emerged about overpromotion by the industry. Overpromotion and overprescribing are both an economic and safety issue: unnecessary drugs waste money and because all drugs are biologically active they pose risks to those who take them.

The pharmaceutical industry directs its extensive marketing efforts at physicians through "detailers" who visit physicians to extol the benefits of their employers' new drugs, provide the physician with samples and gifts, and encourage the physician to prescribe the drugs that their employer is promoting.[15] During hearings held by the Kefauver Committee, evidence was submitted that the pharmaceutical industry spent 25–30 percent of its gross revenue on marketing, although there was some substantial controversy about that figure, in large part because the industry was reluctant to provide financial information.[16] Tom Bleakley, who subsequently became one of the leading Bendectin plaintiff's lawyers, appreciated this aspect of the pharmaceutical industry, as he had worked for several years as a manufacturer's detailer.

Once again, it was the dramatic emergence of another tragedy—thalidomide—that provided the final impetus for passage of the Kefauver-Harris Amendments of 1962.[17] In June 1962 Morton Mintz, a prominent investigative reporter for the *Washington Post*, was tipped off by Kefauver Committee staff persons about the emerging scandal. He authored a page one story in the *Washington Post* about the children in Europe born with seal-like flippers for limbs because their mothers had taken thalidomide during pregnancy.[18]

In October 1962 the Food, Drug, and Cosmetic Act was amended. The amendments required the FDA to approve the safety and, for the first time, the efficacy of each new drug. The 1962 Amendments also provided for a greater oversight role for the FDA in the promotion, including advertising (although limited to written materials and therefore inapplicable to oral statements by detailers),[19] and testing of prescription drugs. Moreover, the 1962 Amendments required the FDA to reexamine all NDAs that had become effective since 1938 to ascertain that the drug met the new efficacy requirement contained in the 1962 legislation.

The retrospective efficacy review requirement, applicable to Bendectin, imposed an enormous burden on the FDA, which responded by contracting out initial review to the National Academy of Sciences. The efficacy review that was conducted by the National Academy of Sciences and the FDA was known as the DESI process (drug effectiveness study implementation). The National Academy of Sciences (NAS) formed thirty panels of experts in different therapeutic areas to examine the data on efficacy for drugs that had first been marketed between 1938 and 1962. The panels then reported to the FDA on their reviews, classifying each drug in one of six categories: effective, probably effective (requiring additional evidence before it can be placed in the "effective" category), possibly effective, ineffective, ineffective as a fixed combination, and effective, but with qualifications. The FDA then undertook to review the NAS panel reports, ultimately issuing DESI notices to manufacturers of drugs that were found wanting. Because of the number of drugs involved (over 4,000 pioneer drugs and many more "me-too" drugs, a drug chemically-equivalent to an already approved drug) the DESI process continued into the 1980s.

Ironically, the 1962 Amendments, made possible by thalidomide, did little to make such a tragedy less likely in the future. The requirement that a drug be proved "safe" remained unchanged from the 1938 Act. Thalidomide would readily have fulfilled the efficacy requirement, as it was a useful sedative. Although thalidomide alerted the world to the role that drugs could play on the developing fetus and contributed to improved teratology testing and methodology (described in the next chapter), the changes it enabled in the 1962 Amendments were largely irrelevant to the concerns highlighted by thalidomide.[20]

The requirement that the efficacy of a drug be demonstrated recognized a fact that had long been appreciated by the pharmaceutical industry and the FDA, but which had not found its way into the Act before 1962. Any drug has a variety of physiological effects on the human body. Some of those effects are benign and may go unnoticed, some of them are beneficial and may be the reason for treatment, some of them are adverse and undesirable. Any assessment of the desirability of a drug requires a comparison of its therapeutic effects—the benefits—with its adverse effects—the costs. That assessment requires information about the efficacy of the drug, the seriousness of the condition for which it is being prescribed, and the frequency of adverse effects and their severity. Logically, an intelligent assessment also requires a comparison of the therapeutic effects and adverse reactions of alternative drugs, but the pharmaceutical industry was successful in blocking inclusion of inter-drug efficacy comparisons as an element of the new drug approval process in the 1962 Amendments.[21]

Nevertheless, with the modifications enacted in the 1962 Amendments, the FDA obtained enormous power and responsibility for the prescription drug industry. The FDA had the authority to determine if a new drug could be marketed, what claims could be made for the drug in advertising and marketing efforts, the information that should be conveyed to physicians about a drug in its labeling,[22] including limitations on use of the drug, and whether a drug should be removed from the market. In exercising these powers, the FDA has significant discretion, even more than is routinely present in the regulatory process, in assessing and balancing the safety and efficacy of the drug. For example, in reviewing the clinical studies conducted by a manufacturer, the FDA might decide that the trials were inadequate to demonstrate the safety or efficacy of a drug, thereby requiring the manufacturer to undertake additional studies. The FDA's discretion was enhanced by informal mechanisms utilized by the Agency, including publicity and regulatory letters.[23] At the same time, there are a number of gaps in the FDA's authority: it cannot order recalls, it does not have subpoena power, and its enforcement budget is often wholly inadequate.

The substantial discretion exercised by the FDA and its use of informal mechanisms such as negotiation with a pharmaceutical company create two very different strata of FDA activity in terms of public knowledge. Decisions to approve drugs, remove drugs from the market, retain them on the market, or to change labeling are public decisions that, in the case of a dangerous or controversial drug, are subject to intense scrutiny by the media, Congress, other public bodies, and consumer organizations. By contrast, much of the FDA's negotiating and jawboning with the industry to reach voluntary agreement occurs without public knowledge. Merrell ceased promoting Bendectin in 1981, at least in part because of quietly applied pressure by the FDA over Merrell's over-promotion of the drug, yet those efforts were in telephone conversations about which the public never knew.

Despite the expanded FDA authority over the pharmaceutical industry, there are limits on its role in ensuring drug safety. A little appreciated yet crucial aspect of FDA regulation of the pharmaceutical industry is that the FDA does not conduct the studies that become the basis of the New Drug Application. Rather, these studies of safety and efficacy are funded and performed or supervised by the manufacturer. Thus the FDA depends on the industry for data and information about the drugs it approves and regulates. There are many forces that influence the quality and objectivity of the studies performed during the clinical development process, some of which raise concern about its reliability. Before detailing those forces however, an understanding of the different phases of testing a new drug is helpful.[24]

The first stage of testing a new compound is in the laboratory with animals or in vitro (test tube) testing of human tissues. The initial laboratory testing is often closely related to research and development efforts conducted by a pharmaceutical company. Only after successful initial laboratory screening does a drug proceed to human trials. Before human experimentation can begin, however, the manufacturer must submit to the FDA an Investigational New Drug (IND) Application, which contains the results of the animal and in vitro testing. This preliminary work is typically performed in-house by the pharmaceutical company sponsoring the drug or is contracted out to a private laboratory.

If the FDA permits further testing, it consists of three phases of human trials. The first stage is designed to assess how humans will tolerate, metabolize, absorb, and eliminate the compound. This stage also examines toxicity but usually does not assess efficacy. Thus the humans who participate in the first phase are usually healthy individuals, who do not suffer from the condition the drug is designed to treat. Participants are carefully monitored to obtain maximum information about the drug's interaction with humans. After the first phase is successfully completed, testing is performed on humans with the disease or condition that the drug is designed to treat to assess its efficacy and safety. The third and largest phase is the clinical testing of the drug by physicians who are supervised by and report to the pharmaceutical company sponsoring the tests. This final phase involves many more subjects (typically 3,000 to 4,000), which provides better information about rarer effects and interactions of the drug and reduces the likelihood that random error will produce spurious results. The studies do not gather as extensive information about individual patients and tend not to be as meticulously performed as the earlier stages because of the large number of physician-investigators involved.[25] The human investigation phases of the testing of a new drug are typically carried out by clinical researchers at university-affiliated hospitals, who contract with the manufacturer to conduct the studies. Sometimes private practitioners are utilized in the final phase of human testing because of the need to obtain large numbers of patients.

After the clinical studies are completed, the sponsor must submit an NDA to the FDA. The NDA contains the results of all animal and human studies, along with information about the proposed uses of the drug and the labeling to be provided. NDAs often comprise multiple volumes made up of tens of thousands of pages.[26] The Bendectin new drug application on file with the FDA in the late 1970s (including supplements from 1956) comprised 250 volumes and approximately 50,000 pages. The FDA must act on the NDA by approving it, disapproving it, or declaring it incomplete. If additional information is submitted after approval of the NDA, a supplemental new drug application is filed.

Several forces contribute to accurate and unbiased testing by the sponsor of a new drug. These include the professionalism of the scientists employed to conduct the studies, the desire of the manufacturer to assess accurately the therapeutic benefits of the drug so as to be able to maximize its potential market, the negative incentives of potential tort liability if the product has undetected adverse effects or risks greater than reported, FDA enforcement of violations of the Act, and the negative good will generated when a drug is revealed to have serious unreported adverse side effects.

Despite those forces, there is the influence of the sponsor's profits that contribute to subconscious biases, overly optimistic interpretation of data, shoddy testing, and even, in several (although a small proportion of) cases, the conscious concealment or falsification of study data submitted to the FDA.[27] Although close observers of the FDA disagree about which of these skewing effects is most prevalent, all agree that they occur. James Goddard, Commissioner of the FDA and later a witness for Merrell in several Bendectin cases, told the pharmaceutical trade association:

I can say that I have been shocked at the quality of many submissions to our I.N.D. staff.

. . .

In addition to the problems of quality, there is the problem of dishonesty in the investigational drug stage.

. . .

I will admit there are gray areas in the IND situation.

But the conscious withholding of unfavorable animal clinical data is not a gray-area matter.

The deliberate choice of clinical investigators known to be more concerned about industry friendships than in developing good data is not a gray-area matter.

. . .

These actions run counter to the law and the ethics governing the drug industry.[28]

A decade later, one of Goddard's successors as FDA commissioner, Alexander Schmidt, agreed that false and misleading reports of studies submitted to the FDA were "serious and grave." He went on to state, "It is certainly more widespread than I would have guessed. I think it represents an area in which we have never been active in regulating, and now clearly we must be."[29]

Even independent researchers hired by the manufacturer, who may have a longstanding relationship with the manufacturer, hope to continue that relationship, and develop personal ties to individuals employed by the manufacturer,[30] may be less than objective in their work, or even innocently suffer from unconscious biases in conducting their studies.[31] A recent analysis of bias in pharmaceutically sponsored studies observed that the industry prefers cooperative investigators, and may employ intimations about future research support to enhance influence over the final content of the published report.[32] An empirical study of the relationship between source of funding and outcome of clinical trials supports these observations: a highly significant correlation between source of funding and the outcome of the study exists. Industry funded studies favored the new therapy being evaluated in 89 percent of the cases. By contrast, studies with general funding favored the new therapy only 61 percent of the time.[33]

Dr. Louis Lasagna, an eminent pharmacologist and critic of the drug regulation system, provides a striking example of the impact of the profit motive in the following report of the reaction of several pharmaceutical companies to a study he had performed:

[T]he firms which stood to gain by the article embraced us with warmth; the others acted as though we were lepers. . . .
It is difficult to believe that the same article could be both a "fine contribution" and an "atrocity"; it seems more likely that one important criteria for evaluating a medical article disregards the validity of its contents, but looks to its effects on corporate earnings.[34]

Most would agree, however, that limits in the capacity of the NDA scientific studies to identify all adverse reactions explain more of the undiscovered drug hazards than does culpable manufacturer conduct. This is so for two reasons. First, it is often difficult to anticipate all of the adverse effects that a drug may cause and to build into the clinical investigations a mechanism to detect those side effects. Second, because even the phase 3 tests are conducted on a limited number of subjects, if a given side effect is rare enough it may not emerge in the clinical testing phase.[35] Thus, inevitably, additional hazards of new drugs emerge as they are put into widespread use in a heterogeneous population. Oral contraceptives had been marketed and used by thousands of women for three years before their tendency to cause blood clots in a small number of users was discovered.[36] These limitations on a complete understanding of a drug's effects are not as sensational as the culpable behavior mentioned previously, but appear to play a greater role in explaining undiscovered adverse effects.

A recent General Accounting Office study of post-marketing hazards documents the inability of the NDA process to identify a large proportion of the significant adverse effects associated with a new drug. The GAO reviewed all prescription drugs approved by the FDA during the decade from 1976 through 1985. By reviewing drugs that were removed from the market or drugs that had undergone a revision in their labeling indicating additional adverse effects, the GAO found that 51.5 percent of 198 prescription drugs approved by the FDA had serious postapproval risks that went undetected in the NDA phase.[37]

Even when the FDA receives solid and thorough data from the investigational studies, it is not infallible and walks a very thin tightrope between delaying or denying approval for beneficial new drugs, on the one hand, and approving drugs that turn out to have unanticipated adverse effects that outweigh any therapeutic benefits. As Richard Merrill, who subsequently became the Chief Counsel of the Food and Drug Administration, wrote, "the conclusion is inescapable that the agency occasionally makes wrong choices even when all of the facts are before it."[38] Those wrong or questionable choices are a function of a complex array of scientific uncertainty, difficult risk-benefit analyses, conflicting attitudes about the proper role of the Agency, and the political and economic forces that buffet the FDA.[39]

Scientific uncertainty is pervasive in the drug regulation field for reasons identified above; no series of clinical trials will reveal all of the hazards associated with use of a drug nor will it necessarily reveal complete efficacy information. Making a decision about whether the therapeutic benefits of a drug outweigh its risks, especially with the uncertainties and incommensurable comparisons involved, is, for many new drugs, an uncertain matter.

That uncertainty, in combination with the FDA's consumer protection function, creates a contrasting problem, one that was forcefully made by critics of the FDA beginning in the 1960s and 1970s. Drug regulation is far too extensive, cumbersome, slow, and costly. Completing the animal and drug studies required and obtaining approval of a NDA typically took 12 years and cost in excess of $200 million (in 1987 dollars) for drugs that began human testing in the period 1970–82.[40] According to one estimate, only one out of 10,000 compounds synthesized in pharmaceutical company laboratories ever makes it to the market. The search for safety has corresponding costs in delay and testing.

Delay in approving drugs for marketing—the "drug lag"—and its consequences in denying Americans prompt access to beneficial new drugs is a frequently heard refrain since Sam Peltzman's pioneering study.[41] Peltzman, an economist at the University of Chicago, found that the 1962 Amendments to the Act resulted in costs of $250 million per year in potential new drugs that were not brought to market and $50 million per year due to decreased competition. Balanced against those losses, Peltzman found less than $100 million per year benefit to consumers from the absence of ineffective drugs that would otherwise have been marketed. An earlier study by Dr. Louis Lasagna found that new drugs reached the United States market from one to two years after they were marketed in European countries.[42]

An important contribution to FDA caution is both Congressional and media scrutiny and criticism, which tends to make the FDA risk averse in reviewing new drug applications. Errors of commission, approving a drug that has serious hazards, result in the harsh glare of adverse publicity and Congressional inquiry. By contrast, errors of omission are rarely revealed or the focus of attention (a recent important exception is the furor over delay in approving drugs for AIDS victims); hence the political consequences for the FDA are quite minimal. And when Frances Kelsey, an FDA official, prevented the marketing of thalidomide, hero status was readily conferred.[43]

Former FDA Commissioner Alexander Schmidt addressed the false negative bias of the FDA in a speech in the mid-1970s:

> For example, in all of FDA's history, I am unable to find a single instance where a Congressional committee investigated the failure of the FDA to approve a new drug. But, the times when hearings have been held to criticize our approval of new drugs have been so frequent that we aren't able to count them . . . . The message to FDA staff could not be clearer. Whenever a controversy over a new drug is resolved by its approval, the Agency and the individuals involved likely will be investigated. Whenever such a drug is disapproved, no inquiry will be made. The Congressional pressure for our negative action on new drug applications is, therefore, intense. And it seems to be increasing as everyone is becoming a self-acclaimed expert on carcinogens and drug testing.[44]

Because of the incompleteness of the NDA process, monitoring of the drug after approval plays an important role in regulatory oversight and protection of the public interest. For a variety of reasons, that monitoring has been less than optimal in identifying post-marketing adverse reactions. The mechanism for tracking a drug's safety in the post-marketing period is the Adverse Drug Experience Report (ADR)[45] or its predecessor, the Drug Experience Report (DER). The ADR is a report by a physician or consumer to the manufacturer of an adverse effect after the use of a pharmaceutical. ADRs do not mean that the effect observed was caused by the drug, but the proximity of time and clinical judgment of the physician is suggestive that there may have been a causal link. The ADR process is voluntary; physicians are urged to report adverse reactions, but are not required to do so. Reports are made to the manufacturer; by law manufacturers must report to the FDA "any adverse event associated with the use of a drug in humans, whether or not considered drug related."[46] In theory at least, the FDA monitors ADRs looking for trends that suggest further investigation.[47]

At every layer, there are forces at work that make (and have made) the

ADR process less than entirely effective in identifying adverse side effects. Consumers are at the base of the ADR pyramid, as they are the ones who suffer the adverse effects. But they are often unaware of any connection between ingestion of a drug and a subsequent adverse reaction. Even if they suspect such a connection, many will not bother to inquire or report to their physician. Physicians, the next layer in the process, also may fail to make a connection between an adverse effect and a prescription drug. Often the underlying condition or disease masks the adverse effect. Or the adverse effect may not manifest itself for a lengthy period of time, as is the case with carcinogens, for example. Moreover, physicians, who do not have a legal obligation to report suspected adverse reactions, are frequently reluctant to report reactions to the manufacturer, because it may implicate them in subsequent litigation.[48] Fewer than 10 percent of doctors do any adverse reaction reporting and those that do only report a portion of the reactions they observe.[49] Inadequate monitoring by the FDA and attention to or analysis of reports that it received has also been reported.[50]

Reporting by manufacturers to the FDA, despite the legal requirement, has been less than perfect. Some notable examples of flagrant manufacturer disregard for this requirement have been documented.[51] More subtle defalcations are harder to detect, impossible to punish through legal process, yet no doubt exist. Countries with nationalized health care and centralized reporting have a considerably more effective post-approval surveillance system than exists in the United States.[52]

Because of these difficulties, virtually all knowledgeable experts agree that the adverse drug reporting system has been inadequate and unreliable.[53] Yet, the adverse drug reporting system played an important role in the genesis of Bendectin litigation, as explained in chapter 6.

The proper role of the FDA in its relationship and dealings with the pharmaceutical industry has long been a festering problem about which there is both internal and external dissension.[54] Some see the FDA as the watchdog of an industry that must be regulated because it poses a threat to the health and safety of the nation. Others, who view pharmaceuticals as making a major contribution to the treatment of disease and thereby the quality of life, would have the FDA play a partnership role with the pharmaceutical industry by coordinating efforts in a cooperative atmosphere. Critics of the FDA complain about its toothlessness in regulating the industry and protecting the American public from such drug fiascos as chloromycetin, Parnate, and MER/29.[55] When the FDA is staffed with people of each of these views, dissension inevitably percolates. Intra-agency suspicions and conflicts may develop in this environment. Sometimes those in subordinate or minority positions will act in covert or subtle ways to further their own views. Indeed, it was several such FDA employees who quietly encouraged and assisted Betty Mekdeci in her search for the cause of David's birth defects.

Of course, much of the disagreement stems from different conceptions of the pharmaceutical industry itself. Those who are suspicious of it regard it as controlled by venal individuals who are motivated predominantly, if not exclusively, by the bottom line, quite naturally view the FDA as drug industry police. Those who believe that the industry is made up of largely reasonable and conscientious individuals, including many physicians and scientists dedicated to improving health care, are inclined to be of the minimalist regulation camp. One of the most extreme members of the former group is Betty Mekdeci, who to this day is persuaded that Merrell employees knew that Bendectin was a teratogen and devoted their efforts before the FDA and in litigation to concealing that fact from others. If she is right, more than police would be required to control the monsters who populate the industry.

In summary, there can be no doubt that FDA regulation provides a significant measure of comfort and safety for consumers and physicians using drugs. Indeed, FDA regulation provided the courts confronting Bendectin litigation with a measure of comfort in deciding the issue of its teratogenicity as explained in chapter 17. Whether the FDA regulates in a way that optimizes therapeutic benefits while minimizing health risks remains one of the significant regulatory controversies of the day. It does, after all, have "a fantastically difficult tightrope to walk," and is subject to the political, economic, and social forces of the day, as the FDA's reaction to AIDS demonstrates.[56] Nevertheless, one can confidently state that despite FDA oversight, some drug calamities are inevitable. One reason for this is the limits on ascertaining the full range of biological effects through existing testing methodologies. The other is the reliance of the FDA on the industry itself to conduct the studies and provide the data for evaluation of the safety and efficacy of drugs, both pre- and post-approval.

Notes

1. The absence of FDA regulation of the Dalkon Shield is explained in MORTON MINTZ, AT ANY COST: CORPORATE GREED, WOMEN, AND THE DALKON SHIELD 54–56, 125–27 (New York: Pantheon Books, 1985).

2. Letter from Richard A. Merrill to author (Mar. 7, 1994); *see also* STEVEN GARBER, PRODUCT LIABILITY AND THE ECONOMICS OF PHARMACEUTICAL AND MEDICAL DEVICES 32–33 (Santa Monica, CA: Rand, 1993).

3. HENRY G. GRABOWSKI & JOHN M. VERNON, THE REGULATION OF PHARMACEUTICALS: BALANCING THE BENEFITS AND RISKS 6–9 (Washington, DC: American Enterprise Institute, 1983).

4. Joseph A. Di Masi et al., *Cost of Innovation in the Pharmaceutical Industry*, 10 J. Health Econ. 107 (1991).

5. *See, e.g.*, Peter Brimelow & Leslie Spencer, *Food and Drugs and Politics*, Forbes, Nov. 22, 1993, at 115.

6. *See generally* Morton Mintz, By Prescription Only: A Report on the Role of the United States Food and Drug Administration, Pharmaceutical Manufacturers, and Others in Connection With the Irrational and Massive Use of Prescription Drugs that May be Worthless, Injurious, or Even Lethal (Boston: Houghton Mifflin, 1967).

7. John K. Iglehart, *The Food and Drug Administration*, 325 New Eng. J. Med. 217 (1991); Orrin Hatch, *The Future Direction of the Food and Drug Administration* 46 Food Drug Cosm. L.J. 15, 15 (1991).

8. A more extensive history of the Food, Drug, and Cosmetic Act can be found in James C. Munch, *A Half-Century of Drug Control*, 11 Food Drug Cosm. L.J. 305 (1956); Frank M. McClellan et al., *Strict Liability for Prescription Drug Injuries: The Improper Marketing Theory*, 26 St. Louis U. L.J. 1, 9–21 (1981); Harry F. Dowling, Medicines for Man: The Development, Regulation, and Use of Prescription Drugs (New York: Knopf, 1970).

9. For an account of the quacks peddling nostrums before the Pure Food and Drug Act of 1906 and the grandiose marketing claims made on their behalf, *see* James H. Young, The Toadstool Millionaires: A Social History of Patent Medicines in America Before Federal Regulation 205–44 (Princeton, NJ: Princeton University Press, 1972).

10. The Supreme Court limited the scope of the Act further when it held that the misbranding provisions were limited to the ingredients of the drug and not the therapeutic claims made by the purveyor. United States v. Johnson, 221 U.S. 488 (1911).

11. Charles O. Jackson, Food and Drug Legislation in the New Deal 151 (Princeton, NJ: Princeton University Press, 1970).

12. *See* Peter Temin, Taking Your Medicine: Drug Regulation in the United States 46–51 (Cambridge, MA: Harvard University Press, 1980).

13. For further detail about the 1938 Amendments, see Peter Temin, *The Origin of Compulsory Drug Prescriptions*, 22 J. L. & Econ. 91 (1979).

14. Milton M. Silverman & Philip R. Lee, Pills, Profits, and Politics 5 (Berkeley: University of California Press, 1974).

15. Richard Harris, The Real Voice (New York: Macmillan, 1964).

16. S. Rep. No. 448, 87th Cong., 1st Sess. 156–64, (1961). Today, the figure is 22 percent. Office of Technology Assessment, Pharmaceutical R & D: Costs, Risks and Rewards (1993).

17. Pub. L. No. 87–781, 76 Stat. 780 (1962).

18. Morton Mintz, *Heroine of FDA Keeps Bad Drug Off Market*, Wash. Post, July 15, 1962, at 1.

For an account of the role of thalidomide in the 1962 amendments to the Food, Drug, and Cosmetic Act, *see* Harris, *supra* note 15; Temin, *supra* note 12, at 123–24.

19. Despite this limitation, the FDA has asserted the authority to regulate non-printed advertisements, including those through broadcase media. As a practical matter, the ability of the FDA to regulate statements made by detailers is quite meager. *See* David G. Adams, *FDA Regulation of Communications on Pharmaceutical Products*, 24 Seton Hall L. Rev. 1399, 1408 (1994).

20. The two exceptions were to provide the FDA with greater authority over

and information about the investigational phase of new drugs to enable it to monitor the manufacturer's clinical studies and, by requiring affirmative FDA approval of an NDA, to facilitate the FDA's demands for additional testing.

21. The FDA has asserted the authority to disapprove an NDA on the grounds of comparative safety with another drug. *See, e.g.,* John C. Ballin, *Who Makes the Therapeutic Decisions?,* 242 JAMA 2875 (1979).

22. In 1986, the FDA adopted a regulation that permits manufacturers to strengthen warnings or omit efficacy claims without prior FDA approval, presumably in instances in which post-marketing surveillance provides new information that should be conveyed to physicians. Subsequent FDA approval is required. *See* Sheila R. Shulman & Marianne E. Ulcickas, *Update on ADR Reporting Regulations: Products Liability Implications,* 3 J. CLIN. RES. & DRUG DEV. 91, 97 & n.10 (1989). For the situation before 1986, see Richard M. Cooper, *Drug Labeling and Products Liability: The Role of the Food and Drug Administration,* 41 FOOD DRUG COSM. L.J. 233 (1986).

23. PETER B. HUTT & RICHARD A. MERRILL, FOOD AND DRUG LAW: CASES AND MATERIALS 1178–1206 (Westbury, NY: Foundation Press, 2d ed. 1991).

24. Modest changes to the pre-approval testing process were promulgated in 1983 and 1987. *See id.* at 517.

25. The IND process is extensively discussed in JERRY T. GIBSON, MEDICATION, LAW AND BEHAVIOR 122–45 (New York: Wiley, 1976); WILLIAM W. WARDELL & LOUIS LASAGNA, REGULATION AND DRUG DEVELOPMENT 19–25 (Washington, DC: American Enterprise Institute, 1975).

26. PATRICIA L. SHANKS, BIOTECHNOLOGY: NEW DEVELOPMENTS IN FEDERAL POLICIES AND REGULATIONS 131 (New York: Practicing Law Institute, 1988).

27. William M. Sage, *Drug Product Liability and Health Care Delivery Systems,* 40 STAN. L. REV. 989, 1019–20 & n.127 (1988); MINTZ, *supra* note 6; Sidney A. Shapiro, *Divorcing Profit Motivation from New Drug Research: A Consideration of Proposals to Provide the FDA with Reliable Test Data,* 1978 DUKE L.J. 155.

28. *Excerpts from Dr. Goddard's Address,* N.Y. TIMES, Apr. 7, 1966, at 24.

29. *Hearings on Preclinical and Clinical Testing by the Pharmaceutical Industry Before the Subcomm. on Health of the Senate Comm. on Labor and Public Welfare and the Subcomm. on Administrative Practice and Procedure of the Senate Comm. on the Judiciary,* 94th Cong., 1st Sess., pt. 3, at 725 (1975).

30. *See* Renée Fox, *Physicians on the Drug Industry Side of the Prescription Blank: Their Dual Commitment to Medical Science and Business,* 2 J. HEALTH & HUM. BEHAV. 3, 11 (1961) (reporting that industry physicians view maintaining personal relationships with academic physicians as "the most important part of [their] job").

31. *See* III REVIEW PANEL ON NEW DRUG REGULATION, PROPOSALS TO PROVIDE THE FDA WITH RELIABLE TEST DATA 17–32 (interim rep. 1977); *The Pharmaceutical Persuaders—The Industry, the Doctor, and the Clinical Trial,* 2 LANCET 421 (1961).

32. Alan L. Hillman et al., *Avoiding Bias in the Conduct and Reporting of Cost-Effectiveness Research Sponsored by Pharmaceutical Companies,* 324 NEW ENG. J. MED. 1362 (1991).

33. Richard A. Davidson, *Source of Funding and Outcome of Clinical Trials,* 1 J. GEN. INT. MED. 155 (1986).

34. *Hearings on Interagency Coordination in Drug Research and Regulation Before the Subcomm. on Reorganization and International Organizations of the Senate Comm. on Governmental Operations,* 88th Cong., 1st Sess., pt. 4, at 1616 (1964) (paper by Louis Lasagna, M.D.).

35. H.R. Rep. No. 931, 91st Cong., 2d Sess. 11–12 (1970).

36. Dowling, *supra* note 8, at 59–60 (1970).

37. General Accounting Office, FDA Drug Review: Postapproval Risks 1976–85 (1990). The GAO defined serious risks as ones requiring withdrawal of the drug, changes in labeling that reflected a serious medical problem, or identification of a serious risk in the FDA Drug Bulletin.

38. Richard A. Merrill, *Compensation for Prescription Drug Injuries*, 59 Va. L. Rev. 1, 16 (1973).

39. For an explanation of the difficulty of risk-benefit analysis in this context, see Stephen G. Breyer, Regulation and Its Reform 147–53 (Cambridge, MA: Harvard University Press, 1982).

40. Di Masi et al., *supra* note 4; *see also* Ronald W. Hansen, *The Pharmaceutical Development Process: Estimates of Development Costs and Times and the Effects of Proposed Regulatory Changes, in* Issues in Pharmaceutical Economics 151 (R. Chien ed., Lexington, MA: Lexington Books, 1979) ($54 million in constant 1976 dollars and over 5 years).

In recent years the FDA has developed a "fast track" for especially promising drugs and is making promising experimental drugs more widely available during the NDA testing process.

41. Sam Peltzman, Regulation of Pharmaceutical Innovation: The 1962 Amendments (Washington, DC: American Enterprise Institute, 1974).

42. Louis Lasagna, *Research, Regulation, and Development of Pharmaceuticals: Past, Present, and Future*, 263 Am. J. Med. Sci. 67 (1972). For a bibliography of literature about the "drug lag," see Hutt & Merrill, *supra* note 23, at 583.

For a list of drugs approved for use in Europe, later removed from the market because of adverse reactions, but never approved by the FDA for sale in the United States, *see* Grabowski & Vernon, *supra* note 3, at 45.

43. As the former chief counsel for the FDA wrote, after reviewing over 100 Congressional investigations of the FDA: "No FDA official has ever been publicly criticized for *refusing to allow* the marketing of a drug. Many, however, have paid the price of public criticism, sometimes accompanied by an innuendo of corruptibility, for approving a product that could cause harm." Richard A. Merrill, *Can the FDA Do Anything Right?*, Va. L. Sch. Rep., Summer 1978, at 19, 22, *quoted in* Sidney A. Shapiro, *Limiting Physician Freedom to Prescribe a Drug for any Purpose: The Need for FDA Regulation* 73 Nw. U. L. Rev. 801, 813 n.86 (1978).

44. Alexander Schmidt, *The FDA Today: Critics, Congress and Consumerism*, speech delivered before the National Press Club, Washington, D.C. (Oct. 29, 1974) *quoted in* Grabowski & Vernon, *supra* note 3, at 5; *see also* Breyer, *supra* note 39, at 132; Herbert Burkholz, The FDA Follies 108–11 (New York: Basic Books, 1994).

45. *See* Postmarketing Reporting of Adverse Drug Experiences, 21 C.F.R. § 314.80 (1994).

46. *Id.*

47. *See* Thomas P. Gross, *The Analysis of Postmarketing Drug Surveillance Data at the U.S. Food and Drug Administration, in* Drug Epidemiology and Post-Marketing Surveillance 1 (Brian L. Strom & Giampaolo Velo eds., New York: Plenum Press, 1992).

48. Mintz, *supra* note 6, at 8; Dowling, *supra* note 8, at 164–66.

49. FDA, New Drug Development in the United States 51 (1990).

50. *See* Daniel W. Sigelman, *Turning the Tables on Drug Companies*, Trial, March 1994, at 72.

51. *See* Merrill, *supra* note 38, at 5–6; FDA, *supra* note 49, at 50 (explaining criminal conviction of pharmaceutical employees who suppressed ADRs for the blood pressure medication Selacryn in the early 1980s).

52. *See* Gerald A. Faich et al., *National Adverse Drug Reaction Surveillance*, 148 ARCH. INTER. MED. 785, 786 (1988) (adverse drug reaction reporting in United States is one-fourth of rate in Great Britain).

53. Shapiro, *supra* note 43, at 813.

The FDA made a number of efforts, beginning in the latter part of the 1980s, to improve the ADR system. *See* Shulman & Ulcickas, *supra* note 22.

54. SUSAN TOLCHIN & MARTIN TOLCHIN, DISMANTLING AMERICA: THE RUSH TO DEREGULATE 1–38 (Boston: Houghton Mifflin, 1983).

55. *See, e.g.*, N.Y. TIMES, Aug. 10, 1960 (former medical officer at FDA claiming it had become "in many of its activities, merely a service bureau" for pharmaceutical industry), *quoted in Interagency Coordination in Drug Research and Regulation: Hearings Before the Subcomm. on Reorg. and Int'l Orgs. of the Senate Comm. on Gov't Operations*, 87th Cong., 2d Sess., pt. 1, at 606 (1962).

56. S. REP. No. 1153, 89th Cong., 2d Sess. 149 (1966) (view of Dr. Louis Lasagna).

Chapter 5
The Wm. S. Merrell Company

The defendant sued by Betty Mekdeci, Richardson-Merrell Inc., was a company with an extensive past. That history played an important role in the initiation and development of Bendectin litigation, and requires some explanation for a full appreciation of its influence. As Professor Joseph Sanders explains: "When hints of trouble emerged concerning Bendectin, many in the plaintiff's bar must have concluded that, with respect to this firm, where there was smoke there must be fire."[1]

Merrell's history included its role as the North American licensee for thalidomide. Merrell also was the manufacturer of MER/29, a widely-hailed anti-cholesterol drug introduced in the 1960s. By the time MER/29 was removed from the market in 1962, thousands of individuals had been harmed by the drug, and fifteen hundred lawsuits ensued. The handful of thalidomide suits and numerous MER/29 suits against Merrell were among the first tort cases against the pharmaceutical industry;[2] thalidomide was the first involving a teratogen, and MER/29 the earliest instance of mass toxic litigation. Each of these pharmaceutical misadventures attracted substantial media attention and published accounts. When Betty Mekdeci contacted attorneys about representing her, Merrell's courtroom history was a matter of public record.

The Corporate Genealogy

Often touted as the first United States pharmaceutical company, the Wm. S. Merrell Company was established in 1828 in Cincinnati, Ohio by a young druggist named William Stanley Merrell.[3] The Wm. S. Merrell Company began as a small retail purveyor of patent medicines but, like a handful of other apothecaries around the world, expanded to producing its own medicaments. These enterprising pharmacists, along with the dye industry (which used chemicals and needed the capability for basic research in that area), and the development of departments of pharmacology in universities, were responsible for the advent of the modern pharmaceutical era, beginning in the late nineteenth century. Initially, the center of the industry was in Germany, because of its concentration of skilled and well-trained chemists. However, because supplies from Germany were cut during both world wars, other countries encouraged and developed domestic pharmaceutical research capabilities. Not until World War II and the refinement of sulfa drugs did the American pharmaceutical industry reach world-class status.

In 1938, the Vick Chemical Company acquired the assets of Wm. S. Merrell, making it a subsidiary of Vick. Vick was primarily involved in the manufacture and sale of household medicinal products and cosmetics (e.g., Vicks VapoRub). Vick traced its lineage back to 1880 when Lunsford Richardson established the company. In the 1930s, Vick became concerned that the cure for the common cold was at hand and decided to diversify into the prescription drug business, leading to its acquisition of Wm. S. Merrell. Thus, in 1956 when Bendectin was introduced to the market, it was a product of the Wm. S. Merrell Company, whose parent was Vick. In 1960 Vick changed its name to Richardson-Merrell Inc., later it combined the Wm. S. Merrell Company and another drug company it had acquired, the National Drug Company, into an operating division named Merrell National Laboratories. At the time, Richardson-Merrell Inc. regularly appeared around 300 on the Fortune 500 list, but fell short of counting itself among the elites of the American pharmaceutical industry, such as Smith, Kline & French and Lederle Laboratories.

Nevertheless, at the beginning of the 1960s Richardson-Merrell Inc., with its well-developed and proficient distribution system, had several drugs in the pipeline that it hoped would catapult it into the first rank of pharmaceutical companies. One of those drugs was MER/29, an anticholesterol drug that Merrell had developed. Another was a drug developed in Germany, but for which Merrell had obtained licensing rights in the United States and Canada: thalidomide. Later sections of this chapter explain Merrell's experience with those drugs.

By 1981, Richardson-Merrell decided to separate its operations into proprietary (over-the-counter) and ethical (prescription) drug organizations. For years the ethical drug business had struggled. The Richardson family was also influenced by the threat of Bendectin litigation.[4] The Merrell National Laboratories division was sold to Dow Chemical Company. Dow merged a small pharmaceutical company that it owned with its new acquisition and changed the name of the new subsidiary to Merrell Dow Pharmaceuticals, Inc., which was the corporate entity sued by Bendectin plaintiffs after 1981.[5]

Thalidomide

The tragic experience with thalidomide cast a pervasive shadow on Bendectin litigation. The obvious connection is that Bendectin was alleged to have much the same impact on the developing fetus as thalidomide had had twenty years before. The periodical *Mother Jones* trumpeted the connection on its cover in November 1980: "In 1960 There Was Thalidomide. In 1980 There Is Bendectin."[6] But the connections and influence were far more subtle and complex: thalidomide played a major role in alerting the world to the risks of exogenous agents on the fetus and spurred major developments in the science of teratology, pharmacology, and toxicology and in the regulation of pharmaceuticals; Chemie Grünenthal, the German pharmaceutical company that developed thalidomide, licensed Merrell to manufacture and distribute thalidomide in Canada and the United States; thalidomide victims brought the first lawsuits over birth defects, and while most of the victims were located in Europe, several North American cases were filed against Merrell; and a number of the lawyers and expert witnesses involved in thalidomide litigation later played key roles in Bendectin litigation.

Thalidomide received more public attention than any other drug in history. The image of horribly deformed children, described by the *Saturday Review* as "cocoons of flesh," was seared into the world's collective consciousness in the 1960s when a number of periodicals published pictures of thalidomide babies. The thalidomide tragedy was extensively investigated, studied, and documented by governments, physicians, journalists, and lawyers. Those accounts, often quite critical—perhaps hypercritical—of the pharmaceutical companies involved, were published in the 1960s and 1970s.

In England, the *Sunday Times* took on the cause of the English victims and championed their efforts to obtain legal redress.[7] By 1980, a team of investigative reporters from the *Sunday Times* had produced a book-length treatment of the entire thalidomide episode that extensively covered virtually all aspects of thalidomide, its toxicity, chemical structure, the psychological impact on families of thalidomide children, and the culpability of Chemie Grünenthal, Distillers Company (Biochemicals) Limited, the English licensee, and Merrell. Henning Sjöström, a Swedish attorney who had represented thalidomide victims in that country, and Robert Nilsson, a physician at the Royal University of Stockholm who had assisted Sjöström with the medical aspects of the case, published another book-length account of thalidomide and the role of the pharmaceutical companies. Two English academics, Harvey Teff and Colin Munro, published a book that focused on the legal aspects of claims by thalidomide victims.[8] Other books about the pharmaceutical industry contained chapters that were devoted to thalidomide, including one authored by Morton Mintz, a prominent investigative reporter for the *Washington Post* and a long-time critic of the pharmaceutical industry. Senator Hubert Humphrey held extensive congressional hearings on the thalidomide episode in the United States, and hundreds of journal, magazine, and newspaper accounts were also published.

The enormous attention paid to thalidomide, the horror of the victims, and the role of the pharmaceutical industry and Merrell specifically in the iatrogenic (injury resulting from medical treatment) nightmare became a matter of public record. That record would cast a long shadow when allegations of Bendectin's teratogenicity emerged in the late 1970s.

The Development and Marketing of Thalidomide

Thalidomide was synthesized in 1954 by Wilhelm Kunz, a pharmacist. Kunz, employed by the German pharmaceutical company Chemie Grünenthal, found that thalidomide was a powerful hypnotic—equivalent to existing barbiturates—but without the hangover effects. Most importantly, thalidomide's therapeutic benefits came without any acute toxic effects. In animal tests Grünenthal could not ascertain a lethal dose for thalidomide, which meant that concerns about overdosing, a serious problem with other hypnotics, were alleviated.[9]

First marketed in October 1957 as a tranquilizer and sleeping aid in Germany, thalidomide was combined with a number of other drugs, including aspirin, for treatment of a variety of common ailments, including colds and the flu. Under German law, thalidomide could be sold as an over-the-counter drug, and when it was exported to Great Britain in 1958 it was sold similarly.

Sales of thalidomide were spurred by an extensive marketing campaign undertaken by Chemie Grünenthal, and its aggressive licensing of the drug in foreign countries. By December 1959, Chemie Grünenthal's sales of thalidomide reached $100,000 per month and within two years sales tripled that in Germany alone. Ultimately, thalidomide was distributed in 40 countries under 50 different trade names.

Chemie Grünenthal's marketing of thalidomide emphasized its nontoxicity—"completely safe" was an early and frequently employed term in thalidomide advertisements. Thalidomide was thus widely used by parents in a liquid form to sedate their children. Indeed, it was characterized as "West Germany's baby sitter."[10] In its enthusiasm to explore all potential markets for its new sedative, Chemie Grünenthal marketed thalidomide to physicians with letters that stated:

In pregnancy and during the lactation period, the female organism is under great strain. Sleeplessness, unrest and tension are constant complaints. The administration of a sedative and hypnotic that will hurt neither mother nor child is often necessary.[11]

The letter went on to specify that thalidomide "does not damage either mother or child," although thalidomide never underwent reproductive testing on pregnant animals by Chemie Grünenthal, Distillers, or Merrell while being actively marketed.

By 1960, sales of thalidomide represented almost 50 percent of Chemie Grünenthal's sales.[12] When a substantial share of a pharmaceutical company's sales or profits derives from a single drug, a strong incentive exists to protect the drug from any threats to its success. Yet at that time, a number of disturbing questions were emerging about thalidomide, although none concerned its possible teratogenicity.

As the use of thalidomide grew through the late 1950s, reports of adverse reactions began to increase. A variety of adverse reactions were reported, including constipation, nausea, and dizziness. The most serious complaint was of peripheral neuritis, an abnormal condition in the nerves of the extremities that is characterized by tingling, or in more serious cases, numbness, muscular pain, cramps, and weakness in the limbs.

Chemie Grünenthal confronted these emerging concerns by minimizing, rationalizing, and distorting the record. In what would later be echoed in allegations in the Bendectin litigation, the *Sunday Times* characterized Chemie Grünenthal's response as the following:

- It lied when doctors wrote asking if they had heard of this sort of side effect before.
- It denied all causal connection between thalidomide and peripheral neuritis.
- It tried to conceal the number of cases that had been reported to the company.
- It tried to suppress publication of reports about thalidomide-induced peripheral neuritis by using influence and by creating diversion and confusion.
- It tried to counter critical reports with favourable ones, and to get them, it was prepared to spend money, use influence, and create distortion.
- It fought to prevent the drug's going on prescription, attacked doctors who advocated this control, and used a private detective to try to discover information that could be used against these doctors.[13]

On December 31, 1960 the first English-language published report raised the connection between thalidomide and peripheral neuritis. Dr. A. Leslie Florence described four cases of peripheral neuritis among his patients and inquired whether other physicians who had placed their patients on long-term thalidomide therapy had noticed similar effects.[14]

Thalidomide in North America

Chemie Grünenthal licensed Merrell to distribute thalidomide in the United States and Canada in 1958 after Smith, Kline & French declined Chemie Grünenthal's offer to be the United States distributor.[15] Smith, Kline's testing of thalidomide revealed no improvement in efficacy over existing drugs. Thalidomide, which was to be marketed in the United States under the trade name Kevadon, was assigned the code name MER 32 by Merrell. Later, in the Bendectin litigation, this code name would be employed when referring to thalidomide to prevent the jury from learning of Merrell's role in thalidomide.

On September 12, 1960, Merrell filed a new drug application (NDA) with the FDA to market thalidomide in the United States. Merrell planned to begin selling thalidomide in March 1961; meeting this target would require rapid consideration and approval of its NDA by the FDA. Although that was not to be in the United States, in April 1961 Merrell had its first success in securing approval to market thalidomide. The Canadian Food and Drug Directorate approved the sale of thalidomide in Canada, and Merrell began selling thalidomide there.

In the United States, Merrell's application was assigned to Dr. Frances Kelsey, a physician and pharmacologist, who had resigned her position at the University of South Dakota Medical School to accept employment with the FDA in 1960. Dr. Kelsey's first major assignment at the FDA was to handle Merrell's application to market the new tranquilizer thalidomide.[16]

Although thalidomide had been approved for sale in Germany and England, the Food, Drug, and Cosmetic Act required Merrell to conduct its own studies of the safety of thalidomide. Merrell's focus in its clinical study was marketing and promotion rather than scientific inquiry. Merrell perverted the regulatory process to enable it to gain a head start in establishing thalidomide as a major new tranquilizer. Merrell's studies, performed by private clinicians, were, in the words of a brochure it prepared to educate its employees about the effort, "To contact Teaching Hospitals . . . for the purpose of selling them Kevadon and providing them with a clinical supply." Rather than being conducted by the medical department, the study was overseen by Merrell's marketing department, with the medical department's role limited to a veto power over the clinicians invited to participate. Merrell instructed the sales people who were to make contacts with clinical investigators that "the main purpose is to establish local studies whose results will be spread among hospital staff members." Investigators could be told they need not report results if they didn't care to do so, an unthinkable condition for any serious study. Placebos were only provided to investigators who requested them.

To maximize its marketing impact, Merrell's thalidomide study was the largest preapproval effort by an American pharmaceutical company by 4 times, involving over 1200 clinicians, 2.5 million pills, and 20,000 patients. One Merrell attorney, later reflecting on the marketing focus of Merrell's thalidomide clinical studies, remarked, "It was a mistake," that "should not have happened."[17]

In Merrell's defense, thalidomide was in wide use in Germany, England, and several other countries at the time Merrell planned and conducted its study. Thalidomide had been tested by Chemie Grünenthal in Germany and Distillers in England, and although Merrell was legally required to conduct its own clinical investigation, it had good reason to believe that nothing untoward would emerge. In Merrell's view, thalidomide had been sufficiently studied in Germany and England, and it used the FDA-required study to introduce the drug and create a favorable climate for marketing thalidomide in the United States. Even though Merrell had a reasonable basis to believe that its clinical study would not reveal anything new, its use of that study for marketing efforts was a perversion of the Food, Drug, and Cosmetic Act.

Dr. Frances Kelsey's first significant communication with Merrell put a chill on Merrell's plans to introduce thalidomide on a fast track. On November 10, 1960, the last day before Merrell's NDA would become effective unless the FDA objected, Kelsey wrote to Merrell and pointed out numerous inadequacies in the NDA, including insufficient data about chronic toxicity, incomplete detail about both the animal and clinical studies that had been performed, and limited information about the drug's stability. These objections extended the effective date for Merrell to market thalidomide for at least another 60 days, but, even more important, served notice on Merrell that the FDA was not going to rubber stamp Merrell's NDA based on the thalidomide experience in Europe.

By all accounts, Merrell had little patience for Dr. Kelsey's requests for additional information and the delays occasioned by them. As early as October 1960, Merrell inquired about who was assigned to review its NDA for thalidomide, as was its right under FDA practice. Thereafter, Merrell engaged in a sustained and determined campaign to truncate review of its NDA not only with Dr. Kelsey, but with her superiors as well. Merrell initiated over fifty contacts with Dr. Kelsey during the 15-month period when thalidomide was under review.[18] In retrospect, Dr. Kelsey, with her characteristic reserve, observed: "Whereas other firms had on occasion applied pressure, in no instances was it as severe as with this application."[19]

In a telephone conversation in February 1961, Merrell's Dr. Joseph Murray pressed Dr. Kelsey for assurances that Merrell's latest thalidomide application would be permitted to become effective. By this time, however, Dr. Kelsey had read Dr. Florence's letter about peripheral neuritis published in the *British Medical Journal*. The report concerned her for two reasons. During the war, Dr. Kelsey had conducted research on quinine and found that drugs that had neurotoxic effects could have other adverse effects as well. Thus Dr. Kelsey was concerned about other side effects that might emerge from thalidomide use. Dr. Kelsey's second concern was about Merrell's good faith: Merrell had provided no information to the FDA about thalidomide and peripheral neuritis in its NDA, despite the published account. Kelsey told Murray of her concerns about peripheral neuritis after he pressed her for the reasons why Merrell's application was deficient. He acknowledged that he was aware of the adverse case reports and that he had written to Chemie Grünenthal for further information. Dr. Kelsey insisted on further animal studies and additional clinical information. Kelsey also decided to proceed with even more caution, concerned now about Merrell's lack of candor in the application process.[20]

Inquiries of Chemie Grünenthal by Dr. Murray elicited the response that while peripheral neuritis was an adverse effect, it was quite rare and reversible on withdrawal of the drug. Neither claim was true: Grünenthal claimed it had knowledge of but 34 cases of peripheral neuritis, but its files contained over 400 reports of the condition.[21] Not surprisingly, Merrell reported back to the FDA with the sanitized information that it received from its licensor, Grünenthal. Merrell also informed Dr. Kelsey that the British and German drug authorities were going to permit the continued marketing of thalidomide with a warning about neurotoxic effects and urged her to adopt the same approach for marketing in the United States. This discussion did nothing to quell Dr. Kelsey's skepticism about the accuracy of the information provided by Merrell. In a memorandum of her meeting with Merrell representatives held on March 30, 1961 regarding the information they had obtained during a recent visit to Europe, Dr. Kelsey wrote: "I had the feeling throughout that they were at no time being wholly frank with me and that this attitude has obtained in all our conferences etc. regarding this drug."[22] Later, Merrell mollified Dr. Kelsey somewhat by explaining that its lines of communications with Chemie Grünenthal had been less than ideal.

Merrell continued to pressure the FDA for approval. In April, Dr. Murray called Dr. Kelsey's immediate supervisor, Dr. Ralph Smith, to inquire whether a decision was forthcoming in light of the information from

Grünenthal provided to Dr. Kelsey in March. Informed that a decision was not imminent, Murray threatened that Merrell would have to contact the FDA Commissioner, George Larrick, to break the logjam. The continuing tension was punctuated by a letter written by Dr. Kelsey to Merrell on May 5, 1961, in which she stated that Merrell's application was "entirely inadequate" because of the absence of sufficient animal studies and scanty clinical information on the incidence of peripheral neuritis and its reversibility. She concluded that "we are much concerned that apparently evidence with respect to the occurrence of peripheral neuritis in England was known to you but not forthrightly disclosed in the application."[23]

After further attempts by a now-angry Merrell to go over Dr. Kelsey's head failed, yet another meeting was held between Dr. Kelsey and representatives of Merrell in May 1961. At this meeting, Dr. Kelsey raised a new area of concern: could thalidomide cross the placental barrier and cause similar neurological damage to the fetus? Kelsey's previous work with quinine had alerted her to the possibility that the fetus might be a different pharmacological entity from the mother.[24]

Over the next several months, Merrell tried to respond to this new area of concern as well as to allay the older concerns about peripheral neuritis. An article published by Dr. Ray Nulsen, a clinical investigator, in the June 1961 issue of the *American Journal of Obstetrics and Gynecology* was submitted to the FDA. Nulsen reported on thalidomide's efficacy and found no adverse effects on the children of women who had taken thalidomide late in their pregnancy. Another meeting was held with the FDA in September to present the results of other clinical investigators' experiences with thalidomide. These efforts were inadequate to assuage Dr. Kelsey's increasing concern about the incidence and reversibility of peripheral neuritis, especially as more reports of such adverse effects were published.

Discovering Thalidomide's Teratogenicity

Meanwhile, independently in Germany and Australia, efforts were being made to track down the cause of a sudden epidemic of children born with limb reduction defects. Although there were many minor variations in the deformity suffered, most were children with phocomelia, one or more limbs that were shortened (sometimes missing) and resembled a seal-like flipper. Phocomelia is extremely rare. Most obstetricians would not confront one case in their professional lifetime.

Yet Dr. William McBride, an ambitious, young (33 years old), and already prominent obstetrician from Sydney, Australia, confronted three cases of phocomelia in the spring of 1961. McBride spent a weekend with the medical records of the three mothers and found one thing in common that raised his suspicions: all three had taken thalidomide. McBride informed the Australian branch of Distillers of his findings and suspicions, but that message apparently was never conveyed to Distillers' main office in London.

McBride's initial attempts to test his hypothesis allayed his fears. During the summer of 1961, McBride found no effect on the offspring of mice and guinea pigs after he fed thalidomide to the mothers. By mid-September, twenty-three women who had taken thalidomide delivered normal children (likely because they took thalidomide after the period when limbs and organs are forming and subject to chemical insult). McBride also consulted with a pharmacologist who perfunctorily dismissed the idea that thalidomide could have a teratogenic effect.

In Germany, Dr. Widukind Lenz, chief of the children's clinic at the Hamburg University Hospital, was consulted in June 1961 by a parent of a child born without arms below the elbows and only three fingers on each hand. The parent had a sister who six weeks before had had a similarly deformed child, and the parent suspected some geographical characteristic was at work. Lenz was astonished when his inquiries revealed numerous other instances of deformities in Munster and throughout Germany. Further investigation uncovered 16 cases of phocomelia in Hamburg. A study of birth records from 1930 to 1955 revealed one case of phocomelia among 212,000 births, yet Lenz estimated there were 50 cases in a thirteen-month period from September 1960 to October 1961.

Lenz was confronted with a classic "cluster" of disease, but uncovering the source of the epidemic was not an easy process. The cluster strongly suggested an environmental agent as the cause, yet there was no reason to suspect drugs. Equally or more plausible were diet, illnesses, radiation, and household cleaners or detergents. Lenz's investigation did not initially focus on drugs, but on November 11, 1961, Lenz interviewed a woman who had borne a phocomelic child. During the interview, the woman volunteered that she had taken thalidomide both before and during her pregnancy, and because she had developed peripheral neuritis had become concerned that the drug might have some effect on her baby even before he was born.

Within four days after this interview, Lenz identified 14 cases of serious birth defects where the mother had taken thalidomide. He called Chemie Grünenthal and laid out his suspicions, evidence, and conclusions. Chemie Grünenthal's response was casual; it offered to send a representative to talk with him in a few days. Concerned by Grünenthal's nonchalant response, Lenz composed and sent a letter to Chemie Grünenthal the next day (November 16) reiterating all that he had relayed over the telephone and creating a documentary record. On November 18, Lenz attended a pediatrics conference and expressed his concerns, albeit without providing the name of the drug he suspected during his presentation. Later, Lenz revealed in private conversations that he suspected thalidomide.

While Lenz was becoming convinced that thalidomide was the culprit, Dr. McBride's concerns were revived when two more women who had taken thalidomide bore children with severe birth defects. He called the Australian office of Distillers and reiterated his concerns, threatening to write letters to medical journals unless action was taken. On November 16, 1961, a Distillers' representative met with McBride. A report of McBride's suspicions was sent to Distillers in London and Chemie Grünenthal in Germany. After the meeting, McBride decided that he could no longer remain silent. Still unsure about the causal relationship and reflecting the prudence of a scientist without convincing evidence, his letter to the *Lancet*, the leading British medical journal, published December 16, 1961, merely reported on his observations and inquired of other readers whether they had noticed similar occurrences:

Sir:
Congenital abnormalities are present in approximately 1.5% of babies. In recent months I have observed that the incidence of multiple severe abnormalities in babies delivered of women who were given the drug thalidomide (Distavil) during pregnancy, as an anti-emetic or as a sedative, to be almost 20%.
   . . .
Have any of your readers seen similar abnormalities in babies delivered of women who have taken this drug during pregnancy?
  W. G. McBride[25]

In Germany, Lenz continued his efforts. During the week of November 20, 1961 Lenz found himself caught up full-time in the thalidomide controversy. Lenz met three times that week with representatives of Chemie Grünenthal and government health officials. Chemie Grünenthal's representatives were generally hostile, searching for flaws in Lenz' research, threatening lawsuits for damage to Grünenthal's business, and refusing to remove thalidomide from the market voluntarily.

Grünenthal executives convened in emergency meetings over the following weekend. Two additional events led them to conclude that thalidomide had to be removed from the market: Dr. McBride's letter, expressing similar concerns to Dr. Lenz's and formulated independently across the world, was revealed and the following day, a German newspaper carried a prominent article about Dr. Lenz and his concerns. The newspaper had been tipped off by a doctor who had attended the pediatrics conference at which Lenz expressed his fears a week earlier. Chemie Grünenthal's Board of Directors decided on November 27, 1961 to remove the drug from the market and notify doctors, pharmacists, and its licensees. Distillers immediately followed suit, notifying its foreign subsidiaries as well as doctors, hospitals, and pharmacists.

At this point suspicions about thalidomide were rampant, but no responsible scientist would conclude that thalidomide's teratogenicity had been proven. A significant piece in that evidentiary puzzle emerged within four weeks, however, when Chemie Grünenthal determined what it had previously not known: thalidomide could cross the placental barrier, as shown by feeding radioactively marked thalidomide to pregnant mice. Thus the developing fetus could be exposed to the chemical agents comprising thalidomide, a necessary but not sufficient condition for it to cause birth defects.

By March 1962 there was little doubt remaining that thalidomide was the teratogenic culprit. Distillers' chief pharmacologist published an article in the *Lancet* on February 10, 1962, marshaling Lenz's, McBride's, and other physicians' findings. The article mentioned an English investigation involving ten cases of children with limb defects. Of these, thalidomide exposure was confirmed in eight of the cases.[26] The next month, a researcher at Distillers found that thalidomide-exposed rabbits produced 13 of 18 kits with severe limb defects.

Thus, eight years after it was synthesized, over four years after it was first marketed, and many months after Dr. McBride's suspicions were first raised, thalidomide's hideous toxicity was uncovered. In one sense, this delay is extraordinary: thalidomide caused birth defects so fearsome that everyone took notice, it increased the relative risk of limb reduction defects by several orders of magnitude, it caused an epidemic that, once noticed, attracted enormous scientific attention, and it had a relatively short latency period, less than nine months. Thalidomide's teratogenicity was exposed initially because of clusters of disease and physicians who investigated those clusters looking for a common thread. No case-control or cohort epidemiological study was ever performed, although more than a hundred papers were published in the aftermath cataloguing the effects of thalidomide on a variety of animal species.

Part of the explanation for the delay in discovering thalidomide's phocomelic effects was a loose confidence in the protection afforded the embryo by the placental barrier. That confidence resulted in laxity even in documenting the drugs provided to pregnant women in their medical records. The absence of rigorous reproductive and teratologic protocols and methodologies at the time also played a role in the delay. Despite considerable advances in the science of uncovering teratogens (and other toxic agents), it is well to recall the words of Frances Kelsey, in her reflections on thalidomide: "With teratogens less potent than thalidomide . . . the difficulties of recognition [are] infinitely greater."[27]

The Legal Sequellae

Merrell was notified of Chemie Grünenthal's actions and the concerns about thalidomide's teratogenicity on November 29, 1961. On November 30, 1961 Dr. Murray called Dr. Kelsey and told her of the emerging concern about thalidomide's teratogenicity, but expressed the hope that the association was merely coincidental. At that point the FDA suspended activity on Merrell's application and awaited further word from Merrell about the connection between thalidomide and birth defects. The United States media initially failed to appreciate or publicize the emerging tragedy, and for several months America remained blissfully oblivious to the catastrophe that was occurring in numerous other parts of the world.

Unlike Chemie Grünenthal and Distillers, Merrell chose not to withdraw thalidomide from the Canadian market. Instead, it wrote "Dear Doctor" letters to physicians informing them of the association that had been found between thalidomide and congenital malformations in Europe and Australia, observing that any causal relationship remained to be proven, but recommending that thalidomide not be provided to pregnant women as a precaution. Thalidomide remained on the Canadian market until March 2, 1962, when the Canadian Food and Drug Directorate requested that thalidomide be withdrawn from the market, and Merrell complied.[28] A week later, the FDA received formal notification from Merrell that it was withdrawing its NDA for thalidomide.

Not until April 1962 did FDA officials appreciate the full extent of thalidomide's dangers. Dr. Helen Taussig, a prominent pediatrician at Johns Hopkins University, returned from Europe where she had confronted the devastation of thalidomide children. She informed Dr. Kelsey and Kelsey's colleague and officemate, Dr. John Nestor, of what she had observed and the virtually inescapable conclusion that thalidomide was responsible. When Dr. Kelsey contacted Merrell to find out where its investigational studies of thalidomide stood, she found out for the first time that over 1,100 United States physicians had received the drug. Further investigation by the FDA revealed that, as late as July 1962, Merrell had not completed its recall of thalidomide from investigators. In August the FDA discovered that 25,000 thalidomide pills were still in the hands of physicians and, even more disturbingly, that over 400 doctors had not contacted patients for whom they had provided the drug because the physicians' records were inadequate to reveal those to whom they had provided it.[29]

Estimates of the number of children afflicted with birth defects due to thalidomide range from 8,000 to 12,000. Children in 46 countries were affected.[30] Germany suffered the vast majority of victims; in England, 400 thalidomide children were born. Seventeen well-documented cases of thalidomide-induced birth defects occurred in the United States, although seven of those cases involved thalidomide that been obtained abroad.[31] Nine other cases of birth defects were suspected of being related to thalidomide, but exposure to thalidomide could not be convincingly established in those cases. Canada had 80 thalidomide-affected children who survived.[32]

Worldwide, a number of legal actions, both criminal and civil, were brought against the manufacturers and distributors of thalidomide. Thalidomide defendants sounded a similar theme in litigation. Thalidomide had been tested by Grünenthal, Distillers, and other licensees and had proved extraordinarily nontoxic. There was no reason for anyone to suspect that it could have an effect on the fetus of a woman who took it. This raised an issue that was to be joined in much of the litigation over thalidomide: what was the state of scientific knowledge about drugs and other chemical agents crossing the placenta and harming the fetus in its own right, as opposed to harming the fetus derivatively by causing harm to the mother? The drug companies affiliated with thalidomide insisted that before thalidomide the placenta was thought to serve as a barrier to toxins, thereby providing a protective shield for the fetus from exogenous agents. The fetus could only be harmed by a toxic substance indirectly as a result of damage to the mother's health. As is often the case in litigation, this position had some truth to it, but appears exaggerated, as was demonstrated in the ensuing years.

Germany played the leading role in criminal prosecutions. Nine Chemie Grünenthal executives were indicted in 1965. The case promised to be lengthy (the prosecutor listed 350 witnesses and 70,000 pages of documentary evidence), arduous (the trial went on for over 2½ years without reaching a conclusion) and, given the number of affected Germans and the severity of their harms, intense, angry, and highly publicized.

As the trial ground on and entered its third year, Grünenthal made an effort to wind up both the criminal and pending civil actions by making a $27 million offer to settle the civil cases, but making clear that the offer was tied to a dismissal of the criminal case. Ultimately, Grünenthal paid German victims $30 million with another $20 million being contributed by the German government. The criminal case was terminated in December 1970, with the consent of the prosecution.

The FDA found two bases for which Merrell might be prosecuted criminally for its role in thalidomide: Merrell had abused the new drug investigation process by using it to premarket thalidomide, and Merrell had made false assertions about the safety of the drug. Prosecutorial authority, however, rested with the United States Department of Justice, which declined in 1964 to pursue the case.[33]

In Britain, government officials declined to conduct a public investigation of Distillers. Thus attention quickly shifted to civil suits against Distillers by victims' families. But the obstacles they faced were significant. Contingent fees are prohibited and two-way fee shifting prevails, making personal injury lawsuits the domain of the very rich and very poor: the rich, because they can afford to finance the cost of civil litigation as well as bear the risk of an adverse decision, which means paying the opponent's costs of litigation; the poor, because Britain provides a means-tested legal aid that enables the poor to obtain legal representation that is paid for with public funds. Legal aid clients are not subject to cost-shifting if they are unsuccessful.

Thus thalidomide plaintiffs in Britain initially were all provided joint counsel who were compensated by legal aid, which incidentally ensured that their case would not be generously staffed or funded.[34] The joint representation of British victims created several conflicts of interest as settlements were negotiated: between victims who were devastatingly injured and those who were not so tragically harmed and between those whose causation cases were stronger and those in which questions arose about the etiology of the claimant's birth defect because of the timing of ingestion and similarity of effects.

Settlements occurred in two waves, the first in 1968 for a group of families who had filed suit within the statute of limitations and the second in 1973 for a larger group of families whose suits were filed after the statute had run. The second group succeeded in obtaining dispensation from the courts to continue their cases because of their delayed knowledge of the facts making up the legal claims. In the end, the average award to each family totaled approximately $125,000, a respectable amount, but a far cry from what was recovered in the United States on behalf of thalidomide victims.

A significant reason for the delay in settlement was due to a conflict among the claimants, a recurrent theme in mass tort litigation when global settlements are proposed. Distillers had developed both an "X" and a "Y" list of children, the former comprising those for whom strong evidence indicated the causal role of thalidomide, the latter including those for whom the evidence was either missing or equivocal. The interests of the "X" group were in strong limits on inclusion in the claimant pool: the smaller the number included, the greater recovery for each. By contrast, the interests of the "Y" group were in broad inclusion for eligibility to receive compensation. Both the question of procedures to assess qualification for inclusion in the compensated group and the carrying out of those procedures delayed the settlement and the ultimate payment of funds to thalidomide families in Great Britain.

Thalidomide litigation in the United States went on for almost twenty years. Merrell settled all of the cases brought against it; only one case proceeded to a jury verdict. Ironically, Merrell settled the last of its thalidomide cases the same week as it entered into a global settlement (later overturned) of all Bendectin cases. Merrell insisted upon, and obtained, confidentiality agreements with the plaintiffs about the financial aspects of the settlements. Only one thalidomide case is contained in the case reporters, and that concerns the procedural question of whether a Canadian plaintiff could pursue her action in the United States.[35]

Thalidomide litigation against Merrell included 13 United States cases. Nate Richter, a leading plaintiffs' lawyer in Philadelphia, agreed to take the first thalidomide case in the United States. Other thalidomide cases followed. Arthur Raynes, a young lawyer in Richter's office, assumed substantial responsibility for Richter's thalidomide cases, and when Raynes left Richter's firm to set up his own office he took the thalidomide clients and cases with him. Although Raynes had one case that proceeded to trial, Merrell settled the case mid-trial after Raynes amassed and presented convincing evidence that the mother had taken thalidomide during the critical period of fetal limb development.

In Cleveland, the law firm of Spangenberg and Traci represented a number of thalidomide victims, largely those from Canada.[36] Facing similar impediments to a tort action as those in Great Britain, thalidomide victims in Canada were the beneficiaries of an ingenious scheme conceived by Professor Alan Linden of Osgoode Hall Law School in Toronto. Linden recommended to Canadian lawyers representing several victims that they locate an American lawyer to represent their clients and bring suit in the United States, where contingent fees were permitted and fee shifting was not. Because the thalidomide sold in Canada had been manufactured by Merrell in Ohio, there was a reasonable basis for jurisdiction in the Ohio courts. Through contacts, Linden located Craig Spangenberg, a personal injury lawyer in Cleveland, who brought suit on behalf of several Canadian victims in federal court in Ohio. During the course of preparing his cases for trial, Spangenberg persuaded Dr. William McBride, the co-discoverer of thalidomide's teratogenicity, to testify as an expert witness at trial.

In Los Angeles, James Butler accepted one thalidomide case, that of Peggy McCarrick, the only United States thalidomide case that resulted in a trial and jury verdict. Butler, the father of nine, was moved when he first met Peggy, who had a shortened leg that ended in a flipper and deformed hip joints. Although he was first consulted when Peggy was 8 years old and when only three months remained before the statute of limitations would bar the claim, Butler agreed to represent the McCarricks, and later represented several British children.

Merrell, convinced that Shirley McCarrick, Peggy's mother, had not taken thalidomide during the period of fetal development of the lower limbs, refused to make any significant settlement offer. Merrell settled all other North American thalidomide cases—the aggressiveness of plaintiffs' lawyers, adverse publicity, and public sympathy for thalidomide victims contributed to this decision. But Merrell was persuaded that Peggy McCarrick's deformities were not due to thalidomide, and in March 1971 the case went to trial in Los Angeles. Dr. Lenz, who had testified against thalidomide manufacturers in a number of cases around the world, appeared on behalf of Merrell and testified that Peggy McCarrick's physical defects were not due to thalidomide. A number of other experts agreed with Dr. Lenz. One of Butler's experts, who also had testified in the Swedish thalidomide cases, was Dr. John Thiersch, director of the Institute of Biological Research and Professor of Clinical Pharmacology at the University of Washington. Dr. Thiersch had been part of a team of researchers who found in 1952 that the drug aminopterin was toxic to the human fetus in doses that did not cause significant reactions in the mother.

After a trial lasting almost three months and in which Butler had Peggy McCarrick make an appearance on her ninth birthday, the jury, by a vote of 10–2, found for the McCarricks and awarded them $2.75 million. The jury's verdict was over $500,000 more than Butler had requested.

The *McCarrick* case had a profound impact on Jim Butler, who not only found himself deeply involved in the plight of a child with severe birth defects, but who also was persuaded that he had met and defeated an evil company that had spread toxic pills throughout the country and attempted to disavow responsibility when called to task. The verdict in *McCarrick* also impressed Merrell officials with the human side of birth defect cases and the impact of the human tragedy on a jury. Although Merrell genuinely believed that it had an open and shut defense, it found itself on the wrong end of a verdict that, for its time, was enormous. Ultimately, after a two-year period during which the trial judge ordered a remittitur (reduction of the amount of damages awarded by the jury) and cross-appeals were pursued, Merrell and the McCarricks settled the case for $600,000. The total amount paid in settlement by Merrell remains confidential, but there is no doubt that for the hundred or so North American (mostly Canadian) victims for whom Merrell was responsible, the sum was substantial. Some settlements were for as much as $1,000,000, and most were for $100,000 or more. The total cost to Merrell of the settlements and defending itself may have reached $50 million.

With the enormity of the financial and public relations consequences of thalidomide, it is not surprising, though no less ironic, that Merrell's attitude toward Dr. Kelsey underwent a transformation. Fred Lamb, general counsel for Merrell, observed: "She's a hero. If it hadn't been for her, we'd be out of business." [37] Thus, the regulatory limitations under which Merrell had earlier chafed saved it untold millions of dollars in liability.

One important episode that emerged from discovery in the United States thalidomide litigation concerned the role of Dr. Ray Nulsen, a physician from Cincinnati, in clinical investigations of thalidomide and his authorship of a paper on thalidomide's safety during pregnancy that was published in the *American Journal of Obstetrics and Gynecology* in 1961.[38] The paper concluded that thalidomide had no deleterious effects on the offspring of mothers who had taken thalidomide during the last trimester of their pregnancy and had been submitted to Canadian and United States drug authorities to support Merrell's application to market thalidomide. Craig Spangenberg, the Canadian thalidomide plaintiffs' attorney who later represented three of Dr. Nulsen's patients, deposed Dr. Nulsen. During Dr. Nulsen's deposition, it emerged that Dr. Pogge, the medical director for Richardson-Merrell, had written the article that bore Nulsen's name. Nulsen stated that he had provided the information for the article to Pogge, but that the information was not in written form; Nulsen testified he had reported to Pogge verbally. Nulsen stated he could not remember whether he kept written records of the patients to whom he had given thalidomide, their personal characteristics, or their self-reported effects of taking thalidomide. Later Nulsen claimed that the written documentation for the article had been destroyed.[39]

The Nulsen episode raised serious questions about the integrity and seriousness of Merrell's clinical testing of new drugs. Industry "ghostwriting" of clinical investigators' journal articles has been condemned as a serious ethical breach.[40] When considered in light of the revelations about MER/29, which was tested by Merrell during the late 1950s, even a fair-minded observer might have concluded that Merrell's scientific operation was not to be trusted.

Craig Spangenberg, a mild mannered lawyer who tends toward understatement and introspection, reflected on his experience with Merrell by commenting, "Merrell did a lot of things. They were really evil. [It was] a bad company." [41]

The Legacy of Thalidomide

Thalidomide caused some of the most horrifying birth defects imaginable: children born with a complete absence of limbs, or flippers attached to the shoulder or lower trunk. It affected legs and arms, fingers and toes. It also affected the development of a number of organs, including the heart, kidney, and digestive tract, depending on the time of ingestion and the corresponding stage of development of the fetus. The vast majority of defects found in thalidomide children, however, upwards of 80 percent, were limb defects.[42] Some of the most severely afflicted fetuses did not survive. One study found a combined stillborn and neonatal death rate of 45 percent after thalidomide exposure, as the fetus or infant could not overcome thalidomide-induced defects, especially of the internal organs.[43]

Thalidomide influenced Bendectin litigation not only because of Merrell's involvement with thalidomide. Thalidomide convincingly demonstrated the ability of drugs and exogenous agents to cross the placental barrier and cause severe birth defects. These birth defects, ones over which the entire western world agonized, had a major impact on thinking and concern about environmental influences on the fetus. Thalidomide provided a major boost to the modern development of teratology, which previously had languished as something of a stepchild in the medical sciences. Thalidomide spurred enhanced concern about the effects of environmental agents on the developing fetus and the development of reproductive testing to better determine whether agents have adverse effects on the fetus.[44] The rapid expansion of animal reproductive testing by the pharmaceutical industry and increased attention to environmental causes of birth defects by epidemiologists reflected this influence.

Thalidomide also provided insight into the psychological impact on parents of bearing a child with birth defects, the sense of guilt, the need to know what was responsible for the child's defect, and the inadequacy of the frequent response to most such inquiries: "We don't know." That pattern would repeat itself in the cycle of Bendectin litigation.

It is often said, not entirely accurately, that thalidomide dispelled a longstanding belief that the placenta served as an impenetrable barrier protecting the human embryo from toxins. Numerous statements exist that thalidomide demonstrated to the world that toxic agents can cross the placenta,[45] and many still believe that to be true.

In retrospect, there is little doubt that many sophisticated physicians and researchers held the belief that the placenta served as a filter for toxic materials.[46] At the same time, as a number of critics of Grünenthal, Distillers, and Merrell have pointed out, science was not completely blind to the possibility that exogenous agents, including drugs, could harm the fetus without causing harm to the mother. To explain this situation requires a bit of the history of teratologic thinking.

The human race, indeed all living species, has always been plagued by congenital malformations. History is replete with reports of children born with birth defects; statues depicting gross abnormalities date back to 6500 B.C. Some of the god-idols of antiquity are believed to have been fashioned in the image of children born with malformations.

At various times, these birth defects have been attributed to such forces as God, Satan, devils, witchcraft, bad thoughts by the mother during pregnancy, and cross-species mating, as well as environmental, genetic, and dietary factors.[47] The Babylonians believed that malformations were meant as a portentous message. Infanticide of children born with birth defects was practiced in a variety of civilizations during history.

By the second half of the nineteenth century, science had a more refined view of birth defects. Scientists were performing experiments with nonmammals such as fish and chicks and inducing teratologic effects with alcohol, chemicals, and nicotine. Researchers nevertheless believed that the mammalian fetus was protected by the placenta in a way that chick embryos in an egg were not.

Mendel's work on plant hybrids, which revealed many of the fundamentals of genetics in the mid- to late nineteenth century, played an important role in teratologic thinking. Several decades after his work, genetics became influential in scientific thinking, making it a common explanation for a wide variety of biologic phenomena, including birth defects.[48] By the 1920s, genetics was believed to be the sole reason for birth defects, and although a few theoreticians hypothesized that agents could pass through the mammalian fetus and harm the embryo, no hard evidence existed.

By the 1930s, a number of clinicians had published papers suggesting that quinine could harm the fetus. These papers were premised on quinine being passed through the placenta and directly affecting the fetus, and cited several instances where that was believed to have occurred.[49]

The modern era of teratology can be traced to the 1940s when experimentalists first studied the effects of diet and exogenous factors on the fetal development of mammals. Several studies found that a variety of agents could cause birth defects in mammals, mostly rodents.[50] In 1948 researchers were able to induce spina bifida in rats with doses of a chemical, trypan blue, that were not toxic to the mother.[51] In the same year, nitrogen mustard was found to cause severe malformations in rats.[52] During the same decade, radiation and german measles were shown to cause birth defects in the human species. In 1952 Dr. John Thiersch, who served as an expert witness in both thalidomide and Bendectin litigation, found that orally administered aminopterin was a human abortifacient and could cause fetal malformations.[53] Yet the mechanisms by which many of these phenomena occurred were not understood, and many researchers and scientists continued to believe that the human embryo was impervious to assault through the placenta, or nearly so with but a few exceptions.[54]

By the 1950s, a number of the larger and more conscientious pharmaceutical companies were conducting reproductive studies of their new drugs on animal species, although the FDA had no protocol for reproductive studies at the time. These studies were by no means routinely performed in the pharmaceutical industry, but Burroughs tested its drug Diaprim on rats for reproductive toxicity because it expected the drug would be used for long-term therapy and Hoffman La Roche commissioned reproductive studies on Librium before it was marketed, as did several other pharmaceutical companies. In 1958, a multi-center collaborative perinatal project began and started gathering data that would address the role of drugs in causing human birth defects. Results from that study, however, were not published until 1977.

Thus the culpability of thalidomide manufacturers for failing to conduct fetal toxicity studies is a matter on which reasonable people can disagree. There can be no doubt, however, that the magnitude of the human tragedy played a remarkable role in the development of the science of teratology. Hundreds of studies were conducted on thalidomide in the years after its teratogenic properties were first identified. Those researchers learned that humans were a species highly sensitive to thalidomide. Scientists also discovered that there was substantial interspecies variation in response to potential teratogens; studies of thalidomide in mice and rats produced no congenital anomalies.[55]

One reason that no birth defects were found in the offspring of rodents is that, rather than causing defects in the fetus that was then born alive, thalidomide killed a proportion of the litter. The dead fetuses were then resorbed into the uterus by the mother. The only evidence of this effect was a reduction in litter size and a modest scar in the uterus.[56] Only reproductive testing of thalidomide in the New Zealand white rabbit produced malformations similar to those found in humans.

Those proposing to expose pregnant women to a drug or other agent became aware that the placenta was not the magical protective barrier that some had thought. Providing pharmacologically active agents to pregnant women was risky business, business that required advance testing. The testing would have to include a variety of animal species and account for the timing of administration in conjunction with embryologic development to examine the variety of birth defects that might occur. Teratologists learned that careful examination was required not only of live-born offspring for defects, but also for the existence of stillborns and fetal resorptions.

Birth defects are an intermediate reaction to toxic agents. In some instances, due to low dose, timing of exposure, or unknown factors, no effects are found. At the other extreme, teratogens may simply kill the fetus.

Epidemiological methodology rapidly improved through the 1960s, as researchers recognized difficulties with recall and other biases and proper definition of the exposure of interest and the outcome to be studied. Epidemiology benefited also from the development of new and improved analytical and statistical methodologies. The importance of using these improved epidemiological tools to examine birth defects and their causes was widely recognized.

Thalidomide was also the paradigmatic "dramatic event," one that affects not only science but political process and regulatory policy. As described in chapter 3, the thalidomide episode played a crucial role in the passage of the Kefauver-Harris amendments to the Food, Drug, and Cosmetic Act. Thalidomide played a continuing role thereafter in FDA policy and regulatory decisions. The FDA became active in recommending methodologic guidelines for adequate reproductive studies. As experience with those recommendations was gained in the mid-1960s, they were modified to reflect those lessons and advances in the scientific frontier. In 1965 the Teratology Society was formed and began publishing a journal devoted to that specialty. Physicians, aware of the risks to the fetus, became more cautious about prescribing drugs for their pregnant patients.[57] Thalidomide also spawned psychosocial research into the impact on the family and physician when a major tragedy occurs.

Ethel Roskies, a Canadian sociologist, conducted a study of families of thalidomide victims in Canada.[58] Roskies, after a number of interviews, was stunned by the variety of reactions among mothers of thalidomide children, ranging from extreme shock requiring emotional retreat and gradual assimilation of the reality and its consequences, to accepting the event as a challenge to be confronted and overcome, to quiet resignation by one poor farm mother, who accepted her child as just one more of life's difficulties.[59] Roskies, who limited her study to Canadian thalidomide victims, was unaware of the couple from Belgium who poisoned their daughter born without legs.[60] Frustrated by her inability to order and categorize these reactions, Roskies inquired: "How can one remain faithful to the oscillation, change, and confusion so evident in the data, and, at the same time, make this material coherent?"[61] She found solace in the observation of another researcher, faced with similar difficulties: "The . . . paradox of ordering reality versus the unreality of order taunts the investigator who wishes somehow to describe objectively the course of events."[62]

Despite the insight that generalizations about the initial reactions of families of congenitally malformed children are dangerous, two important findings emerged from Roskies's research. First, virtually all physicians involved in these births suffered tremendous turmoil. When the possible role of thalidomide emerged, the predominant reaction of physicians who had prescribed the drug was not to mention the possibility of thalidomide's role to the parents. When patients inquired, physicians would deny that thalidomide was the cause of the child's birth defects, instead blaming genetic factors, denying sometimes even that thalidomide had been prescribed.[63] Personal, professional, and potential legal consequences were all at work in this disavowal epiphenomenon.

Second, many women, upon learning that thalidomide was responsible for their child's birth defects, reported that initially they were quite relieved: a pharmaceutical cause meant that uncertainty about the cause was removed and guilt at the possibility that the source was genetic was relieved. Among those afflicted with tragedy, the unanswered question of "Why?" is often wrapped up with self-blame. "[M]any parents believed that something must have been wrong with *them*, and they blamed themselves, or each other, for the child's deformities. 'It's all your fault,' the mother of a severely brain-damaged boy was told. 'It's inherited from your family.' "[64]

The initial reaction of relief was then followed in a number of cases with anger at the physician who had prescribed the drug or at the manufacturer of the drug, mistrust of medical treatment generally, and even guilt at having taken the drug during pregnancy.

Thus thalidomide stood figuratively omnipresent when Bendectin litigation began. Thalidomide provided an attractive allegory for lawyers contemplating suit against Merrell over Bendectin. An international contingent of lawyers and expert witnesses gained experience in litigation over a teratogen. But the framework for Bendectin litigation requires consideration of yet another drug debacle, one that ironically got crowded out of the media's pharmaceutical reporting in 1962, because thalidomide took center stage that year.

MER/29

If Merrell's culpability in connection with thalidomide was ambiguous, its conduct in the development, testing, and marketing of MER/29 was not. In the late 1950s (at the same time that it first marketed Bendectin), Merrell developed a compound that promised to be a breakthrough drug. By this time cholesterol had been identified as contributing to heart disease and atherosclerosis, and a drug that could be safely used to reduce cholesterol levels had a huge potential market. In laboratory tests on animals, MER/29 (or triparanol, its generic name) had significantly reduced cholesterol levels. Before Merrell could submit its new drug application to the FDA, however, Merrell had to conduct tests to demonstrate the safety of MER/29 in humans.[65]

From 1956 to 1959 Merrell conducted both animal and human clinical testing. The animal tests were performed by the scientific staff of Merrell, and the human-clinical studies were performed by physicians selected by Merrell. Merrell filed its new drug application for MER/29 in June of 1959 and followed up by sponsoring a medical conference on MER/29 designed to familiarize cardiologists with its new drug.[66] Merrell paid travel expenses and consultation fees to those physicians in attendance.

Ironically, in light of later developments, the Chair of the Conference, Dr. Irving S. Wright of Cornell Medical School, lauded the careful scrutiny of MER/29:

If more drugs had been subjected to this kind of review early in their life histories, many mistakes and millions of dollars would have been spared physicians, patients, and pharmaceutical companies. This is the way a new drug should be reviewed, critically and without bias, so that new directions for investigation and evaluation may be pointed out.[67]

Merrell's NDA became effective in April 1960, although not without some controversy at the FDA. Critics there questioned whether long-term studies of MER/29's safety should be conducted since patients would take it for prolonged periods. Nevertheless the FDA indicated that it would not oppose Merrell's new drug application, and Merrell began marketing its drug aggressively as the first safe drug to reduce cholesterol.[68] Merrell was quite successful: within 18 months 400,000 persons had used the drug. By June 30, 1961, after its first full fiscal year on the market, MER/29 was Merrell's largest selling pharmaceutical and accounted for 13 percent of its prescription drug sales.

Ten months later MER/29 was removed from the market as reports of adverse side effects, the most serious of which was cataracts, multiplied.

Although a few physicians and pharmacologists had earlier expressed concerns both about the safety and efficacy of MER/29, a significant event raising a cloud over the drug occurred in January 1961, curiously enough in the laboratories of a competitor of Merrell, Merck & Co. Merck had synthesized its own triparanol and had conducted long-term toxicity tests on animals. Those studies found that both dogs and rats suffered increases in cataracts. Merck reported these findings to Merrell and invited Merrell to come to its labs and review Merck's findings, an invitation Merrell accepted. Although Merrell had previously found cataracts in two dogs in its own MER/29 studies, no report was made to the FDA. Because Merrell believed that it produced a purer version of MER/

29 than Merck, Merrell began another study to see if it could replicate the Merck result. Later, in October 1961, the Mayo Clinic reported that two of its patients on MER/29 therapy had developed cataracts; both patients had also suffered from hair and skin changes.

At the FDA, due to staff turnover, a new official was assigned responsibility for MER/29. Dr. John Nestor, Dr. Kelsey's officemate and a person who by inclination believed in aggressive oversight of the pharmaceutical industry, assumed responsibility for MER/29 in late 1961.[69] Almost immediately Nestor urged his superiors to halt the sale of MER/29, but he was overruled. Nestor was successful in strongarming Merrell into putting warnings on its labeling and sending out "Dear Doctor" letters on December 1, 1961. The letter advised physicians that some patients on MER/29 therapy had developed cataracts.

A crucial development in the withdrawal of MER/29 occurred fortuitously in February 1962. An FDA employee in Cincinnati met the husband of a former Merrell employee while car-pooling to work one day. The husband explained that his wife, Beulah Jordan, had been employed in the toxicology-pathology department at Merrell. Jordan claimed that she resigned because she had been directed by Evert Van Maanen, who directed Merrell's Biological Sciences Department, to change data on animal studies that were to be submitted to the FDA. The FDA employee, concerned about conditions at Merrell, made arrangements to interview Jordan and forwarded his report to Washington, DC, where it came to the attention of Nestor. The report arrived on Nestor's desk shortly after the allegations of thalidomide's teratogenicity had surfaced and after Merrell had requested Dr. Kelsey to hold the NDA for thalidomide in abeyance.[70]

On April 9, 1962 Nestor and Edwin Goldenthal, an FDA pharmacologist who had opposed the marketing of MER/29, arrived unannounced at Merrell's headquarters in Cincinnati to investigate its laboratory data and results on MER/29. During that search, Nestor and Goldenthal obtained all the data underlying Merrell's animal tests of MER/29.[71] Within two days Merrell agreed voluntarily to remove MER/29 from the market.[72]

Merrell, recognizing the potential civil and criminal difficulties it was facing, hired the New York City law firm of Davis, Polk & Wardwell to represent it. Davis, Polk is among the handful of elite corporate law firms in this country and had provided legal advice on corporate matters to Merrell for a number of years. John Davis, the first name partner in the firm, was the Democratic candidate for President in 1924 who ran against Calvin Coolidge. Lawrence E. Walsh, who later served as the Iran Contra special prosecutor, was the partner who headed the defense team at Davis, Polk. Walsh had sterling credentials: a former federal judge, he had just completed a three-year stint in Washington, DC as Deputy Attorney General in the United States Department of Justice.

In December 1963 a federal grand jury returned a criminal indictment against Richardson-Merrell, Wm. S. Merrell, and three Merrell employees, including Harold Werner, the Vice-President in charge of research, and Van Maanen. All of the charges alleged violations of the federal False Writing Statute,[73] which prohibits intentionally providing false information to the government or withholding information that the law requires to be provided to the government. The essence of the charges was that the defendants had failed to notify the FDA of the true results of six animal studies which Merrell had conducted and which had resulted in a variety of adverse side effects, including fetal mortality in a study of pregnant rats who were given MER/29. The indictment alleged that Merrell had deliberately changed dosages, timing, body weights, and adverse effects (including eliminating reports on the development of cataracts in the two dogs) and concocted data for animals that had died and that never existed, all to minimize MER/29's toxicity in its submissions to the FDA.

Several months later, all defendants pleaded nolo contendere (no contest) to the criminal charges, virtually the equivalent of a guilty plea. The primary difference between the nolo and guilty pleas is that the nolo plea cannot be used in subsequent civil litigation to prove the defendants engaged in the acts alleged. Instead, civil plaintiffs have to prove their cases. The two corporate entities were fined the maximum amount and the individuals were given six months probation, a mild sentence that perhaps confirmed Merrell's sagacity in hiring Davis, Polk and Walsh as its lawyers.

MER/29 became the first drug to generate large-scale tort litigation. Estimates are that 4,000 to 5,000 persons suffered adverse side effects from MER/29. The most serious was cataracts; other side effects included lost, thinned, or changed color of hair and mild to severe skin reactions. Only in rare instances were those affected unable to work, in some cases the adverse effects were reversible, and medical expenses to treat the adverse effects were quite modest. While these consequences were serious for the victims who suffered them, they were far from the magnitude of adverse effects suffered with thalidomide and alleged later in Bendectin litigation. The absence of more serious consequences meant modest potential compensatory damage awards in lawsuits on behalf of the victims, putting pressure on the plaintiffs' lawyers to find economical means to prepare their cases. It also stimulated the impetus for seeking punitive damages against Merrell.

In the first case of plaintiffs' attorney cooperation in a mass toxic products liability case, a MER/29 group was formed in 1963 to investigate the extent to which jointly-conducted efforts could be economically pursued, while at the same time (because this was to be done consensually) leaving control over each individual case with the plaintiff's attorney. Traditionally, the primary obstacle to consolidated or coordinated litigation in personal injury cases has been the insistence of the plaintiffs' attorneys on maintaining control over the course of their clients' cases. This insistence stems in part from the culture of rugged individualism in the plaintiffs' bar; it views itself as a bastion of opposition to the establishment, protecting the ordinary citizen from the evils of the powerful corporate establishment. Consistent with that conception, plaintiffs' attorneys work alone or in smaller groups than their counterparts representing corporate or insurance interests. Serving the legal needs of corporate America requires specialization and the capacity to bring several lawyers together on large projects. The advent of the large law firm in the late nineteenth century served that need.[74] By contrast, personal injury clients' needs can be served by a single lawyer, or at least could, until the advent of the mass toxic substances litigations of the past few decades.

To a significant extent, opposition to collective adjudication is economic; class or group efforts reduce the amount of legal work available and make it more difficult to charge a full contingent fee. Another impediment to cooperative efforts occurs when a small number of attorneys have invested time and developed information crucial to the prosecution of that genre of cases. In those situations, the attorneys view their efforts as investments yielding proprietary information that they are loath to share. This phenomenon has been evident in asbestos litigation, and generally seems more prevalent where litigation over a common agent or subject begins slowly with only a limited number of attorneys involved for a period of time. If the efforts of the MER/29 group to expedite and streamline litigation were to be successful, it would have to be because of its appeal to individual plaintiffs' attorneys who would decide that it was in both the attorney's and the client's interest to participate.

Thus, as might be expected, the coordinated efforts on behalf of MER/29 plaintiffs were relatively modest. Each plaintiff's attorney retained ultimate control over settlement and any trial that was required. Ultimately, almost 300 attorneys representing over 75 percent of the plaintiffs became members of the MER/29 group. Although the topic was discussed, the MER/29 group never attempted a class action or other form of consolidated litigation, and Merrell, although appreciating the efficiency advantages of some form of consolidation, was ambivalent because of concerns that a jury might be prejudiced by the number of victims before it. In a few jurisdictions with a large MER/29 docket, all cases were assigned for pretrial proceedings to the same judge.

In the end, the MER/29 group set up an organization that was funded by a per-plaintiff charge paid by each participating attorney. Paul Rheingold, a young lawyer who later rose to prominence in the plaintiffs' bar, organized the group and became the administrative head of the group. Lou Ashe, a partner of Melvin Belli, was also active in early efforts to coordinate MER/29 litigation. The group's greatest contribution was in conducting unified discovery of common issues relating to liability for compensatory and punitive damages, including depositions of defendant's employees, government employees, and other scientific witnesses, developing a document depository that contained all of Merrell's files relating to MER/29, and preparing a uniform set of interrogatories to Merrell.[75] In addition, a newsletter with information about settlements, trials, medical information, key regulatory developments, and copies of legal documents that had been filed in MER/29 cases was prepared and circulated periodically to members of the group.

The vast majority of cases were settled; by 1967 only 11 cases had been tried. The outcomes of the tried cases showed that Merrell had its greatest success in the early cases—the first three resulted in verdicts for Merrell—but later cases tended to favor plaintiffs, either because the plaintiffs' attorneys became better educated or Merrell became less able to control which cases proceeded to trial.

One significant legacy of the MER/29 litigation was the first award of punitive damages in a products liability case. In *Toole v. Richardson-Merrell Inc.*[76] the California Court of Appeals approved an award of $250,000 in punitive damages. In a paragraph that reflected its repugnance at Merrell's conduct, the court summed up the evidence that supported the jury's award of punitive damages:

> In our case there is evidence from which the jury could conclude that [Merrell] brought its drug to market, and maintained it on the market, in reckless disregard of the possibility that it would visit serious injury upon persons using it. Besides the falsification of test data under the direction of Dr. Van Maanen and the withholding from the FDA and the medical profession of vital information concerning blood changes and eye opacities in test animals, there was evidence that, after Dr. Fox reported eye opacities and blindness in her test animals, and after Merck, Sharp & Dohme had made a similar report, [Merrell] continued to represent to the medical profession that MER/29 was a proven drug, remarkably free from side effects, virtually nontoxic, having a specific and completely safe action. In light of [Merrell]'s knowledge, the jury could infer that these statements were recklessly made, with wanton disregard for the safety of all who might use the drug. Moreover, similar representations continued to be made even after the first report of cataracts in a human had been received and after [Merrell]'s later tests confirmed the presence of eye opacities in virtually all test

animals. When respectable medical publications began to challenge the toxicity and efficacy of MER/29, [Merrell]'s salesmen were instructed to blame side effects on other drugs, or at least to suggest that as a good possibility. Even after a number of cases of cataracts in humans from use of MER/29 had been reported to [Merrell], and when its own tests had established blindness in its test animals, [Merrell] continued to defend sale of its drug. When in November 1961 Dr. Nestor of the FDA expressed the opinion that MER/29 should be withdrawn from the market he was told by Vice President Woodward, in President Getman's presence, that MER/29 " . . . was the biggest and most important drug in Merrell history. . . ." and that the company intended " . . . to defend it at every step. . . ." and would withdraw the drug from the market voluntarily only when it determined that its inherent risk outweighed its efficacy. In December 1961 the FDA compelled [Merrell] to issue a drastic warning letter notifying the medical profession of known cases of cataract in humans from use of the drug. [Merrell] nevertheless continued with plans vigorously to promote its sale.[77]

That paragraph, published in 1967, was permanently enshrined in law libraries across the country and available for any attorney conducting even cursory research. Not only did Merrell's conduct become well known within the plaintiffs' bar, it also created a wall of suspicion at the FDA in its dealings with Merrell: the Medical Director of the FDA informed the Agency's employees:

As you may know, we have recently obtained evidence that the Wm. S. Merrell Co. falsified data submitted as part of the New Drug Application for MER/29. In view of this we cannot consider the information submitted by this firm as reliable without thorough verification.[78]

One observer estimated Merrell's total payout for MER/29 claims at $50 million.[79] Along with its costs for North American thalidomide claimants, Merrell's products liability costs for these two drugs were in the neighborhood of $100 million.

Bendectin

In 1953, Dr. Raymond Pogge, the Medical Research Director at Merrell, conceived of an antinauseant drug that could be used to treat morning sickness in women.[80] Because of the four million pregnancies per year in the United States and the large number of women who suffer from morning sickness, the potential market for this drug was quite attractive. Over the next three years, Pogge, in consultation with colleagues at Merrell, developed a combination drug designed to treat morning sickness.

Morning sickness is a common affliction, a loose classification that includes nausea, vomiting, or both, suffered by pregnant women. The precise cause of morning sickness is unknown, although the best informed theory is that it is related to the level of placental hormones. Obstetricians estimate that between 50 and 90 percent of pregnant women suffer from some degree of morning sickness. A great deal of variability exists among women: some suffer only the mildest symptoms, others are virtually disabled, while a few suffer such severe and unremitting vomiting that they lose weight and become dehydrated, posing a risk both to themselves and their fetuses. Patients with the most severe reaction, known as hyperemesis gravidarum, constitute less than one percent of all pregnancies. They often require hospitalization to rehydrate them intravenously and to monitor possible complications in other organs. For most women, the symptoms reach an apex in months two through four of their pregnancies, usually waning or ending around 16 weeks of pregnancy. Women with morning sickness have every bit as successful pregnancies as those women who do not suffer from it; some studies show that women who suffer morning sickness have better outcomes, as a group, in terms of miscarriages and premature deliveries, than those who do not suffer from it.

The drug that Dr. Pogge developed for morning sickness, Bendectin, consisted of a fixed-ratio combination of three drugs: pyridoxine (Vitamin B6), which had been sold since the 1930s, dicyclomine hydrochloride, marketed under the trade name Bentyl by Merrell since 1950, and doxylamine succinate, an antihistamine marketed as Decapryn by Merrell since 1948. The theory behind this combination was to combine an antispasmodic (Bentyl) that calmed the gastrointestinal tract, with an antihistamine (Decapryn) known to have antinauseant effects and pyridoxine, which was also thought to have antinauseant properties. In 1976 Bentyl was removed from Bendectin because efficacy studies conducted pursuant to the 1962 Amendments to the Food, Drug, and Cosmetic Act revealed that it did not contribute to the efficacy of the drug.[81] Thereafter Bendectin was manufactured and sold as a two ingredient drug.

On July 2, 1956 Merrell filed an NDA for Bendectin. Four weeks later, the FDA informed Merrell that it would not object to the NDA, thereby permitting it to become effective. Bendectin was marketed in the prethalidomide era, as an antiemetic for pregnant women suffering from nausea and vomiting. It contained no labeling precaution about adverse effects or cautionary statement about unknown risks to the mother or fetus, although its three ingredients had been the subject of only casual toxicity testing and no reproductive tests. Bendectin's labeling remained that way for over twenty years. Bendectin was distributed in 22 other countries as well, including England and Canada.

Because the three ingredients had each been in use and because the prevailing pharmacologic belief at the time was that the fetus was protected by the placenta, Bendectin was not tested for teratogenicity before it was marketed as a prescription drug in 1956.

A fixed-ratio combination drug to treat morning sickness in pregnant women is not without its problems. First, combination drugs are generally disfavored by pharmacologists.[82] Because of the fixed ratio in a combination drug, the prescriber cannot adjust the proportion of any of the ingredients where appropriate, thereby subjecting some patients to an excess of one component or not enough of another. Second, morning sickness is a transient condition that resolves itself and rarely causes lasting harm. The majority of pregnant women with morning sickness manage their discomfort without medical intervention.[83] Adjustments in diet or eating schedule are often sufficient, and emetral, a cola-like syrup, provides relief for some women. The American Medical Association has advised physicians that less than one percent of pregnant women have symptoms severe enough to justify drug intervention.[84] Similarly, the well-respected *Medical Letter* advised physicians: "Unless a drug is urgently needed, it should not be administered during pregnancy, especially during the first trimester. . . ."[85]

But the reality is that many pregnant women seek relief from their physicians for the discomfort of nausea associated with pregnancy. At the height of its popularity, Bendectin was used by over 30 percent of pregnant women in the United States.[86] A review of Bendectin performed by eight leading academic pharmacologists, obstetricians, and pediatricians, after observing there was little scientific evidence to support the need for treatment of morning sickness, recognized the significance of patient demand:

[I]n the pragmatic world of medicine the condition of nausea and vomiting of pregnancy will be treated by physicians, as patients demand relief from the discomfort and disruption of life style. Demand is an important part of the rationale for the use of Bendectin in the treatment of significant nausea and vomiting of pregnancy.[87]

Thus, women like Betty Mekdeci could call their physician's office, complain of morning sickness, and obtain a prescription over the telephone. Some 36 million pregnant women took Bendectin worldwide during the 27 years it was marketed.

Notes

1. Joseph Sanders, *The Bendectin Litigation: A Case Study in the Life Cycle of Mass Torts*, 43 HASTINGS L.J. 301, 316 (1992).
2. Some widely scattered tort suits had been brought against drug companies

since the 1940s. *See* William Prosser, *The Assault upon the Citadel (Strict Liability to the Consumer)*, 69 YALE L.J. 1139 (1960); Craig Spangenberg, *Aspects of Warranties Relating to Defective Prescription Drugs*, 37 COLO. L. REV. 194, 199 n. 19 (1965). A number of suits were also brought against Parke Davis over its drug Chloromycetin.

3. Schieffelin & Co. was founded in 1781, fifty years before Wm. S. Merrell. HARRY F. DOWLING, MEDICINES FOR MAN: THE DEVELOPMENT, REGULATION, AND USE OF PRESCRIPTION DRUGS 40 (New York: Knopf, 1970).

4. Carol Loomis, *Richardson-Merrell Unswallows a Pill*, FORTUNE, Jan. 12, 1981, at 54.

5. Eight years later, Merrell Dow and Marion Laboratories, a Kansas City pharmaceutical company, formed Marion Merrell Dow Inc. Merrell Dow became a wholly owned subsidiary of Marion Merrell Dow. In 1995 Hoechst A.G., a German pharmaceutical company, purchased the stock of Marion Merrell Dow, making it a subsidiary of Hoechst.

6. MOTHER JONES, Nov. 1980.

7. HARVEY TEFF & COLIN MUNRO, THALIDOMIDE: THE LEGAL AFTERMATH (Farnborough, England: Saxon House, 1976).

8. Much of this section is based on the accounts of thalidomide contained in these three sources: HENNING SJÖSTRÖM & ROBERT NILSSON, THALIDOMIDE AND THE POWER OF THE DRUG COMPANIES (Harmondsworth: Penguin, 1972); THE INSIGHT TEAM OF THE SUNDAY TIMES, SUFFER THE CHILDREN: THE STORY OF THALIDOMIDE (London: Andre Deutsch, 1979) [hereinafter INSIGHT TEAM]; TEFF AND MUNRO, *supra* note 7.

9. Questions both about the efficacy of thalidomide and its nontoxicity were later raised in several accounts of the thalidomide tragedy. *See* SJÖSTRÖM & NILSSON, *supra* note 8; INSIGHT TEAM, *supra* note 8.

10. Richard McFadyen, *Thalidomide in America: A Brush with Tragedy*, 11 CLIO MEDICA 79, 79 (1976).

11. SJÖSTRÖM & NILSSON, *supra* note 8, at 194.

12. *Id.* at 54.

13. INSIGHT TEAM, *supra* note 8, at 41.

14. A. L. Florence, *Is Thalidomide to Blame?*, 2 BRIT. MED. J. 1954 (1960).

15. *Interagency Coordination in Drug Research and Regulation: Hearings Before the Subcomm. on Reorg. and Int'l Orgs. of the Senate Comm. on Gov't Operations*, 87th Cong., 2d Sess., pt.1, at 275–76 (1963) (reprint of letter from W. A. Munns, President of Smith, Kline & French, to Senator Hubert Humphrey, dated August 27, 1962) [hereinafter Interagency Coordination].

16. RICHARD HARRIS, THE REAL VOICE 184 (New York: Macmillan, 1964). For an excellent account of the thalidomide experience in the United States, see McFadyen, *supra* note 10.

17. Telephone interview with Richard E. Nolan (Apr. 13, 1994).

18. S. REP. No. 1153, 89th Cong., 2d Sess. 18 (1966); Interagency Coordination, *supra* note 15, at 81–100.

19. McFadyen, *supra* note 10, at 80. Several years later, in 1966, Dr. James Goddard, then the Commissioner of the FDA lectured the pharmaceutical industry: "I am deeply disturbed at the constant direct personal pressure some industry representatives have placed on our people." RALPH A. FINE, THE GREAT DRUG DECEPTION 203 (New York: Stein & Day, 1972).

20. Subsequently, in 1962, the FDA investigated how much information about adverse effects had been passed to Merrell from Distillers and Chemie Grünen-

thal that had not been revealed in Merrell's NDAs. Those investigators determined that Merrell first found out about the peripheral neuritis concerns from the published reports and that Merrell was first informed about teratogenic concerns in late November 1961, after thalidomide was withdrawn from the market by Grünenthal. McFadyen, *supra* note 10, at 88.

21. INSIGHT TEAM, *supra* note 8, at 77.

22. SJÖSTRÖM & NILSSON, *supra* note 8, at 118.

23. *Id.* at 121.

24. Helen B. Taussig, *The Thalidomide Syndrome*, SCI. AM., Aug. 1962, at 29, 34.

25. William G. McBride, *Thalidomide and Congenital Abnormalities*, 2 LANCET 1358 (1961).

26. A.L. Speirs, *Thalidomide and Congenital Abnormalities*, 1 LANCET 303 (1962).

27. Frances O. Kelsey, *Events After Thalidomide*, 46 J. DENT. RES. 1201, 1204 (Supp. 1967).

28. FINE, *supra* note 19, at 179.

29. McFadyen, *supra* note 10, at 85.

30. INSIGHT TEAM, *supra* note 8; TEFF & MUNRO, *supra* note 7.

31. S. REP. No. 1153, 89th Cong., 2d Sess. 12 (1966).

32. JEAN WEBB, THE THALIDOMIDE PROBLEM IN CANADA (1964).

33. McFadyen, *supra* note 10, at 88.

34. For an account of one parent's struggle to obtain compensation for his thalidomide-affected daughter, see DAVID MASON, THALIDOMIDE: MY FIGHT (London: Allen & Unwin, 1976).

35. Henry v. Richardson-Merrell Inc., 508 F.2d 28 (3d Cir. 1975).

36. This account of the North American litigation is drawn from INSIGHT TEAM, *supra* note 8, at 128–36; interviews with James Butler, Merrell, and Craig Spangenberg; and discovery documents produced in the MDL-486 litigation.

37. Mark Dowie & Carolyn Marshall, *The Bendectin Cover-up*, MOTHER JONES, Nov. 1980, at 43, 45.

38. R.O. Nulsen, *Trial of Thalidomide in Insomnia Associated with the Third Trimester*, 81 AM. J. OBSTET. & GYN. 1245 (1961).

39. SJÖSTRÖM & NILSSON, *supra* note 8, at 123–27; INSIGHT TEAM, *supra* note 8, at 81–85.

40. S. REP. No. 1153, 89th Cong., 2d Sess. 224–25 (1966).

41. Telephone interview with Craig Spangenberg (Feb. 6, 1992).

42. INSIGHT TEAM, *supra* note 8, at 113, 265–68; ETHEL ROSKIES, ABNORMALITY AND NORMALITY: THE MOTHERING OF THALIDOMIDE CHILDREN 2 (Ithaca, NY: Cornell University Press, 1972).

43. Richard W. Smithells, *Defects and Disabilities of Thalidomide*, 1 BRIT. MED. J. 269 (1973).

44. Kelsey, *supra* note 27, at 1201.

45. "The discovery that thalidomide, a pharmacodynamic drug, produces congenital malformations was a shock, since these effects had previously been associated only with substances that interfere with the synthesis of protein and nucleic acids." R. Brodie, *Idiosyncracy and Intolerance, in* DRUG RESPONSES IN MAN (Gordon E.W. Wolstenholme & Ruth Porter eds., London: Churchill, 1967); Taussig, *supra* note 24, at 35 ("until recently no thought had been given to the need for the testing of drugs for potential harmfulness to the human embryo").

46. Editorial, *Teratology*, 1 LANCET 530 (1969); Taussig, *supra* note 24; S. REP. No. 1153, 89th Cong., 2d Sess. 25–26 (1966).

47. The Bible contains an admonition to the wife of Manoah, who anticipated

becoming pregnant, "Now therefore, beware, I pray thee, and drink not wine nor strong drink and eat not any unclean thing." Judges 13:4.

48. Josef Warkany, *History of Teratology, in* HANDBOOK OF TERATOLOGY 1 (James Wilson & F. Clarke Fraser eds., New York: Plenum Press, 1977).

49. *See, e.g.*, H. Marshall Taylor, *Prenatal Medication as a Possible Etiologic Factor of Deafness in the New-Born*, 20 ARCH. OTOLARYNGOLOGY 790 (1934).

50. JOSEF WARKANY, CONGENITAL MALFORMATIONS, NOTES AND COMMENTS 29–35 (Chicago: Yeat Book Medical, 1971).

51. Joseph Gillman et al., *A Preliminary Report on Hydrocephalus, Spina Bifida, and Other Congenital Anomalies in the Rat Produced by Trypan Blue*, 13 S. AFRICAN J. MED. SCI. 47 (1948).

52. D. Haskin, *Some Effects of Nitrogen Mustard on the Development of External Body Form in the Fetal Rat*, 102 ANAT. REC. 493 (1948).

53. John B. Thiersch, *Therapeutic Abortions With a Folic Acid Antagonist*, 63 AM. J. OBSTET. & GYNEC. 1298 (1952).

54. James G. Wilson, *Current Status of Teratology, in* HANDBOOK OF TERATOLOGY 47, 48 (James Wilson & F. Clarke Fraser eds., New York: Plenum Press, 1977).

55. INSIGHT TEAM, *supra* note 8, at 49–50, 270.

56. *Id.* at 272.

57. Wilson, *supra* note 54, at 48.

58. ROSKIES, *supra* note 42, at 2.

59. *See also* INSIGHT TEAM, *supra* note 8, at 114.

60. *Id.*

61. ROSKIES, *supra* note 42, at 55.

62. FRED DAVIS, PASSAGE THROUGH CRISIS: POLIO VICTIMS AND THEIR FAMILIES (Indianapolis: Bobbs-Merril, 1963).

63. *See, e.g.*, Jane E. Brody, *Thalidomide Trial Hears Evidence on Baby Born Without Arms*, N.Y. TIMES, Mar. 11, 1969, at 27 (prescribing physician in first American thalidomide trial denied that mother had been provided thalidomide).

64. INSIGHT TEAM, *supra* note 8, at 116.

65. The account of MER/29 in this section was drawn from FINE, *supra* note 19; Paul D. Rheingold, *The MER/29 Story—An Instance of Successful Mass Disaster Litigation*, 56 CALIF. L. REV. 116 (1968); MORTON MINTZ, BY PRESCRIPTION ONLY 230–47d (Boston: Houghton Mifflin, 1967); Sanford J. Ungar, *Get Away With What You Can, in* IN THE NAME OF PROFIT 106 (R. Heilbroner ed., Garden City, NY: Doubleday, 1972); MILTON SILVERMAN & PHILIP LEE, PILLS, PROFITS, AND POLITICS 89–94 (Berkeley: University of California Press, 1974); Roginsky v. Richardson-Merrell, Inc., 378 F.2d 832 (2d Cir. 1967); Toole v. Richardson-Merrell Inc., 60 Cal. Rptr. 398 (1967).

66. 2 PROGRESS IN CARDIOVASCULAR DISEASE 485 (New York: Grune & Stratton, 1959).

67. *Id.* at 648.

68. *See* Toole v. Richardson-Merrell Inc., 60 Cal. Rptr. 398, 405 (1967) ("MER/29 was introduced to the market by the greatest promotional and advertising effort ever made by [Merrell] in support of a product. . . . Doctors were bombarded with sales promotion, and subjected to brainwashing sessions with detailmen (salesmen). One advertising brochure stated that MER/29 was ' . . . virtually nontoxic and remarkably free from side effects even on prolonged clinical use.' ").

69. Dr. Nestor's role in the events leading to the removal of MER/29 from the market is detailed in FINE, *supra* note 19, at 20–21, 34–35.

70. *See* JOHN BRAITHWAITE, CORPORATE CRIME IN THE PHARMACEUTICAL INDUSTRY 60–63 (Boston: Routledge & Kegan Paul, 1984).

71. *See* Fine, *supra* note 19, at 20–21, 34–35.

72. INSIGHT TEAM, *supra* note 8, at 67.

73. 18 U.S.C. § 1001 (1964); *see generally* George Rosner, *Criminal Liability for Deceiving the Food & Drug Administration*, 20 FOOD DRUG COSM. L.J. 446 (1965).

74. *See* Wayne K. Hobson, *Symbol of the New Profession: Emergence of the Large Law Firm 1870–1915, in* THE NEW HIGH PRIESTS: LAWYERS IN POST-CIVIL WAR AMERICA (Gerard W. Gawalt ed., Westport, CT: Greenwood Press, 1984).

75. Rheingold, *supra* note 65, at 127–30.

76. 60 Cal. Rptr. 398 (1967).

77. *Id.* at 416.

A contrary result, rejecting punitive damages, was reached by the Second Circuit in an opinion written by Judge Henry Friendly. Roginsky v. Richardson-Merrell, Inc., 378 F.2d 832, 850 (2d Cir. 1967). A jury awarded punitive damages in a third case as well. Those punitive damage awards raised a number of issues about the imposition of punitive damages in products liability cases, especially in multiple cases for the same underlying conduct, that are being hotly debated today. *See, e.g.,* 2 AMERICAN LAW INSTITUTE REPORTERS' STUDY, ENTERPRISE LIABILITY FOR PERSONAL INJURY: APPROACHES TO LEGAL AND INSTITUTIONAL CHANGE 260–64 (1991).

78. FINE, *supra* note 19, at 184; *Hearings Before the Subcomm. on Reorg. and Int'l Orgs. of the Senate Comm. on Gov't Operations*, 88th Cong., 1st Sess., pt.3, at 907 (Mar. 20, 1963).

79. FINE, *supra* note 19, at 166; *see also* SILVERMAN & LEE, *supra* note 65, at 92 (estimate of $45–55 million).

80. *See* Deposition of Dr. Raymond Pogge at 3, 12, 28–31, MDL-486 (S.D.Ohio, June 28, 1983).

81. Milan Korcok, *The Bendectin Debate*, 123 CAN. MED. ASS'N J. 922, 923 (1980).

82. SILVERMAN & LEE, *supra* note 65, at 109–10.

83. The information about morning sickness is from Judy Folkenberg, *Mal de Mere: Simple Remedies Best for Morning Sickness*, 22 FDA CONSUMER 26 (Nov. 1988).

84. AMA DEPARTMENT OF DRUGS, AMA DRUG EVALUATIONS 417 (Chicago: American Medical Association, 4th ed. 1980).

85. *Drugs in Pregnancy*, 14 MEDICAL LETTER 94, 94 (Dec. 8, 1972).

86. 11 FDA DRUG BULLETIN 1 (1981).

87. BIO/BASICS INTERNATIONAL CORP., BENDECTIN PEER GROUP REPORT 6–7 (1975).

Chapter 6
A Mother's Quest

Very shortly after David's birth in March 1975, Betty Mekdeci became consumed with his birth defects. Initially, her efforts focused on pursuing appropriate medical and surgical care for David's shortened forearm, malformed hand, and concave chest. She was also concerned about other, as yet unidentified, health problems he might have. Betty Mekdeci took David to plastic surgeons, orthopedists, and hand surgeons in Orlando, Gainesville, and Memphis, Tennessee, where she had grown up. She contacted and consulted with a number of other doctors as well.[1] Because of conflicting advice that made her cautious about proceeding with any radical surgery or medical treatment, Mekdeci's effort evolved into an attempt to clarify the diagnosis of his condition and determine its cause.

Mekdeci's efforts to discover more about David's birth defects rapidly became a major focus in her life. When the doctors with whom she initially consulted about David's condition provided few answers and little guidance, she began researching birth defects at the Orlando Public Library. When the resources there quickly proved inadequate, she obtained medical texts through interlibrary loan. When she identified physicians and scientists who specialized in studying birth defects and their causes through her research, she expanded her inquiries by writing to virtually anyone whom she thought might be able to help her in her quest to better understand David's birth defects.

Mekdeci read and absorbed an enormous amount of information about birth defects, the mechanisms by which they are caused, and much of what was known by experts in the field and what was not known. Later, when Mekdeci shared the fruits of her research with her attorneys, they were stunned at the expertise she had developed and her encyclopedic capacity to retain what she had learned. The science spanned the intersection of a number of medical and scientific fields, including teratology, the study of birth defects, embryology, the study of the development of the fetus, toxicology, the study of substances that are poisonous, epidemiology, the study of the source of disease in human beings, and pharmacology, the study of the effects of drugs on human beings.

As studies of thalidomide families revealed, the desire to understand the source of a child's birth defect is a strong one in most families. But Betty Mekdeci's efforts, by any measure, far surpassed any victim's family's previous efforts. Assisted by her mother, Sara Irby, she devoted herself to investigating and learning everything she could about the cause of David's birth defects. Perhaps identifying some exogenous cause would answer the question and relieve the doubts that haunt many parents of children born with birth defects. Perhaps the process of and efforts required in identifying the cause of David's birth defects would prove a mother's devotion to and love for her child. Perhaps identifying the cause could prevent future tragedies, a purpose that Mekdeci embraced with an organization she founded in 1980, the Association of Birth Defect Children. Perhaps it was the unique individual who was Betty Mekdeci. As she explained several years later to one of her attorneys: "It's just my personality. Whatever I'm doing—even if it's making candles in the yard. I made candles and I was obsessed with making candles."[2] Perhaps without knowing why, Mekdeci summoned all her considerable energy and intellectual resources and poured her heart and soul into finding out why her child was born with a shortened right arm and caved-in chest.

Because of the number of drugs she had taken during her pregnancy, Mekdeci inquired of her obstetrician whether those might have contributed to David's birth defects. His responses, which she perceived as defensive, led to further questioning about possible causes of David's birth defects. The obstetrican responded that the closest thing he had seen to David's birth defects were the thalidomide children. When orthopedic specialists examined David, they inquired about the drugs that Mekdeci had taken during her pregnancy. Betty Mekdeci decided to explore the possibility that drugs were responsible for David's birth defects. Before David Mekdeci was six months old, Betty Mekdeci had written to the FDA and obtained preliminary information about the drugs she had taken during her pregnancy.

But the going was slow in obtaining information from the FDA. In addition to overcoming the ennui of any large governmental bureaucracy, Mekdeci was hampered because several drugs were involved and the requests spanned a number of different organizational divisions within the FDA. Thus her follow up requests for information were ignored or referred because the information was located in another division of the

FDA. Also complicating her attempts to obtain information about Bendectin was that it was a combination of three distinct drugs, each of which had separate files in the FDA, along with an NDA for Bendectin. At one point, frustrated with the FDA's lack of responsiveness, Mekdeci sent an 8 × 10 photograph of David displaying his birth defects to the Commissioner of the FDA, Alexander Schmidt, with a letter complaining about the unresponsiveness of the FDA to her requests for information.

Betty Mekdeci and her mother followed every lead and clue that they could identify. When they read about birth defects in a medical text or journal article, they fired off a letter to the author inquiring about the drugs Mekdeci had taken and David's birth defects. Numerous contacts by telephone and letter were made with dozens of individual employees at the FDA. Organizations that might provide helpful information were canvassed. Before they were through, Mekdeci and her mother wrote to the March of Dimes, experts at numerous medical schools, authors of journal articles or letters about birth defects, state health departments, members of Congress, public health organizations including the World Health Organization, Ralph Nader's medical and health organization, a similar organization in Canada, syndicated physician-columnists, and several foreign drug regulatory agencies, seeking assistance in pinpointing the cause of David's birth defects. Mekdeci also wrote to Dr. Helen Taussig, the Johns Hopkins pediatrician who had been instrumental in making America aware of the consequences of thalidomide in Europe. Dozens of additional letters were sent to the FDA inquiring about the drugs that Mekdeci had taken and tests that had been performed of the toxicity and teratogenicity of the drugs. Mekdeci requested copies of adverse drug experience lists and case reports, animal and human studies, and FDA reports and summaries of those studies.

Many of the Mekdeci-Irby inquiries went unanswered. But two related themes emerged from the responses that they did receive. One was how little is known about the causes of birth defects. The second was that although the drugs that Mekdeci had taken during pregnancy were a possible source of her son's birth defects, there was little or no hard evidence to support that suspicion and there was no way, given existing scientific knowledge, to determine whether they were the cause. Sometimes those responses added the epidemiological dictum that even if a drug were teratogenic, there would be no way to determine whether the drug was responsible for any given individual's defects, because of the possibility of other causes.

Mekdeci was quickly confronted with the huge gap in our knowledge about the sources of birth defects. She also became aware of a matter that many women would later learn in the publicity about Bendectin litigation: existing scientific methods are incapable of ascertaining whether some low level of risk exists in any given agent, including one prescribed for mothers during the period when the fetus is forming organs and hence susceptible to chemical insult. Mekdeci also found out how little in the way of hard scientific evidence existed about the risks of Bendectin and its components. Surely a person with less determination and drive than Betty Mekdeci would have accepted the futility of the effort by this point.

Despite the emerging uncertainty, Mekdeci pursued her campaign unflaggingly. Dissatisfied with the response she initially received from the March of Dimes that there was no epidemiological evidence and incomplete animal studies about the effect of the drugs she had taken on unborn fetuses, she wrote again. The reply came from the head of Medical Services for the March of Dimes: "I realize that you are looking for a final, complete and specific answer, but it is impossible for anyone to give you this." [3]

However, a few responses provided hints of suspicion—nothing definitive or even strong—but strands that enabled an individual intent on discovering the cause of her son's birth defects to begin to believe that clues were emerging from a murky background. The science of embryology quickly narrowed the field of non-genetic agents that could be responsible for congenital organ defects such as David's. In the summer of 1976, Mekdeci learned the chronology of development of the fetus; experts agreed that a teratogen could not cause a birth defect in an organ once it was fully formed (the critical period in the development of limbs is 24 to 36 days after conception). Thalidomide, with its extraordinary teratogenic potency, had left the world with that legacy of learning. Thus Betty Mekdeci quickly limited her inquiries to Actifed, Bendectin, and Erythromycin, even though she had taken half a dozen other drugs during her pregnancy. Later, timing also eliminated Erythromycin, leaving Bendectin and Actifed as the only drugs that were potential causes of David's birth defects.

A response from an English institute of adverse drug reactions alerted Mekdeci to isolated associations that had been found between some antihistamines and birth defects;[4] doxylamine, one of the components in Bendectin, is an antihistamine. Mekdeci found a letter written by Dr. Donald Patterson and published in 1969 in the *Canadian Medical Association Journal* that reported on a child born with congenital malformities whose mother had taken Bendectin during her pregnancy. Mekdeci immediately began corresponding with Dr. Patterson, ultimately persuading him to write another letter to the CMA Journal in 1977 reporting on another case of Bendectin-associated malformations, as well as adverse case reports Mekdeci had obtained from the FDA.[5]

During her investigation, Betty Mekdeci discovered a powerful legal tool to help her. Congress enacted the Freedom of Information Act (FOIA) [6] in 1966 to give citizens greater access to government information. FOIA created a right of access to any federal agency records not protected from disclosure by nine statutory exemptions. In 1974 FOIA was amended because of complaints that responses to requests were too slow and renewed public concern about government secrecy in the wake of the Watergate scandal.[7] Since the 1974 amendments, use of FOIA has grown dramatically; requests to the FDA alone went from 2,600 annually before the 1974 amendments to 33,000 annually in the early 1980s.[8] The vast majority of those requests, however, are by pharmaceutical companies regulated by the FDA. Nevertheless, Betty Mekdeci employed the FOIA after its liberalization, which enabled her to obtain information from the FDA. Her first FOIA request to the FDA was prompted by the suggestion of a sympathetic FDA employee with whom she had spoken. It yielded a list of adverse drug reports for Actifed, Bendectin, and Erythromycin in the summer of 1976.

Of 140 reports, 86 or over one-half, involved birth defects in the offspring of women who took Bendectin. By contrast, none of the adverse drug reports for Actifed and Erythromycin involved congenital defects. Of course, that disparity might be explained by the fact that Bendectin was the only drug whose purpose was to treat morning sickness, and therefore one would expect it to be used more frequently by pregnant women.

Betty Mekdeci also discovered the inadequacies in the drug adverse reporting system in this country. She obtained copies of Congressional hearings that identified the flaws, backlogs, and inadequate resources of the system. That deficiency persuaded her, no doubt correctly, that the adverse reactions she had uncovered were only a small portion of the total that existed. She also obtained one of the early animal reproduction tests of Bendectin performed by Merrell and discovered that because the pregnant rabbits were housed outside, all but two of them died before delivering offspring. In a scathing letter to the FDA, she commented that "I could have done better tests . . . in my garage."

Informal contacts with FDA employees also assisted Mekdeci in her investigations. In telephone conversations with individuals at the FDA, Mekdeci learned about which medical journals to review, which divisions at the FDA had information about the drugs she had taken, and how to fashion her FOIA requests. A handful of FDA employees were sympathetic to and supportive of her efforts, and Mekdeci has since reported that one FDA employee told her confidentially to focus her efforts on investigating Bendectin as the cause of David's birth defects. Mekdeci had managed to tap into a vein of FDA employees who felt the FDA was not aggressive enough in protecting consumers and who vented their discontent by quietly encouraging and assisting consumers who contacted them. Without the assistance of those individuals, who educated Mekdeci about where to look for evidence, how to obtain it, and from whom to seek assistance, her quest might have ended unfulfilled. As she put it in a letter to her lawyers, "we would never have gotten this far without their help and encouragement." [9]

Through telephone conversations with FDA employees, Mekdeci also learned that the FDA was completing its efficacy review—known as DESI—of Bendectin. The DESI process examined the efficacy of drugs that had been marketed before the 1962 amendments to the Food, Drug, and Cosmetic Act and was mandated by those amendments. Because of the number of drugs involved (over 4,000 original drugs plus many more "me too" drugs), the DESI process was delayed for a number of drugs and not completed until the 1980s. The National Academy of Sciences panel to which the FDA delegated initial review of the efficacy record on Bendectin concluded that it was only "probably effective" and commented on the scantiness of evidence submitted by Merrell and the undesirability of fixed combination drugs generally. After review of the National Academy of Sciences recommendation, the FDA downgraded the evaluation of Bendectin to only "possibly effective," thereby requiring Merrell to present additional evidence of Bendectin's efficacy. Merrell then conducted additional controlled efficacy studies, which found that doxylamine, and to a lesser extent pyridoxine, were of benefit in the treatment of nausea and vomiting of pregnancy, but that dicyclomine did not measurably improve the efficacy of Bendectin. [10]

Merrell decided to reformulate Bendectin to remove the dicyclomine component in 1975. But the laborious pace of the FDA and questions about labeling modifications and whether the Bendectin trade name should be changed delayed the reformulation until November 1976.

Betty Mekdeci first heard of the possible change in the formulation of Bendectin from FDA employees in early 1976. Later she obtained an internal FDA memorandum prepared by James Morrison, the special assistant to the Director of the Bureau of Drugs, in October 1976. In that memorandum of a meeting at which the issue of whether Merrell could continue to market the reformulated drug under the name Bendectin was discussed, Morrison summarized the sense of the meeting: "Concern was expressed by Compliance that the approval of the improved, safer product should not be unnecessarily delayed for labeling purposes."

Mekdeci, aware that DESI was concerned only with efficacy and not safety, immediately suspected that the reformulation under DESI was a cover for removing the teratogenic component of Bendectin. [11] The change in Bendectin's formulation had another important impact on future litigation: plaintiffs were differentiated. Some, like Mekdeci, had taken the three-component Bendectin formulation. Others, who used Bendectin after the reformulation, only received the two-component version.

In early 1977 Mekdeci located Dr. Richard Burack, author of *The Handbook of Prescription Drugs*, published initially in 1967. Mekdeci first contacted him with an inquiry about the change in ingredients in Bendectin, but quickly found a sympathetic ear for her suspicions about Bendectin's teratogenicity. Burack encouraged her to continue to pursue the FDA both to obtain further information and to pressure it to reconsider Bendectin's safety. After Mekdeci obtained a copy of a letter from an Italian lawyer to Merrell that suggested that a suit had been brought against Merrell in Italy for birth defects caused by Bendectin, Dr. Burack agreed to contact the Italian lawyer to obtain additional information.[12] Burack continued to consult with Mekdeci as she amassed additional information about Bendectin.

When Merrell discovered that Mekdeci had been inquiring about Bendectin from the FDA (FOIA requires that each agency keep a public log of requests for information; Merrell periodically reviewed that log), John Page, the Vice-President of Medical Research at Merrell, contacted her. Page sent Mekdeci copies of the Bunde-Bowles study and three additional epidemiological studies which had been published and which tended to exonerate Bendectin as a teratogen.[13] Burack then assisted Mekdeci in critically reviewing those studies and pointing out flaws and possible biases that might have skewed the results. Burack explained to Mekdeci his suspicion that some of the researchers had connections to or were being paid by Merrell for their research work. Burack also obtained correspondence by physicians who had written to Merrell inquiring about an association between birth defects and Bendectin. He became convinced that Merrell was unforthright in its responses (having seen the list of adverse reactions that Mekdeci had obtained from the FDA) and eagerly informed Mekdeci of his view.

Burack also educated Mekdeci about thalidomide and the terrible consequences that it had wrought in Europe in the early 1960s. Mekdeci obtained a book written by a lawyer and doctor about thalidomide, *Thalidomide and the Power of the Drug Companies*.[14] Reading the book, she was impressed with the difficulties of identifying thalidomide as a teratogen and the role of several of the drug companies involved, which was to stonewall and deny thalidomide's hazards until the evidence became overwhelming. She also learned of Merrell's involvement with thalidomide in Canada and the United States. The thalidomide episode not only fueled Mekdeci's suspicions about drugs, it also provided a link to the manufacturer of Bendectin.

One contact with a foreign health agency in Australia yielded the address of Dr. William McBride, one of the two physicians credited with identifying thalidomide's teratogenicity. Dr. McBride's response to Betty Mekdeci's letter informing him of her suspicions gave succor to Mrs. Mekdeci's campaign:

I have seen several children with birth deformities whose mothers have taken Debendox [the name under which Bendectin was marketed in Australia] during pregnancy. I will write to the F.D.A. for this information.

Later Dr. McBride would testify as an expert on behalf of Betty Mekdeci in her lawsuit against Merrell.

Not only did Betty Mekdeci's search for the cause of David's birth defects require enormous energy in pursuing leads, extensive and exhaustive research, a strong dose of distrust, perseverance in following up on inquiries that went unanswered, and a keen intelligence to absorb what she received, it also required a measure of cognitive dissonance to discard the evidence that was not consistent with the beliefs she was forming that drugs, and specifically Bendectin, were responsible for David's birth defects. It is hard to pinpoint precisely when Mekdeci became convinced that Bendectin was the cause of David's birth defects; likely this conviction was evolutionary rather than revolutionary. At that point, however, Mekdeci's emphasis was on the evidence pointing toward Bendectin's teratogenicity and discounting anything contrary.

To be sure, there were threads and strands to support Mekdeci's beliefs, and the contrary evidence of Bendectin's safety was exceedingly thin. At the time she began her investigation, there was but one epidemiological study of Bendectin that had been published, by Drs. Bunde and Bowles, employees of Merrell, in 1963. Even at the time she filed suit, there were but three additional epidemiological studies that examined Bendectin's teratogenicity.

There was much to criticize in the Bunde-Bowles study. Some flaws were apparent from the face of the published report; others required examination of the data gathered by the authors, which awaited subsequent litigation. From the published report, however, Dr. Burack might have explained the following to Betty Mekdeci. The Bunde-Bowles study was not peer reviewed and had been published in a third-rate journal. The exposed and unexposed cohorts came from records of private obstetricians recommended by the Merrell marketing department who were known to be major Bendectin users. A cohort study such as the one Bunde and Bowles performed had an exceedingly small chance of identifying a small to modest association with most specific birth defects. The control group was not matched with the exposed cohort in terms of other risk factors, such as age, other drugs taken, and diabetes. Nor did the study attempt to account for those factors and determine whether they played a role in the outcome. The study examined only live births, thereby neglecting the possibility of an excess rate of miscarriages or still-births. The definition of exposure was too broad, including the entire first trimester, thereby including many women in the exposed cohort who should not have been. Moreover, the overall defect rate among the exposed cohort and all women was .5 and .72 percent respectively, rates that were so low compared to general population figures that they strongly suggested substantial ascertainment error (accurately determining the disease being studied) in the study. Many of these criticisms had been raised by a Merrell consultant, Richard Smithells, who reviewed the Bunde-Bowles study for Merrell in 1973.[15]

Of the three other studies Merrell sent Mekdeci in an attempt to persuade her that Bendectin was not teratogenic, one, published in 1976, confirmed the meager scientific record: "published studies on the possibility of deleterious effects of [a number of drugs prescribed for morning sickness for years] on the development of the human embryo and fetus are sparse."[16] The study included 10,000 live births, of which 600 involved mothers who had taken Bendectin. The authors concluded: "On the basis of our present findings supported by these additional independent sources [Bunde-Bowles] conducted elsewhere, it is our conclusion that . . . Bendectin when taken in the doses recommended for pregnant women [is] not teratogenic."[17] But as Betty Mekdeci found out from those helping her, the study aggregated all birth defects studied, rather than separating out distinct classes of defects. If an agent causes only one type of defect, this aggregation will tend to mask any effect that may exist. Although the study found that the overall incidence of serious birth defects was lower among women who had taken Bendectin than among those who had not, it also found that the incidence of birth defects discovered at one month of age for those Bendectin mothers who had taken the drug during the first six weeks of their pregnancy, the period of greatest sensitivity, was 1.9 times the rate in the control group. Yet, because of the small numbers of women involved, this number was based on but one serious congenital anomaly among 36 women taking Bendectin during the first six weeks, raising serious doubts about the stability of this finding.

The second study, an offshoot of the Collaborative Perinatal Project, a major effort to investigate factors in pregnancy that were associated with neurological defects in offspring, was completed and published in 1977. It was a broadbased study of numerous drugs and their association with a wide array of birth defects. Data gathered from 12 major hospitals during 1959 to 1965 that comprised over 50,000 births were pooled and analyzed for a variety of purposes. The authors primarily investigated the association between classes of drugs, such as antihistamines, and birth defects. Dicyclomine and doxylamine were among the drugs that were included in the study, and generally were not associated with significant increases in birth defects. Although the drugs were treated separately in the analysis, most of the mothers who had taken doxylamine and dicyclomine had taken them together as Bendectin, along with pyridoxine, which was not included in the study. Consequently, although specific results were reported separately for doxylamine and dicyclomine, they tended to be quite similar. Thus doxylamine was not associated with an increase in the incidence of pectus excavatum, one of David's birth defects. However, some excess relative risks were found, including 1.37 for doxylamine and minor malformations as a group; 1.63 for doxylamine and clubfoot; 1.46 for dicyclomine and minor malformations as a group; 8.2 and 8.8 for doxylamine and dicyclomine respectively for macrocephaly (an enlarged brain and head involving developmental disabilities); and 12 for dicyclomine and diaphragmatic hernias. While the study tended to exonerate Bendectin as a limb defect teratogen, it had several inadequacies and raised some suspicions. Its focus was not on Bendectin or its components, and it did not systematically examine their association with all birth defects, although some were examined and reported. The exposure definition included taking the drug at any time during the first four lunar months of pregnancy, too long a period that would, as was the case in the two prior studies, dilute any real association. The excess associations found for dicyclomine and doxylamine were striking, but ultimately not very convincing because of the number of associations investigated and the likelihood that simply through random error some associations would emerge. Because of the number of associations investigated, this study would have to be viewed as an initial investigation designed to identify relationships that should be pursued in further studies.

The third study provided by Merrell had been performed in 1965 and was identified as a study of the teratogenicity of Meclizine, an unrelated drug that was suspected of being teratogenic.[18] The study compared pregnant women who had taken Meclizine with pregnant women who had taken any of ten other antinauseant drugs (Bendectin was one of the drugs in this category) and pregnant women who had taken no drugs. This study's focus on another drug and failure to disaggregate results with Bendectin provided little evidence either way about the safety of Bendectin. As more studies were completed and published through the 1980s, Merrell ceased relying on or even referring to this study.

The perfect epidemiological study that provides open and shut answers to causal questions has yet to be performed. Methodological error is to epidemiology as credibility is to eyewitness testimony; both forms of evidence must be discounted by their respective flaws. Betty Mekdeci, with help from Dr. Burack and others, was able to identify several flaws in the epidemiology she was provided, not to mention the overall paucity of evidence. Yet her belief in Bendectin's teratogenicity relied on evidence that was, on balance, less salient even than the studies she discounted.

Thus Betty Mekdeci found support in a 1970 study of limb reduction defects among children born in Canada.[19] The pilot study's purpose was to investigate the feasibility of a reporting system for congenital anomalies that would permit identifying changes in their incidence. The study included 29 children born with limb deficiencies, of which three mothers had taken Bendectin and three mothers had taken other antinauseants, which could have meant other non-Bendectin antinauseants or antinauseants that were unknown. But without information about the number of women who were taking Bendectin at the time, i.e., a control group, this information is meaningless in attempting to assess Bendectin's teratogenicity. That is, if 10 percent of all women were taking Bendectin and 10 percent of those with limb anomalies were taking Bendectin, one would be hard pressed to draw any conclusion of teratogenicity. The study concluded: "The preliminary investigation to date has provided no evidence to identify a specific etiologic agent."[20]

Similarly Betty Mekdeci's reliance on the 86 congenital malformations she found in the adverse drug reaction data from the FDA might be impressive to one unschooled in etiologic inquiry. But adverse drug reports, aside from the difficulties with underreporting, represent a numerator without a denominator. Without knowledge of how many pregnant women are taking Bendectin, the number of birth defects suffered by those who do is very poor evidence of teratogenicity.[21] While Mekdeci surely did not appreciate this point when she first received the FDA print-outs in the summer of 1976, she was later informed. On September 6, 1977 Dr. Dwight T. Janerich, the Director of Genetic Oncology for the New York Department of Health wrote to Mrs. Mekdeci:

> Without information on the total number of pregnant women exposed to Bendectin over all the time it has been marketed, it is impossible to evaluate the occurrence of 130 cases of congenital malformations. Bendectin was on the market when the thalidomide tragedy occurred. It is prescribed for symptoms similar to those for which thalidomide was used. This could account for a biased reporting. It could also account for the association with limb reduction defects.[22]

Dr. Janerich added to his letter the observation that

> Finally, in interviewing literally hundreds of mothers of children born with birth defects, we found many mothers "know" what caused their child's problem. Some of their explanations are quite good. It is easier to deal with a cause than to accept the fact that no one will ever know.

Mekdeci continued searching for further evidence, hoping either to find the figurative "smoking gun" or in more laborious fashion additional pieces to fit into the mosaic that would reveal the causal chain for David's birth defects. Most responses that Mekdeci received revealed new avenues for inquiry and search, and Mekdeci unrelentingly followed up on them. At one point, frustrated with her inability to obtain information from the FDA pursuant to additional FOIA requests, Mekdeci wrote complaint letters to a variety of Senators, Representatives, and FDA officials. One person she wrote to was Dr. Richard Crout, the Director of the Bureau of Drugs, which encompassed all of the divisions of the FDA with which Mekdeci had been dealing. Some of the sympathetic FDA employees with whom she had talked had urged her, confidentially, to contact Crout, who oversaw the FDA's regulation of the pharmaceutical industry. When she did not receive a prompt response to her letter, she called Dr. Crout, but ended up speaking to James Morrison, the special assistant to Dr. Crout. Morrison was quite impressed with the data that Mrs. Mekdeci had uncovered about the reports of birth defects of women who had taken Bendectin. Morrison was also struck with her knowledge and articulateness in discussing her concerns. Morrison had a personal interest too: his stepson had a birth defect similar to David Mekdeci's.

Morrison consulted with Dr. Crout, who then wrote to Mekdeci stating that he would have epidemiologists within the FDA review available information as well as consult with outside experts to determine if there was a genuine problem with Bendectin. Crout cautioned Mekdeci that if Bendectin were toxic, it was likely to be at such a level that existing test methods could not detect it. Nevertheless, he promised to investigate further. Crout commended Mekdeci for her interest and persistence and encouraged her to keep in touch with his office. He closed with a handwritten note expressing his personal interest in the matter because he, like Morrison, had a child with a birth defect in his own family.

Crout and Morrison consulted with Dr. Godfrey Oakley at the Centers for Disease Control in Atlanta. Oakley, who was Chief of the Etiologic Studies Section in the Birth Defects Branch of the Bureau of Epidemiology in the federal government's premier agency for monitoring disease and its causes, had more expertise in the area than those at the FDA. Oakley explained to Crout that he was not impressed by the adverse drug reports of birth defects, especially the ones involving limb defects, because the most obvious, serious, and dramatic adverse effects—such as birth defects—tend to be the ones that are reported and get into the adverse drug reporting system. Although Oakley agreed that further epidemiological inquiry was justified, which he then undertook with a colleague at the CDC, he was not alarmed by Mekdeci's findings. Morrison relayed this information to Mekdeci, but came away with the impression that by this time she had become convinced that Bendectin was responsible for David's birth defects.

Dr. Oakley also contacted Mrs. Mekdeci to discuss her concerns and explained that there was no evidence to implicate Bendectin in David's birth defects, but then went on to sound a familiar refrain: the difficulties of determining weak effects. Even if Bendectin increased the incidence of a type of birth defect by 20 percent over the background rate, it would be virtually impossible to detect through existing epidemiological methods.

Dr. Burack, who was familiar with a number of government officials in Washington because of his pharmacologic work, provided Mekdeci a measure of access in Congress. Dr. Burack knew Benjamin Gordon, an economist who was on the staff of the United States Senate Subcommittee on Antitrust and Monopolies, the same subcommittee that Estes Kefauver had chaired in 1962 when extensive amendments to the Food Drug and Cosmetic Act had been enacted in the wake of the thalidomide tragedy. The subcommittee continued to play a watchdog role for the pharmaceutical industry and the FDA. Burack contacted Gordon and told him about his and Mekdeci's suspicions about Bendectin. At Burack's suggestion, Mekdeci wrote to Ben Gordon, who, like many others, was impressed with Mekdeci's accumulated knowledge and acumen in a complex scientific field.

Gordon provided a copy of Mekdeci's letter to Norman Gorin, a producer for *60 Minutes* who was in Washington investigating another story for *60 Minutes*. Gorin was also impressed both with the letter from the mother of a child who believed that drugs had caused her son's birth defects. Gorin sensed a compelling program, in the finest *60 Minutes* style: the program would raise issues not only of the safety of drugs, but the competence and effectiveness of the FDA in regulating the pharmaceutical industry and insuring drug safety. *60 Minutes* had long had an interest in the FDA and had aired a number of shows critical of its performance. Gorin was quickly able to obtain additional information about the adverse drug reaction reports for Bendectin. With them in hand he flew to Orlando in March 1977 to interview Betty Mekdeci.

Gorin came away from his interview enormously impressed with the self-taught expertise of Betty Mekdeci. She was energized, propelled, and indefatigable in searching out everyone that she thought might help her in her crusade. She had taught herself a great deal about teratology and pharmacology after contacting people from around the world. Gorin went back to New York to discuss the story with Mike Wallace, but left behind a copy of the adverse drug reports on Bendectin that he had obtained from the FDA. Those adverse drug reports revealed that approximately one-half of the birth defects involved limb defects, an astonishingly high percentage, far in excess of that found in the general population. That datum heavily influenced Betty Mekdeci and, subsequently, her lawyers. It cannot be explained on the same basis as the number of birth defects identified in adverse reports of Bendectin—that Bendectin is used exclusively in pregnancy and therefore is likely to result in numerous coincidental associations with birth defects. Limb defects make up a very small percentage of all birth defects, and the 50 percent rate in the Bendectin adverse drug reports was much larger than would be expected. Merrell subsequently hypothesized that the impact of thalidomide on the public and the concomitant association of drugs with limb defects explains the disparity, but the hypothesis remains no more than that.

Gorin obtained other Merrell interoffice memoranda that convinced him that Merrell had adopted a "circle the wagons" mentality. When he also found out about Merrell's involvement with MER/29, Gorin concluded that he had a "delicious story." Meanwhile, Gorin's contacts enabled him to obtain extensive information contained in FDA files and from others; one FDA official commented that CBS knew more about the FDA's Bendectin files than the FDA did. Gorin shared much of the fruits of his research with Mekdeci. She felt she had finally found a sympathetic and well-connected ally in her efforts to demonstrate the teratogenicity of Bendectin.

Mike Wallace concurred with Gorin's judgment about the program, and a decision was made to do a *60 Minutes* segment on Bendectin, Betty Mekdeci, and birth defects.

In the spring of 1977 Wallace, Gorin, and a CBS production crew flew to Orlando. Mekdeci was not without some turmoil about this imminent national attention to her cause. By this time she had hired attorneys who were preparing to file her case in court. They were leery of her making public statements that might hurt the case in the future.[23] As her attorneys informed her, the Actifed that Mekdeci had taken was still under suspicion, and prematurely focusing on Bendectin could hurt the strength of the case against Burroughs Wellcome, the manufacturer of Actifed, if subsequent evidence emerged that pointed to Actifed. Other statements that Mekdeci might make could only harm her lawsuit and could not be of benefit. On the other hand, national exposure of Bendectin's teratogenicity on the highly rated *60 Minutes* program meant saving other parents and children the anguish with which the Mekdecis had lived. The acclaim due a concerned mother, without any formal scientific training, for uncovering the teratogenic effect of a drug for morning sickness that had been sold for over twenty years virtually without suspicion provided additional motivation for cooperating with CBS.

Mekdeci's attorneys gave the O.K., no doubt aware that the national exposure would produce many more potential Bendectin plaintiffs. Mike Wallace conducted a lengthy interview at the Mekdecis' home. Betty Mekdeci looked forward to the fall of 1977 when the segment was to be aired.

Gorin contacted both Merrell and Richard Crout at the FDA about participating in interviews that would be aired as part of the *60 Minutes* program. The request to the FDA caused much anguish, as the FDA felt that *60 Minutes'* propensity for sensationalism had resulted in unfair treatment and criticism of the FDA in the past. Crout requested that Marion Finkel, then an Associate Director in the Bureau of Drugs, prepare a statement about Bendectin that would be released to CBS. Merrell was contacted to provide information and a meeting of FDA and Merrell officials was held, with a mutual interest of minimizing the sensationalization and criticism of Bendectin that they feared *60 Minutes* would provoke. Ultimately, Crout refused to appear for an interview, concerned that Wallace and *60 Minutes* had already made up their minds and that Crout would be unable to explain the complex scientific issues in the limited time available.

Merrell did cooperate with *60 Minutes* and an interview of the chief medical officer and another corporate official was conducted and taped. Merrell pointed out that no epidemiological study had found an increased association between Bendectin and birth defects, and also explained the limited utility of adverse drug reports (which had most impressed Gorin when he first obtained them) in ascertaining the teratogenicity of a drug. Gorin came away from the interview believing that Merrell "had stonewalled us."

As Gorin investigated further and spoke with experts in the epidemiology and teratology fields, he began to have doubts. Godfrey Oakley at the Centers for Disease Control explained to Gorin the difficulty of drawing a causal inference from adverse drug effect reports. Discussions with other experts confirmed this difficulty as well as further emphasized to Gorin the absence of any studies finding an association between Bendectin and birth defects. Gorin became concerned about airing a program that might cause anguish to mothers of children with birth defects who had taken Bendectin as well as the possible reaction of pregnant women who had previously taken Bendectin who might obtain abortions, fearful that they were carrying a fetus with defects. Gorin received a letter from Dr. Tommy N. Evans, Chair of the Department of Gynecology & Obstetrics at Wayne State University in Detroit, that expressed these concerns:

Anxiety, to some degree, is present in most pregnant women. Many women have natural fears of being unable to carry a pregnancy to a normal termination or fears of having an infant with birth defects. In women with these fears, open or suppressed, there is the risk of creating feelings of guilt or personal responsibility if the pregnancy is complicated or ends with a less than perfect or normal outcome for the mother and her infant.

There is a real possibility that harm could be done to some of these women by a public TV program on this subject if not kept in medical balance. Some patients could be expected to make the irrational decision to seek abortion while others could become clinically depressed or disturbed to the point of requiring medical treatment.

. . .

It is our understanding that the topic of "morning sickness" might be included in this CBS program. It is further understood that the fetal safety of the drug Bendectin might be inferentially questioned. This widely prescribed drug has been available by prescription for about two decades in the United States and worldwide for almost as long. To our knowledge, either by personal use or by that of our colleagues, as well as the occasional epidemiologic reports in the literature, Bendectin has a demonstrated record of reasonable safety. To the best of our knowledge, there is no evidence that Bendectin has a harmful effect on the fetus. To raise now, even inferentially, a question regarding the safety of Bendectin in pregnancy without complete review of the epidemiologic studies on this drug could cause unnecessary anxiety for thousands of women. There is suggestive information that the condition of moderate or severe nausea and vomiting of pregnancy are a greater risk to the woman and her fetus than the medication.

The letter was cosigned by forty other prominent obstetricians, solicited by Evans to join him in the letter.

Ultimately, Gorin and others at CBS decided not to air the Bendectin segment because of the inconclusiveness of the scientific evidence. Betty Mekdeci was greatly disappointed. After overcoming her attorneys' reservations, she had anticipated the publicity with much satisfaction.

Betty Mekdeci had contemplated a lawsuit, even in the early stages of her search for the origin of David's birth defects, indeed before she had uncovered any evidence to fuel her suspicions. Although in the early stages of her investigation she was unsure who the defendant might be, she nevertheless contacted a local attorney who agreed to look into the possibility of a lawsuit. Dissatisfied with the lawyer's progress, which consisted of little more than obtaining copies of relevant medical records, she perfunctorily fired him. She promptly found another lawyer to represent her and just as promptly terminated him, after he described her situation as "an interesting social problem." Mekdeci didn't want philosophers or social analysts; she wanted someone who would provide legal expertise and assist her in her crusade to identify who and what was responsible for David's birth defects. She went on to retain a third set of lawyers, but a pattern of stormy relationships was established that would dog her to the very end of her suit against Merrell in 1983.

Among the many persons whom she consulted and received advice from, one counseled her that if she was serious about a suit she needed a specialist, a name like Melvin Belli in the personal injury field, to take on such a significant case against the pharmaceutical industry. Melvin Belli was a household name, and Mekdeci, in her own unselfconscious and energetic style, promptly wrote to Belli, requesting that he take on her case. His response, in the summer of 1976, made a lasting impression on Betty Mekdeci. If Melvin Belli, the King of Torts, agreed to represent her, she must have a valid claim, went her thinking. Not only did this reaffirm her faith that it was a drug that caused David's birth defects, but she would have the best personal injury lawyer in America on her side in demonstrating that fact in a courtroom. Mekdeci was convinced that she was about to be involved in "very heady" litigation, with a master lawyer shepherding her through it.

Belli, whose home base was in San Francisco, explained to Mrs. Mekdeci that he would represent her, her husband, and David and try their case in court. Because of his busy schedule, distance from Florida, and difficulties of establishing necessary proof, he would arrange for two other law firms in Florida to assist in the pretrial proceedings. Gerald Tobin, a former state court judge in Florida, of Tobin & Fisch, would take on the role of preparing the pleadings and other legal documents that would be required. Tobin recognized the need to find someone with expertise in pharmaceutical or medical personal injury claims to also be involved in representing the Mekdecis. Arthur Tifford, who worked in Tobin's office and who later became one of the primary lawyers working on the Mekdecis' case, recommended George Kokus, an attorney with whom Tifford had practiced in the United States Attorney's office in Miami.

George Kokus and Arthur Cohen, two personal injury lawyers who had their own firm and specialized in medical malpractice work, agreed to conduct the pretrial discovery required to prepare the case for trial. Kokus and Cohen had been classmates at the University of Miami Law School; Kokus had gone to work for the United States Attorney in Miami upon graduation from law school, where he received significant trial experience. Kokus is gruff and coarse, and with a heavy-set build, he cuts an unimposing image—one that belies his acuity. Arthur Cohen had been a practicing physician for 17 years. He was drawn to law school by a fascination with the law, an insatiable desire to argue, and a garrulous, aggressive personality. Upon graduation from law school, he put his medical training to work as a medical malpractice lawyer. When George Kokus decided it was time to leave government service, Kokus accepted Cohen's invitation to join him in his practice.

Mekdeci readily agreed to this triumvirate arrangement. She was ecstatic that Belli had agreed to represent her, and she recognized the advantages of having local lawyers performing the legal work necessary to prepare her case for trial. The written agreement that Michael and Betty Mekdeci signed only provided for legal representation by Tobin and Fisch. The omission of Belli would have significant repercussions later when all the Mekdecis' lawyers sought to withdraw from representing the Mekdecis. Like other personal injury plaintiffs, the Mekdecis agreed to pay their lawyers a fee only if the lawsuit was successful. Because this would be a groundbreaking and complicated lawsuit, the fee was set at 50 percent of any recovery—the typical contingent fee is in the 25 to 40 percent range.

The contingent fee that the Mekdecis agreed to pay is virtually unique to the United States; most other Western countries prohibit attorneys from entering into such an arrangement. It is universally the fee arrangement of choice in personal injury litigation in this country.[24] The contingent fee is justified because of the access it provides to the legal system: most persons with valid claims would be unable to pay their attorneys, especially if they are ultimately unsuccessful in their suit. The primary criticism of the arrangement is that by giving the attorney a stake in the outcome of the case, conflicts of interest may be created between client and attorney.[25] This could occur where additional attorney efforts might produce a marginally higher recovery, benefiting the client, but with opportunity costs to the attorney greater than the attorney's share of the enhanced recovery. This situation is particularly likely to arise in deciding whether to reject a settlement offer and go to trial, as trials require large time investments by attorneys.

Behind this facade of simplicity, the attorney who is paid a contingent fee is providing a number of services. First, like the lawyers who defended Merrell and were paid an hourly fee, Belli and his co-counsel provided legal services to the Mekdecis. However, unlike the hourly-rate attorney, the contingent-fee attorney also provides an insurance function. The attorney, rather than the client, assumes the risk of an adverse outcome that is insufficient to pay for the legal services provided. The contingent-fee attorney also provides a financing function. By delaying payment for services until a recovery is obtained and advancing the costs of the suit until then, the attorney finances the costs of legal services during the course of the litigation. Contingent fee attorneys are compensated for these services through an equity interest in the client's case.[26]

In one sense, the contingent fee increases the number of suits that are brought—indeed critics have castigated it for its tendency to clog the courts. In a society that widely perceives itself as overly litigious, this is a significant criticism. This criticism, however, is really nothing more than an attack on the contingent fee fulfilling its function of providing access to the legal system for those who would not otherwise be able to proceed if required to pay an hourly fee.

Contingent fee attorneys also serve as gatekeepers to the legal system. Because they are paid only if the case is successfully concluded or settled, incentives exist not to accept cases that are unmeritorious.[27] Many plaintiffs' attorneys, especially prominent and successful ones like Belli, accept only a small fraction of the cases about which they are consulted. But at the outset of a case, before the opportunity to conduct formal discovery, substantial uncertainty may exist as to how strong a given case will turn out. No doubt attorneys make mistakes in their evaluation of cases, and the temptation to take high stakes, yet low-likelihood-of-success cases also explains why contingent-fee attorneys, despite their self interest in screening unmeritorious and weak cases, may nevertheless sometimes accept them.[28]

The allure of high stakes, marginal cases is enhanced by the possibility of repeat business. Getting in on the ground floor of mass tort cases where there are many potential plaintiffs promises lucrative returns. Contingent fees are rarely discounted to reflect economies of scale. Melvin Belli, characteristically, has sought to be among the first involved in a number of mass torts, including the Hyatt Regency Skywalk litigation, Bhopal, and several commercial airline crashes. The most notorious example of Belli failing to exercise selectivity in choosing clients occurred in the cigarette litigation, where Belli solicited a plaintiff in 1979 while lecturing at hospices. He filed suit in 1982 on behalf of John Galbraith, who had quite a weak case: he had a medical history of non-tobacco diseases, including tuberculosis, chronic fibrosis, and heart disease. No autopsy was performed, in part because Belli counseled the family against it, concerned that the results would reveal the death was caused by hereditary disease rather than lung cancer.[29] Because of his eagerness to be in the vanguard of the second wave of tobacco lawsuits, Belli pushed the case to an early trial. Not surprisingly, he lost the case because the jury believed that Galbraith's smoking was not the cause of his death.[30]

The primary difficulty with contingent fees is the potential wedge it may create between attorney and client interests when the attorney has a financial stake in the outcome of the case. There are two primary concerns: the attorney's incentive to maximize the client's recovery may be dulled by self-interest, and the attorney may have different priorities with regard to settlement than the client.

The first concern is that as the return for hours invested by a plaintiff's attorney drops off (presumably like any scarce resource, the yield declines as additional units of input are invested) the attorney's incentive to continue investing in the case ends before the client would like. Thus the attorney will devote his or her efforts to other cases where the return on the investment of time is greater, rather than maximizing the first client's recovery.[31] An empirical study of lawyer effort found some evidence that this phenomenon occurs, especially in small stakes cases.[32]

The second concern involves different tolerances for risk by attorney and client in evaluating the desirability of settlement. Risk aversion is a preference not to gamble, even though the expected return is equivalent to the certain investment. Thus, a risk averse individual would choose a certain $500 payment over a 50 percent probability of obtaining a $1,000 payment. Most of us are risk averse—particularly when the stakes are large, as they often are in personal injury cases—as evidenced by the prevalence of insurance in modern society. Risk aversion also generally correlates negatively with income; those with less wealth will be more protective of it and less willing to risk a loss.

Unlike the personal injury plaintiff who has only one opportunity to recover, contingent fee attorneys are diversified by virtue of having a substantial number of cases. Thus, the client who would prefer to settle on a discounted basis from the projected recovery may have a conflict with his attorney who would prefer the potentially larger recovery at trial to settlement. A conflict with contrary positions may develop: the client is willing to assume the risk of trial, but the attorney's efforts required to prepare the case for trial exceed his share of the additional recovery.[33] Because of disparities in knowledge, the client is not likely to be an effective monitor of the attorney when this conflict arises.

Timing also may result in conflict, with the victim preferring a rapid recovery to pay medical bills, obtain occupational therapy, and replace lost wages.[34] On the other hand, most attorneys have sufficient assets or ability to borrow that there is not an impelling need to settle each case at an early point.

A third concern, especially among lawyers' organizations, about contingent fees is one of image and professionalism. The concept of attorney as professional does not fit neatly within the concept of attorney as financier or entrepreneur. But the Pollyanna view that attorneys (and other professionals) are different in kind from others engaged in private commerce has been greatly eroded in recent years.

Across a wide swath of the legal profession are incidents that seem more compatible with profit-oriented commerce than the preferred image of professional dedicated to client service: widespread attorney advertising, modern marketing strategies employed by law firms, compensation tied to procuring clients rather than representing them, the decline of lawyer loyalty to law firms and concomitant bidding for them (and their clients) by other law firms, franchising of law firms, and class actions proceeding with attorneys financing, directing, and acting as the only real parties in interest in litigation.[35]

In the mass toxic substances arena, cases such as those involving Agent Orange, asbestos, the Dalkon Shield, and Bendectin demand huge investments of money and labor to pursue adequately. The issue of whether mass cases such as that of Bendectin should be pursued essentially as business propositions by entrepreneurial lawyers is one of the hard questions that later emerged in the Bendectin multidistrict litigation and continues to be raised as new mass toxic substances—most recently breast implants—emerge.

In addition to the 50 percent contingency provision, the agreement that the Mekdecis signed provided that they would pay all the costs of the suit. Those costs, which include expert witness fees, deposition costs, copying charges, and travel expenses for their attorneys, would later exceed $100,000, a sum well beyond the means of the Mekdecis and the vast majority of personal injury plaintiffs. This barrier was solved by her attorneys agreeing to advance the money required to pay the costs during the litigation. If a successful result was achieved the costs could be deducted from the recovery, but if the suit were ultimately unsuccessful, existing professional ethical rules required that "the client remains ultimately liable" for the costs.[36]

The requirement that clients fund their lawsuits arose from longstanding prohibitions on champerty and maintenance that barred strangers and lawyers from stirring up litigation by purchasing a claim or providing the funding for a claim. The prohibition also was designed to prevent attorneys from obtaining a financial stake in a case that could create incentives contrary to the client's interests, similar to the concerns about the effects of contingent fees. The bar to advancing costs was modified in 1969 when the American Bar Association permitted attorneys to advance the costs, but with the "client remain ultimately liable" qualification.[37] Nevertheless, the Mekdecis were not required by their lawyers to repay the costs if the suit was unsuccessful, a clear violation of ethical limitations then in force.

In violating the proscription on funding litigation, Belli, Tobin, Cohen, and Kokus were not alone. One commentator on contingent attorney's fees commented in 1964 that the requirement was honored only in the breach by contingent fee attorneys,[38] and two decades later, despite still being prohibited, another commentator reported that the practice still "flourishes."[39] The reason for flouting this ethical proscription is plain: if observed it would have an impact on potential plaintiffs not dissimilar from that of the English rules on attorney's fees, which prohibit contingent fees and permit the victorious party to recover a large portion of the winner's fees from the loser. The risk of being responsible for those costs keeps all but the wealthy, risk-prone, and possessors of sure-thing claims from pursuing them.

But if the contingent fee is tolerated because of the access it provides, the prohibition of attorneys assuming the responsibility for costs in a day when an ordinary products liability case may cost $50,000 or more to finance and a groundbreaking case twice that amount or more—the first cigarette case in which a jury returned a plaintiff's verdict cost the attorneys $500,000 in out-of-pocket costs[40]—seems long of tooth and antithetical to the principle of open access to courts that has long been a staple of American procedure. Moreover, once contingent fees are permitted, with their potential to create a cleavage between client's and attorney's interests, permitting attorneys to assume the costs of litigation only has a modest and marginal impact on those concerns.

By the late 1980s most states had changed their rules on responsibility for costs and the arrangements with the Mekdecis would have been proper under those subsequent modifications.[41] But the sidestepping of ethical limitations was but the first of a number of far more dubious ethical actions by the Mekdecis' lawyers that would emerge in later stages of the case.

Despite the extraordinary efforts by Mrs. Mekdeci, her attorneys began with very little solid evidence in 1976 when they initially agreed to represent her. George Kokus and Arthur Cohen, when contacted by Tifford, thought about whether they wanted to get involved in what was likely to be a difficult, expensive, and protracted piece of litigation. There was very little information available about Merrell's decision to market Bendectin, its awareness of scientific evidence that Bendectin was dangerous, or even that Bendectin was responsible for the birth defects that Betty Mekdeci believed it was. Nevertheless, Kokus and Cohen learned of Merrell's role with thalidomide in the United States and that it had left thalidomide on the market in Canada longer than any other company that distributed it elsewhere in the world. They also found out about Merrell's involvement in MER/29, the fraud for which it had pleaded nolo contendere, and the extensive civil litigation by MER/29 victims. Kokus felt that a pattern of corporate conduct was established that at least justified further investigation. That search for fire among the corporate smoke would be facilitated after a lawsuit was filed and formal discovery was available from Merrell. Perhaps most significantly, Betty Mekdeci represented the potential for many more clients: by the mid-1970s as many as 25 percent of pregnant women in the United States were taking Bendectin. This meant the possibility of numerous future suits—suits in which

Mekdeci's lawyers would be advantaged in signing on clients and pursuing their cases—and collecting a contingent fee—based on their pioneering work in the Mekdeci case.

A complaint was filed in the United States District Court for the Middle District of Florida, the federal district court that encompasses Orlando, on June 20, 1977. Betty, Michael, and David Mekdeci were named as plaintiffs and Merrell National Laboratories, a Division of Richardson-Merrell, Inc. and Burroughs Wellcome and Company, the manufacturer of Actifed, were named as defendants. Although the suit would be governed by state law, it was permitted in federal court based on diversity of citizenship, a jurisdictional grant to the federal courts that permits them to hear cases involving parties who are citizens of different states.

Notes

1. Much of this chapter is based on Depositions and Trial Testimony of Elizabeth Mekdeci, Mekdeci v. Merrell National Laboratories, No. 77-255-Orl-Civ-Y (M.D. Fla. Jan. 12, Jan. 18, and Apr. 12, 1978, July 3, 1979, and Feb. 5–6, 1980) and the documentary exhibits thereto; Interview with James Morrison, Deputy Director of Drug Standards, Bureau of Drugs, FDA (May 9, 1990); Interview with Elizabeth Mekdeci (Dec. 28, 1989); Interview with Arthur Tifford, Attorney for Elizabeth Mekdeci (Jan. 2, 1989); Interview with George Kokus, Attorney for Elizabeth Mekdeci (Mar. 24, 1990); Telephone Interview with Norman Gorin, Executive Producer, *60 Minutes* (Aug. 27, 1990).

2. Interview of Elizabeth Mekdeci by attorney Doug Peters (Aug. 11, 1980).

3. Letter from Arthur J. Salisbury to Elizabeth Mekdeci (Mar. 17, 1976).

4. Letter from C.H. Ashton to Mrs. E. W. Irby (Sept. 30, 1976).

5. D.C. Patterson, *Congenital Malformities Associated with Bendectin*, 116 CAN. MED. ASS'N J. 1348 (1977).

6. 5 U.S.C. § 552 (1988).

7. ROBERT F. BOUCHARD & JUSTIN D. FRANKLIN, GUIDEBOOK TO THE FREEDOM OF INFORMATION AND PRIVACY ACTS 9 (New York: C. Boardman, 1980).

8. William H. Miller, *Will Someone Leash Corporate Snooping?*, INDUSTRY WEEK, June 27, 1983, at 94.

9. Letter from Elizabeth Mekdeci to attorney Gerald Tobin (Dec. 19, 1976).

10. Interview with James Morrison, Deputy Director of Drug Standards, FDA (May 9, 1990); Internal Memorandum of Merrell (Dec. 11, 1975).

11. Subsequently, Morrison insisted that the reference to "safer product" had nothing to do with new toxicity information, but simply reflected the universal fact that any active ingredient has potential side effects, and if the component is not contributing to efficacy then removing it always results in a safer product. Interview with James Morrison, Deputy Director of Drug Standards, FDA (May 9, 1990).

12. In 1973 Merrell's Italian subsidiary had received an inquiry from an attorney who represented a child born with a defect of the left forearm and hand. That inquiry resulted in a change in the labeling for Bendectin in Italy, but no lawsuit or settlement.

13. Carl A. Bunde & D.M. Bowles, *A Technique for Controlled Survey of Case Records*, 5 CURRENT THERAPEUTIC RES. 245 (1963); OLLIE HEINONEN ET AL., BIRTH DEFECTS AND DRUGS IN PREGNANCY (Littleton, MA: Publishing Sciences Group, 1977); Lucille Milkovich & Bea van den Berg, *An Evaluation of the Teratogenicity of Certain Antinauseant Drugs*, 125 AM. J. OF OBSTET. & GYN. 244 (1976); J. Yerushalmy & Lucille Milkovich, *Evaluation of the Teratogenic Effect of Meclizine in Man*, 93 AM. J. OBSTET. & GYN. 553 (1965).

14. HENNING SJÖSTRÖM & ROBERT NILSSON, THALIDOMIDE AND THE POWER OF THE DRUG COMPANIES (Harmondsworth: Penguin, 1972).

15. Letter from Richard W. Smithells, Merrell consultant, to Mark T. Hoekenga, Vice-President, Research, Medical & Regulatory Affairs, Merrell National Laboratories (Aug. 29, 1973).

16. Milkovich & van den Berg, *supra* note 13, at 244.

17. *Id.* at 247–48.

18. Yerushalmy & Milkovich, *supra* note 13.

19. Philip Banister, *Congenital Malformations: Preliminary Report of an Investigation of Reduction Deformities of the Limbs, Triggered by a Pilot Surveillance System*, 103 CAN. MED. ASS'N J. 466 (1970).

20. *Id.* at 471.

21. *See, e.g.*, Jeffrey L. Carlson & Brian L. Strom, *Screening for Unknown Effects of Newly Marketed Drugs*, in DRUG EPIDEMIOLOGY AND POST-MARKETING SURVEILLANCE 73, 74 (Brian L. Strom & Giampaolo Velo eds., New York: Plenum Press, 1992) ("Without an incidence rate, one cannot determine whether the adverse outcome occurs more commonly than it would have been expected to occur spontaneously").

22. Letter from Dr. Dwight T. Janerich to Mrs. Michael E. Mekdeci (Sept. 6, 1977).

23. Their fears were well-founded. In October 1979 an article about Bendectin in the *National Enquirer* included a segment about the Urland family and their seven-year-old born with a missing arm. In 1987 the Third Circuit Court of Appeals affirmed the dismissal of their lawsuit against Merrell because it was filed after the statute of limitations had expired. The article in the *National Enquirer* played a major role in the court's determination of when the Urlands first knew of Bendectin's involvement, thereby starting the statute of limitations clock. Urland v. Merrell-Dow Pharmaceuticals, Inc., 822 F.2d 1268 (3d Cir. 1987).

24. *See* Marc Franklin et al., *Accidents, Money, and the Law: A Study of the Economics of Personal Injury Litigation*, 61 COLUM. L. REV. 1, 22 n.103 (1961).

25. *See* Kevin M. Clermont & John D. Currivan, *Improving on the Contingent Fee*, 63 CORNELL L. REV. 529 (1978).

26. *See* Geoffrey P. Miller, *Some Agency Problems in Settlement*, 16 J. LEGAL STUD. 189 (1987).

27. *See* Michael J. Saks, *Do We Really Know Anything About the Behavior of the Tort System—And Why Not?*, 140 U. PA. L. REV. 1147, 1190–92 (1992).

28. For an analysis of the economic incentives that might affect a plaintiff's lawyer's decision, *see* John C. Coffee, *Understanding the Plaintiff's Attorney: The Implications of Economic Theory for Private Enforcement of Law Through Class and Derivative Actions*, 86 COLUM. L. REV. 669 (1986).

29. JOHN A. JENKINS, THE LITIGATORS: INSIDE THE POWERFUL WORLD OF AMERICA'S HIGH-STAKES TRIAL LAWYERS 144 (New York: Doubleday, 1989).

30. Robert A. Rabin, *A Sociolegal History of the Tobacco Tort Litigation*, 44 STAN. L. REV. 853, 870 (1992); Deborah Graham, *Plaintiffs' Lawyers Undaunted by Tobacco*

Defeats, LEGAL TIMES, Jan. 27, 1986, at 2; Linda Deutsch, *Seeking the Culprit in a Smoker's Death*, NAT'L L.J., Jan. 6, 1986, at 13.

31. Earl Johnson, Jr., *Lawyers' Choice: A Theoretical Appraisal of Litigation Investment Decisions*, 15 L. & SOC. REV. 567, 588 (1980–81); Murray L. Schwartz & Daniel J.B. Mitchell, *An Economic Analysis of the Contingent Fee in Personal-Injury Litigation*, 22 STAN. L. REV. 1125, 1133–36 (1970).

32. HERBERT M. KRITZER ET AL., THE IMPACT OF FEE ARRANGEMENT ON LAWYER EFFORT 17 (Santa Monica, CA: Rand, 1986).

33. *See* DOUGLAS E. ROSENTHAL, LAWYER AND CLIENT: WHO'S IN CHARGE? 96–99 (New York: Russell Sage Foundation, 1974); Miller, *supra* note 26.

34. For those injured in the workplace, the existence of worker's compensation provides for this need. Tort suits against third parties on behalf of injured workers thus probably do not have this divergence of attorney and client interest.

35. *See, e.g., In re* Oracle Securities, 136 F.R.D. 639 (N.D. Cal. 1991) (conducting an auction of plaintiffs' class action attorneys to determine which one will be appointed to represent the class and recover fees for representing it).

36. MODEL CODE OF PROFESSIONAL RESPONSIBILITY DR 5-103(B) (Chicago: ABA, 1977).

37. Mark Lynch, *Ethical Rules in Flux: Advancing Costs of Litigation*, LITIG., Winter 1981, at 19.

38. FREDERICK B. MACKINNON, CONTINGENT FEES FOR LEGAL SERVICES 69 (Chicago: Aldine Publishing, 1964).

39. Lynch, *supra* note 37, at 20.

40. Morton Mintz, *Winning Lawyer Hasn't Quit Fight Against Tobacco Firms*, WASHINGTON POST, June 19, 1988, at H4.

41. MODEL RULES OF PROFESSIONAL CONDUCT Rule 1.8(e) (Chicago: ABA, 1983) (permitting attorneys to pay costs with repayment contingent on recovery); Rand v. Monsanto, 926 F.2d 596, 600 (7th Cir. 1991).

Chapter 7
The *Mekdeci* Case

Only God knows whether Bendectin causes birth defects.
—Judge Walter Hoffman, Trial judge in
Mekdeci v. Merrell National Laboratories[1]

The filing of the *Mekdeci* complaint in 1977 was the beginning of a lengthy and tortuous case that was not finally resolved until 1983.[2] The initial stages of the case entailed extensive discovery by both sides. The discovery rules afford parties an opportunity to obtain evidence both from adversaries and independent witnesses. That evidence may assist the party obtaining it in proving its case or reveal evidence that an opponent intends to rely on at trial.

Betty Mekdeci and her lawyers were plainly the underdogs. George Kokus and Arthur Cohen undertook to conduct the pretrial discovery and preparation for trial, but they were handicapped by several factors. As plaintiffs, Cohen and Kokus had the burden of introducing evidence to establish the Mekdecis' claims—it was their burden to develop adequate evidence to demonstrate that the Mekdecis should win. Merrell could, at least in theory, remain entirely passive and succeed if the Mekdecis were unsuccessful in developing sufficient evidence to permit a verdict in their favor. Despite Betty Mekdeci's extensive research efforts, Cohen and Kokus believed they did not have enough evidence to succeed when the complaint was filed in the fall of 1977. Cohen and Kokus had very little to establish that Merrell had acted improperly in developing or marketing Bendectin. Causation remained a major obstacle, with only a variety of hints and suspicions and not even an expert witness identified who would testify that Bendectin was responsible for David's birth defects. Discovery would make or break the case.

In order to develop the evidence that would be required, Cohen and Kokus had to identify and sift through a massive amount of documentation and witnesses. They were stunningly understaffed to perform the work that was required. Cohen and Kokus were the only two lawyers in their firm, and their existing clients and cases demanded significant portions of their time. Gerald Tobin never was actively involved in the *Mekdeci* case (a matter of considerable annoyance to Cohen and Kokus, since he was to share in any attorney's fees recovered), and only Arthur Tifford provided assistance to Cohen and Kokus in their trial preparations.

Cohen's and Kokus's task was made more difficult because the *Mekdeci* case was the seminal Bendectin case. No prior discovery had been conducted, no one had previously pursued the numerous blind alleys and empty avenues of inquiry that existed. This meant the universe of inquiry was huge, with little guidance available as to what course would be most fruitful.

Beyond understaffing, vast quantities of information to obtain, review, and assess, and the burden of developing a successful case, Cohen and Kokus faced financial exigencies that severely squeezed their ability to prepare and try the case. The original agreement was that the expenses of preparing the case would be shared pro rata by each of the three attorney groups: Belli, Cohen and Kokus, and Tobin. Yet Gerald Tobin never paid his full share, and when Arthur Tifford left Tobin's firm and agreed to assume a share of Tobin's fees, he was delinquent in paying his share of the expenses of suit. Expenses were considerable, for copying costs, payments to expert witnesses retained to testify for Mekdeci and to Merrell's experts for their time at discovery depositions, fees of court reporters who transcribed pretrial depositions, and costs for attorney travel during discovery.

By contrast, Merrell's defense team from the prestigious New York law firm of Davis, Polk & Wardwell was amply staffed and abundantly funded. For Merrell, the *Mekdeci* case posed threats that loomed much larger than any judgment in that case, and thereby justified extensive—virtually unlimited—defense efforts. Lawrence E. (Ed) Walsh, with impeccable credentials, was the lead lawyer for Merrell.

Shortly after graduation from Columbia University Law School in the 1930s, Walsh went to work for the then-Manhattan District Attorney, Thomas Dewey, who was fighting Tammany Hall corruption. In the early 1940s he did a brief stint at Davis, Polk, before returning to work for his former boss, Thomas Dewey, who had been elected Governor of New York. President Eisenhower appointed Walsh a federal judge in 1954, and in 1957, William Rogers, the Attorney General and a friend and former colleague of Walsh's, persuaded him to resign to become second in command at the Justice Department. Among Walsh's assignments at Justice was supervision of the process of selecting federal judges. When John Kennedy was elected President in 1960, Walsh returned to Davis, Polk and shortly thereafter became outside counsel for Merrell—just in time to represent it in the criminal prosecution arising out of MER/29. In 1964 Walsh became a member of Merrell's Board of Directors. After his retirement from Davis, Polk and at the age of 75, he was appointed by a panel of federal judges as the special prosecutor for the Iran Contra affair in December 1986. He spent the next eight years and the twilight of his legal career exhibiting his characteristic thoroughness in his legal work, albeit with uncharacteristic public controversy.[3]

Walsh is known as a courtly, meticulous, and intense lawyer who, despite his unassuming manner, has a backbone of steel. He is compulsive in his preparation for a case, insisting that every fact, legal issue, and development be thoroughly considered and pursued. He readily acknowledges his trait of being overdemanding of those who work for him and having little patience for those who fail to meet his standards. Merrell's defense would not suffer from lack of immaculate preparation, generous staffing, excellent lawyering, or ample funding.[4]

In contrast to Cohen and Kokus, Walsh had the luxury of assembling a team of lawyers at Davis, Polk to work on the *Mekdeci* case. They included Alfred Schretter, who had assisted Walsh in defending Merrell in the MER/29 litigation, as well as Mark Austrian, a young litigator at Davis, Polk. When the work became heavy, other lawyers in the firm (at the time comprised of approximately 100 lawyers) were called on for temporary assistance. Unlike the Mekdecis' lawyers who were paying the expenses of trial preparation out of their own pockets, Walsh and his colleagues billed Merrell for costs that were incurred during pretrial preparations, at trial, and thereafter. The David and Goliath metaphor reasonably captures the difference between the Mekdecis' lawyers and Merrell's lawyers, although the slingshot employed by Cohen and Kokus would have been an economy model and, as George Kokus explains, "Goliath wasn't as rich as Merrell."

Davis, Polk's numerical and financial superiority was demonstrated early in the case when in October, 1977 it served on Cohen and Kokus a 117-page set of interrogatories (questions that an opponent must answer under oath) that contained 170 separate items ("normal" discovery in a birth defect case according to one Merrell lawyer).[5] Remarkably, answers to the interrogatories were filed on time, which may be more of a tribute to Betty Mekdeci and her devotion to the cause than to her attorneys' knowledge or efforts at that early stage. The answer to one interrogatory, which inquired about the plaintiffs' evidence that Bendectin causes birth defects, revealed the challenge the Mekdecis' lawyers faced. The answer consisted of a reference to Dr. Patterson's case reports in the *Canadian Medical Journal*, the reports of adverse drug reactions, and an attack on the Bunde-Bowles study Merrell had performed.

Throughout the early phases of discovery, Merrell was the aggressor, engaging in wide-ranging, extensive, and meticulous discovery. Because Merrell would be exonerated if another cause of David's birth defects could be identified and because genetic factors are known to play a role in a portion of birth defects, Merrell sought medical histories and information from the entire Mekdeci family. Merrell also insisted on comprehensive medical examinations of each of the Mekdecis by a physician it hired.

The first round of depositions were conducted by Merrell and focused on the Mekdeci family. Merrell's attorneys deposed Betty Mekdeci on three separate occasions, the first of which, in January 1978, continued for over three days. Ed Walsh inquired in painstaking detail about everything from Mekdeci's employment history, to when she got pregnant, to how she obtained Bendectin, to the details of her search for the cause of David's birth defects, to her family tree. For each relative Betty Mekdeci identified, Walsh sought his or her address, educational background, employment, health, and any birth anomalies. Merrell also conducted the deposition of Michael Mekdeci, both Betty's and Michael's parents, and Betty's doctors, including a psychiatrist whom she had seen in the wake of the failure of her first marriage. No stone was left unturned in defending Merrell.

Toward the end of her first deposition, after three days of patient and searching questioning by Ed Walsh, Betty Mekdeci, never at a loss for words, eloquently and passionately lectured Walsh about Merrell's deficiencies in testing and providing information about Bendectin:

Here is a company who has been in thalidomide, involved with thalidomide, and they know that the only animal that had the identical deformity to man was one species of macaque monkey. Rats and rabbits did not demonstrate the typical limb deformity of phocomelia. The closest that they got to any kind of limb deformity was in rabbits, and that was not phocomelia. . . .

All right. They never went to higher animals. Here's a company who knows all about thalidomide, yet they haven't got the money to go to higher animals. . . .

. . . I feel like there were certainly enough [adverse reactions] reported, given our bad reporting system, incidences of a specific type of birth defect to have warranted some kind of acknowledgement of this on the labeling and to physicians. I think I should have had the choice to make up my mind whether I wanted to take this drug based on the fact of what you had in your files and what the FDA had. Then if I wanted to go ahead and take it and take my chances, we wouldn't be sitting across from each other. But, it's not fair for you to have this knowledge, whether or not you have established in your minds this causal relationship, and not share it with the medical community and with the public who is going to be consuming this stuff.[6]

Even after suit was filed, Betty Mekdeci continued her efforts to find additional evidence helpful to her case. At the same time, she was an active client who insisted that she be kept informed about developments in her case, and quickly informed her lawyers when she was dissatisfied with their efforts or responses. She forwarded suggestions to her lawyers, identified scientific sources that she recommended they obtain and consult, and prodded them to be more aggressive in their efforts on her behalf. Indeed, as late as the spring of 1978, Betty Mekdeci was still pulling the laboring oar in efforts to develop evidence of Bendectin's teratogenicity.

Dissatisfied with several aspects of her attorneys' performance, she wrote a four-page letter of complaint to Melvin Belli, whom she still viewed as the lead lawyer on her case. The letter detailed her numerous complaints. The Florida lawyers' investigation into the medical aspects of the case was inadequate, her telephone calls and letters went mostly unanswered, discovery from Merrell had not been pursued, her lawyers had yet to take their first deposition, the rift between Cohen and Kokus and Gerald Tobin because of Tobin's lack of commitment had become evident, Dr. William McBride, the hero of the thalidomide tragedy, had not been contacted by her lawyers after his favorable response to her about Bendectin, and the Florida lawyers had ignored her suggestion that they consult with Paul Rheingold, the lawyer who had coordinated the plaintiffs' efforts in MER/29, in the hope that he might provide helpful information about how to pursue discovery against Merrell.

Despite the number of complaints, Betty Mekdeci's irritation was a product of her impatience with her attorneys' efforts to prepare her case for trial and their cavalier treatment of her, by failing to respond to her inquiries and to keep her informed of their efforts. Had Betty Mekdeci been a mid-level manager at a corporation that was a repeat client, her lawyers would have been accommodating and attentive, if not fawning. But the contrast with most personal injury plaintiffs is stark—communication is casual, phone calls often go unreturned, and attention is reserved for important phases such as a serious settlement offer or final preparation for trial. Personal injury plaintiffs simply do not have the benefit (and leverage) of controlling future business in the way organizational clients do.

Belli's response sought to soothe Betty Mekdeci and reassure her about the extensive efforts made by her lawyers. Betty Mekdeci's letter did have the effect of bringing to a head dissatisfaction with Gerald Tobin's lack of engagement in the case (he was seeking election as a judge), and his removal as liaison and nominal head of the Florida lawyers' efforts.

Much of Cohen's and Kokus's early effort in the *Mekdeci* case was focused on identifying expert witnesses who would testify at trial. Because of his medical background, Arthur Cohen was assigned responsibility for the medical and pharmaceutical aspects of the case. Dr. Roger Palmer, a pharmacologist at the University of Miami who had previously been employed as an expert witness by Arthur Cohen, was contacted and asked to review the Bendectin studies. But he was slow in gathering information and responding to anxious inquiries from Cohen, making evident the need to locate others who might assist. Cohen contacted a number of physicians that Betty Mekdeci had identified, including William McBride, Donald Patterson, the Canadian physician who had published adverse reaction reports about Bendectin, and others.

But by mid-1978 Betty Mekdeci's lawyers were becoming discouraged in their efforts to develop evidence to prove causation, that is, that David's birth defects were the result of Betty's use of Bendectin. Melvin Belli wrote to Betty Mekdeci: "I know proximate cause is nice to have specifically, but if you don't have it you go to trial on what you've got rather than wait indefinitely for something that may not come down." Moreover, the *Mekdeci* case was more difficult than other Bendectin cases might have been because of facts peculiar to the case: David's birth defects were not bilateral, and most of the limb defects found in thalidomide children affected both the right and left sides.[7] Teratologists theorized that, if a chemical agent were responsible for birth defects, its presence in the womb would act equally on both sides of the developing fetus. In addition, Betty Mekdeci had taken a number of drugs during her pregnancy, which provided Merrell the opportunity to point to alternative possible causes of David's birth defects.

At this point, other lawyers might have chosen to cut their losses and dismiss the case or seek a nominal settlement from the defendant. In fact, Cohen and Kokus did just that with Burroughs Wellcome, agreeing to dismiss it from the case. Nothing helpful to indict Actifed had turned up, the experts that Cohen and Kokus consulted were pessimistic, and the *Mekdeci* team lacked the resources to fight a war on two separate fronts. Merrell decided not to resist Burroughs Wellcome's dismissal from the case, as that would avoid the specter of the two defendants inadvertently helping the plaintiff by pointing fingers at each other. The dismissal left unconstrained authority over the defense at trial to Merrell.

But there were forces that prevented dismissal of the Mekdecis' case against Merrell. The lawyers knew that Betty Mekdeci would never agree to abandon the claim. She retained the conviction, which her lawyers were increasingly doubting, that there was a "smoking gun" document somewhere "out there" that would break open the case against Bendectin if only it could be found in time for trial. She wrote in one letter to her lawyers: "I am absolutely convinced that this drug can and does deform certain babies and every day it is left on the market means more heartache, pain and suffering for unsuspecting parents and perhaps a lifetime of being deformed and crippled for the 'lucky' babies that live." She concluded her letter by inquiring whether the reason that causation was so difficult to prove was because the medical community that had "handed [Bendectin] out like candy" could simply not bring itself to believe that it had harmful effects.

Mekdeci's lawyers hoped to put Merrell's corporate character on trial before the jury, thereby diminishing the significance of causation. Some torts scholars have suggested that the causation inquiry is not as objective and purely factual as might appear. Professor Wayne Thode, for example, has argued that a drunk and speeding driver who ran into a child who darted into the path of the car might be found liable even if a sober driver observing the speed limit could not have avoided the child.[8] The culpability of the driver and the danger his actions pose to others makes this a sympathetic case even though it could be not said that the drunkenness or speeding caused the child's injuries. Jury researchers have also proposed a model of decision-making that supports this view. In this account, jurors construct a plausible story to account for the evidence and reach a verdict consistent with the legal instructions they are given. In the construction of a story, jurors may commingle evidence on different elements, such as liability and causation.[9] While the researchers' formal modeling occurred afterwards, the plaintiffs' lawyers reached the same conclusions based on experience and intuition. Cohen and Kokus hoped to shore up their otherwise weak case on causation with evidence of Merrell's culpability.

Although Cohen and Kokus were having difficulty gathering evidence to prove causation, Merrell's evidence tending to exonerate Bendectin was less than compelling, although it improved during the period before trial. Perhaps most important for Cohen, Kokus, and Belli was the realization that, even though the *Mekdeci* case might be a long shot, the potential stakes were enormous, involving thousands of other families with birth defects where Bendectin was implicated.

With many areas unexplored in the fall of 1978 and early 1979, Cohen and Kokus stepped up their efforts to uncover additional evidence that might improve their chances of succeeding in the *Mekdeci* case. Facing a scheduled trial date of summer 1979, Cohen and Kokus sought a delay, in a series of motions that began in January 1979. Merrell, seeking to maximize its resource advantage, resisted each plaintiff motion for a continuance.

During discovery, Merrell made available a copy of its new drug application for Bendectin on file with the FDA. The NDA was massive, comprising 250 volumes and 54,000 pages of information. Separate NDAs for the two major components in Bendectin, doxylamine and dicyclomine, also consisted of tens of thousands of densely packed pages as well. George Kokus rented a microfilm machine, packed it in his car, and drove to Davis, Polk's office in New York to copy the NDAs, which he then brought back to his office in Florida for review. Copying the NDAs required two trips by Kokus spanning the months of February and March of 1979. Copying and reviewing the NDAs was a massive, labor intensive task, that strained Cohen and Kokus and their capacity to keep up with the demands of a case whose complexity was geometrically expanding.

The review of documents produced by Merrell resulted in the strongest piece of evidence Cohen and Kokus found in the *Mekdeci* case. In the wake of thalidomide, Merrell recognized that it would have to perform teratology testing on Bendectin, which at that point had been successfully marketed for five years. Because rodents had proved a poor model for predicting human response to thalidomide, Merrell assigned a young scientist, Dr. Robert Staples, a reproductive physiologist, to conduct a teratology study of Bendectin on rabbits. Staples's memorandum (which was stamped "Rough Draft"), after noting malformations found in the kits of rabbits fed the highest doses of Bendectin, observed that "sternal changes noted involving shifted ossification centers by past experience could point to the possibility of more severe alterations should increased doses be employed." The "past experience" referred to by Staples was to a thalidomide study he had completed the year before. In that study Staples found sternal malformations in the kits of rabbits fed thalidomide and noted a shifted ossification in one of the kits that was autopsied.[10] Other researchers had found sternal ossification anomalies in certain sensitive rat strains exposed to thalidomide.[11]

Staples concluded his report: "These possibilities can be answered only upon further experimentation employing increased dosage." Yet no further animal studies of Bendectin were performed by Merrell in response to Staples' recommendation.

The Staples study appeared to be the smoking gun for which all litigators long. If there is a trial lawyers' heaven, it is littered with smoking guns—documents that provide devastating evidence against the opposing party and in the opponent's hand. Subsequent investigation revealed that Merrell did not submit the study to the FDA upon its completion, instead waiting three years before submitting it and then in conjunction with its NDA for doxylamine, rather than Bendectin. Most suspiciously,

Dr. Staples's recommendations for further study were removed, and modifications were made in the data reported to the FDA.

Roger Palmer, who reviewed the studies and lab notebooks kept by Staples and his assistant, later reported to Cohen and Kokus on a number of abnormalities and wasted fetuses that were reflected in lab notebooks but not included in the final study as submitted and published.

The plaintiffs immediately characterized these changes and omissions as sanitizing the data, while Merrell claimed that it was a legitimate reclassification by Dr. Dorsey Holtkamp, a Merrell endocrinologist who headed the department conducting the research, performed after Staples left Merrell's employ. But, even if Merrell's explanation of good faith reviewing and editing is accepted, the better course would have been to report *both* Staples's original findings and the subsequent corrections, along with an explanation for the reclassifications.

Other aspects of Merrell's corporate behavior fed the plaintiffs' lawyers' predisposition that the defendant was an irresponsible, if not evil, corporate character. Discovery of Merrell's correspondence and memoranda revealed that it managed, perhaps more accurately micromanaged, inquiries from doctors who had patients with birth defects after Bendectin exposure. This was the same malfeasance, persuading doctors to reclassify their call as an "inquiry" rather than an adverse report so the calls would not have to be reported to the FDA, as occurred with MER/29. Similarly, Merrell denied to inquiring physicians that similar reports of birth defects had been received and reassured them with the Bunde-Bowles study. But Dr. Palmer, who reviewed the study, told Cohen and Kokus that the Bunde-Bowles study was plagued with faulty methodology that made it a poor vehicle for establishing the safety of Bendectin.

Cohen and Kokus also discovered that the letter that Dr. Tommy Evans had written to CBS about its proposed Bendectin program was orchestrated by Merrell. Merrell employees had helped draft the letter, identified prominent physicians who were approached about co-signing the letter, and wrote thank you notes to the doctors who signed the letter. After CBS decided not to air the show, Merrell wrote a "Dear Tommy" letter thanking him for his "continuing help to Merrell as a consultant." This episode contributed to the plaintiffs' belief that Merrell was a master at manipulating the medical profession and its views about the safety of Bendectin. To be sure, the doctors who signed the Evans letter appear genuinely to have believed the views expressed in it. Yet Merrell's behind-the-scenes manipulation added another tinge of taint to feed the lawyers' predispositions.

Other discovery supported these views. Dorsey Holtkamp, who reclassified Dr. Staples's findings and later became director of medical research at Merrell, was deposed by Arthur Cohen on June 21, 1979. He testified:

Q. Was Merrell or, at least you, as a scientist, were you of the opinion in 1963, let's say the end of '63, that the relationship between Thalidomide and malformations in man was only a possible relationship?
Answer. Yes.
Q. You didn't think that had been established?
Answer. Correct.
Q. When did you believe it was established that Thalidomide was teratogenic in man?
Answer. I am not convinced that has ever been established to this date.[12]

The Staples study, Merrell's manipulation of physicians' inquiries, the weakness of the Bunde-Bowles study, Merrell's behind-the-scenes role in the Tommy Evans letter, and testimony like Dorsey Holtkamp's, which is virtually identical to the tobacco industry's longstanding denials that the causal relationship between smoking and lung cancer has been proved, fueled Cohen, Kokus, and the Mekdecis' resolve to pursue the case.

A significant development complicating preparation for trial was the publication of several additional studies of birth defects and drugs in the late 1970s. One study by a British researcher, Richard Smithells, focused on Bendectin and concluded that the results suggested that Bendectin was not teratogenic.[13] Another study found a statistically significant association between Bendectin and congenital heart defects, but the authors cautioned that the outcome might have been spurious and required further study before any inference of causation was justified.[14] (David's doctors had told his parents that he might have a congenital heart anomaly, but were equivocal when pressed during litigation.) A preliminary report of a study by two researchers at the Centers for Disease Control, Godfrey Oakley and Jose Cordero, became available on the eve of trial. The Oakley study was particularly important because it was a case-control study and therefore had greater power to reveal an association between Bendectin and birth defects, if one existed. The authors concluded that their study did not establish any causal relationship between Bendectin and major birth defects and that it suggested first trimester exposures to Bendectin confer little if any risk for the birth defects studied.[15] Each of these studies meant additional depositions and investigation into the study and its implications.

On April 6, 1979 the court scheduled the trial to begin July 16, 1979, with a final pretrial conference to discuss the issues and facilitate the smooth conduct of the trial set for July 5, 1979. The proximity of the trial induced a flurry of activity in the case, as both sides scrambled to get ready for a difficult and complex trial. Merrell needed to depose the experts that the Mekdecis had located who would testify on their behalf; Cohen and Kokus needed to do the same with Merrell's experts, as well as conduct depositions of a number of Merrell officials who were involved in the development, testing, marketing, and oversight of Bendectin.

In the frenetic pace during the early summer of 1979 Merrell attempted to obtain information that it had been seeking for 18 months: the costs of David's medical treatment and other expenses attributable to his birth defects. Most of the expenses had been paid by the Mekdecis' insurance company, and the task of researching and itemizing those costs had been a low priority. In the end, Merrell did not insist on an accounting of the costs. Instead it agreed to a stipulation that the Mekdecis' out-of-pocket expenses were $20,000, a paltry sum by comparison to the other damages sought in the suit. The casual $20,000 stipulation, however, later played an important role in the jury's verdict.

The Mekdecis' lawyers quickly realized that they would be unable to keep up with the pace required, which Davis, Polk artfully accelerated. Merrell designated every expert witness it might conceivably ask to testify, thereby overwhelming plaintiffs with the number that had to be deposed. At one point, depositions of three separate witnesses were scheduled in Miami, Boston, and Bethesda, Maryland on the same day. Davis, Polk noticed a fourth deposition of one of the Mekdecis' experts for the same day in Detroit, Michigan. As plaintiffs' motion seeking to delay the deposition argued with simple logic: "The law of mathematics dictates that the three attorneys [working on behalf of the Mekdecis] cannot be in four or more cities on the same date at the same time." Over thirty deposition notices were filed and served during May and June, 1979.

At the Pretrial Conference, George Kokus expressed his fatigue and frustration in trying to meet the demands of the supercharged schedule for trial:

Your Honor, there have been depositions which we had to cancel. There are at least 25 expert witnesses of the Defendant who we never took the deposition of because it was physically impossible. The three [plaintiffs'] attorneys traveled all around the world to take these depositions within the deadlines set by the Court.

Quite frankly, we took the depositions of very few of their experts because we didn't have the manpower and sometimes there were as many as five or six depositions set on a day and we had many other—according to the pre-trial Order, there were many other things we had to get done and it was physically impossible.

What Kokus did not mention were the extraordinary financial demands imposed on his firm by the *Mekdeci* case. Cohen and Kokus were paying most of the expenses of discovery, though in theory they were being shared three ways with Belli and Tobin. Those expenses—including travel, deposition transcripts, experts, and numerous miscellaneous items—reflected the breadth of discovery and the careening pace at which they were proceeding. The greatest costs were yet to come—the opportunity costs incurred by Cohen and Kokus over the next year while they devoted virtually full-time efforts to finish preparation for and conduct the trial. That meant virtually closing up their malpractice and personal injury practice. Yet, there was a silver lining that Cohen and Kokus reassured themselves with: *Mekdeci* was just the first of many future Bendectin cases. Their investment in *Mekdeci* would pay off well into the future.

In May 1979 plaintiffs sought a continuance of the trial. The nominal reason was that Melvin Belli, who still was to lead the trial team, had a conflict with other cases that he was scheduled to try during the same period. A delay would also have the beneficent effect of providing additional time for the plaintiffs' lawyers to complete their trial preparations. That task appeared close to impossible, given the remaining work, the demands that Merrell's attorneys put on plaintiffs' attorneys to respond to their discovery requests and motions, and the limited resources available to them to meet these challenges. Belli's affidavit in support of the motion to delay the start of the trial added, "However, I will be available to participate in the trial of this matter during the month of August." On May 14, 1979 Judge Young denied the plaintiffs' motion; he was holding the parties' feet to the fire. This inflexible approach was a significant detriment to the plaintiffs, who did not have the resources or capacity that Merrell did.

By this point Betty Mekdeci had become concerned that Melvin Belli would default on his agreement to try her case. She wrote him in May 1979 expressing that concern and challenging him with the knowledge she had recently gained from a book about personal injury litigation: "Will you in fact try our case in court should we come to trial? Or has our case simply been as the book put it 'farmed out' to Tobin and Fisch who gave your office a referral fee for the use of your name?" Referral fees were unethical arrangements that would subject an attorney to disciplinary procedures, yet were commonly employed. Belli responded reassuringly, if ambiguously, "we are actively in this case and intend to participate in the trial unless we can get a satisfactory settlement."

The final pretrial conference was held on July 11, 1979—a mere five days before the trial was scheduled to begin. At that time, it became clear that the trial would have to be delayed because of incomplete discovery of expert witnesses, pending disputes over document discovery, and additional witnesses who had been identified. Because of the need to address those matters, Judge Young, the Chief Judge of the federal district court and the judge to whom the *Mekdeci* case was assigned for trial, post-poned the trial until August 7, 1979, which only modestly reduced the severe pressure on the parties to complete their trial preparations.

The day before the final pretrial conference, Merrell had served an important motion, seeking to have excluded from trial any reference to thalidomide or MER/29. Merrell's arguments were quite sound. The is-sue of Merrell's culpability and Bendectin's toxicity were distinct from those relating to thalidomide and MER/29. Reference to thalidomide at trial might improperly influence the jury with respect to Bendectin and its teratogenicity. Evidence of Merrell's culpability with regard to MER/29, and to a lesser extent thalidomide, might persuade the jury that Merrell was nefarious or worse. Most jurors would tend to be less con-cerned about wrongly deciding a case against a party it viewed as evil, regardless of the evidence about Bendectin. To put the point another way, the jury would be biased in favor of the plaintiff because of the bad character of Merrell.

The plaintiffs' strongest rejoinder was that evidence that Merrell had deceived the FDA with regard to MER/29 tended to show that it engaged in the same conduct with regard to Bendectin. The Staples study, con-ducted in 1963, demonstrated a chronological proximity between Mer-rell's deceptive behavior in MER/29 and Bendectin. Evidentiary rules, however, declare that prior bad acts by an individual cannot be intro-duced to prove that the individual acted in the same fashion at some later point in time. This prohibited "propensity inference" from bad acts or a bad character reflects the concern that a jury will be inclined to rule against the bad actor, not because of the merits of the case, but because it dislikes the evildoer.

The exclusion of this evidence comes at the cost of sacrificing evidence that might be relevant and probative—a person who has cheated at cards in the past is more likely to cheat at cards in the future than an honest card player—but the prejudicial effect and the consequent adverse im-pact on accuracy is thought to outweigh the consequences of excluding the evidence. Although this rule is most applicable to individuals and their behavior, Merrell, as a corporate defendant, had a stronger claim for exclusion. The wrongdoing in the MER/29 and thalidomide cases was by individual employees of Merrell. If the evidence would be ex-cluded if there were a trial of those individuals for other wrongdoing, it surely had even less value in assessing subsequent behavior of a corpo-ration made up of many individuals.

Judge Young did not rule on Merrell's motion at the pretrial confer-ence. Later, however, before the trial began in January 1980, evidence of Merrell's connection to thalidomide and MER/29 was excluded. Plain-tiffs had lost one of the significant rounds of ammunition they had counted on, indeed, a bullet that had helped persuade the lawyers to become involved in the *Mekdeci* case in the beginning.

Another significant event at the pretrial hearing was the first public intimation that Melvin Belli might not be present to try the case. Judge Young inquired: "Who is going to be the main trial attorney for the Plaintiffs, are you Mr. Belli?" George Kokus interjected: "I think the easiest way to do that—I would be considered lead counsel as far as the responsibility for the overall conduct of the case."[16]

In August, at the time of the rescheduled trial, the court once again postponed the trial at the request of plaintiffs. The parties had been arguing over expert witnesses at trial and recent document production. They were plainly not ready to proceed to trial in an organized and efficient fashion. Constraints on available court time dictated delaying the case until January, and Judge Young was hopeful that arrangements could be made for a visiting judge to try the lengthy case, so as not to disturb the regular docket of pending criminal and civil cases. The trial was put off until January 1980.

In the months before trial, the first national publicity about Bendectin's safety emerged. The Orlando papers had reported on the filing of the Mekdecis' suit, but with the cancellation of the *60 Minutes* program there had been no national publicity about Bendectin or its accusers. The *National Enquirer* became interested in Bendectin (after being alerted by Melvin Belli) when the *Mekdeci* case was filed and had assigned a number of researchers and reporters to investigate. In October 1979 the *Enquirer* published a sensationalized story that trumpeted the "New Thalidomide Scandal—Experts Reveal." The story defined "teratogen," as "an agent that causes 'the formation or bringing forth of monsters,'" a reference to its Greek etymology that ignored its broader contemporary usage, which includes any environmental factor that interferes with the normal development of the fetus. The story chronicled each Merrell transgression discovered by Betty Mekdeci's lawyers in the preparation for trial and carefully marshaled statements by physicians and researchers in a fashion that gave the impression that Bendectin was a modern version of thalidomide.

Later, in 1980, the leftish and progressive magazine *Mother Jones* published another article, entitled "The Bendectin Cover-Up." The authors highlighted the existence of birth defect children born to women who took Bendectin, overstated the associations researchers had found between Bendectin and birth defects, and breathlessly concluded that Bendectin was "a modern-day horror story of corporate [Merrell] and bureaucratic [FDA] irresponsibility."[17] Even the *New York Times* got into the act, publishing a lengthy article in the Sunday Magazine about Bendectin that featured a picture of then five-year-old David Mekdeci and sympathetically recounted Betty Mekdeci's efforts and lawsuit.[18]

The national publicity, especially the *Enquirer* article, had an important effect on the evolution of Bendectin litigation. In response to the publicity (as Belli had hoped) many more women emerged who had taken Bendectin and borne children with congenital anomalies. Some of these women wrote to Betty Mekdeci, who shortly after the first trial formed the Association of Bendectin Children (later expanded to the Association of Birth Defect Children), an organization dedicated to the cause of children born with birth defects due to exposure to Bendectin. Mrs. Mekdeci forwarded the names of these women to her attorneys, who were accumulating potential plaintiffs for future cases. Dozens and perhaps hundreds of future cases were identified in this manner. Other than *Mekdeci*, not a single Bendectin case was filed until after the *National Enquirer* article.[19]

In November, Cohen and Kokus informed Betty Mekdeci that Melvin Belli would not be present to try her case, because he had a conflicting trial. Mekdeci reports she "pitched a fit," and repeatedly called Belli seeking to persuade him to change his mind. Similar efforts by Arthur Cohen were met with a crashing telephone receiver response. A number of people associated with the *Mekdeci* case have hypothesized why Belli, who was 73 at the time, decided not to participate in the trial; none is very persuasive. The most popular explanation is a lack of confidence in his ability to get up to speed and handle a complex case that would require a two month trial. But Belli could have played the role of lead counsel, conducted voir dire (questioning potential jurors), given the opening argument, and left the more technical and grueling aspects to Cohen and Kokus. In the end, Belli's default may have been a more prosaic matter of bottom-line economics. Belli had numerous cases pending around the country and was constantly faced with conflicting trials. The resolution of those conflicts required a business judgment about which case held more potential. The *Mekdeci* case was going to be a difficult one, Betty Mekdeci was anything but a grateful, doting client, and Cohen and Kokus had immersed themselves in the case from its beginning. Other more promising Bendectin cases would emerge, so Belli went off to Rockville, Maryland to try a case that began at the same time as the *Mekdeci* trial. Nevertheless, a number of observers familiar with both Belli and the *Mekdeci* trial feel that the Mekdecis were better served by Cohen and Kokus than they would have been with Belli as the chief trial lawyer.

Belli's default would subsequently cause him considerable public embarrassment. The *American Lawyer*, a widely-circulated legal newsmagazine with muckraking tendencies, published an article entitled "Melvin

Belli's Bait and Switch" that detailed Belli's failure to appear and his subsequent attempt to withdraw from the *Mekdeci* case. The first page of the article was illustrated with an empty suit of armor and a pinstripe-suited lawyer escaping and running off. Belli later justified his failure to appear by explaining that he had appeared ready for trial in August, but the judge rescheduled the trial until January.[20] The difficulty with Belli's explanation is that the August trial date was postponed at the request of the plaintiffs,[21] and his name was on the request.

With Belli out of the trial, Cohen and Kokus, with the assistance of Arthur Tifford, geared up to try the case but remained understaffed. A week before the *Mekdeci* trial started, Belli called Allen Eaton, a Washington, DC lawyer experienced in food and drug law and pharmaceutical litigation. Eaton had just completed the trial of a personal injury drug case in Pennsylvania, and Belli explained the need for additional help at trial. Eaton, after a stint with a major Washington law firm, had formed his own firm five years previously and was struggling to establish his practice. The prospect of involvement in future Bendectin cases, part of the promise of the *Mekdeci* case, was quite attractive. Moreover, Eaton was familiar with Merrell. Eaton had represented John Nestor, the FDA employee who had investigated MER/29 and the officemate of Frances Kelsey, and other FDA employees who claimed that they were mistreated by their superiors because of their strict treatment of favored pharmaceutical companies. On the weekend before the trial began, Eaton flew to Florida to assist Cohen, Kokus, and Tifford in trying *Mekdeci*. His role was primarily behind the scenes, preparing written motions, responding to Merrell's motions, and conducting necessary legal research, but he would later play a central role in the MDL-486 litigation.

The trial began on January 22, 1980, and ended two months later on March 21, 1980.[22] Any trial, even for a few days, is a grueling, demanding, and tiring challenge for attorneys. The length of the *Mekdeci* trial, the tremendous stakes involved for both sides and the concomitant contentiousness, the last-minute discovery (depositions of some witnesses were taken during the trial), and the long trial days commanded by a trial judge who was in a hurry to complete the trial made the *Mekdeci* trial even more so.

Judge Walter Hoffman, a 73-year-old senior federal judge from Norfolk, Virginia, presided over the trial. A short, affable, portly individual, often jocular in his exchanges with attorneys, he nevertheless maintained tight control of the trial proceedings. Hoffman preferred informality and self-deprecation to imperiousness, and often employed humor to leaven the combative atmosphere in the courtroom. He was appointed to the federal bench in the 1950s and immediately became embroiled in civil rights cases in which his decisions ordering integration drew resentment from a community deeply rooted in southern traditions. Hoffman's most notable case was the criminal tax prosecution of Vice-President Spiro Agnew, in which Hoffman approved a deal that permitted Agnew to escape incarceration in exchange for his resignation as Vice-President of the United States. Scrupulously fair, Hoffman had an open mind and was always willing to be persuaded that his initial inclination was wrong. Both sides would get an opportunity to make their case before an impartial arbiter.

Hoffman agreed to travel to Florida and try the case at the request of Judge Young, who was concerned about the impact on other cases if he became engaged in a two month trial. Ironically, just before heading to Orlando to preside over the *Mekdeci* case, Judge Hoffman found out that his daughter-in-law, who was five months pregnant, had taken Bendectin earlier in her pregnancy.[23]

The Mekdecis, their lawyers, representatives from Merrell, Ed Walsh, four other Davis, Polk attorneys and two Orlando attorneys representing Merrell, and reporters from across North America and Europe were present when the trial began. Interest was especially high in western Europe, where the thalidomide tragedy was still vivid, and Bendectin was widely distributed. David Wright, a senior reporter for the *National Enquirer*, who had become friendly with Betty Mekdeci and sympathetic to her cause, attended the trial. A number of plaintiffs' lawyers who were interested in the Mekdecis' case and future Bendectin litigation, including Jim Butler and Art Raynes, both plaintiffs' lawyers in thalidomide litigation against Merrell, also monitored the trial.

Merrell was well-staffed, highly organized, and prepared to the hilt— a fine-tuned litigation machine. By contrast, the Mekdecis' attorneys struggled financially, were often caught flat-footed when new matters were raised, and confronted organizational difficulties frequently. They would sometimes require a delay in the proceedings to locate a document, among the thousands in their files, that was unexpectedly needed. Merrell ordered daily copy of the trial transcript from the court stenographers, a costly option, requiring a team of six court reporters to shuttle in and out of the courtroom. The disparity in resources that marked the pretrial phases in the case continued through the trial.

The plaintiffs' primary strategy was to put Merrell on trial, emphasizing the changes in the Staples' study, the delay in submitting it to the FDA, the poor quality of the Bunde-Bowles study, the clustering of limb defects among the adverse drug reports, and Merrell's disingenuous responses to doctors who called with an adverse reaction and inquired about Bendectin and birth defects. That thrust was necessitated by the absence of any definitive or even strongly supportive evidence of Bendectin's teratogenicity on which plaintiffs could rely. Plaintiffs also attempted the awkward undertaking of attacking the epidemiology studies that exonerated Bendectin before Merrell introduced them. One lesson Cohen and Kokus learned from this cumbersome effort was to delay their critique of the epidemiology until rebuttal (after defendant's evidence), which is the way most subsequent Bendectin cases were tried.

Not surprisingly, given Cohen's and Kokus's experience as malpractice lawyers, much of their case was cast in a malpractice mold. Dr. Roger Palmer, their leadoff witness, testified that Merrell's deficiencies in obtaining and reporting adverse drug reports were below the standard found in the pharmaceutical industry, thereby adapting the malpractice standard to a pharmaceutical case. The plaintiffs' experts opined that David's birth defects were caused by Bendectin "to a reasonable degree of medical certainty," the talismanic invocation required by the law in malpractice cases, but which is otherwise meaningless in the medical profession.

Experts were brought in to testify that Bendectin was a weak teratogen; one estimated that Bendectin might increase the number of birth defects by 5 percent. That possibility was not precluded by the epidemiological studies Merrell introduced. As the plaintiffs' experts pointed out, the power of the epidemiological studies (because of the small number in the exposed group and the small incidence of limb reduction defects) and biases (especially recall) left a band of uncertainty that plaintiffs exploited. Yet the plaintiffs' "weak teratogenicity" evidence should have been insufficient to meet their burden of proof on causation—a 5 percent increase in birth defects, even if established, would not be adequate to demonstrate that David's birth defects were more likely than not caused by Bendectin. Rather, it would indicate a less than 5 percent chance that it was. Nevertheless, several plaintiffs' experts testified that in their opinion David's birth defects were caused by the Bendectin Betty Mekdeci took during her pregnancy.

One such expert was Dr. Alan Done, a pediatrician and pharmacologist at Wayne State University Medical School. Done would play a major role in future Bendectin litigation. He had excellent credentials: stints as a faculty member at the University of Utah and Stanford University, service for several years in the Bureau of Drugs at the FDA, and a host of publications. His specific interest and research focused on the area of drug toxicity in children. Ultimately, however, Done's propensity to exaggerate his credentials and his increasing reliance on income from serving as an expert witness created problems with his effectiveness and credibility.

Done testified that in his opinion Bendectin was a teratogen that had caused David Mekdeci's birth defects. His testimony focused almost exclusively on the former question, with the latter being virtually an afterthought. Done relied on the Staples study, the clustering of limb defects in the adverse drug reports that Betty Mekdeci had uncovered, and his reanalyses and recalculation of the data in the epidemiology studies that had been performed. Done's testimony about his reanalyses was close to indecipherable, as he corrected errors in his calculations, transposed decimal points, and apologized for sloppy mathematics. Done responded characteristically to George Kokus's request that he use a uniform rate for birth defects based on the number of defects per thousand live births:

> I think, if you want to chance my fouling up the mathematics again, but that's all right.
> .4 to .8, .4 to .6—I'm sorry. That's .1 percent, so it would be one. I'm sorry, one per thousand. 2.3—this, incidentally is a study in which the possibility of ingestion of this or other drugs like it could not be ruled out, but I still included it. Four. I'm sorry. That's of anomalies.
> The births, .6 and I made a mistake here. I'm sorry. That 2.3 was of anomalies, not of births.[24]

No jury could possibly have understood Done, nor could Merrell's attorneys have conducted an intelligent cross-examination of this testimony. This poorly prepared and confusing testimony by an important expert witness highlights the need for requiring that expert witnesses prepare a thorough and detailed written report of their opinions and the bases for those opinions in advance of trial. Preparation in advance, committing it to paper, and providing the reports to opposing counsel during discovery would do much to improve the quality of expert witness testimony and the ability of attorneys on cross-examination to reveal the weaknesses in the expert's opinions and reasoning process.[25] If experts were limited in their testimony to those matters fairly encompassed in their report, opposing attorneys would be better prepared and better able to demonstrate the weaknesses in the expert's testimony.

Merrell was in a poor position to take advantage of the weaknesses in the plaintiffs' evidence on specific causation. For Merrell, the future of Bendectin was riding on the outcome of the *Mekdeci* trial. A victory that thoroughly vindicated Bendectin was required. Conceding that Bendectin was a weak teratogen and defending on the ground that it did not cause David's birth defects would be a financial and public relations disaster for Merrell and Bendectin. Although legally parties may argue alternatively—Bendectin doesn't cause birth defects, but even if it does, it didn't cause David's birth defects—even that course was risky because Merrell felt that it had to exonerate its drug in the trial.[26] Moreover, that approach posed two risks. First, the jury might misinterpret the alternative argument as a concession on the original position. Second, recent research into jury decision making suggests that juries do not carefully segregate each legal element in the case.[27] As Professor Sanders has observed, this version of events, anchored on a statistically based specific causation argument, "is risky because it relies too heavily upon the jury's willingness to separate each element of the tort and find for the defendant if the plaintiff fails to prevail on every element."[28]

Thus Merrell's strategy was to emphasize the epidemiological studies that had been performed by several researchers. Ed Walsh hammered home the point that none of these studies had identified a statistically significant association between Bendectin and birth defects.[29] If Merrell could convince the jury (or the court, as it did in other cases) that a statistically significant epidemiological study was required to demonstrate causation, it would vindicate Bendectin and provide a defense not only in the *Mekdeci* case, but applicable in future cases as well. Merrell continued with the strategy developed in *Mekdeci* through to the end of Bendectin litigation: unless a statistically significant epidemiological study found an association, Bendectin could not be found to cause birth defects.

For months George Kokus had tried to persuade Frances DaCosta, a retired FDA pharmacologist, to testify at the *Mekdeci* trial. In 1968 DaCosta had reviewed the animal studies submitted by Merrell, including the modified Staples study of rabbits, and written a report on their toxicological implications. DaCosta told Kokus that if she had seen the original, unmodified Staples study, she would have recommended that Bendectin's FDA approval be withdrawn or at least that a birth defect warning be provided. Yet DaCosta was reluctant to testify, disinclined to become involved in a major lawsuit with its attendant publicity and unpleasant cross-examination. Allen Eaton's involvement in the case proved crucial, as he was able to call on his former FDA clients to prevail on DaCosta to testify, which she agreed to do as the trial began. Over Walsh's strenuous objections, Judge Hoffman permitted the Mekdecis to add DaCosta to their witness list for trial.

Perhaps the most dramatic aspect of the *Mekdeci* trial was the squaring off of two of the medical heros of the thalidomide tragedy. Dr. William McBride traveled from Australia and testified on behalf of the Mekdecis that Bendectin was a weak teratogen. Several weeks later, Dr. Widukind Lenz, McBride's co-discoverer from Germany, appeared to testify on behalf of Merrell. Lenz, who had been barred from testifying on behalf of thalidomide victims in Germany because of his apparent bias on their behalf, had previously testified for Merrell in *McCarrick*, the sole United States thalidomide case to go to trial. Lenz testified that in his opinion David Mekdeci's birth defect was Poland's syndrome, a birth defect that was not associated with thalidomide or other drugs. Because Poland's syndrome characteristically involves unilateral defects, Lenz's view was that Bendectin could not be responsible for David's birth defects.

The plaintiffs rested on February 13, 1980, after a short yet poignant appearance by David Mekdeci in the courtroom. Merrell began its defense by calling a number of company employees and former employees, including Dr. Staples, to explain their involvement in the Bendectin studies that were performed by Merrell. Staples testified that he did not believe Bendectin was a teratogen based on the results of his study. The testimony of the first outside researcher who published a study of Bendectin (in 1978), Richard Smithells, turned out to be disastrous for Merrell.

Smithells, who had conducted extensive research on thalidomide, explained during direct examination that he had studied pregnant women in Leeds and Liverpool, England. The study concluded that the results tended to exonerate Bendectin as a teratogen, consistent with the prior studies of Bunde and Bowles in 1963 and the 1976 study by Milkovich and van den Berg. Smithells's study corrected for one bias that existed in both of the prior studies. Because of the records kept by Britain's National Health Service for all prescription drugs, Smithells was able to determine the time during pregnancy when a woman received Bendectin. Thus Smithells was able to exclude women as exposed who had taken the drug outside the period of organogenesis, but this made no difference in the incidence of birth defects that he found.

During discovery, George Kokus had obtained copies of correspondence between Smithells and Merrell. Kokus introduced a letter that Smithells had sent to Merrell requesting additional financial support for his Bendectin study. Smithells sought a $26,000 endowment for his university, which, he wrote,

is a larger sum than you suggested in your letter but I think anything smaller could only be used on an annual basis for a limited time. For this I would not, of course, be ungrateful. Much clearly depends on the value of this publication to Merrell-National Labs. If it may save the company large sums in California Courts (which is rather what I thought when we undertook the study) they may feel magnanimous. If with the passage of time the study is of no significance I can only regard the figure you suggest as generous and welcome.[30]

Smithells's letter could be read to mean that he was selling favorable studies to Merrell and that was precisely the impression that Kokus fostered with the jury. Kokus also hammered home that Smithells had omitted mentioning Merrell's name in the acknowledgments of his study even though it had provided funding for the study.

Kokus also elicited from Smithells his criticism of the Bunde-Bowles study. Smithells had been consulted by Merrell in the early 1970s, and he responded by identifying and explaining to Merrell the weaknesses in the study and his conclusion that Bunde-Bowles was inadequate to address the question of whether Bendectin was associated with birth defects at a modest or low rate. Those methodological inadequacies tracked the testimony of the Mekdecis' experts who criticized the Bunde-Bowles study.

Toward the end of his cross-examination of Smithells, Kokus surprised Smithells with a coup that rivaled a Perry Mason cross-examination. Smithells's control group consisted of all births in Leeds and Lancaster in 1975. After obtaining Smithells's affirmation of the importance of a control group to compare to the Bendectin-exposed group, Kokus inquired, "if it [Bendectin] was available to the comparison group, your study—it would be relatively useless?"

Smithells agreed: "If that was true, it would make the study totally useless." Kokus then revealed what he had been informed by Betty Mekdeci and confirmed the night before from a British newspaper: Bendectin, known as Debendox in England, was available over the counter there. Judge Hoffman gasped, "Oh my God." Later, after a recess in which Smithells regained his composure and regrouped, he explained that it was unlikely that many women bought Debendox over the counter, because it was cheaper to obtain by prescription through the National Health Service. But the damage was done to Dr. Smithells and his study. Dr. Smithells did not appear as an expert witness in any of the subsequent Bendectin trials.

Merrell spared no expense in presenting its case. Merrell brought to the trial at least one of the authors of each epidemiology study of Bendectin. Ollie Heinonen, from Finland, testified about the study that he performed. Smithells was the second international epidemiological researcher who testified on behalf of Merrell. Lucille Milkovich, from the west coast, testified about the study she had performed. Depositions of her co-author, Bea van den Berg, and Godfrey Oakley, of the CDC, were also read to the jury. Merrell employees and former employees who had been involved in the development or testing of Bendectin were brought to trial to "tell the story" of Bendectin. Dr. Brian MacMahon, head of the Department of Epidemiology at the Harvard School of Public Health, testified to the concept of statistical significance and confidence intervals, stressing their importance in analyzing any study.

Merrell also relied heavily on a statement about Bendectin issued by the FDA in 1977. The statement had been prepared by the FDA's Marion Finkel, after the FDA decided not to provide an interview to Mike Wallace in conjunction with the *60 Minutes* program planned on Bendectin. The FDA was concerned that *60 Minutes* would sensationalize the dangers of Bendectin, and the statement was prepared to quell fears that might result.

The "Statement on Bendectin" reiterated that the drug was approved by the FDA for nausea and vomiting of pregnancy. It was supportive of the safety of Bendectin, referring to the negative epidemiological studies and dismissing the significance of the adverse drug reports as evidence of teratogenicity.

Testimony concluded on Thursday, March 14, 1980. The six-person jury (four men and two women) began its deliberations in the late morning of Monday, March 17, 1980, after Judge Hoffman finished instructing them. The jury continued deliberating a second day and by the end of the day had still not reached a verdict, an unusually long time for a jury to deliberate, even in as lengthy a case as *Mekdeci.* At the end of the second day, the jury sent Judge Hoffman a note stating that it had been unable to resolve the central question in the case—whether Bendectin caused David's birth defects. The source of the difficulty was the intrinsic pharmacological reality that all drugs have some, albeit small, risk:

> We have failed to reach a consensus as to whether Bendectin has a better than even chance of causing the birth defects of David Mekdeci. The difference of opinion stems from the fact that there was testimony presented which indicated that any drug or chemical has a slight chance of causing birth defects if ingested during the critical period of pregnancy.

The jury's conundrum was prescient: the epidemiological evidence in the case could not rule out the possibility that Bendectin increased the risk of a birth defect in some small measure. But whether one could translate that possibility into a conclusion that it was more likely than not that Bendectin caused David's birth defect was a much more difficult proposition. Walter Seacat, Professor of Mathematics and Statistics at the University of Central Florida and the foreperson of the jury, likely deserves the credit for the jury's acuity.

Judge Hoffman was most reluctant to declare a mistrial, which would require the parties to retry the two-month case at a later date. Too much time (and money) had been expended on the trial to squander it by declaring a mistrial. He told the jury that it would break for the night and resume deliberating on Wednesday. Wednesday came and went without a verdict, but on Thursday morning the jury sent a question to the judge inquiring if it could render a verdict "with a rationale for such verdict." As the jury perceptively observed in its note, "these parties represent not only themselves, but a society in which they are an integral part."

Judge Hoffman told the jury it could not return a rationale with its verdict. Thirty minutes later, a mistrial began to look likely when the jury sent another note that it was "hopelessly deadlocked." The difficulty was that Grover Ashcraft, a farmer and former mayor of a small town outside Orlando, had decided that plaintiffs should prevail. Initially the lone juror for plaintiffs, Ashcraft was able to obtain some support from a few of the jurors as the week wore on. However, by Friday, it was apparent that the two women jurors were adamantly opposed to a plaintiffs' verdict. One of them had several daughters who had used Bendectin and all her grandchildren "were perfect." At that point the possibility of a very small award of damages to "send a message" was discussed. Ashcraft realized that if he insisted on a full award of damages he would force a mistrial. The $20,000 medical expenses stipulation provided a convenient figure. On Friday, in its fifth day of deliberations, the jury returned its verdict. The verdict form contained a space for the jury to designate the prevailing party, which was filled in with "plaintiff," and then left unchanged the next paragraph of the form, which contained the $20,000 in stipulated medical expenses. "Nothing" was filled in on the line for the amount of damages due to David.

The jury's verdict was hopelessly problematical. Did the designation of "plaintiff" mean all three plaintiffs, just David, or just the parents? If intended to cover all three, it was plainly an inadequate amount, since the parties had agreed that the medical expenses alone were $20,000, and Merrell had not disputed that David had suffered a serious injury for which he would be entitled to compensation if liability existed. Concluding that it was intended to be an award to David alone was dubious, because the jury had filled in "nothing" as the damages awarded to him. Finally, if intended to mean just the parents, the jury's verdict was both internally inconsistent and legally erroneous. Inconsistent, because there was no basis in the evidence to conclude that the parents were entitled to recover and David was not. If Bendectin caused David's birth defects, both the parents and David were entitled to recover. If Bendectin did not cause David's birth defects, neither should recover. The verdict was legally erroneous, because under existing Florida law the parents' claim was derivative of their child's. To put it in simpler terms, the parents could not recover *unless* David also recovered.

Both sides seized on the uncertainty and equivocation in the verdict. The Mekdecis, their lawyers, and several journalists who were sympathetic to their cause held a victory celebration that night. Betty Mekdeci put on a brave face with the media and claimed that the favorable verdict was more important than "a lot of money." "I'm delighted with the verdict. I'd rather give this to my son than a million dollars." "It means the drug is unsafe," interpreted George Kokus, while Ed Walsh reached a contrary conclusion: "it seems to be a vindication of the drug." Merrell's marketing department informed its sales force: "The verdict of the jury is a clear vindication of Bendectin. The denial of any award to the child can only mean that Bendectin did not cause his birth defects." A more accurate sense of Merrell's view of the verdict may be reflected in the statement of Robert Irvine, Merrell's Director of Communication: "We're disappointed with the verdict; we feel it's contrary to the evidence."[31]

Judge Hoffman was plainly troubled by the verdict. He recognized its ambiguity and inconsistency. More importantly, the history of the jury's difficult deliberations pointed strongly to a jury compromise, a result not of mutually arriving at a considered decision after give-and-take, but rather accepting an outcome that neither of the contending factions agreed with, but which was somewhere between the conflicting views. Compromise verdicts thus challenge a fundamental tenet of the jury system: verdicts are reached based on discussion and persuasion that leads to a considered consensus. Although jury compromises are common in personal injury litigation, they are frequently hidden in general verdicts, which only provide the prevailing party and the damages if the plaintiff prevails. Those bottom-line forms do not reveal the basis of the jury's decision. The amorphousness of damages law, which gives the jury substantial discretion in determining an appropriate amount to award for nonpecuniary injuries, assists juries in hiding their compromises. But the $20,000 amount, in light of the medical expenses stipulation and the no damages award to David, strongly signaled a jury compromise, a legally impermissible outcome. Everyone went home appreciating that the jury's verdict was not likely to be the last word in the *Mekdeci* case. Nor was the *Mekdeci* case to be the last word on Bendectin litigation. Arthur Cohen and George Kokus announced that they were ready to file several additional Bendectin cases.[32]

Notes

1. Davin Light, *Scientists Disagree, But Jury Will Tackle Bendectin Enigma*, ORLANDO SENTINEL STAR, Mar. 16, 1980.

2. The account of the pretrial discovery period was drawn from pretrial conference transcripts in Mekdeci v. Merrell National Laboratories, Civ. No. 77-255-Orl-Civ-Y (M.D. Fla.), correspondence of Betty Mekdeci, her attorneys, and Merrell's attorneys, docket entries in Mekdeci v. Merrell Laboratories, and interviews with Betty Mekdeci, George Kokus, Arthur Tifford, and Alfred Schretter.

3. *See* Scott Spencer, *Lawrence Walsh's Last Battle*, N.Y. TIMES, July 4, 1993, at § 6, p. 11.

4. The background information about Walsh is contained in Steve Lichtman, *Have Brief, Will Travel*, NEW REPUBLIC, Aug. 24, 1987, at 14; Christopher Drew, *Iran-Probe Counsel Defends Credentials*, CHICAGO TRIB., Jan. 19, 1987, at 1.

5. Letter from Alfred E. Schretter to author (Apr. 28, 1994).

6. Deposition of Elizabeth Mekdeci at 568–70, Mekdeci v. Merrell National Laboratories (M.D. Fla. Jan. 20, 1978).

7. Richard Smithells, *Defects and Disabilities of Thalidomide Children,* 1 BRIT. MED. J. 269, 272 (1973).

8. E. Wayne Thode, *The Indefensible Use of the Hypothetical Case to Determine Cause in Fact,* 46 TEX. L. REV. 423 (1968).

9. *See* Joseph Sanders, *From Science to Evidence: The Testimony on Causation in the Bendectin Cases,* 46 STAN. L. REV. 1, 51–53 (1993).

10. Robert E. Staples & Dorsey E. Holtkamp, *Effects of Parental Thalidomide Treatment on Gestation and Fetal Development,* 2 EXP. & MOLEC. PATH. SUPP. 81, 94–96 (1963).

11. THE INSIGHT TEAM OF THE SUNDAY TIMES, SUFFER THE CHILDREN: THE STORY OF THALIDOMIDE 272 (London: Andre Deutsch, 1979).

12. Deposition of Dorsey Holtkamp at 78, Mekdeci v. Merrell National Laboratories (M.D. Fla. June 21, 1979).

13. Richard Smithells & Sheila Sheppard, *Teratogenicity Testing in Humans: A Method Demonstrating Safety of Bendectin,* 17 TERATOLOGY 31 (1978).

14. Kenneth Rothman et al., *Exogenous Hormones and Other Drug Exposures of Children with Congenital Heart Disease,* 109 AM. J. EPIDEMIOL. 433 (1979).

15. Jose F. Cordero et al., *Is Bendectin a Teratogen?,* 245 JAMA 2307, 2310 (1981).

16. Transcript of Pretrial Hearing at 13, Mekdeci v. Merrell National Laboratories (M.D. Fla. July 11, 1979).

17. Mark Dowie & Carolyn Marshall, *The Bendectin Cover-Up,* MOTHER JONES, Nov. 1980, at 43.

18. John de St. Jorre, *The Morning Sickness Drug Controversy,* N.Y. TIMES, Oct. 12, 1980 (Magazine), at 11.

19. Defendant's Memorandum as to Common Issues for Consolidated Trial at 4, MDL-486 (S.D. Ohio Dec. 15, 1983).

20. Edward J. Burke, *The Brawl Over Bendectin,* NAT'L L.J., Apr. 6, 1981, at 12, col. 2.

21. Plaintiffs' Motion for Extraordinary Relief and to Reopen Discovery, Mekdeci v. Merrell National Laboratories (M.D. Fla. July 31, 1979).

22. The account of the trial is based on interviews with the individuals identified in note 2, as well as the transcripts of the trial and newspaper reports published in the Orlando Sentinel Star.

23. Davin Light, *Bendectin Judge Tried Other Famous Cases,* ORLANDO SENTINEL STAR, Mar. 30, 1980.

24. Transcript of Trial at Vol. 13, pp. 44–45, Mekdeci v. Merrell National Laboratories (M.D. Fla. Jan. 30, 1980).

25. In December 1993 the Federal Rules of Civil Procedure were amended to require the exchange of experts' reports by adversaries at least 90 days before trial. Fed. R. Civ. P. 26(a)(2).

26. Sanders, *supra* note 9, at 57 & n.255 (explaining that consistency is an important value in jury decision making and that Bendectin juries may perceive alternative arguments as inconsistent).

27. *See, e.g.,* Nancy Pennington & Reid Hastie, *Explaining the Evidence: Tests of the Story Model for Juror Decision Making,* 58 J. PERSONALITY & SOC. PSYCH. 189 (1992); Richard Lempert, *Telling Tales in Court: Trial Procedure and the Story Model,* 13 CARDOZO L. REV. 559 (1991); *see also* Sanders, *supra* note 9, at 51–52.

28. Sanders, *supra* note 9, at 57.

29. A claim that was incorrect. One study published before the *Mekdeci* trial found a statistically significant association between Bendectin and congenital heart defects, although the authors were skeptical about whether this represented a true causal relationship. Rothman et al., *supra* note 14.

However, because the Mekdecis' lawyers chose not to introduce evidence about David's possible heart anomaly, this error was inconsequential.

30. Letter from R.W. Smithells to Mark T. Hoekenga, Merrell National Laboratories (Jan. 26, 1977).

31. Most of this information is contained in Davin Light, *Bendectin Jury Awards Orlando Family $20,000*, ORLANDO SENTINEL STAR, Mar. 22, 1980, at C1.

32. *Id.*

Chapter 8
The Unraveling of *Mekdeci*

Neither side was entirely happy with the jury's verdict, although the appropriate post-trial course for each was unclear. Merrell was concerned that the verdict was technically for the plaintiff. The decision might be the basis for future plaintiffs to seek to foreclose Merrell from arguing that it was not negligent or that Bendectin did not have the capacity to cause birth defects. This was a real concern, because just one year earlier, the United States Supreme Court had approved of the use of a procedural device—offensive collateral estoppel—to permit a plaintiff to prevent a defendant who had previously litigated and lost on an issue from relitigating that issue in the new plaintiff's case.[1] If lower courts permitted the use of that procedural device in future Bendectin cases, Merrell would have its strongest defense—Bendectin does not cause birth defects—unavailable. Moreover, the adverse verdict was sure to damage Bendectin sales, which had already been hurt by publicity generated by *Mekdeci.*

The Mekdecis were delighted at the apparent victory on the matter of liability. But the damage award wouldn't begin even to reimburse the lawyers for the expenses they had incurred in preparing and trying the case, approximately $150,000. Since the expenses were to be repaid first, the Mekdecis would receive nothing, the lawyers would receive nothing for their time, and there would be $130,000 in out-of-pocket loss in the case. Although technically the Mekdecis were responsible for that, the lawyers knew they would have to bear it. Yet the lawyers had other cases they were preparing to file, cases that were more attractive than the *Mekdeci* case. They had little stomach to retry the *Mekdeci* case, with its demands on their time, preferring to pursue what they viewed as stronger cases. Judge Hoffman's transparent skepticism about their punitive damages case contributed to the lack of interest in pursuing the *Mekdeci* case, as punitive damages was the most promising route to recovery of substantial damages.

The Mekdecis sought a limited new trial in which the only matter to be retried would be the amount of damages. Merrell sought only a judgment notwithstanding the verdict—an outright dismissal of the Mekdecis' case, despite the jury's verdict. Neither side asked Judge Hoffman for the most obvious solution to the jury's problematical verdict: a new trial of all issues. The Mekdecis were anxious to retain the jury's determination that Merrell was liable—a finding they were not confident would be replicated in a second trial. Thus they sought a retrial limited to the amount of damage. Merrell preferred to live with the $20,000 verdict, rather than to seek another trial in which the plaintiffs could again attempt to recover the $10 million for which they had originally sued. Thus Merrell argued that Judge Hoffman should not order a costly new trial, even though the jury's verdict was a compromise.

While an inadequate award of damages does not automatically mean that the verdict was an improper compromise, and thus a limited new trial might be appropriate, there was no question that the Mekdeci jury had compromised. The five days of deliberations were unusually long for a jury in any case and indicated strife among the jury members. The jury's notes to Judge Hoffman, especially the one reporting that they were "hopelessly deadlocked," added another piece to the compromise jigsaw puzzle. Judge Hoffman's instructions to the jury after its report of the deadlock, urging them to continue deliberating so as reach a verdict and avoid the need for a new trial also pointed toward compromise. The fact that the amount awarded ($20,000) was the stipulated amount of medical expenses, but ignored any physical or emotional suffering by David Mekdeci and his family, any lost earnings prospects, and any future medical care that he might require, completed the picture. Judge Hoffman had no choice but to order a complete new trial with the compromise verdict staring him in the face.

On May 12, 1980 Judge Hoffman announced that he was denying both sides' post-trial motions and ordering a new trial on all issues. The retrial was scheduled for January 26, 1981. Judge Hoffman also made explicit a matter he had hinted at previously: if the jury had awarded punitive damages, he would have overturned them as legally improper. This served as an invitation to Davis, Polk to file a motion for partial summary judgment (a request that the court rule on the matter without submission to the jury) on the punitive damage claim and notice to Cohen and Kokus that any retrial would, even if successful, provide a limited award of damages.[2]

One week later Cohen, Kokus, and Eaton filed another Bendectin case, *Koller v. Richardson-Merrell, Inc.*, in federal court in Washington, DC. The lawyers viewed *Koller* as the attractive, path-breaking case that *Mek-*

deci unfortunately was not. Cynthia Koller was a nurse and had taken only Bendectin during her pregnancy, thereby precluding Merrell from calling into question the effect of other drugs, as occurred in *Mekdeci*. Anne Koller was born with severe bilateral limb reduction defects, a condition that avoided the defense that drugs do not cause unilateral birth defects. Cohen et al. were anxious to try the *Koller* case because they felt it would give them the unequivocal win that they would need to soften up Merrell on settlements and provide badly needed funds to finance future cases.

The conflict between *Koller* and *Mekdeci* illustrates an important facet of mass toxic litigation that often is overlooked. Cases are not, despite the assumption of many, homogenous, and serious conflicts emerge between stronger and weaker cases. This phenomenon, which bodes poorly for mass resolution techniques such as the class action, would play a prominent role in the course of the Bendectin multidistrict proceedings in Cincinnati.

Open conflict developed between Betty Mekdeci and her lawyers over the retrial. She welcomed another trial and held out the hope that Melvin Belli would appear to try it. Perhaps most important, Betty Mekdeci felt that she deserved to be the first successful plaintiff and to be rewarded publicly with the credit for having exposed Bendectin as a teratogen. She had earned the right, through her years of unflagging effort, to the acclaim that would be accorded to the individual who uncovered this teratogen (Frances Kelsey had been lionized for protecting the United States from thalidomide). Meanwhile, Cohen and Kokus were adamantly determined to avoid or at least postpone the retrial, preferring to pursue other cases that held more promise. Arthur Cohen, with his abrasive and belligerent personality, could irritate people without trying, and Betty Mekdeci had difficulty holding a telephone conversation without one hanging up on the other.

A major difficulty was that Betty Mekdeci was anything but the typical client: she was smart, independent, critical—perhaps hypercritical—, stubborn, and would not accede to her attorneys' advice on how to proceed with her case. As Betty Mekdeci wrote to Arthur Cohen in the midst of their clash over the retrial:

You and your associates are used to clients who are the passive recipients of your advice. We are emphasizing that we are the parties to this action and that we deserve and intend to participate in all decision making in our litigation.[3]

Convinced of the merits of her claim, Betty Mekdeci considered anything less than an unconditional victory to reflect inadequacies by her attorneys. She was outspoken in informing them of her views. Melvin

Belli's desertion of her and her case still rankled her; criticizing the performance of Cohen and Kokus gave greater substance to that dereliction. Cohen and Kokus in turn had invested much of themselves and their money in the case and were not impervious to this criticism, which served to provoke them.

Betty Mekdeci developed a litany of criticisms of her attorneys' handling of the first trial: Only 161 of 1,000 exhibits that had been marked and identified were admitted into evidence. She felt that additional discovery should have been pursued, such as a deposition of the employee in charge of Merrell's adverse drug reaction. Cohen and Kokus put on no evidence about David's heart defect, a defect which doctors could not confidently confirm and were only willing to say was possible. Similarly, no evidence was introduced about David's lost earning capacity. She criticized Cohen and Kokus for their emphasis on the Staples study, thereby neglecting causation. Betty Mekdeci even told another attorney that she felt that having a Jewish attorney (Arthur Cohen) and a black attorney (Allen Eaton) presenting her case to a conservative Orlando jury was poor strategy.[4] Her disparagement and carping especially rankled Arthur Cohen. He resented her second-guessing and recriminating, after he and Kokus had practically shut down their practice for a year to pursue her case. That resentment and anger eased any qualms that Cohen and Kokus might have had about seeking to abandon her case.

Arthur Cohen attempted to maneuver Betty Mekdeci into dismissing him, Kokus, and Tifford as her attorneys. This strategy was necessary because attorneys have an ethical obligation to continue representing their clients and may not terminate the attorney client relationship, absent certain exceptions such as the client unreasonably impeding the attorney's efforts. In addition, once attorneys have represented a client in a lawsuit, their withdrawal requires court approval, which is often difficult to obtain when there is no other attorney willing to take over the representation.[5] But Betty Mekdeci was merely insisting that her attorneys continue to prosecute her case. Her attorneys' desire not to do so, based on a belief that better cases were available to pursue, merely created a conflict of interest between the attorneys and the Mekdecis that was plainly insufficient to permit withdrawal without the client's permission. Mekdeci foiled Cohen's gambit by writing to him and the court reaffirming that she intended to have her lawyers continue in their representation of her.

The schism between the Mekdecis and their lawyers emerged publicly on July 24, 1980 when the lawyers asked the court to relieve them from representing the Mekdecis any further. Mekdeci asserted that the motion was a bombshell to her; she had no clue her lawyers were going to seek to abandon her until she received notice of the motion in the mail. While that may literally be true, she knew that she and her attorneys had come to an impasse on when her case should be retried and relations had been tense and difficult for many months.

The withdrawal motion was discussed at a pretrial hearing before both Judge Hoffman and Judge Young (who was to preside at the retrial), five days later in July. At the hearing, a Davis, Polk lawyer provided the court with a copy of a London *Observer* interview with Melvin Belli, in which he was quoted as stating: "Our client was too demanding and too hard to work with. Hers wasn't that good a case, and we want to get on with the 200 other Debendox cases we are preparing." [6] Belli's public statements and denigration of the Mekdecis' case was a stunning breach of ethical norms for attorneys who owe a duty of zealous representation to their clients and have an obligation not to prejudice or damage the client during the course of that representation. His statement also confirmed what had become obvious over the months since the *Mekdeci* verdict: the Mekdecis' lawyers had a conflict between their own interests in pursuing other cases and their obligations to the Mekdecis. Belli compounded his brazen ethical transgressions after the second trial, by writing to 200 potential Bendectin plaintiffs explaining: "The unfortunate thing about the *Mekdeci* case was that it should never have been the *first* case tried, because the mother took other drugs as well as Bendectin and there were other factors wrong with the *Mekdeci* case." [7]

Merrell, anticipating the *Mekdeci* case rupturing, argued that there should be no delay in the scheduled retrial. A clean victory at the retrial would provide a significant public statement about Bendectin's safety and only begin to repair the publicity damage and lost sales. Moreover, a victory might dampen plaintiffs' lawyers enthusiasm for pursuing Bendectin cases.

Because the withdrawal motion unenlighteningly cited only "irreconcilable differences," and Mrs. Mekdeci had not spoken with her attorneys about the motion, another hearing was scheduled in August to give the Mekdecis an opportunity to consult with their lawyers about the motion (which plainly should have been done before the motion was ever filed in court) and decide whether they would oppose the motion or obtain new counsel. Mrs. Mekdeci was informed that the retrial date in January was firm and would not be rescheduled even if she obtained new counsel.

In the interim, Betty Mekdeci contacted the Detroit law firm of Charfoos, Christensen, Gilbert & Archer, a well-known plaintiffs' personal injury firm. Sam Charfoos, the founder of the firm, had collaborated with Melvin Belli in establishing the American Trial Lawyers Association, an organization of plaintiffs' personal injury and criminal defense lawyers. However, in the late 1970s, Charfoos's son, Larry, had publicly criticized Belli, stating that he was over the hill and afraid to try cases. As a consequence, there was enmity between Belli and the Charfoos firm.

The Charfoos firm had already begun investigating several Bendectin cases when Betty Mekdeci called. Tom Bleakley and Doug Peters, attorneys at Charfoos, had looked into Bendectin. The firm's interest in the *Mekdeci* case was heightened because a successful first case would enhance the value of its own cases.

At the August hearing, Charfoos lawyer Doug Peters attended, indicated the firm's interest in representing the Mekdecis, and requested additional time to review the case. Judge Young then turned to Arthur Cohen and questioned him sharply: "The point that I'm concerned with, Mr. Cohen, is whether these other cases are resulting in a conflict of interest that you and your colleagues might have in the representation of Mrs. Mekdeci." Cohen responded unequivocally: "I can answer that question quite frankly flat out no, sir. They do not represent any conflict." Earlier Cohen had asserted that "we are not filing our Motion to Withdraw as Counsel because we want to litigate other cases."[8] Cohen's statements to the court were disingenuous at best, outright misrepresentations at worst.

In his no-nonsense fashion, Judge Young laid out for Arthur Cohen the situation: if the Mekdecis were able to obtain new counsel to represent them at the second trial, Cohen et al. would be permitted to withdraw. If new counsel were not obtained, Cohen would remain in the case. Another hearing was scheduled for two weeks later.

To this point in time, Cohen had still not revealed the specifics of his reasons for seeking to withdraw. On August 21, 1980 he provided a confidential statement to the court explaining the reasons for the withdrawal motion. Cohen cited disagreements over trial strategy at the first trial, Betty Mekdeci's criticism of the lawyers handling of the trial, her refusal to meet with the lawyers after Judge Hoffman ordered a new trial and subsequent termination of the telephone conversation with Arthur Cohen, and her allegations that counsel had a conflict of interest with their other Bendectin cases. This was all pretty thin grounds in support of the attorneys' request to abandon her case. Relations with Betty Mekdeci had been stormy from early in the relationship in 1977. She had criticized her Florida attorneys a number of times during pretrial preparations, at one point appealing to Melvin Belli to intervene with them. Closer to the truth of the reason for seeking withdrawal may have been a matter raised obliquely in the last paragraph of the letter stating the lawyers' grounds. Cohen mentioned the commitment of time and money required for the first trial, and asserted that requiring them to "double such commitment . . . would be unconscionable." Cohen might have added that this was especially so for a case in which they had lost confidence, were afraid they would be barred from even seeking punitive damages, and which they felt was not the best one to pursue to enhance the value of the numerous Bendectin cases they were stockpiling. The contingent fee arrangement, with the attorneys bearing the risk of covering trial expenses if the case was lost, created yet another gap in the mutuality-of-interest wall of attorney and client.

The second hearing in August was exceedingly delicate and awkward. The Charfoos firm was representing the Mekdecis in their opposition to the withdrawal motion by Kokus et al. At the same time, Cohen and Kokus were representing the Mekdecis on matters related to preparation for the second trial, a trial they were desperately trying to avoid. Betty Mekdeci was ambivalent about the withdrawal, recognizing that if new counsel were substituted, delay of her retrial might be required but the alternative necessarily would require continuing with attorneys with whom her relationship was irreparably blighted. Meanwhile Arthur Cohen was horrified that the withdrawal question was to be heard in front of Merrell's lawyers.

Merrell's lawyers strongly resisted any in camera proceeding (a private meeting in judge's chambers) that would exclude them. They were deeply suspicious that the motivation for the withdrawal motion was that Cohen and Kokus had uncovered some new fact that rendered the *Mekdeci* case unmeritorious. If that were the case, they wanted to obtain that information. In any case, they were not unhappy about the *Mekdeci* case self-destructing before their eyes.

Doug Peters of Charfoos stated that his firm was willing to undertake representation of the Mekdecis in the retrial, but adamantly insisted that the trial be put off for an additional six months. (A major reason for Peters's request was Betty Mekdeci's criticism of Cohen and Kokus in their preparation for the second trial and her suggestion of additional leads to pursue.) Every time that Peters attempted to explain to the court reasons why extra time was required, Arthur Cohen interrupted and objected, furious at this thinly veiled criticism of his efforts at the first trial. Later, the Eleventh Circuit Court of Appeals went out of its way to comment that "Cohen obstructed the proceedings at every possible juncture."[9]

In the end, Judges Hoffman and Young refused the continuance the Charfoos firm requested, and the firm declined to represent the Mekdecis. After the second trial, the denial of the continuance sought by Charfoos was raised before the Eleventh Circuit, which upheld the trial court, but not without reluctance. Appellate courts are loath to reverse trial courts on matters relating to the day-to-day scheduling and management of litigation—such decisions are wisely left to the discretion of the trial judge and rarely affect the outcome of a case. Moreover, the *Mekdeci* retrial presented a significant demand on the resources of the federal court in Orlando—it would require two full months of a judge's time, while criminal cases, motions, conferences, and other matters would have to be heard by other judges. Yet the *Mekdeci* case, which was the first of its kind, implicating important public health issues and a significant schism between client and attorneys, deserved some special treatment to ensure that it was fully and fairly litigated. The Eleventh Circuit acknowledged that "the interests in favor of a fair trial [generally outweigh] the interests in favor of an immediate trial," but relied on the Charfoos take-it-or-leave condition of a six month continuance to conclude that the district court "did not abuse its discretion in refusing to accede to that demand."[10] Had reversal not meant a third rendition of this two-month trial, the Eleventh Circuit might well have done so.

Ironically, even if Betty Mekdeci had acceded to Cohen and Kokus' request to seek a continuance of her case, they would not have been able to obtain one. The January date was set in stone, as the denial of Charfoos' request for a continuance demonstrated.

The refusal to order a continuance left Cohen, Kokus, and Tifford representing clients they fervently did not want to represent. Over the remaining months before the second trial, they would make two more motions in the trial court seeking to withdraw, seek mandamus (an extraordinary form of appeal that is only rarely available) from the Eleventh Circuit, and appeal to the Eleventh Circuit as well. Their efforts prompted Betty Mekdeci to write to Doug Peters: "Wish they were working as hard getting ready to try our case as they are getting out of it." None of those efforts was successful, but in the course of them Cohen, Kokus, and Tifford raised another objection to going forward with the retrial in January.

On December 31, 1980 they pleaded impecunity as a ground for seeking withdrawal, or, alternatively, continuing the trial, following through on a threat they had made to the Mekdecis in October.[11] The attorneys asserted that they did not have the money to pay for a second trial, and if forced to proceed to trial they would try a "paper" case, relying on reading the transcript from the previous trial, rather than putting on live witnesses. Such a presentation would be devastating to the chances for success, as sterile recitations from a transcript are terribly tedious, leaving jurors bored and inattentive to evidence presented in that fashion.

The withdrawal episode drew harsh criticism from the Eleventh Circuit in 1983 when it affirmed the lower court's decision on behalf of Merrell:

> Our conclusion [that the Mekdecis were not entitled to a new trial based on inadequate representation in the second trial] in no way suggests that we condone the conduct of the plaintiffs' original attorneys. On the contrary, we agree that the present record raises disturbing questions on the propriety of the lawyers' actions. The attorneys' various antics create the impression that they may have been more concerned with bettering their position in other Bendectin cases, rather than with fulfilling their professional responsibilities to the Mekdecis, who ironically made it possible for the lawyers to obtain the other cases in the first place. Additionally, there are indications that several, if not all, of the attorneys may have breached their contractual obligations to the plaintiffs.[12]

The withdrawal episode also reveals a significant aspect of mass tort litigation that distinguishes it from other forms of litigation, especially public interest litigation. Numerous unaffiliated attorneys compete to establish their expertise and success in an apparently emerging field. Both competitive incentives to lead the pack and ethical obligations once the attorney has agreed to represent a client impede careful case selection. In that respect, mass tort attorneys suffer a disadvantage that their defendant adversaries, the government, and other civil rights litigators do not.[13] As Professor Rabin reports, Melvin Belli, anxious to become involved in the "second wave" of cigarette litigation, took on a 70-year-old lung cancer victim who had died without being autopsied, had suffered from several non-cigarette related diseases, and had a treating physician who did not believe that smoking was a direct cause of his patient's death.[14]

The second trial, in which Cohen, Kokus, and Tifford largely made good on their threats, was anticlimactic. Kokus and Tifford appeared for the trial; Cohen remained in Miami to attend to Kokus & Cohen's practice. Large portions of the transcript of the first trial were read, with Kokus reading the questions that had been asked at the first trial and Tifford, sitting on the witness stand, reading the answers. In an ironic twist, when one or the other of them was not present, Lynn Busath, an attorney with Davis, Polk, would fill in playing the role of the plaintiffs' witness. Betty Mekdeci viewed the contrived and stilted proceedings with anguish, but with little recourse. Her appeals to Kokus were met with a hostility that was evident to courthouse observers. Kokus, himself, lived in a camper-trailer that he parked in a hotel parking lot to burnish the image of the financially wrung-out lawyer.

Betty Mekdeci repeatedly telephoned and wrote Melvin Belli, who had carefully kept his distance, importuning him to assist. Belli had written to her stating emphatically that he would not appear for the second trial, but offering the same "assistance, financial and otherwise" provided for the first trial, a promise that he partially fulfilled by sending a check for $25,000 in the midst of the second trial. After receiving Belli's check, Kokus arranged for Roger Palmer and Alan Done to appear and testify at the trial.

Whether Cohen and Kokus had the $70,000 that it would have cost to put on a live case remains unclear. What is plain is that Melvin Belli deserves a large share of the blame for the paper trial. He was the lawyer who the Mekdecis had hired, he had chosen the Florida lawyers to associate with, and he had ample financial resources to fund the trial. Funding the second trial would have been a minimal hardship to him compared to Cohen and Kokus. Yet he contributed only $25,000 and not until after much pleading by Betty Mekdeci and in the midst of the trial.

The trial continued longer even than the first trial, lasting over nine weeks. Merrell tried the case every bit as thoroughly and cautiously as it had the first, with the additional recognition after the first verdict of the difficult task it faced to succeed in persuading a jury. Yet, in the end, the outcome was, if not a foregone conclusion, not difficult to anticipate. The jury deliberated for only two hours before returning a verdict for Merrell. By this time however, a solo victory was too meager an obstacle to stop the Bendectin litigation train in its tracks. Too many plaintiffs lawyers had identified too many potential plaintiffs and invested too much time and money in the cause to abandon it at this point. Perhaps if Merrell had won a string of four, five, or six jury verdicts it would have quelled plaintiffs' lawyers' efforts. But Merrell didn't.

On April 9, 1981 Merrell filed a request for reimbursement of costs in the amount of $206,122 that it had incurred in connection with the two trials. Federal law provides that a successful party may recover costs for a very limited category of items, which represents only a small portion of the expenses that are typically incurred. While Merrell was plainly within its legal rights in seeking to recover these costs, the effort was a plain signal that Merrell was playing hardball and serving notice that it did not look benignly on the *Mekdeci* suit, despite having prevailed. Judge Young later slashed the cost recovery by Merrell to $6,000, a great relief to the Mekdecis, but still a substantial burden for a middle class family to bear.

But the $200,000 in costs represented only the tip of the iceberg for Merrell in defending the *Mekdeci* case. Merrell's general counsel reported to the FDA that Merrell had spent over $1,000,000 just in defending the case through the first trial. Another Merrell spokesperson put the final tab at "several million dollars," to defend the entire *Mekdeci* case, including the two trials and appellate proceedings.[15] That is a stunning figure—no doubt more than the case could have been settled for. Yet it represents not only the risk Merrell assessed the *Mekdeci* case as posing, but the implications of that case for future litigation. In that respect, Betty Mekdeci and her attorneys faced a defense that was of an effort and size that reflected much more than the single claim being asserted.

The bill of costs episode in which Merrell sought recovery of over $200,000 in costs from the Mekdecis after the second trial gives some appreciation of the overwhelming costs of complicated toxic substances litigation for ordinary citizens. Although the costs were ultimately reduced to $6,000, even that sum represented an enormous burden to the Mekdecis. The Mekdecis' concern throughout this episode was exacerbated by the tenuous relationship they had with their attorneys, whom they did not entirely trust to protect their interest. Interestingly, after vigorously pursuing the assessment of costs, Merrell never attempted to collect on the $6,000 cost award, although it did file its judgment as a lien on the Mekdecis' home.

In a television interview after the jury verdict, Betty Mekdeci scornfully characterized the proceeding as the "Untrial."

Notes

1. Parklane Hosiery v. Shore, 439 U.S. 322 (1979).
2. Subsequently, on the eve of the second trial, Judge Hoffman granted Merrell's motion, dismissing the punitive damages claim.
3. Letter from Mrs. Elizabeth Mekdeci to attorney Arthur Cohen (July 12, 1980).
4. Memorandum of attorney Douglas Peters (Aug. 5, 1980) (summarizing interview with Mrs. Elizabeth Mekdeci).
5. MODEL CODE OF PROFESSIONAL RESPONSIBILITY DR 2-110 (Chicago: ABA, 1981); MODEL RULES OF PROFESSIONAL CONDUCT Rule 1.16 (Chicago: ABA, 1983).
6. LONDON OBSERVER, July 27, 1980.
7. Letter from Melvin M. Belli to Philip Davis (June 22, 1981).
8. Transcript of Proceedings at 17–18, Mekdeci v. Merrell National Laboratories, Case No. 77-255-Orl-Civ-Y (M.D. Fla. Aug. 11, 1980).
9. Mekdeci v. Merrell National Laboratories, 711 F.2d 1510, 1517 n.9 (11th Cir. 1983).
10. *Id.* at 1520.
11. That same month, Allen Eaton appeared at a hearing in the *Koller* case, urging the trial judge to schedule a prompt trial date.
12. Mekdeci v. Merrell National Laboratories, 711 F.2d at 1523.
13. For an account of case selection difficulties in asbestos and tobacco litigation, see Robert Rabin, *A Sociolegal History of the Tobacco Tort Litigation*, 44 STAN. L. REV. 853, 870 (1992); PAUL BRODEUR, OUTRAGEOUS MISCONDUCT 31–36 (New York: Pantheon, 1985).
14. Rabin, *supra* note 13, at 870.
15. Jim Nesbitt, *Drug Manufacturer Will Ask Couple Who Lost Lawsuit to Pay Court Costs*, ORLANDO SENTINEL, Dec. 15, 1983.

Chapter 9
The Proliferation of Bendectin Litigation

Belli, Cohen, and Kokus were sophisticated enough personal injury lawyers to appreciate the potential of Bendectin litigation. Belli, especially, had a history of aggressively seeking to be at the vanguard of mass litigation. Once there, Belli had a knack for garnering attention and publicity to attract clients (he had contacted the *National Enquirer* and interested it in Bendectin and the *Mekdeci* case), thereby enabling him to play a prominent role in mass disaster litigation.[1] In the late 1970s and early 1980s the efforts of Belli, Cohen, and Kokus, national media attention, and the first *Mekdeci* verdict went a long way toward expanding Bendectin litigation. Even an FDA hearing in the Fall of 1980 on the safety of Bendectin, that largely exonerated it, could not derail the efforts of this small group of plaintiffs' lawyers and the large number of parents with birth defect children who had become aware of the claims about Bendectin's teratogenicity.

The national publicity about the *Mekdeci* case generated dozens of inquiries to Betty Mekdeci and her lawyers.[2] Roger Palmer, one of the Mekdecis' expert witnesses, received over a hundred inquiries after he was identified in an article about the *Mekdeci* case. Cohen, Kokus, Tifford, and Belli were assiduously gathering names of families that had inquired about the role of Bendectin in causing birth defects in the hope of using the information and human capital they had acquired during the *Mekdeci* case.

Melvin Belli sought additional Bendectin clients with the ethically dubious and thinly disguised technique of placing advertisements in daily newspapers seeking subjects who had been exposed to Bendectin for "epidemiological and statistical purposes."[3] These advertisements were plainly for the purpose of attracting Bendectin clients. Shortly after Belli first ran these advertisements, Cohen and Kokus followed suit and began running their own similar solicitations. These advertisements were misleading in that they could not possibly form the basis for any legitimate study—the haphazard and self-selected responses would fatally bias any legitimate scientific inquiry. Moreover, the timing of the advertisements—they continued to run even after the *Mekdeci* trial was underway—made any use of the responses for evidentiary purposes implausible at best. The ethics of the scheme aside,[4] the effort does demonstrate the financial incentives that encourage plaintiffs lawyers' attempts to amortize their considerable investment of money and time by attracting additional clients in mass tort contexts.

After the conclusion of the first *Mekdeci* trial, George Kokus and Melvin Belli went to Europe to attempt to identify additional potential plaintiffs. The British press pounced on the *Mekdeci* case and the questions raised about Bendectin's safety. Kokus went to England and Scotland, and Belli went to England and West Germany, where many still remembered thalidomide with horror.[5] While there, Kokus and Belli courted the press, publicized their "victory" in the *Mekdeci* case, and gathered names of families for whom they would later file suit.

When George Kokus's international efforts began to pay off, he associated with a New York lawyer, Lee Goldsmith, who was also a physician. Cases were filed in New York; Goldsmith agreed to share expenses with Kokus. A number of these cases were filed early in 1981, and later others were filed in the United States as well. A United States forum was attractive for a number of reasons. First, much of the evidence of Merrell's activities with Bendectin and bearing on causation had already been developed here. Second, standards for tort liability in Europe were well behind the advances that had taken place in the United States. More significantly, the United States is the only country in the western world that routinely affords a right to a jury trial in civil cases. The commitment to jury trials, along with the vague standards for determining non-pecuniary damages, means that there is far more discretion afforded in the awarding of damages in this country.[6] In England, by contrast, judges award damages based on prior cases and tend to be comparatively parsimonious in their awards.[7] Professor Patrick Atiyah estimated the maximum award for pain and suffering to be under $200,000.[8] Punitive damages are permitted only in rare circumstances.[9] As a result, damage awards in the United States tend to be much more generous than in England or on the Continent. Finally, the availability of contingent fee arrangements in the United States and the practice of lawyers financing the costs of a case make legal services in personal injury cases far more accessible in the United States than in other countries. As might be expected, foreign citizens whose injuries have some connection to the United States have aggressively sought out American courts. As Lord

Denning aptly put it: "As a moth is drawn to the light, so is a litigant drawn to the United States." [10]

Kokus still had the *Koller* case pending, but was unable to attend to it because of the second *Mekdeci* trial. Kokus brought James Butler into the case in January 1981. Butler, from Los Angeles, had played a prominent role in the United States thalidomide litigation and thus had expertise in the birth defect area. More importantly, Butler had the capacity to provide significant financing for the *Koller* case—a necessity if the case was to be pursued adequately against the seemingly unlimited resources of Merrell. Moreover, Butler was a true believer. His response to the scientific community's view that 60 to 70 percent of birth defects are of unknown origin is unequivocal: "They call them GOKS, that means, 'God only knows,' but I know it's drugs, it has to be." [11] Meanwhile Butler had filed his own Bendectin case against Merrell, *Cordova*, in California in 1979.

Other United States lawyers had become aware of the *Mekdeci* case, the questions it raised about Bendectin's safety, and the $20,000 verdict in the first trial. A number filed Bendectin suits, which were dispersed across the country. Russell Tritico, a lawyer from Louisiana, had attended the *Mekdeci* trial and filed one of the early cases in the wake of the first *Mekdeci* verdict. Tom Bleakley and Doug Peters, attorneys at the Charfoos firm, which had considered taking over the representation of Mrs. Mekdeci, filed several cases in Michigan in 1980. Stanley Chesley, the "Master of Disaster" from Cincinnati, filed his first Bendectin case, *Holly Beth Thomas v. Merrell National Laboratories*, on February 12, 1981. The *Thomas* case was assigned to Judge Carl Rubin of the Southern District Court of Ohio in Cincinnati, the same judge who had presided over Chesley's class action on behalf of the victims of the Beverly Hills Supper Club fire in Kentucky. Chesley and Rubin each played a major role in the consolidated MDL-486 proceeding detailed in chapters 10–14.

Joan Oxendine, a nurse-practitioner who lived in Mitchellville, Maryland, read the *National Enquirer* article about Bendectin in October 1979. Her daughter, Mary, had been born in 1971 with limb reduction defects, and Joan had taken Bendectin during her pregnancy. The Oxendines located a Washington DC lawyer named Barry Nace, and he filed suit on their behalf in January 1982 against Merrell and Upjohn (Joan Oxendine had also taken a drug produced by Upjohn during her pregnancy) in the District of Columbia Superior Court. Because Upjohn refused to join Merrell's request to transfer the case to federal court, the case was litigated in the local District of Columbia courts. Upjohn's strategical decision on this procedural matter turned out to have a decisive impact on the outcome of the *Oxendine* case, as explained in chapter 16.

In the fall of 1980 an FDA hearing on Bendectin was held that promised to have a major impact on future Bendectin litigation. For a variety of reasons—political, scientific, legal, and public opinion—the FDA had become uneasy about Bendectin. In 1977, when *60 Minutes* was investigating Bendectin, the FDA refused a live interview but prepared a "Statement on Bendectin," which reviewed the adverse drug reports for Bendectin, summarized the existing studies of its teratogenicity, and concluded on an optimistic note: "If Bendectin is associated with any risk to an unborn child, the risk is so small that it cannot be detected by the large scale studies [that have been performed]."[12] Later, in 1979, the FDA had a staff pharmacologist review the animal toxicology studies to determine if additional testing would be prudent.[13]

After the first *Mekdeci* trial, the FDA was contacted by Congressman Don Edwards of California, whose interest in Bendectin resulted from a grandchild with birth defects. Edwards had obtained information about the evidence put on at the *Mekdeci* trial, as well as one observer's claim that, "MER-29, thalidomide and Bendectin—all products of the same manufacturer which were developed at the same time—have a common thread in the failure to reveal necessary evidence on which the FDA can make a determination as to the safety of the drug."[14] Edwards criticized the FDA for its complacency about Bendectin and urged it to conduct a comprehensive investigation. Doug Walgren, another member of Congress, had a staff member who became interested in Bendectin because she had a child with birth defects. Walgren lent his support to Edwards' efforts with the FDA and considered holding hearings in a science subcommittee that Walgren chaired. Walgren was assisted in his Bendectin initiatives by Dr. John Nestor, who had played a critical role in uncovering Merrell's MER/29 activities.[15]

In addition to Congressional interest, public concern about Bendectin, and the possibility that some teratogenic risk existed, the FDA was troubled by Merrell's marketing and promotion of Bendectin. The FDA requested that Merrell cease marketing efforts to physicians that made it appear "as if almost every pregnant woman were a candidate for this drug . . . in contravention of good medical practice which dictated that exposure to drugs during pregnancy be minimized."[16]

On September 15, 1980 the FDA convened its Fertility and Maternal Health Drugs Advisory Committee. The Committee was made up of several academic obstetricians and gynecologists, a neonatalogist, and a statistician; several consultants also assisted the Committee, including an epidemiologist. The Committee was to hold two days of hearings and advise the FDA on whether the existing scientific studies indicated an association with birth defects, whether additional studies of Bendectin should be conducted, and whether the labeling of Bendectin required modification.

The hearing was fraught with tension: contending factions of experts, as well as Merrell representatives and plaintiffs' lawyers interested in Bendectin, were present and anxious to further their position. Merrell had over 14 employees present, including David Sharrock, its chief executive officer. Journalists from around the world were present, anticipating a human interest story of major proportion. Many authors of Bendectin studies, expert witnesses from *Mekdeci*, and others who reviewed the studies or who were conducting studies testified during the hearings. After a controversial and at times raucous two days of hearings, the Committee concluded:

> [T]he data presented to date do not demonstrate an association of increased risk for human birth defects with the use of bendectin [*sic*]. The committee notices with concern two studies that suggest an association between Bendectin and certain anomalies. Therefore, a residual uncertainty regarding a possible relationship does exist.[17]

The apparent contradiction between the first two sentences of the Committee's response is explained by the form of the question put to the Committee by the FDA.[18] The question inquired into an association between Bendectin and birth defects. The first sentence of the Committee's response addressed the question of whether Bendectin was a general teratogen, that is, caused an increase in all birth defects. Far more likely, however, is that an agent will have a specific effect, that is, increase the risk of a single or related group of birth defects. Two studies presented at the hearings found an association between Bendectin and a specific birth defect, one heart disease and the other cleft palates, which explains the second sentence of the Committee's answer. Both of those studies were case-control studies and deemed less than conclusive evidence of an association by their authors.[19] The Committee also recommended that Bendectin remain on the market, but that the label on Bendectin be modified to state that it should only be used for those patients whose morning sickness was "unresponsive to conservative (non-drug) measures." [20]

The Advisory Committee's recommendations disappointed those affiliated with the plaintiff side who were hoping that it would recommend removal of Bendectin from the market. But the momentum that had developed for bringing suit against Merrell was not quelled. The lack of evidence did not make the studies that existed any stronger or bias-free than they had previously been, and several plaintiffs lawyers were becoming more sophisticated in their appreciation of the way in which the probity of those studies could be attacked or limited. The recent emergence of the cleft lip association found in a British study, along with the reasons that led the *Mekdeci* team of lawyers to pursue that case initially, were sufficient to overcome the new obstacle raised by the Advisory Committee's conclusion.

After the Advisory Committee's hearings and recommendations, Bendectin labeling for the first time contained information about the teratogenic studies that had been performed, that those studies had generally not identified an association with birth defects, but were of insufficient power to identify even a doubling of specific types of birth defects. The caution also provided the dictum that: "Bendectin should be used only when clearly needed for the treatment of nausea and vomiting of pregnancy not responsive to conservative (non-drug) measures."

The Advisory Committee's recommendations reassured Dow Chemical Company, which had been negotiating to acquire the ethical pharmaceutical business of Richardson-Merrell, in the hope of developing synergies with Dow's chemical expertise and a small drug company that it owned. Dow was chary about completing the acquisition because of potential liability implicated by Bendectin litigation. Dow itself had been enmeshed in another mass toxic case since 1979, the Agent Orange litigation, and was unwilling to buy into another one. Dow officials attended the Advisory Committee Hearings anonymously and their concerns were assuaged. In March 1981 the pharmaceutical division of Richardson-Merrell became a subsidiary of Dow, named Merrell-Dow Pharmaceuticals Inc.

By 1981 Merrell recognized that it could not continue to litigate Bendectin cases one-by-one. Many of the researchers who had been called on to testify about their Bendectin work were unwilling to testify repetitively in future lawsuits. Numerous corporate officials had been deposed in *Mekdeci* and *Koller* and responding to the discovery demands of plaintiffs, as well as the information needs of its own lawyers, diverted Merrell employees from the pharmaceutical business to the litigation business. While that had seemed a reasonable cost to pay in light of the threat posed by the *Mekdeci* case, the proliferation of actions and concomitant discovery requests required some action to mitigate the litigation demands of multiple, geographically dispersed cases on the company and its counsel.

Merrell's solution was to seek consolidation of all of the cases pending in federal courts in a single forum. Section 1407 of title 28 of the United States Code, enacted in 1968, permits the transfer of related cases with a common issue to a single district court.[21] The Judicial Panel on Multidistrict Litigation, made up of seven federal judges, is vested with the authority to issue consolidation orders when the convenience of the parties and witnesses and efficiency in adjudication will be served. Significantly, the statute only authorizes consolidation for pretrial proceedings, including discovery, but not for trial. Moreover, the authority to transfer is limited to federal cases; no provision exists to consolidate cases pending in state courts. On September 25, 1981 Merrell requested that the Multidistrict Panel consolidate 48 pending federal lawsuits. Merrell asked that the cases be transferred to federal court in Cincinnati, the location of its corporate headquarters.

Notes

1. JOHN A. JENKINS, THE LITIGATORS: INSIDE THE POWERFUL WORLD OF AMERICA'S HIGH-STAKES TRIAL LAWYERS 76, 140–42 (New York: Doubleday, 1989).

2. In addition to the *National Enquirer* and *Mother Jones* article, the *New York Times* Sunday Magazine ran a largely sympathetic article in October, 1980. John de St. Jorre, *The Morning Sickness Controversy*, N.Y. TIMES, Oct. 12, 1980 (Magazine), at 13.

3. *E.g.*, SAN FRANCISCO CHRONICLE, Feb. 21, 1980, at 9; *see* Edward J. Burke, *The Brawl Over Bendectin*, NAT'L L.J., Apr. 6, 1981, at 1.

4. The ABA Code of Professional Responsibility barred lawyers from recommending themselves for employment to a non-lawyer, in effect prohibiting solicitation of clients. In a disciplinary matter in which Belli was the principle, the California Supreme Court in 1974 decreed that public statements whose purpose is primarily to solicit legal business are unethical. Belli v. State Bar, 519 P.2d 575 (Cal. 1974). In two cases in 1978, the United States Supreme Court addressed the first amendment limitations on state ethical restrictions on solicitation. The court held that an ACLU attorney writing a letter offering legal services, where the solicitation was not for gain and the solicitation was not in person, could not be proscribed, but that a face-to-face, for-profit solicitation could be prohibited. *In re* Primus, 436 U.S. 412 (1978); Ohralik v. Ohio State Bar, 436 U.S. 447 (1978). Thus Belli's advertisements in 1980 fell in the for-profit, written solicitation gap that remained after the Court's two opinions. In Zauderer v. Office of Disciplinary Counsel, 471 U.S. 626 (1985), decided five years after Belli's advertisements, the Court addressed the uncertainty left by *Primus* and *Ohralik*. The Court held that advertisements motivated by private gain that offered legal services to Dalkon Shield IUD victims were protected by the first amendment, provided the advertising was truthful and non-deceptive, a condition that Belli's solicitations, designed to evade the then-existing anti-solicitation rules, did not fulfill. *See generally* Eric S. Roth, *Confronting Solicitation of Mass Disaster Victims*, 2 GEO. J. LEGAL ETHICS 967 (1989).

5. Milan Korcok, *The Bendectin Debate*, 123 CAN. MED. ASS'N J. 922, 928 (Nov. 8, 1980).

6. *See* Randall R. Bovbjerg et al., *Valuing Life and Limb in Tort: Scheduling "Pain and Suffering,"* 83 Nw. U. L. REV. 908 (1989).

7. DAN CASSIDY, LIABILITY EXPOSURES 49 (London: Witherby, 1989).

8. P.S. Atiyah, *Tort Law and the Alternatives: Some Anglo-American Comparisons*, 1987 DUKE L.J. 1002, 1023.

9. *Id.* at 1024.

10. Smith, Kline & French Laboratories Ltd. v. Bloch, 1983 W.L.R. 730, 733 (Eng. C.A. 1982).

11. David Lauter, *Bendectin Trial Disintegrates; Allegations of Misconduct Mar "Perfect Case,"* NAT'L L.J., Feb. 21, 1983, at 1.

12. FDA, Statement on Bendectin (undated).

13. FDA Internal Memorandum re: Bendectin Teratology Studies, NDA 10–598 (Dec. 4, 1979).

14. Letter from Representative Don Edwards to FDA Commissioner Jere E. Goyan (May 7, 1980).

15. Henry H. Dausch & Mary L. Richardson, Memorandum of Meeting (Apr. 8, 1982).

16. Memorandum of Peter H. Rheinstein, Director, FDA Division of Drug Advertising, of telephone conversation with Fred Lamb, General Counsel, Merrell Laboratories, re: Proposed Action on Bendectin Promotional Campaign (May 30, 1980).

17. FDA Fertility and Maternal Health Drug Advisory Committee, Unedited Answers to Questions Submitted to the Committee (Sept. 15–16, 1980).

18. The question posed to the Advisory Committee was: "Do the animal and human data reviewed by you and presented to you support the conclusion that Bendectin is associated with an increased risk for human birth defects?"

19. J. Golding et al., *Maternal Anti-nauseants and Clefts of Lip and Palate,* 2 HUMAN TOXICOL. 63 (1983) (the Golding study was presented as an unpublished work to the Advisory Committee in 1980); Kenneth Rothman et al., *Exogenous Hormones and Other Drug Exposures of Children with Congenital Heart Disease,* 109 AM. J. EPIDEMIOL. 433 (1979).

20. FDA Fertility and Maternal Health Drug Advisory Committee, *supra* note 17.

21. *See generally,* Judith Resnik, *From "Cases" to "Litigation,"* 54 LAW & CONTEMP. PROBS. 5, 29–35 (1991); Stanley Weigel, *The Judicial Panel on Multidistrict Litigation, Transferor Courts and Transferee Courts,* 78 F.R.D. 575 (1978); Note, *The Judicial Panel and the Conduct of Multidistrict Litigation,* 87 HARV. L. REV. 1001 (1974).

Chapter 10
Litigating a Multidistrict Case

By the time of its multidistrict motion, Merrell had decided to change counsel in defending new Bendectin lawsuits. Ed Walsh was facing mandatory retirement, and Davis, Polk's legal services were exorbitantly expensive (the *Koller* case reportedly cost Merrell $7 million in fees, after Davis, Polk reduced its initial bill of $12 million). Dow had purchased Merrell, and it did not have the same relationship with Walsh and Davis, Polk that Merrell had. Frank Woodside, a lawyer at Dinsmore & Shohl, a prominent Cincinnati law firm, was hired as Merrell's new primary defense counsel for Bendectin litigation. Woodside, who was also trained as a physician, had successfully represented Proctor & Gamble in lawsuits over its Rely tampons by toxic shock victims. Other lawyers were hired on the east and west coasts to try cases that remained outside the consolidated proceedings, and local counsel were employed for individual cases to handle individual discovery and routine legal matters.

Woodside is an engaging character, with an impish smile, a disarming, folksy manner, and a well-developed sense of humor. More comfortable in gold chains (albeit tasteful ones) than French cuffs and cufflinks, Woodside more resembles a plaintiff's lawyer than he does the straight-laced mien of an Ed Walsh. Genuinely comfortable in the courtroom where he tones down his out-of-court persona and becomes more staid, Woodside tries more cases than most civil litigators. He has developed a national reputation based on his successes in trying Rely tampon and Bendectin cases and was later chosen by Dow Corning to supervise its defense in the breast implant cases.

The Multidistrict Decision

Merrell's consolidation motion was preceded by extensive informal discussions between Merrell and plaintiffs' lawyers, who did not oppose the
motion. Opposing parties frequently agree on consolidation, but the
real dispute emerges over where the consolidated proceedings will take
place. Merrell preferred Cincinnati, where its headquarters and its primary lawyer were located.

Venue (the choice of locale for the trial) is an important strategical
concern for parties involved in a lawsuit, primarily because of the implications about the potential jury pool. But that concern was not present,
as the multidistrict consolidation would not be for trial purposes, as explained later. Thus, while some plaintiffs' lawyers preferred New York or
Washington, DC as the location for transfer, most acquiesced in Cincinnati for several reasons.[1] Stanley Chesley, who would later assume the
role of first among equals on the committee appointed to conduct pretrial proceedings on behalf of plaintiffs, was located in Cincinnati, as was
Merrell and the vast majority of documents that would be produced as
part of the discovery process.

Chesley and Frank Woodside arranged to meet with Carl Rubin, the
Chief Judge of the federal district court that encompassed Cincinnati.
Chesley was familiar with Judge Rubin from previous cases. Chesley had
initially made his mark in the mass tort arena in litigation spawned by
the Beverly Hills Supper Club fire in Kentucky that killed 165 patrons.
Rubin was assigned to preside over the federal cases, which ultimately
resulted in a recovery of $49 million. Chesley shared in a $5 million attorneys' fee award in that case and established a reputation as a major
player in mass tort litigation. Chesley was later recruited to participate in
the Agent Orange litigation because he could provide badly-needed financing[2] and has played a major role in most of the significant mass torts
since, including Bhopal, the Pan Am crash in Lockerbie, Scotland, the
MGM Grand Hotel, the San Juan Dupont Plaza hotel fire, and most recently, breast implants.[3]

Chesley's role in consolidating mass torts and settling them on a universal basis has thrust him into a highly controversial role among the
plaintiffs' bar. Chesley is one of a new breed of lawyer-businessman-
entrepreneur who is more comfortable calculating the present value of
a structured settlement than taking the deposition of an opposing expert. Those who have observed his legal work are unimpressed with his
technical skills, but Chesley readily concedes that he's interested in big
ideas, not the details required to litigate a case meticulously. Chesley
vehemently argues his mass resolution philosophy, making broad pronouncements and incanting the term "global resolution" with a reli-

gious fervor. Plaintiffs become commodities who are accumulated as inventory to be sold when a sufficiently attractive offer of settlement is made.[4] A measure of Chesley's commitment to collective treatment of suits and disregard for traditional individualistic procedure is that Chesley could not remember the name of the first Bendectin client on whose behalf he filed suit, several years after the multidistrict litigation concluded. Chesley's mass resolution style often puts him at odds with other plaintiffs' lawyers because of the threat he poses to their ability to maintain control over their individual cases and fee arrangements and their commitment to individual resolution.[5]

By contrast with Chesley, traditional plaintiffs' lawyers view themselves as the protector of individuals, representing the underdog to obtain justice against the establishment. "As they view it, gigantic and heartless insurance companies will grind down helpless victims unless modern gladiators—they themselves—intervene to protect the injured party, poor and outgunned as he or she is."[6] One malpractice lawyer describes his role: "The opportunity I have as a trial lawyer to give a client a better and fuller life through an adequate damage award gives me immense satisfaction. I regard it as a badge of honor to walk into a courtroom to do battle on behalf of individuals who have been maimed or killed by malpractice and other forms of negligence."[7] Chesley and his collective litigation philosophy does not mesh well with the vision of the traditional plaintiff's lawyer.

There was one red flag about Judge Rubin's conduct of the *Beverly Hills Supper Club* case that might have concerned Chesley and other plaintiffs' lawyers. Judge Rubin ruled that the trial would be trifurcated, with the question of whether the defendants' aluminum wiring was the cause of the fire being tried first, and the issue of breach of duty (and culpability) being tried separately later, if the jury found causation in the first proceeding. Damages would be resolved in yet a third phase, if necessary. That trifurcation order was the first instance of cleaving the determination of liability into separate hearings.[8] After the jury's verdict for the defendants in the causation trial was overturned on appeal for different reasons, a new trial was conducted by another judge without bifurcation. That procedural change was viewed as critical to the plaintiffs' verdict in the second trial by most lawyers associated with the case.[9]

Once again, however, Rubin's trial habits were not central, as the multidistrict consolidation was not for trial purposes. Chesley liked Rubin's no-nonsense, organized style (Rubin has published and hands out to new attorneys appearing before him a pamphlet containing rules for proceeding in his court), his policy of permitting broad discovery to the parties, a practice of running a very tight courtroom and imposing strict deadlines, and a strong commitment to the jury system.[10] (In twenty years of judging, Rubin has overturned only 3 of an estimated 400 jury verdicts.[11]) Rubin can be impatient—he's quite direct and doesn't waste time getting to the point. Those who cross him or fail to abide by his rules usually decide that the wrath they have incurred is not worth the advantage obtained. Perhaps most important, Rubin had a demonstrated willingness to be procedurally innovative. In the *Beverly Hills Supper Club* case, Rubin had certified an unusual class action that facilitated a large settlement between several defendants and the plaintiffs.

After being approached by Woodside and Chesley, Rubin indicated to them that he would be willing to handle the multidistrict Bendectin litigation, his first experience with a multidistrict case.[12] On February 9, 1982 the Multidistrict Panel transferred 45 cases to the Southern District of Ohio, after concluding that the common question of whether birth defects were caused by Bendectin justified coordinated discovery and pretrial proceedings before Judge Rubin.[13] Thus began "MDL-486," the case file number assigned to the consolidated proceedings. Subsequently, the Panel issued orders transferring hundreds of later-filed cases to Judge Rubin. The landscape of Bendectin litigation was transformed from individual case skirmishes to a mass toxic substances war.

In theory, the transfer of cases in a multidistrict proceeding is only for pretrial purposes, with the cases to be returned to their original district for trial. The reason for the retransfer is to preserve a home, presumably convenient (and often strategically favorable) forum for the plaintiff filing the suit, who traditionally is afforded the choice of forum. The reality is that very few multidistrict cases are returned to their home fora, because they are resolved without the need for trial. If a case is settled or dismissed before trial, that will occur in the transferee court, and there remains nothing to retransfer to the original court.

Although they did not appreciate it at the time, the MDL-486 participants were about to embark on a proceeding that would result in a trial involving 1,100 plaintiffs, raise important questions about the structure of mass toxic substances cases and trials that are still being debated in other cases today, produce a $120-million dollar settlement, only to be upset by an appellate court, and serve as virtually a laboratory experiment for aggregate adjudication of mass toxic cases.

Organizing Plaintiffs' Lawyers

From the time of Merrell's motion for multidistrict consolidation, Stanley Chesley took the lead in organizing the plaintiffs' lawyers who were interested in Bendectin litigation. Meetings were held to discuss how to respond to the motion and to begin preliminary planning if the consolidation motion were granted. From these meetings, five attorneys emerged who took charge of the multidistrict proceedings on behalf of the plaintiffs.

George Kokus, because of the expertise he developed in the *Mekdeci* case, was an obvious choice. Kokus, who was financially devastated by the *Mekdeci* case, limped into MDL-486 hoping to recoup some of his investment of time, expenses, and human capital in the *Mekdeci* case. Arthur Cohen remained in Miami, attempting to resurrect their malpractice and personal injury practice. Tom Bleakley, who had developed several Bendectin cases while at the Charfoos firm in Detroit, was a second. Bleakley had spent time in medical school (though he hadn't graduated), worked as a detail person in the pharmaceutical industry for several years and gravitated toward litigating drug cases on behalf of plaintiffs. Bleakley had been involved in the first multidistrict pharmaceutical case, involving Cleocin in Detroit.[14] Jim Butler, the old warrior who had battled Merrell over thalidomide and who was involved in several other individual Bendectin cases, was the third. Stanley Chesley was a newcomer to Bendectin. But he was willing to undertake a substantial role in financing the case, a crucial matter if plaintiffs were going to litigate on anything approaching a level playing field. Later, Allen Eaton was added for his expertise in food and drug law, his experience in the *Mekdeci* and *Koller* cases, and because he was genuinely liked by the other attorneys involved.

These five lawyers were confirmed as the Plaintiff's Lead Counsel Committee (PLCC) by Judge Rubin when no other plaintiffs' lawyers objected to their appointment. At the time, lead counsel were elected by the parties (really their attorneys) in the action, subject to review and confirmation by the trial judge.[15] Kokus, Eaton, Bleakley, and Butler controlled a substantial number of the existing Bendectin cases. Other attorneys' acquiescence in Kokus et al.'s appointment as lead counsel reflected their prominence in Bendectin litigation at that time and the other attorneys' willingness to join forces with Chesley. But Bendectin litigation would evolve considerably, with new attorneys, notably Barry Nace, later emerging as major figures. But at the time of selection of lead counsel, Nace had just filed his first Bendectin case in Washington, DC.

The role of lead counsel in a multidistrict proceeding is blurred. In a class action, one set of lawyers represents all members of the class in all aspects of the class action. Unlike a class action, the MDL-486 consolidation technically involved lawyers for all of the plaintiffs. Yet even with the initial 45 cases (the number continued to grow), it would be infeasible and uneconomical to have that number of attorneys participating in the consolidated proceedings, even though their clients' cases were at stake. Yet the cases would return to their home districts for trial, at least in theory. And there remained individual issues in each case, such as damages, that would not be the subject of discovery or trial preparation in the multidistrict proceedings. The precise scope of authority of lead counsel and the indistinct seam between their work on common issues and what remains for the attorneys for individual plaintiffs remains problematical.[16] In some measure this uncertainty arose in MDL-486 because of the difficulties in identifying which issues were common and which were individual, as explained in chapter 12. One limitation on lead counsel's authority, however, was clear: they had no authority to enter into a settlement on behalf of the Bendectin claimants that they did not individually represent.

Complicating the role of the PLCC appointed by Judge Rubin was the absence of any preexisting organizational structure among the five of them. Unlike a single firm, in which a hierarchical structure exists to provide leadership and authority, the five attorneys on the lead counsel committee were from independent firms, with equal authority.

No organizational mechanism exists to resolve disagreements and disputes that develop among lead counsel, to coordinate their efforts, to avoid the cumbersomeness of drafting by committee, to discipline shirkers, or to tame raging egos.[17] Even identifying and developing the issues in a coherent, consistent, and logical manner is better performed in a hierarchical structure.[18] The Bendectin cases filed by each member of the PLCC were not uniform. For example, as a result of his globe-trotting after the first *Mekdeci* trial, George Kokus had a large proportion of foreign plaintiff cases. These differences in case characteristics created different interests among the five lead lawyers—differences that sometimes erupted into conflicts. Even such a mundane problem as access to the case files and discovery materials has to be solved if five geographically dispersed attorneys are to conduct a major multi-party products liability case.[19] By contrast, Merrell had no such organizational impediments: Frank Woodside headed up a team of attorneys at Cincinnati's Dinsmore & Shohl.

To be sure, mutual self-interest served a disciplining role for the PLCC. All would be better off in their own individual cases if the multidistrict proceedings were fruitful. The possibility of working together again in another mass tort case was sufficiently remote, however, that it contributed little to mutual cooperation.[20] Kokus's, Eaton's, and, to a lesser extent, Bleakley's dependence on Chesley's purse strings also served as an authority surrogate. Moreover, the PLCC expected to recover attorneys' fees for their efforts from any recovery by individual plaintiffs whom they did not represent. There was much discussion among the members of the PLCC about what percentage of the recovery it would seek as fees. This was a delicate matter, as those fees would reduce the fees recovered by attorneys for individual plaintiffs. Yet the PLCC, in conducting pretrial discovery on the common issues, would provide a public good from which all Bendectin cases would presumably benefit. Discussion focused on a range of 7 to 10 percent of the recovery, which would constitute about one-third of the total attorney's fee. Ultimately, of course, the authority to determine the fees awarded to the PLCC for its efforts on common issues was Judge Rubin's.[21]

The Growth of Scientific Evidence

On the causation front, there was a great deal of activity during the period from the end of the second *Mekdeci* trial until the conclusion of discovery in MDL-486. The years 1981–84 were the three most prolific years for Bendectin research, both epidemiological and toxicological. Here, as Professor Joseph Sanders has written, "science was driven by the law."[22] Bendectin litigation made the drug a hot topic, attracting researchers' interest. At the same time, the FDA, under pressure from Don Edwards and Doug Walgren in Congress and with the recommendation of its 1980 Advisory Committee, was both sponsoring research and encouraging Merrell to initiate and support additional studies of Bendectin. While most of the studies tended to exonerate Bendectin (almost a dozen negative studies, mostly case-control studies, were published during this period),[23] a few raised additional questions about the safety of Bendectin, although none provided decisive evidence of teratogenicity.

The most significant concerns were raised by an epidemiological study conducted by two Yale epidemiologists, a German study of Wistar rats, a study of monkeys conducted at the Primate Research Center at the University of California, and a study of rats cosponsored by the National Center for Toxicological Research. Drs. Michael Bracken and Brenda Eskenazi, prompted by the attention to and litigation over Bendectin, analyzed a data set they had compiled earlier and found that the risk of pyloric stenosis was more than quadrupled among mothers of children exposed to Bendectin.[24] Pyloric stenosis is a blockage in the stomach that prevents digestion and results in forceful projectile vomiting. The condition, once diagnosed, can be readily corrected by minor surgery, but can be fatal if untreated. The Bracken and Eskenazi study was based on births between 1974 and 1976 and hence involved the three-ingredient version of Bendectin, rather than the two-ingredient version marketed after 1976. Bracken and Eskenazi also found a tripling of heart valve anomalies among exposed infants. Both of the findings were statistically significant, but the authors stopped short of concluding they had identified a causal connection, stating it was "unclear" whether the strong association they found was a result of a causal relationship. The authors concluded that "the physician should carefully weigh the hazards of maternal nausea and vomiting during pregnancy against the risk of a mal-formation that can be treated." [25]

The association identified by Eskenazi and Bracken led two other re-search groups to pursue the relationship between pyloric stenosis and Bendectin. A group of researchers examined records of a large HMO and found a similar increased risk of pyloric stenosis in mothers who had ingested Bendectin during their pregnancy.[26] The study covered births between 1977 and 1982, and thus involved the two-ingredient version of Bendectin. Perhaps most significantly, these researchers found a dose-related association between Bendectin and pyloric stenosis. However, they did not conclude the association was necessarily causal, primarily because of the concern that severe vomiting during pregnancy may have been a confounding factor (i.e., the true cause of pyloric stenosis is vom-iting, and pregnant women taking Bendectin vomit more than those who do not take Bendectin).

Yet another larger study by a third group of researchers found no in-creased association between Bendectin and pyloric stenosis.[27] This study, which was also motivated by Bracken and Eskenazi's findings, examined subjects who were exposed to both the two- and three-ingredient ver-sions of Bendectin. The study identified ten times as many children with pyloric stenosis as the Bracken study, thereby reducing the likelihood that random chance affected the outcome. But the study also was subject to criticism because it had a broad definition of exposure—any time dur-ing pregnancy—that might have diluted any effect, was partially funded by Merrell, and relied on maternal recall after birth to determine expo-sure to drugs. In sum, the three studies together raised disquieting con-cerns about Bendectin and pyloric stenosis, but did not resolve them.

A German study of rats found an association between doxylamine and diaphragmatic hernia. The authors of the study concluded: "In the pres-ent case, doxylamine succinate looks like a mild clearcut teratogen in Wistar rats." [28] In a subsequent study, the authors were unable to repli-cate the association with diaphragmatic hernias but concluded that the outcome was probably due to the different strains of rats (and their dif-ferent genetic susceptibilities) used in the two studies. Assuming a no-effect threshold dose and using a crude extrapolation from the high doses employed in the rat studies, the authors nevertheless concluded that Bendectin was unlikely to be teratogenic at the doses recommended for pregnant women.

The primate study raised questions about a heart defect that involves a hole between the left and right ventricle, which was found dispropor-tionately in prenatal fetuses exposed to Bendectin. Since exposed mon-keys who went to full term did not display this effect, the authors suggested that the drug delayed the closure of the heart wall during the early prenatal period, but that it spontaneously resolved itself by full term. Finally, a study sponsored by the National Center for Toxicological Research found an increased rate of malformations in rats, but at a dose that also induced maternal toxicity, suggesting that the malformations were a result of maternal distress rather than a direct teratogenic effect.[29]

These studies, particularly the epidemiological ones on pyloric stenosis, had a significant impact on MDL-486. First, these and other studies that emerged required the lawyers to absorb, study, and ultimately conduct discovery about them. Second, the ones that indicated possibilities of Bendectin's teratogenicity gave the PLCC renewed hope in the merits of the case. Third, the findings about specific effects and diseases emphasized that studies that did not disaggregate by type of defect might miss the trees for the forest. Toxic agents tend to have a specific effect or a related pattern of effects, rather than exhibiting transtoxicity. A study that found no overall increase in malformations might simply be diluting and masking a real but rare and specific effect. This specificity-of-effect phenomenon then revealed that all Bendectin claimants were not created equal: some studies tended to exonerate Bendectin with regard to certain defects, while others might support a contrary conclusion for different defects.

The Breadth and Depth of Discovery

Discovery in MDL-486 was far broader in scope and probed more deeply than had occurred in *Mekdeci*. In part this was due to the PLCC deciding to start afresh with discovery—to cast a wide net that would uncover evidence that might have been missed in the *Mekdeci* case. If there were any hidden smoking guns, the PLCC was determined to locate them. In part, the PLCC benefited from Cohen's and Kokus's efforts in *Mekdeci* (as well as the ongoing discovery in *Koller*), which revealed additional avenues of investigation—other Merrell employees and knowledgeable individuals to depose and additional documentation to seek. In part, the PLCC's better staffing and funding permitted the exploration of a variety of avenues that were beyond Cohen's and Kokus's means. Yet another reason for expanded discovery was the variety of plaintiffs and birth defects that were consolidated in MDL-486. These different birth defects, with potentially distinct causal questions and evidence implicated, expanded the breadth of relevant scientific evidence. Finally, the growth of Bendectin-science, as explained above, required significant efforts by both sides in the case.

The plaintiffs' efforts included requesting testing, marketing, sales, and drug experience reports from each of 22 foreign subsidiaries of Merrell in Europe, Africa, Australia, and South America. This request imposed huge labor, logistical, and language burdens on Dinsmore & Shohl to identify and catalog documents responsive to the request. In addition, the plaintiffs' lawyers spent four months at Merrell's headquarters during which 500,000 documents were produced for their review. Ninety-three discovery depositions were taken, and numerous other videotaped depositions were conducted to preserve testimony to be used at the individual trials after the cases were remanded to their transferor courts.

An intriguing line of documents obtained from Merrell revealed that it was well aware of the inadequacy of the Bendectin teratology studies in the 1970s. It had hired Dr. H. Tuchmann-Duplessis, a French teratologist, as a consultant in 1973. Tuchmann-Duplessis, after reviewing the Bendectin teratology studies, informed Merrell that in his view the studies available were inadequate to justify a conclusion about Bendectin's lack of teratogenicity. The additional studies that he recommended performing were not concluded for almost ten years, until 1982. The PLCC also found a review of the Bunde-Bowles study that Merrell had commissioned Dr. Richard Smithells to perform in 1973. Smithells criticized the methodology of Bunde-Bowles and informed Merrell of its inadequacy to support the safety of Bendectin.

The PLCC, convinced that a weak link in Merrell's defense was the Bunde-Bowles study, conducted extensive discovery in that area. Patient records from each of the participating physicians were sought and analyzed to determine if they matched the data provided for the study. Depositions of medical secretaries were taken to ascertain their methods for preparing and reporting the data.

Tom Bleakley found out from Art Raynes, one of the American thalidomide lawyers, about Merrell's ghostwriting of an article favorably evaluating thalidomide, nominally written by an independent Cincinnati obstetrician, Dr. Ray Nulsen. The PLCC found during discovery that Merrell and Nulsen had done the same thing in a laudatory article about Bendectin published in 1957.[30] Allen Eaton also found evidence (an internal Davis, Polk memorandum) that Nulsen, along with Dr. Bunde, had been involved in a proposal to destroy documents that indicated adverse reactions occurred in Nulsen's clinical thalidomide trials, birth defects that were not reported in his data.[31] Incidents like these fertilized the belief of plaintiffs' lawyers that the history of Merrell and its Bendectin testing went beyond shoddiness and across the malevolent line. Of course, Merrell's peccancy was an independent question from whether Bendectin caused birth defects, a matter which the PLCC inevitably could not avoid.

In addition to the consolidated discovery, information about the individual plaintiffs and the circumstances surrounding their injuries and

damages would be required before those cases could be tried. Recognizing this, Merrell had its local counsel, supervised by Dinsmore & Shohl,
initiate discovery over individual issues in each pending case. Detailed
interrogatories were sent to each plaintiff, inquiring into the medical
history of each family member, the circumstances of use of Bendectin,
and other matters that might provide Merrell a defense. The PLCC
viewed this discovery as beyond its responsibility, and the attorneys for
individual plaintiffs, with the cases transferred to Cincinnati, were out of
the loop and uninterested in investing themselves in discovery. Because
the multidistrict consolidation statute requires that entire cases be transferred, rather than only the common issues in those cases, supervision of
discovery over case-specific matters was the responsibility of Judge Rubin.
The PLCC attempted to persuade Rubin to suspend individual discovery
until the common issues discovery was completed. However, Rubin's
scheduling orders contemplated that when the cases were remanded to
their home districts they would be ready for trial. Thus, he insisted that
discovery proceed on two fronts: the common issues discovery on Merrell's liability and the teratogenicity of Bendectin and local discovery
over case-specific matters.

In the midst of this discovery, a critical new development required the
attention of the MDL-486 attorneys. On June 9, 1983 the proceedings in
MDL-486 were punctuated by a dramatic announcement: Merrell would
cease manufacturing Bendectin, thereby effectively withdrawing it from
the market.

Notes

1. Although the Panel is not bound by the parties' views, it tends to ratify transfers to which the parties have agreed. *See, e.g., In re* Brown Co. Sec. Litig., 325 F.
Supp. 307, 308 (J.P.M.L. 1971).

2. PETER H. SCHUCK, AGENT ORANGE ON TRIAL 109, 121 (Cambridge, MA:
Belknap Press of Harvard University Press, 1987).

3. For discussion of Chesley's role in these mass tort cases, see Alison Frankel,
Et Tu Stan?, AM. LAW., Jan./Feb. 1994.

4. *Cf.* JOHN A. JENKINS, THE LITIGATORS: INSIDE THE POWERFUL WORLD OF
AMERICA'S HIGH-STAKES TRIAL LAWYERS 108 (New York: Doubleday, 1989)
(plaintiffs in mass tort case are "commodities to be traded and fought over").

5. *See* Frankel, *supra* note 3, at 68.

6. JEFFREY O'CONNELL, THE LAWSUIT LOTTERY 147 (New York: Free Press,
1979).

7. STANLEY M. ROSENBLATT, TRIAL LAWYER 11–12 (Secaucus, NJ: Lyle Stuart,
1984).

8. *But see* Beeck v. Aquaslide-N-Dive Corp., 562 F.2d 537 (8th Cir. 1977) (separate trial on the issue of whether defendant manufactured the product that
caused plaintiff's injury, a limited, specific, and largely collateral subissue).

9. Andrew Wolfson, *After 8 Years, a Complex Case Comes to an End*, NAT'L L.J., Aug. 19, 1985, at 6.

10. Carl B. Rubin, *The Jury System: An Unbelievable Success*, 18 OHIO N.U.L. REV. 743, 744 (1992) ("the jury system is without question the greatest way to decide questions of fact that has ever been created").

11. *Id.* at 745.

12. The Multidistrict Panel doesn't assign a consolidated case to a judge without obtaining the approval of that judge first. DAVID F. HERR, MULTIDISTRICT LITIGATION 167 (Boston: Little, Brown, 1986).

13. *In re* Richardson-Merrell Inc., 533 F. Supp. 489 (J.P.M.L. 1982).

14. HERR, *supra* note 12, at 90 n.23.

15. MANUAL FOR COMPLEX LITIGATION § 1.92 (St. Paul, MN: West Publishing, 5th ed. 1982). A subsequent version of the Manual gives the judge the authority to select counsel, albeit after canvassing and considering the attorneys' suggestions. MANUAL FOR COMPLEX LITIGATION (SECOND) § 20.224 (Philadelphia: American Law Institute-American Bar Association Committee on Continuing Professional Education, 1985).

16. *See, e.g.*, Vincent v. Hughes Air West, Inc., 557 F.2d 759 (9th Cir. 1977); Feldman v. Hanley, 49 F.R.D. 48, 51 (S.D.N.Y. 1969).

17. *See* John C. Coffee Jr., *Rethinking the Class Action: A Policy Primer on Reform*, 62 IND. L.J. 625, 640–41 (1987) (recognizing the organizational difficulties that develop with an "ad hoc" law firm appointed to litigate a class action or consolidated case).

18. *See* Jay Tidmarsh, *Unattainable Justice: The Form of Complex Litigation and the Limits of Judicial Power*, 60 GEO. WASH. L. REV. 1683, 1759 (1992); MARVIN E. SHAW, GROUP DYNAMICS: THE PSYCHOLOGY OF SMALL GROUP BEHAVIOR 315 (New York: McGraw-Hill, 3d ed. 1981) ("Although . . . coordination is possible without a formal group leader, it is probable that effective group action seldom occurs unless someone in the group directs the various activities of group members").

19. *Cf.* Mary Twitchell, *The Ethical Dilemmas of Lawyers on Teams*, 72 MINN. L. REV. 697, 764–66 (1988) (discussing suboptimal communication and coordination of lawyers working together in a group effort).

20. ROBERT AXELROD, THE EVOLUTION OF COOPERATION 20 (New York: Basic Books, 1984).

21. *See* Vincent v. Hughes Air West, Inc., 557 F.2d 759, 768–73 (9th Cir. 1977) (trial court had authority to award fees to lead counsel from recovery of each individual plaintiff); John C. Coffee, *The Regulation of Entrepreneurial Litigation: Balancing Fairness and Efficiency in the Large Class Action*, 54 U. CHI. L. REV. 877, 911 nn.80–81 (1987).

22. Joseph Sanders, *The Bendectin Litigation: A Case Study in the Life Cycle of Mass Torts*, 43 HAST. L.J. 301, 346 (1992).

23. *See* Sanders, *supra* note 22, at 395 (Table 2).

24. Brenda Eskenazi & Michael B. Bracken, *Bendectin (Debendox) as a Risk Factor for Pyloric Stenosis*, 144 AM J. OBSTET. & GYN. 919 (1982).

25. *Id.* at 924.

26. Pamela Aselton et al., *Pyloric Stenosis and Maternal Bendectin Exposure*, 120 AM. J. EPIDEMIOL. 251 (1984).

27. Allen A. Mitchell et al., *Birth Defects in Relation to Bendectin Use in Pregnancy II. Pyloric Stenosis*, 147 AM. J. OBSTET. & GYN. 737 (1983).

28. Reimar Roll & G. Matthiaschk, *Embryotoxicity and Reproduction Studies with*

Doxylamine Succinate in Mice and Rats (1981) (unpublished), *cited in* Public Citizen Health Research Group, Petition Requesting the Immediate Removal of Bendectin and All Other Fixed-Combination Drugs Containing Doxylamine and Pyridoxine from the Market (June 25, 1982).

29. Rochelle W. Tyl et al., *Developmental Toxicity Evaluation of Bendectin in CD Rats*, 37 TERATOLOGY 539 (1988) (study performed in 1982–83).

30. Roy Nulsen, *Bendectin in the Treatment of Nausea of Pregnancy*, 53 OHIO MED. J. 665 (1957). Dr. Pogge admitted ghostwriting the "first draft" of the article. Deposition of Raymond C. Pogge at 69, *In re* Richardson-Merrell, Inc. "Bendectin" Products Liability Litigation, MDL-486 (S.D. Ohio July 7, 1983).

31. Transcript of In Chambers Proceedings, MDL-486 (S.D. Ohio Feb. 22, 1984).

Chapter 11
The Withdrawal of Bendectin

At a press conference on June 9, 1983 David Sharrock, president of Merrell's United States subsidiary, announced Merrell would cease producing Bendectin.[1] Merrell's cessation effectively removed Bendectin from the market.[2] The removal of a pharmaceutical product from the market is ordinarily a routine and common occurrence when a drug is no longer an economically viable product. Withdrawal rarely attracts much attention or involves much planning. Bendectin's removal, because of the legal, regulatory, political, and public relations situation, was the aberration.

Merrell arranged for Dr. Charles Flowers, Vice-President of the American College of Obstetricians and Gynecologists and Chair of the Department of Obstetrics and Gynecology at the University of Alabama, to accompany Sharrock at the press conference and make a brief statement decrying the loss of a valuable drug. Flowers was paid for his appearance and had previously served as a paid consultant to Merrell on regulatory matters, but these facts were not disclosed.[3] Ominously, Flowers predicted that "Birth defects may well increase,"[4] a prophecy that was widely repeated.[5] Later, the college issued a statement that the loss of Bendectin would create "a significant therapeutic gap,"[6] echoing a phrase that Merrell had employed in announcing its decision to pharmacists.

Sharrock emphasized that Bendectin was safe and its removal was a result of business, rather than medical, concerns. He blamed the withdrawal on "these litigious times," a phrase that the media adopted and reported nationally. Bendectin was a victim, according to Merrell, of the high costs of defending against unmeritorious claims.

Sharrock explained that Merrell's liability insurance premiums for Bendectin were approaching its gross sales of Bendectin. Despite two substantial price increases in 1982 and 1983, Merrell anticipated that it would lose money on Bendectin in 1983. Litigation was costly in two respects: large numbers of lawyers had to be hired and paid to defend Merrell in the increasing number of cases, and litigation was distracting many Merrell employees from their usual responsibilities, impeding Merrell's ability to develop new and beneficial drugs. Sharrock concluded by once again denouncing the contemporary tort system and its impact:

> Summarizing then, I think there are lessons in this for all of us. America is a litigious society. Unfortunately, consumers—the ultimate beneficiaries of drugs—will increasingly see the real cost of defending products against unsubstantiated claims. In fact, as in the case of Bendectin, such claims can ultimately deny the public the use of needed therapy.

Merrell's adversaries in Bendectin litigation had a diametrically different view. Betty Mekdeci was ecstatic about the withdrawal, announcing to the media that the withdrawal was a victory in her battle with Merrell.[7] The Health Research Group, a Ralph Nader-affiliated institution that serves as a consumer advocate on medical issues, hailed the action, concluding that it would spare hundreds of thousands of pregnant women and their fetuses the risk of an unsafe drug.

The PLCC and other plaintiffs' lawyers suspected that Merrell's explanation was a cover for more ominous motivations for the withdrawal. The withdrawal was announced 13 days after Barry Nace had obtained a $750,000 judgment in *Oxendine*, a Bendectin case that had remained in the local District of Columbia courts. Many believed that Merrell's decision was a response to the *Oxendine* outcome. In addition, the withdrawal convinced many that there were hidden teratologic skeletons in Merrell's closet. Barry Nace's comments on the withdrawal reflected the thinking of others: "It is obviously an admission to me. You don't withdraw a drug unless you have a problem with it."[8] Jim Butler was the least restrained; he wrote to other lawyers that Merrell's explanation "is a bold-faced lie. The drug is a teratogen and has caused untold misery in thousands of children over the past 25 years."[9] Publicly, he exulted that the decision was "fantastic."

There was a small germ of a basis for Butler's hyperbolic claims. A number of studies that called Bendectin's safety into question had emerged in the early 1980s, as detailed in chapter 10. One study published in 1982 by Eskenazi and Bracken had found an association between Bendectin and pyloric stenosis. Another study was begun to further examine the connection. One month before Merrell's announcement of the withdrawal, an advisory committee, consisting of Merrell representatives, FDA officials, and other experts met with the principal investigator of the second study who reported that his preliminary analysis indicated a strong association between pyloric stenosis and Bendectin, confirming the Eskenazi and Bracken study.[10]

The withdrawal provided a new optimism to the PLCC, which then proceeded to seek evidence that would support their suspicions, and a new discovery tangent ensued. The PLCC sought documents that might bear either on Merrell's purported explanation for the withdrawal or might reveal more damaging motivations. Jim Butler deposed David Sharrock for a full day, interrogating him about the decision to withdraw Bendectin.

In the end, the truth resided neither in Merrell's announcement nor in the PLCC's suspicions.[11] The PLCC was dead wrong in its suspicions that *Oxendine* had motivated the withdrawal and that Merrell's new concerns about the safety of Bendectin motivated the withdrawal.

Merrell's inaccuracy in its account of the withdrawal was far more subtle, omitting important forces at work in order to further its propaganda efforts to make Bendectin a martyr of tort law. Merrell's undertaking has achieved enormous success.[12] A more accurate explanation of the forces leading to withdrawal requires tracing Bendectin litigation back to the mid-1970s, when Betty Mekdeci began her crusade and the effect of her efforts on Bendectin sales.

Worldwide sales of Bendectin for 1983 were projected at $21.2 million, with Merrell squeaking out a thin $1.1 million profit. Insurance premiums were eating up an increasing proportion of those gross revenues—Merrell's insurance premiums increased several hundred percent to $10.4 million for United States coverage in 1983. Significantly, its excess insurer, Lloyd's, was threatening to withdraw coverage or exclude Bendectin from coverage if it remained on the market. Because its insurance was written on an "occurrence" basis, Merrell had adequate coverage for suits arising from births that had already occurred, but was facing the prospect of inadequate coverage for suits arising from future sales. While David Sharrock's statement that liability insurance costs almost equalled gross sales was not quite right, the financial picture for Bendectin was gloomy.

What David Sharrock did not share with his audience when he announced the withdrawal of Bendectin was the declining sales of Bendectin beginning in 1980 or the reasons for that decline.[13] Total U.S. sales of Bendectin were in excess of 100 million tablets from 1973 to 1980, hitting a high of 133 million in 1979. At that time, 30 percent of all pregnant women in the United States took Bendectin. In 1980 Bendectin usage declined by over 20 percent and the following year by another 60 percent. Although the percentage of pregnant women using Bendectin increased slightly in 1982 over the prior year, it still was only 50 to

67 percent of the usage for the decade from 1969 to 1979. One Merrell sales forecast concluded that by 1985 sales of Bendectin would be 15 to 20 percent of what they were in 1979.

What explains this dramatic decline? One must return to Betty Mekdeci and her lawsuit against Merrell. That lawsuit spawned national publicity in late 1979 and 1980, ranging from the sensational (*National Enquirer*) to the leftist investigational (*Mother Jones*) to the mainstream (*New York Times*).[14] That publicity, Merrell discovered, had an appreciable impact on Bendectin sales.

To cope with this decline in sales and the increasing cost of defending Bendectin suits, Merrell instituted two large price increases, in March 1982 and again in January 1983. The wholesale price of Bendectin increased during this period from $16 per 100 tablets to almost $50 for 90 tablets. By 1983 Bendectin cost consumers about $1.00 per tablet. By contrast, as Merrell realized, a consumer could put together a home-made Bendectin "cocktail" by purchasing Unisom, an over-the-counter sleep aid consisting of doxylamine, and Vitamin B-6 tablets for about one-fourth the cost of Bendectin.

The FDA Advisory Committee Hearing on Bendectin in 1980 also had a significant impact on Bendectin sales, albeit indirectly. The Advisory Committee recommended that Bendectin's labeling be modified to provide that it should only be used by patients whose morning sickness could not be controlled by more conservative measures. When this recommendation was implemented, the indications for use of Bendectin were narrowed and the reporting of teratologic studies were expanded to explain the positive animal studies as well as the few epidemiological studies that had found associations with specific birth defects. Merrell provided a summary of this information in a patient package insert that was provided to all women who received Bendectin. One textbook in obstetrics and gynecology added a comment about the adverse case reports of birth defects, "equivocal or contradictory" studies, and FDA consideration of a warning about the teratogenic uncertainty of Bendectin.[15]

Sales of Bendectin also declined because Merrell decided to cease advertising and promotional efforts for Bendectin. The FDA had been concerned about Merrell's over-promotion of Bendectin since 1980, because some of Merrell's materials suggested that virtually every pregnant woman might benefit from taking Bendectin. The FDA employed informal pressure to convince Merrell to tone down its promotional claims, which culminated with Merrell ceasing its promotional efforts for Bendectin.[16]

Merrell anticipated further reductions in sales in response to new warnings for Bendectin about which it was negotiating with the FDA. The new warnings, to be included in the drug's labeling and a "Dear Doctor" letter, would explain the results of the studies of pyloric stenosis that had been recently completed.

In addition to the precipitous drop in sales, Bendectin had become a good will albatross for Merrell. The adverse publicity about risk had harmed its reputation, even among women who continued to use Bendectin, as they dealt with their anxiety because of the residual doubt about Bendectin's safety. The adverse publicity also harmed Merrell in the medical community, and the two rapid and steep increases in price were unpopular with pharmacists, physicians, and consumers.

Thus, what many careful and conservative physicians had long counseled came about. Bendectin was no longer profligately prescribed for every pregnant woman with nausea. Physicians, aware of concerns being raised through new labeling, became more cautious in their prescribing practices. Pregnant women, too, became less willing to take Bendectin (or any drugs), concerned about harming their unborn children. No doubt some of that concern was fed by the frenzied and exaggerated reports of the *National Enquirer* and similar media. No doubt some overreacted to the information about the uncertain residual risk. But the reduction in use surely brought Bendectin consumption closer to what it should have been than in the earlier and profligate days. The response to the increases in price also demonstrated to Merrell that there is price elasticity in the demand for at least some pharmaceuticals. Bendectin sales would never return to the halcyon days when over 30 percent of all pregnant women in the United States took it.

While Merrell was not entirely forthcoming about the reasons for withdrawing Bendectin, it was entirely straightforward in its denials that the *Oxendine* verdict or the new epidemiological study of pyloric stenosis were responsible for its decision. Internal Merrell planning documents reveal that David Sharrock began thinking about withdrawal as early as December 1982, well before either event. Merrell made the final decision to withdraw Bendectin from the market on May 4, 1983 and spent five weeks of extensive and meticulous efforts planning the event. Bendectin's withdrawal was not a precipitous decision.

The extensive efforts by Merrell planning the withdrawal, and the documentation of those efforts, provides a case study on one controversial aspect of products liability law. Rule 407 of the Federal Rules of Evidence bars the introduction of evidence of subsequent remedial measures performed by a defendant to prove "negligence or culpable conduct." Rule 407 was drafted without consideration of strict products liability, and courts have wrestled with whether it should be read to bar such evidence when plaintiffs seek to use it in a strict liability case. Many courts have, sensibly, considered the purposes of Rule 407, which rests primarily on a policy to encourage individuals to take precautions when they become aware of a hazard. The concern is that a potential defendant, aware that a subsequent remedial measure may be used against it in a lawsuit, will desist from taking that action because of the adverse impact in a later lawsuit.

The courts that have confronted the admissibility of subsequent remedial measure evidence in strict products liability cases have reached different outcomes. The reasoning of the courts departs on their intuition about the empirical impact of the admissibility rule adopted. One school of thought, exemplified in Judge Posner's opinion in *Flaminio v. Honda Motor Co.*,[17] contends that admitting such evidence will have precisely the adverse effect to that which prompted adoption of the rule:

Especially in a product case, the accident may have been readily avoidable either by eliminating some defect or by warning the consumer of some inherent danger, and in such a case the failure to apply Rule 407 might deter subsequent remedial measures just as much as in a negligence case.[18]

The contrary view is that far more important factors are at work in the decision of a manufacturer whether to take steps to reduce the risk associated with a product:

The contemporary corporate mass producer of goods, the normal products liability defendant, manufactures tens of thousands of units of goods; it is manifestly unrealistic to suggest that such a producer will forego making improvements in its product, and risk innumerable additional lawsuits and the attendant adverse effect upon its public image, simply because evidence of adoption of such improvements may be admitted in an action founded on strict liability for recovery on an injury that preceded the improvement.[19]

Of course, in Merrell's view, the withdrawal of Bendectin was not a subsequent remedial measure, as Merrell argued that the withdrawal did not reduce risk because Bendectin was perfectly safe. But, the PLCC argued otherwise, and Merrell was ultimately confronted by the PLCC over admissibility on the Rule 407 battlefield. Merrell's failure to even consider the Rule 407 implication of its cessation of Bendectin production provides one case study of the unimportance of Rule 407 in corporate decision making.

Bendectin's withdrawal was a careful, meticulously planned event. In making the decision, Merrell analyzed the financial, public relations, legal, and political consequences. The plan addressed all of Merrell's affected internal and external constituencies, including Congress, the FDA, employees, its Board of Directors, market analysts, insurers, stockholders, clinical investigators, pharmacists, physicians, and lawyers. In implementing the decision, Merrell left no stone unturned. Office space was obtained to accommodate 15 employees to answer 28 toll free hot lines that were established to handle inquiries from consumers, pharmacists, and physicians. Merrell recognized that the withdrawal would be seized upon by plaintiffs lawyers and predicted their reaction:

> The product liability lawyers involved in the Bendectin litigation will seek to use the company's decision to remove Bendectin from the marketplace as evidence that the product causes birth defects. There is probably no way to prevent this from happening, because some in this group will be undeterred by the facts
> . . . .
> Plaintiffs' counsel will no doubt seek to uncover, through discovery, documents relating to the decision to discontinue Bendectin in hope that they can find some admission about liability.[20]

Yet with all of its extensive efforts, there is not a single mention of Rule 407, its application to the withdrawal decision, the body of law that had developed on this question, or the implications for the existing Bendectin litigation. The impact of Rule 407 on Merrell's decision to withdraw Bendectin was nil.

Surprisingly, Merrell resisted producing its withdrawal planning documents in MDL-486 when the PLCC sought it. Merrell's claim was that the documents were protected by the work product doctrine that shields the efforts of attorneys or their agents in preparing a lawsuit. The argument was that because the decision to withdraw the drug was a result of litigation, the planning and decision process were protected from discovery. The argument was legally dubious and strategically misguided. In claiming work product protection, Merrell's argument turned on its head the concept of protecting efforts *to prepare* for or conduct litigation, by seeking protection for business planning that was *the result* of litigation.[21]

Claiming work product protection was of dubious judgment, because the documentation would have demonstrated to the PLCC that the decision to withdraw Bendectin was motivated by financial concerns and not safety concerns or FDA pressure. Indeed, Arthur Hull Hayes, Chair of the FDA at the time, was most concerned to emphasize that Merrell's decision was voluntary and entirely independent of the FDA when he was first informed of the withdrawal in a meeting with Merrell the day before the public announcement.

One aspect of Merrell's plan, however, might have been of mild embarrassment to it. Merrell anticipated the political benefit it might gain from making Bendectin into a victim of an expansive, extravagant tort system and overzealous attorneys, and sought to capitalize on that prospect. Merrell's plans included prompting sympathetic editorials in medical journals that would tell the story of a safe and effective drug—the only one approved for morning sickness—being driven from the market because of unjustified products liability lawsuits. Doctors would be receptive to such a story, Merrell believed, because of their own discontent with malpractice liability and escalating insurance premiums. Detailpersons could be used to reinforce the message that Merrell sought to convey. Meetings with leaders in the medical community were contemplated. Merrell considered sponsoring symposia to address issues such as the impact of litigation on the delivery of health care. On the legal reform front, Bendectin would make an excellent example in support of federal products liability legislation, which had been introduced and debated in Congress since the late 1970s.

One final effect of Bendectin's withdrawal deserves mention. The withdrawal set the stage for the development of critical evidence that one informed observer, Judge Carl Rubin, believes made the difference in the subsequent MDL-486 trial.

Notes

1. The account of the cessation announcement is drawn from Statement by David B. Sharrock, President of Merrell-Dow Pharmaceuticals, U.S.A., announcing company's decision to discontinue production of Bendectin (June 9, 1983).

2. Ceasing production of Bendectin rather than withdrawing it from the market by abandoning its New Drug Application on file with the FDA left Merrell with more flexibility in marketing Bendectin in the future or overseas, as well as providing greater confidentiality for proprietary information in the NDA. Memorandum, Merrell T-Project 7–8 (undated).

3. *See* Transcript of Trial at 2751, 2778, Richardson v. Richardson-Merrell, Inc., Civ. No. 83-3505 (D.D.C. Aug. 25 & 26, 1986).

4. Andrew Skolnick, *Key Witness Against Morning Sickness Drug Faces Scientific Fraud Charges*, 263 JAMA 1468, 1469 (1990).

5. *See, e.g.*, PETER W. HUBER, GALILEO'S REVENGE: JUNK SCIENCE IN THE COURTROOM 129 (New York: Basic Books, 1991); David Williams, *How Nader Killed a Beneficial Drug*, HUM. EVENTS, Jan. 14, 1984, at 10–11.

6. Jane E. Brody, *Shadow of Doubt Wipes Out Bendectin*, N.Y. TIMES, June 19, 1983, at § IV3.

7. Jonathan Susskind, *Maker Ends Bendectin Production*, ORLANDO SENTINEL, June 10, 1983, at A1.

8. Bill Densmore, *Premium Hikes Force Dow to Halt Bendectin Production*, BUSINESS INSURANCE, June 20, 1983, at 25.

9. Letter from James G. Butler to attorney Wylie Aitken, et al. (June 23, 1983).

10. Memorandum of Meeting (BCDSP) (May 9, 1983) (authored by Charles Anello, FDA).

11. The explanation of the reasons for Merrell's withdrawal is based on documents prepared by Merrell in planning the cessation of production. Those documents were submitted to the MDL-486 court in camera.

12. *See, e.g.*, Elkins v. Richardson-Merrell, Inc., 8 F.3d 1068, 1069 (6th Cir. 1993) ("Faced with costly litigation . . . Merrell-Dow voluntarily withdrew the drug from the market in 1983"); Note, *A Question of Competence: The Judicial Role in the Regulation of Pharmaceuticals*, 103 Harv. L. Rev. 773, 775 (1990) (claiming Bendectin withdrawal is symbolic of a "developing crisis in health care"); David

Williams, *How Nader Killed a Beneficial Drug*, Hum. Events, Jan. 14, 1984, at 10–11; *see also* chapter 18.

13. The next day, the *New York Times* reported that "use of the drug has dropped off considerably in the last few years," apparently based on information provided by the FDA. *Company Stops Making Morning Sickness Drug*, N.Y. Times, June 10, 1983, at A16.

14. The first story was published in the *National Enquirer*. *New Thalidomide Scandal—Experts Reveal*, Nat'l Enquirer, Oct. 1979, at 1. The *National Enquirer* was alerted to the *Mekdeci* case and the Bendectin story by Melvin Belli. Telephone interview with Mrs. Elizabeth Mekdeci (Mar. 8, 1994).

15. Ralph C. Benson, Current Obstetrics & Gynecologic Diagnosis & Treatment 625 n.* (Los Altos, CA: Lange Medical Publications, 4th ed. 1982).

16. Deposition of David Sharrock at 78, MDL-486 (S.D. Ohio July 8, 1983); Memorandum of telephone conversation between Peter Rheinstein, FDA and Fred Lamb, Merrell National Laboratories (May 30, 1983).

17. 733 F.2d 463 (7th Cir. 1984).

18. *Id.* at 470.

19. Ault v. International Harvester Co., 528 P.2d 1148, 1152 (Cal. 1974); *see also* Sanderson v. Steve Snyder Enterprises, Inc., 491 A.2d 389, 395 (Conn. 1985) ("it is unlikely that any evidentiary use of subsequent remedial measures will discourage a designer or manufacturer from taking them").

20. Merrell Dow Pharmaceuticals, T-Project 30 (undated).

21. *See* Simon v. G. D. Searle & Co., 816 F.2d 397, 401 (8th Cir. 1986) (risk management documents prepared for financial oversight of defendant's products liability cases were not protected by work product doctrine), *cert. denied*, 484 U.S. 917 (1987); *accord In re* Pfizer Inc. Securities Litigation, 1993 U.S. Dist. LEXIS 18215 (S.D.N.Y. 1993). *But see* Rhone-Poulenc Rover Inc. v. The Home Indemnity Co., 139 F.R.D. 609 (E.D. Pa. 1991) (holding risk management estimates protected by work product doctrine; otherwise financing and planning a defense by an insurance company would be "extremely hazardous").

Chapter 12
Forging a Mass Toxic Substances Trial[1]

From the beginning of the MDL-486 litigation, Judge Rubin sent a clear message to the lawyers that it would not languish. At the first pretrial conference he announced to the assembled lawyers that they would have 18 months to complete discovery, at which time the non-Ohio cases would be returned to their home courts and the individual trials of the Ohio cases would begin. Even at that early stage, when the number of MDL-486 cases was still small, it became apparent that a significant proportion would be filed in the Southern District of Ohio. Lawyers who were not interested in or capable of trying Bendectin cases would either refer their clients to Stanley Chesley or associate with him, and those cases were filed in Cincinnati.

There was little reason for Judge Rubin or the parties to consider a multi-plaintiff trial at the outset of MDL-486. All non-Ohio cases would be returned to their home districts, unless a settlement or dismissal occurred, and would be tried there. Moreover, with only 45 cases nationwide, the necessity for a consolidated or class action trial was less than apparent.

Heedless about a common trial, the Multidistrict Panel had only casually considered the issues common to all the plaintiffs' suits. The Panel stated in its transfer order: "Common factual questions arise from the allegations in each action that birth defects were caused by the mother's ingestion during pregnancy of Bendectin . . . . "[2] That haphazard characterization masked the complexity of identifying a common issue for all claims, given the differences among various birth defects and the structure of the scientific evidence. During the ensuing years, the participants in MDL-486 would struggle to identify the common issues with a precision that would permit a consolidated trial.

The impetus for a mass trial emerged as more cases were filed during the MDL-486 proceedings. About a year after the multidistrict consolidation there were 100 Bendectin cases filed in the Southern District of Ohio and 130 other cases that had been transferred there pursuant to the Panel's orders. Some form of trial that could resolve more than one case at a time began to look considerably more attractive, especially to Judge Rubin, who mused about the possibility that trying each case separately might "immobilize me for the balance of my judicial career." [3] But at the time, the parties were still at an embryonic stage in their conceptualization of the issues that would have to be tried, those that might be common (and therefore susceptible to a mass trial) and those that were peculiar to each individual case and would require individualized determinations, such as damages.[4] The complexity, along with the dramatic increase in the number of Bendectin cases, resulted in a circuitous route to a consolidated trial of some 1,100 plaintiffs in 1985.

How did a small multidistrict case grow by over an order of magnitude within three years? Two reasons emerge. Stanley Chesley and the PLCC endeavored to encourage as many case filings as possible. The motivation was partially financial and partially tactical. The PLCC convinced Judge Rubin to issue an order assessing a $500 levy on each case in the multidistrict proceedings to defray the costs of discovery. In addition to the capitation fee (which most individual plaintiffs' attorneys ignored), attorneys fees awarded to the PLCC would be a function of the number of cases involved and the total recovery. The tactical motivation developed later during the discovery proceedings when the common issues discovery was heavy. Reversing the usual situation, the PLCC felt that it had Frank Woodside and his firm understaffed and scrambling to keep up with the demands of completing discovery within Judge Rubin's deadlines. Chesley and the PLCC hoped that encouraging individual plaintiffs' attorneys to engage in individual discovery in their home districts with obstetricians who had prescribed Bendectin, physicians who treated the birth defects, and others would contribute to overwhelming Woodside and distracting him from his multidistrict efforts.

In addition to burdening Woodside with supervising extensive local discovery, Chesley hoped that more cases would foster a greater interest by Merrell in settlement. As the stakes increase, settlement becomes more attractive to those who are risk averse. By increasing the number of claimants and the potential recovery, Chesley hoped to make settlement more attractive to Merrell.

Thus Chesley periodically sent letters to all plaintiffs' attorneys urging them to file their cases promptly. Typically, these solicitations were accompanied by a rose-colored lens assessment of the course of proceedings. As late as the spring of 1984, just a few months before trial was scheduled to begin, Chesley wrote: "We are confident of a favorable outcome at trial . . . ."

The second reason for the growth of Bendectin cases was an unequivocal plaintiff's verdict in *Oxendine v. Merrell Dow Pharmaceuticals Inc.*, on May 27, 1983. Barry Nace filed *Oxendine* in the local court in Washington, DC, and the case could not be transferred and consolidated in the MDL-486 proceeding. *Oxendine* remained in the local District of Columbia court, and the case proceeded to trial against Merrell. The jury found that Bendectin caused Mary Oxendine's birth defects and assessed damages at $750,000.[5]

The *Oxendine* verdict and the subsequent withdrawal of Bendectin provided a boost to the plaintiff's efforts. As explained in chapter 11, the PLCC was convinced that the withdrawal of Bendectin reflected a new and devastating development with regard to its teratogenicity. *Oxendine* demonstrated that Bendectin cases were winnable. Over a hundred new cases poured into the multidistrict proceedings during the summer of 1983 in response to these developments. By the fall of 1983, the MDL-486 docket contained hundreds of individual actions filed by numerous law firms scattered across the United States. Not incidentally, the PLCC brought new energy and dedication to the common issues discovery.

The increase in the number of cases, especially those filed in Ohio, generated a rethinking of the individual trial plan. Judge Rubin had the authority to consolidate all the Southern District of Ohio cases not only for pretrial purposes, but for trial as well.[6] In addition to the efficiency of a collective trial, Judge Rubin raised another apprehension:

> [I]f you have a common issue of liability and you submit it to five juries, you can get five different viewpoints and somebody, I think, gets hurt. . . . I think that doesn't make sense. If the issue is common, let's select one jury and try that issue.[7]

Judge Rubin became convinced that individual trials for each claimant were unrealistic and infeasible. He encouraged the parties to identify a collective mechanism to meet the demands of the increasing number of Bendectin cases. A pattern developed at the periodic pretrial conferences as the parties struggled to respond, rarely finding common ground. Judge Rubin would unleash his assault weapon and threaten all the attorneys with it: If no agreement were forthcoming, he would try all of the cases individually, one after another. He would continue by proceeding to determine the number of pending cases, divide by 50 (on the assumption that an individual case could be tried in a week), and use that number as the number of years that he and the attorneys would be together in his courtroom trying Bendectin cases. By the fall of 1983, with 360 cases pending, Judge Rubin was threatening seven years of Bendectin trials, one after a mind-numbing other.

The PLCC responded to Judge Rubin's urgings by proposing that a sample of cases be selected and tried. Stanley Chesley was familiar with the test case concept from his involvement in the Agent Orange litigation, where Judge Weinstein adopted that structure to try the causal issues.[8] Crucial to the PLCC's strategy was to present to the jury plaintiffs with a variety of birth defects who would demonstrate the heart-rending consequences of the drug. As Tom Bleakley wrote to other members of the PLCC: "The presence of real children in [the trial] would be the humanizing factor that, in my opinion, is essential to the litigation."[9] Thus emerged the PLCC's position that the consolidated trial proceed by trying a dozen or two sample cases that would represent different classes of birth defects and resolve the question of Bendectin's teratogenicity for each of those classes. Separate damages determinations would later be required, but the hope was that the resolution of those cases would serve as a practical barometer for settling the remainder of the cases. Throughout the common trial discussions, the PLCC adhered to its sample trial proposal.

Merrell was genuinely conflicted about its preferences. The primary concern was that a common issues trial in Ohio would subject Merrell to enormous risk without equivalent benefit. Merrell knew that there were thousands upon thousands of potential claims lurking in the shadows of past Bendectin use. With approximately 100,000 children born with birth defects each year, Bendectin use ranging from 10 to 30 percent among pregnant women, and an 18-year statute of limitations in most states, the magnitude of potential claims was staggering. Losing a common issues trial in Ohio could estop Merrell, based on the doctrine of offensive collateral estoppel, from contesting Bendectin's teratogenicity in all later claims. Of course, the same risk existed even in an individual case, such as *Oxendine.*

Collateral estoppel permits—with qualifications—the resolution of an issue in one case to be employed in a subsequent case. The Supreme Court had approved this use of collateral estoppel—by a new plaintiff against a party who had previously lost on the issue—for federal claims in 1979, and a number of state courts had followed suit.[10] To some, offensive collateral estoppel provided an efficient mechanism for resolving mass tort claims. Indeed, offensive collateral estoppel had been employed by a beleaguered federal trial judge in asbestos litigation, and although that decision was reversed, collateral estoppel posed a significant risk for Merrell.[11] The risk was not reciprocal, however, because litigants cannot be estopped based on the outcome of a case in which they were not parties. Thus, all those claimants who were not a party to a common issues trial could not be estopped by a decision favorable to Merrell in a common trial, but they were able to use an adverse decision against Merrell as the basis for estoppel.[12]

On the other hand, Merrell had already tasted the sour consequences of individual case adjudications. That experience led it to seek multidistrict consolidation to avoid the debilitating effects of defending itself repeatedly throughout the country.

Merrell's concerns led it to two dramatically inconsistent positions. First, Merrell requested that Judge Rubin certify Bendectin litigation as a class action. Merrell sought a class that would consist of all those with claims that Bendectin had caused a child's birth defects. Consistent with its concern about future claims, Merrell advocated a mandatory class that would include the cases of all claimants. Because Bendectin had been removed from the market, the class included virtually all claimants save a small number then in utero who would later be born. Unlike the more typical class action, no claimants would be permitted to choose to exclude themselves from the class action suit. This arrangement would ensure that Merrell would not face asymmetrical risks at the trial. Consistent with its advocacy for certification of a mandatory class, Merrell characterized the common issue as "whether Bendectin has been proven to be a human teratogen and, if so, the nature of the birth defects it is alleged to cause." [13]

But a mandatory class is unusual and reserved for extraordinary situations such as when there are so many claimants to a limited fund that it may be exhausted before all claimants have the opportunity to come forward.[14] Merrell made only a half-hearted attempt to argue that it fell within this category, and it was reduced to asserting that Judge Rubin should ignore the decisions of two courts of appeals that had earlier overturned mandatory classes in mass tort actions, in the Dalkon Shield and Hyatt Regency Skywalk cases.[15] The PLCC had an easy time arguing that certifying a mandatory class was improper (although nine months later, after settlement, it would take a contrary position).

Judge Rubin refused to certify a class action as the means to a common issues trial. In doing so he raised a concern that the parties had not addressed, namely the problem of differences in state law. Federal courts sitting in diversity are obligated to apply the substantive law (and choice of law) of the state in which they sit. Most states would apply their own substantive law to a case involving a resident plaintiff injured in that state. With hundreds of cases that had been filed in federal courts nationwide, Judge Rubin would be forced to apply different substantive law to different class members, a confusing and largely unmanageable task when a jury trial is required. The concern about differing state law was not unique to a class action; virtually any attempt at a common issues trial for multi-state plaintiffs would suffer this infirmity.[16]

After Judge Rubin's denial of a class action, Merrell reverted to a diametrically inconsistent position, that "causation is not an issue that is susceptible of trial on a consolidated basis. The issue as to whether Bendectin has caused any particular plaintiff's birth defect can only be decided after an analysis of the facts and circumstances of the individual case."[17] Driven by the concern that an adverse determination on causation would be used against it in subsequent litigation, Merrell argued that there were no common causation questions.[18]

Frank Woodside thereafter repeatedly stressed to Judge Rubin the individualistic aspect of causation in the Bendectin cases. He could do this because there were individual aspects to the causation question, though there were also common aspects. Thus Woodside could point out that a small proportion of birth defects were known to be of genetic or environmental causes. In each case, the question whether one of the known causes of the plaintiff's birth defect might explain it was an individual issue. Another individual issue Woodside repeatedly stressed to Judge Rubin was whether a plaintiff's mother took Bendectin during the period of organogenesis.

Woodside's instincts in emphasizing the individual aspects of causation were quite sound. Merrell had a much stronger case on the question whether Bendectin caused a given child's birth defects than on whether Bendectin was capable of causing birth defects. Although most of the epidemiological studies conducted of Bendectin did not find substantial associations between Bendectin and birth defects, they were not powerful enough to rule out the possibility that Bendectin had a weak teratogenic effect.[19] With that lack of power, along with some of the toxicology studies, plaintiffs might make a plausible case that Bendectin was capable of causing birth defects, however weakly. Of course, any such determination in a common issues case would draw new Bendectin cases galore, even if Merrell would still have specific causation to litigate in individual resolutions after the MDL-486 common issues trial.

The advocacy by the parties and lack of clear understanding about the scientific structure of evidence of causation did little to clarify the issues for Judge Rubin. At one point, he inquired of counsel: "It can't be a teratogen in one instance and not the other, can it?" Stanley Chesley quickly jumped in and agreed, out of either ignorance or advocacy. Jim Butler interrupted to correct Chesley and explain, correctly, that a teratogen, like any toxic agent, does not necessarily affect everyone. Cigarette smoking vastly increases the risk of lung cancer, but the great bulk of smokers do not get lung cancer. In response to Butler, Judge Rubin inquired: "Then it is not a common issue?" Woodside responded, "That is our position. You now perceive our problem." What Woodside glossed over is that while the teratogenicity of Bendectin is not a sufficient condition for plaintiffs to prevail on causation it is a necessary one. Moreover, the issue was sufficiently in doubt that a trial on that question alone might provide an efficient mechanism for resolving the plaintiffs' claims, especially if the jury were to find that Bendectin was not a teratogen, thereby foreclosing recovery and concluding the cases.

By the end of 1983 Judge Rubin was determined to conduct some form of common issues trial, even if he was perplexed about what those common issues were. On November 16, 1983 he issued an order consolidating for trial all cases that had been filed in the Northern or Southern Districts of Ohio.[20] In addition, all non-Ohio cases that had been transferred pursuant to the multidistrict litigation could choose to participate in the common issues trial. To do so, however, the plaintiffs would have to consent to the use of Ohio law in litigating the common issues. If the plaintiffs lost in the common issues trial, that would resolve their cases; if they succeeded, the cases would be returned to their home districts to address the remaining individual issues. In essence, Judge Rubin created a nonmandatory class, similar to a class defined by rule 23(b)(3) of the Federal Rules of Civil Procedure but requiring claimants affirmatively to opt into the class, reversing the rule 23(b)(3) presumption that claimants are included in the class unless they opt out. While providing a framework for a common issues trial, Judge Rubin deferred to the parties on the question of what the common issues would be.

The parties' responses only further muddied the common issues waters. Merrell nominally opposed the trial of any general causation question and continued to insist that causation was an individual matter, while suggesting that trying the issue whether scientific evidence established that Bendectin caused a recognizable pattern of birth defects would be appropriate. By contrast, the PLCC's proposed common issues included several specifications of negligent wrongdoing by Merrell, breach of warranty, strict liability, fraud, and a curious causation issue that would have resolved all plaintiffs' causation questions in one miraculous fell swoop: "Whether Merrell's acts of omission and commission were substantial contributing factors in the development of birth defects of the minor plaintiffs."

Judge Rubin attempted to fill the common issues vacuum left by the parties inability to agree. After acknowledging their failure to concur, he set forth the three common issues that he would try in the consolidated trial: 1) whether Bendectin causes any of nine distinct types of birth defects (such as limb, genito-urinary, or heart defects); 2) whether Bendectin is unreasonably dangerous; and 3) whether Merrell provided adequate warnings of Bendectin's dangers.

The nine categories Judge Rubin employed derived from an earlier settlement effort he had made. In an attempt to facilitate a settlement, Judge Rubin had written to the parties recommending subclasses be established and asking that the PLCC separate all plaintiffs into separate categories by type of birth defect.[21] The categories the PLCC employed in its response were the categories Judge Rubin subsequently employed in his order setting the common issues.[22] Unfortunately, the taxonomy employed by the PLCC was not prepared with common causal mechanisms in mind. As one expert at trial explained, a single category contained a variety of birth defects that have very different causes.[23] Thus it would have been preferable to have selected the categories based on what was known about the causal mechanisms of birth defects or based on the scientific evidence that would be introduced rather than the categories constructed by the PLCC to facilitate settlement discussions. Unfortunately, because of the parties' failure to agree on the common issues, Judge Rubin was operating without the input of counsel and their access to scientific information.

The common issues trial was scheduled to begin on June 11, 1984. Non-Ohio plaintiffs could choose to participate in the trial before February 1, 1984; anyone who had previously chosen to opt in could void that choice before May 1, 1984. MDL-486 was in the home-stretch of its race toward trial.

Judge Rubin repeatedly advocated the use of court-appointed experts in the common issues trial. He even wrote to the FDA and AMA seeking their assistance in locating appropriate individuals. Expressing great skepticism about the credibility of experts hired by the parties, Judge Rubin paraphrased an apprehension expressed by Learned Hand eighty years previously: "[A] jury of six people who know even less about teratology than I do are going to have to make a decision as to which experts to believe."[24]

The PLCC, facing FDA approval of Bendectin that had been repeatedly examined and reaffirmed, the development of a large body of epidemiological evidence in the early 1980s, and the emerging consensus within the teratology and epidemiology fields that Bendectin was not a teratogen, strenuously resisted Judge Rubin's suggestions. The PLCC was forced to argue that virtually all experts were tainted by some connection to Merrell, and that no independent unbiased experts were available. There was some basis to their claim: Merrell had funded a number of the researchers who had studied Bendectin and had contacted and hired others to serve as expert witnesses on its behalf.[25] Merrell also had established relationships with many other prominent obstetricians and pediatricians. Yet, ultimately, the PLCC's claim was just not credible. Judge Rubin expressed his incredulity: "I simply refuse to believe that nowhere in this world can I find people who have no particular axe to grind and who can advise me without any interest in the outcome of what the case is all about." [26] Despite his convictions, Judge Rubin, like so many other judges, never did appoint any experts in MDL-486, and the case was tried with experts hired only by the parties.

During the late winter and spring of 1984 three significant developments had a major impact on MDL-486. The first occurred at a pretrial conference when Judge Rubin had an epistemological epiphany about the causation issues in MDL-486; the second involved a series of evidentiary rulings by Judge Rubin in anticipation of trial; and the final matter concerned Stanley Chesley and Frank Woodside's settlement efforts.

Judge Rubin's epiphany occurred at a pretrial conference on March 19, 1984, when he realized for the first time that causation would be dispositive of all plaintiffs' liability claims if the jury found for Merrell. This recognition occurred when Stanley Chesley pointed out to Judge Rubin that his common issues order omitted trial of the plaintiffs' negligence claims, which provided an alternative theory for holding Merrell liable. At that point Frank Woodside interceded to assert that the causation question that Judge Rubin was to try would be dispositive of *all* theories of liability. In other words, liability and causation are independent and each essential elements for a plaintiff to recover. Rubin, confused, responded by inquiring whether there could be negligence if there was no causation. Once again, Woodside explained that a lack of causation would be dispositive. Judge Rubin began to see through the fog, remarking "this is like looking at something through field glasses and it gets in and out of focus."

When Judge Rubin finally absorbed Woodside's point, Fed. R. Civ. P. 42(b) provided the instrument for putting this newfound knowledge to work. Issues related to liability and causation could be separated for trial, and the causation question tried first. With two months left before the beginning of the trial, Judge Rubin ordered a bifurcated trial, with "all issues involving causation" to be tried first and all liability (i.e., breach of duty) matters tried later.

Judge Rubin's "trifurcation" of the MDL-486 trial, as the Sixth Circuit Court of Appeals later characterized it,[27] was probably the most important and most controversial of his many rulings during the course of the case. The separation of causation and liability meant that the purely scientific question of whether Bendectin increased the risk of various birth defects would be presented separately to the jury. Rubin's decision "trifurcated" the case because, after those two issues were resolved, damages would have to be addressed in individualized hearings. As Rubin observed in his Order: "Should plaintiffs prevail upon causation issues, the jury will hear and then consider the [liability matters]. A defendant's verdict on the issue of causation will terminate the trial."[28]

While Judge Rubin's observations about the implications of a defense verdict on the "can it cause" issue were correct, his belief that all causation issues could be resolved in the common issues trial was not. Although the parties' advocacy efforts obscured it, a finding that Bendectin caused birth defects would not conclude the question of causation. Even if Bendectin causes birth defects, it plainly does not cause every birth defect, as all of the birth defects with which Bendectin was implicated had existed long before Bendectin was formulated. In short, there were no "signature" birth defects that necessarily implied Bendectin etiology, as exists, for example, with asbestos and asbestosis. Thus a secondary question for every Bendectin claimant was whether that individual's birth defect was caused by Bendectin or whether Bendectin was an innocent merely along for a ride that would have terminated at the same destination.[29] The structure of the scientific evidence to be presented in MDL-486 would not address that question, and it would necessarily arise if plaintiffs succeeded in the general causation phase. Indeed, Judge Rubin had not so much trifurcated MDL-486, as he had "polyfurcated" it, with several additional phases of trials required if plaintiffs succeeded in each of the prior ones.

The structure ultimately settled upon by Judge Rubin was devastating to the PLCC for two reasons. First, trying causation alone meant that plaintiffs would not be able to present evidence of Merrell's culpability to the jury during the first phase of the trifurcated procedure. To personal injury lawyers, negligence or fault is "hot," while strict liability and, a fortiori, causation is "cold."[30] Juries, reflecting human nature, are provoked by a highly culpable defendant, but Judge Rubin's bifurcation order meant that the plaintiffs would not be able to present that evidence while trying the most problematical aspect of their case—causation. The initial causation trial would be a cold, analytical, and scientific inquiry about Bendectin and birth defects.

The PLCC repeatedly complained about the "sterile laboratory atmosphere" this would create and referred to an earlier case that Judge Rubin had bifurcated, the *In re Beverly Hills Fire Litigation*.[31] Although the Court of Appeals had upheld Rubin's bifurcation decision, it expressed concern that bifurcation "may deprive plaintiffs of their legitimate right to place before the jury the circumstances and atmosphere of the entire cause of action . . . replacing it with a sterile or laboratory atmosphere in which causation is parted from the reality of injury." [32] The concern of the court appears to be that the jury should fully appreciate the consequences and importance of its causation inquiry. Because of the infamy of the Beverly Hills Supper Club fire, the court expressed the view that Judge Rubin had not abused his discretion, but at the same time indicated uneasiness with the bifurcated proceeding. The strongest argument the PLCC could muster was that for it to show the inadequacy of studies exonerating Bendectin as a teratogen required evidence of improper and inadequate test methods. Judge Rubin was unyielding:

> I don't care if they were improper, Mr. Eaton. Let me assume for a moment that Merrell Dow puts out a sugar pill. And they advertise it as a great diet reducer. It isn't worth a damn. They don't test it. They crush some sugar and put it in a pill and put it on the market. You come along and say, "Hey, that doesn't work. You guys didn't test it." They say "Yep, that's right, we didn't test it." That's got nothing to do with it. If it doesn't cause birth defects, Mr. Eaton, it doesn't matter what they did. [33]

Judge Rubin's response missed the key point Allen Eaton was trying to make. Merrell's misfeasance had nothing to do with the efficacy of Bendectin but bore on the probative value of the tests it had performed to assess Bendectin's teratogenicity. Yet, although Judge Rubin excluded evidence that tended to show fraud or impropriety in Merrell's scientific testing (the Smithells letter seeking funds in exchange for a favorable study was excluded), he did permit plaintiffs to explore inadequacies and errors in the design and conduct of studies of Bendectin, including the one performed for Merrell by Bunde and Bowles. [34]

The second problem with the structure of the trial was the ethical dilemma it posed for the PLCC. Causation was actually to be tried as nine subissues, with each of nine broad categories of birth defects separately considered. As Tom Bleakley had recognized a year earlier, [35] the scientific evidence and expert witnesses were not consistent across all birth defects. For some birth defects there was a stronger scientific basis for a finding of causation; for others there was a weaker one. Some witnesses who might be helpful on one category of birth defect could be harmful on others. Decisions had to be made about which defects to emphasize, whether to sponsor or attack studies that lumped all birth defects together in investigating Bendectin, and more generally to emphasize or play down the concept of specificity of effect—the idea that most toxins cause a specific effect or pattern of effects and not shotgun effects. Yet these decisions pitted some subgroup of Bendectin claimants against another subgroup, all of whom the PLCC would be representing at trial.

Perhaps the best indication of the PLCC's antipathy to the MDL-486 trial structure was how they voted with their cases. Jim Butler, Tom Bleakley, and George Kokus all decided to pull their cases out of the common issues trial. Stanley Chesley, who had filed his cases in Ohio, didn't have that option. Other lawyers, who were knowledgeable about Bendectin litigation and who felt capable of trying individual cases, like Art Tifford and Barry Nace, also kept their cases out of the MDL-486 trial.

While the trifurcation decision was the most significant in structuring the trial, several other rulings by Judge Rubin had an important impact on the trial. In the spring of 1984, during the final lap of pretrial preparation, Merrell filed a flurry of motions addressing the admissibility of various pieces of evidence. This effort succeeded in whittling away at some of the most powerful, yet dubiously relevant, pieces of the plaintiffs' case.

The first matter involved Judge Rubin's dogged insistence that thalidomide and MER/29 would not rear their heads in the consolidated trial. That decision was first made early in the discovery proceedings and consistently adhered to by Judge Rubin, despite repeated attempts by the PLCC to have him reconsider. Judge Rubin's ruling was consistent with similar decisions in *Mekdeci* (where the evidence was excluded at trial) and *Koller* (where Judge Johnson ruled it not discoverable), but nevertheless a bitter disappointment to the PLCC. As late as a month before the trial was scheduled to begin Judge Rubin reiterated his views to the PLCC: "The first time you mention Thalidomide, I will declare a mistrial." [36]

The second decision concerned the admissibility of Merrell's withdrawal of Bendectin from the market. Plaintiffs sought to introduce this evidence because the jury might draw the intimation that the withdrawal was motivated by concern about the drug's teratogenicity. Merrell was very apprehensive that that was precisely the inference a jury might draw and consequently argued vigorously for its exclusion. Judge Rubin had already provided his preliminary inclination to do just that in July 1983 right after the withdrawal was announced. He confirmed that inclination and granted Merrell's motion to exclude any evidence about Bendectin's withdrawal.

Merrell next sought to prevent the PLCC from introducing any epidemiological study unless it found an association that was statistically significant at the .95 level. As mentioned in chapter 3, statistical significance is used as an instrument to address sampling error. It assesses the plausibility that any positive association found in a study would have occurred if Bendectin truly is not a teratogen. While statistical significance played no role in the MDL-486 trial because Judge Rubin denied the motion, [37] the effort was a continuation of Merrell's strategy throughout the Bendectin litigation to persuade courts to reject any study that found an association between Bendectin and birth defects unless the finding was statistically significant. Merrell had first succeeded in this effort in the *Koller* case. There Judge Johnson not only ruled that any epidemiological study used by plaintiffs had to be statistically significant at the .95 level, but also held on her own initiative that any attack by the plaintiff on an epidemiological study that found no association between Bendectin and birth defects could not be made unless the errors identified would result in a statistically significant finding.[38] As chapter 17 explains, Merrell had additional successes in this effort in later Bendectin cases, and the issue remains a controversial one in the law applied to toxic substances cases.

Frank Woodside argued that the scientific community requires that an association be statistically significant at the .95 level before it is accepted as real rather than as a spurious result. Since the causation question to be tried was a scientific question, Woodside reasoned, its conventions should be employed as well. Contrary to Woodside's claims, however, the question how much random error the legal system should tolerate and how it should trade off different kinds of random error is a legal question, not a scientific one.[39] The relatively conservative requirement of significance at the .95 level (to which many biostatisticians no longer adhere) screens out evidence that may be quite valuable in trying to determine whether a causal relationship exists. Although quite unsophisticated about statistical techniques, Judge Rubin intuitively smelled a rat: "There's something about this, Dr. Woodside, that troubles me. . . . I think you are engrafting a scientific concept on legal principles and it doesn't work."[40] Ultimately, Judge Rubin denied Merrell's motion.[41]

The final issue concerned the presence of the children-plaintiffs in the courtroom. Initially the question arose merely as one of logistics—the courtroom was not large enough to accommodate several hundred children. Judge Rubin announced his intention to exclude all children who were so young that they could not be of assistance to counsel at trial. The PLCC recommended that five representative plaintiffs for each of the nine categories of birth defects be permitted in the courtroom. Frank Woodside urged Rubin to exclude all children, but Rubin temporized—requesting the parties to provide briefs on the issue—vaguely aware that there might be applicable precedent he should consider.

The underlying concern is the ages-old problem of sympathy for the injured plaintiff overcoming rational assessment of the evidence.[42] The concern was well put 150 years ago in *Haring v. New York & Erie R.R. Co.*,[43] in one of the first cases the common law courts confronted involving the remarkable technological development of the railroad:

We can not shut our eyes that in certain controversies between the weak and the strong—between a humble individual and a gigantic corporation, the sympathies of the human mind naturally, honestly and generously, run to the assistance and support of the feeble . . . ; compassion will sometimes exercise over the deliberations of a jury, an influence which, however honorable to them as philanthropists, is wholly inconsistent with the principles of law and the ends of justice.[44]

Injured plaintiffs at trial and the emotional reaction to them and the conflict with legal principles reflect a larger paradox. When confronted with paying for safety precautions ex ante—say for mine safety—society will spend only a fraction of what it spends for rescue after a cave-in when an identifiable life is at stake. No one inquires whether rescue efforts are "worth it" in the ex post situation.[45] Injured plaintiffs are the courtroom legal analog of the trapped coal miner.

The Court of Appeals in the Agent Orange litigation justified the $180 million settlement on concerns that jury sympathy might result in an erroneous verdict. Although the court was persuaded that defendants should prevail on the merits, it recognized that the settlement nevertheless reflected a real concern by defendants. Recognizing that the "settlement was essentially a payment of nuisance value," juror sympathy for the injured plaintiffs nevertheless created a real but small risk of a verdict adverse to the defendants.[46]

Yet the adjudicatory process has long protected this advantage for tort plaintiffs.[47] Because a plaintiff's physical condition is always relevant to the appropriate damages to be awarded and there has been strong reluctance to bifurcating an individual case, the plaintiff's presence is invariably justified. Beyond the evidentiary value, there is the principle that the opportunity to be present and observe when one's rights are being adjudicated is fundamental to the concept of due process. Also justifying the presence of the plaintiff is the assistance she may provide to her attorney during the procedure. Thus tort plaintiffs almost always benefit from the sympathy factor, however powerful with the given jury. This bias is often justified by pointing to the countervailing force of defendants' greater resources available to devote to defending themselves,[48] a justification that, however legitimate, surely had less force in the MDL-486 aggregated proceeding.

After the trifurcation decision, the presence of children in the courtroom during the causation phase could hardly be justified either because their condition was relevant to the jury's inquiry or because they could be of assistance to their attorneys, who were trying the scientific question whether Bendectin was capable of causing birth defects. Indeed, for many of the younger children, their presence could not even be justified on the ground that presence and cognition of the proceedings is an important procedural right. Judge Rubin excluded all children under 10 as well as all children with visible birth defects from the causation hearing.

Sensitive to their (and their parents') interests, Rubin arranged for a separate room in the courtroom to be outfitted with closed-circuit television, equipped with a telephone line to the PLCC in the courtroom, and staffed with experienced nurses so that parents could attend the trial if they desired.[49]

On June 11, 1984 Judge Rubin, the lawyers for both sides, representatives of Merrell, many plaintiffs, potential jurors, and the media gathered in courtroom 805 of the United States Courthouse in Cincinnati for the commencement of the *Bendectin Products Liability Litigation* trial. The first order was selection of the jury, which proceeded for two days. However, before the next stage—opening statements—commenced, Judge Rubin issued a curious order. Several pending criminal cases required attention because of the federal Speedy Trial Act. The Bendectin trial required continuation until July 23, 1984 to accommodate the criminal cases.

The invocation of the Speedy Trial Act was a ruse; Rubin was far too competent a manager of his docket to permit an interruption of a major multidistrict trial he had planned for months. In fact, Frank Woodside and Stanley Chesley had agreed to a settlement in principle, and more time was required to hammer out the details. MDL-486 entered the settlement phase.

Notes

1. This chapter is based on transcripts of pretrial conferences in MDL-486, correspondence among the attorneys involved in the case, motions, and documents filed in the case, and interviews with Judge Carl Rubin, Frank Woodside, George Kokus, Thomas Bleakley, and Stanley Chesley.

2. *In re* Richardson-Merrell Inc. Products Liability Litigation, 533 F. Supp. 489, 490 (J.P.M.L. 1982).

3. Transcript of Pretrial Conference at 27, *In re* Richardson-Merrell, Inc. "Bendectin" Products Liability Litigation, MDL-486 (S.D. Ohio July 1, 1983).

4. *But see* Cimino v. Raymark Industries, 751 F. Supp. 649, 664–65 (E.D. Tex. 1990) (employing statistical techniques to extrapolate damage awards based on damage awards in a representative sample of cases); *see also* Michael J. Saks & Peter D. Blanck, *Justice Improved: The Unrecognized Benefits of Aggregation and Sampling in the Trial of Mass Torts*, 44 STAN. L. REV. 815 (1992); Robert G. Bone, *Statistical Adjudication: Rights, Justice, and Utility in a World of Process Scarcity*, 46 VAND. L. REV. 561 (1993).

5. The judgment against Merrell was reduced by the $300,000 settlement with Upjohn. Letter from Alfred Schretter, Attorney for Marion Merrell Dow to author (June 11, 1994).

6. *See* Fed. R. Civ. P. 42(a); 28 U.S.C. § 1404(b) (1988 & Supp. 1995).

7. Transcript of Pretrial Conference at 39, *In re* Richardson-Merrell, Inc. "Bendectin" Products Liability Litigation, MDL-486 (S.D. Ohio Apr. 30, 1982).

For an account of five juries hearing the identical evidence simultaneously and doing precisely what Judge Rubin described, *see* Michael D. Green, *The Inability of Offensive Collateral Estoppel to Fulfill Its Promise: An Examination of Estoppel in Asbestos Litigation*, 70 Iowa L. Rev. 141, 221–23, 228–35 (1984).

8. *In re* "Agent Orange" Products Liability Litigation, 100 F.R.D. 718 (E.D.N.Y. 1983).

9. Letter to PLCC from Tom Bleakley (Nov. 28, 1983).

10. *See* Parklane Hosiery Co. v. Shore, 439 U.S. 322 (1979). The question whether federal or state preclusion laws apply where one of the courts involved is a federal court sitting in diversity is a complicated one that the Supreme Court has not yet resolved. *See* Stephen B. Burbank, *Interjurisdictional Preclusion, Full Faith and Credit and Federal Common Law: A General Approach*, 71 Cornell L. Rev. 733 (1986); Ronan E. Degnan, *Federalized Res Judicata*, 85 Yale L.J. 741 (1976).

11. *See* Green, *supra* note 7.

12. Precisely because of the concern that some claimants might sit on the sidelines and await the outcome of another trial, the Supreme Court had suggested in *Parklane* that this might be a situation where nonparties should not be permitted to employ offensive collateral estoppel.

13. Defendant Merrell Dow Pharmaceuticals Inc.'s Response to the Court's Order to Show Cause at 3, *In re* Richardson-Merrell, Inc. "Bendectin" Products Liability Litigation, MDL-486 (S.D. Ohio Sept. 30, 1983).

14. For the arguments in favor of employing mandatory classes in mass tort cases, see Note, *Class Certification in Mass Accident Cases Under Rule 23(b)(1)*, 96 Harv. L. Rev. 1143 (1983). Virtually all of the benefits touted can be obtained through multi-district transfer, consolidation or optional class actions, and informal cooperation among plaintiffs' attorneys.

15. *In re* Northern District of California Dalkon Shield IUD Products Liability Litigation, 693 F.2d 847 (9th Cir.), *cert. denied*, 459 U.S. 1171 (1983); *In re* Federal Skywalk Cases, 680 F.2d 1175 (8th Cir.), *cert. denied*, 459 U.S. 988 (1982).

16. *See generally* Barbara Atwood, *The Choice-of-Law Dilemma in Mass Tort Litigation: Kicking Around* Erie, Klaxon, *and* Van Dusen, 19 Conn. L. Rev. 9 (1986); Friedrich K. Juenger, *Mass Disasters and the Conflict of Laws*, 1989 U. Ill. L. Rev. 105 (1989); William D. Torchiana, Comment, *Choice of Law and the Multistate Class: Forum Interests in Matters Distant*, 134 U. Pa. L. Rev. 913 (1986). A proposal to solve the choice of law problem for multi-state mass torts is contained in American Law Institute, Complex Litigation Project § 6.01 (Philadelphia: American Law Institute, Proposed Final Draft 1993).

17. Defendant's Memorandum as to Common Issue of Liability for Consolidated Trial at 14, *In re* Richardson-Merrell, Inc. "Bendectin" Products Liability Litigation, MDL-486 (S.D. Ohio Dec. 15, 1983).

18. *Id.* at 2.

19. Professor Joseph Sanders, who has reviewed the expert testimony in six Bendectin trials, reports that "Merrell also increasingly based its entire case on general causation . . . . Merrell offered . . . very limited evidence disputing specific causation." Nor did Merrell argue that any relative risk less than 2.0 would be inadequate to prove individual causation by a preponderance of the evidence. Joseph Sanders, *From Science to Evidence: The Testimony on Causation in Bendectin Cases*, 46 Stan. L. Rev. 1, 55, 57 (1993).

20. Judge Rubin assumed that all cases filed in Ohio would be governed by Ohio law. That assumption failed to take into account that many of those cases arose in other states and were referred to Stanley Chesley to be filed in Cincinnati. As Merrell later pointed out to Judge Rubin, Ohio would likely apply the law of the state where the plaintiff resided and the child suffered the birth defect.

Mitchell v. General Motors Corp., 439 F. Supp. 24, 27 (N.D. Ohio 1977). Thus, at least some of those cases might have been governed by other states' substantive law.

21. Letter from Judge Carl B. Rubin to Frank C. Woodside & Stanley M. Chesley (Dec. 8, 1983).

22. Order, *In re* Richardson-Merrell, Inc. "Bendectin" Products Liability Litigation, MDL-486 (S.D. Ohio Dec. 29, 1983).

23. Transcript of Trial at 1998, *In re* Richardson-Merrell, Inc. "Bendectin" Products Liability Litigation, MDL-486 (S.D. Ohio Feb. 21, 1985) (testimony of Brian MacMahon).

24. Transcript of Pretrial Conference at 21, *In re* Richardson-Merrell, Inc. "Bendectin" Products Liability Litigation, MDL-486 (S.D. Ohio Apr. 29, 1983). Hand's admonition is contained in Learned Hand, *Historical and Practical Considerations Regarding Expert Testimony,* 15 Harv. L. Rev. 40, 54–55 (1901).

25. Letter from W. Glenn Forrester, attorney for Marion Merrell Dow, to author (Nov. 29, 1994).

26. Transcript of Pretrial Conference at 26, *In re* Richardson-Merrell, Inc. "Bendectin" Products Liability Litigation, MDL-486 (S.D. Ohio Apr. 29, 1983).

27. *In re* Bendectin Litigation, 857 F.2d 290, 306 (6th Cir. 1988), *cert. denied,* 488 U.S. 1006 (1989).

28. Order, *In re* Richardson-Merrell, Inc. "Bendectin" Products Liability Litigation, MDL-486 (S.D. Ohio Apr. 12, 1984).

29. *See* chapter 3.

30. *See* Paul D. Rheingold, *The Expanding Liability of the Product Supplier: A Primer,* 2 Hofstra L. Rev. 521, 531–32 (1974).

31. 695 F.2d 207 (6th Cir. 1982), *cert. denied,* 461 U.S. 929 (1983).

32. *Id.* at 217.

33. Transcript of Final Pretrial Conference at 3, *In re* Richardson-Merrell, Inc. "Bendectin" Products Liability Litigation, MDL-486 (S.D. Ohio May 11, 1984).

34. *In re* Bendectin Litigation, 857 F.2d 290, 317–19 (6th Cir. 1988), *cert. denied,* 488 U.S. 1006 (1989).

35. Memorandum to Plaintiff's Bendectin head counsel by Tom Bleakley (Apr. 5, 1983).

36. Transcript of Final Pretrial Conference at 5, *In re* Richardson-Merrell, Inc. "Bendectin" Products Liability Litigation, MDL-486 (S.D. Ohio May 11, 1984).

37. Order, *In re* Richardson-Merrell, Inc. "Bendectin" Products Liability Litigation, MDL-486 (S.D. Ohio Feb. 19, 1985) (Docket No. 2862).

38. Memorandum Opinion, Koller v. Richardson-Merrell Inc., Civ. No. 80–1258 (D.D.C. Feb. 26, 1983).

39. *See* Michael D. Green, *Expert Witnesses and Sufficiency of Evidence in Toxic Substances Litigation: The Legacy of Bendectin and* Agent Orange *Litigation,* 86 Nw. U. L. Rev. 643 (1992).

40. Transcript of Final Pretrial Hearing at 45, *In re* Richardson-Merrell, Inc. "Bendectin" Products Liability Litigation, MDL-486 (S.D. Ohio May 11, 1984).

41. Order, *In re* Richardson-Merrell, Inc. "Bendectin" Products Liability Litigation, MDL-486 (S.D. Ohio Feb. 19, 1985) (Docket No. 2862).

42. *But see* Valerie P. Hans, *Attitudes Toward Corporate Responsibility: A Psycholegal Perspective,* 69 Neb. L. Rev. 158, 176–77 (1990); Valerie P. Hans & William S. Lofquist, *Jurors' Judgments of Business Liability in Tort Cases: Implications for the Litigation Explosion Debate,* 26 Law & Soc'y Rev. 85, 94 (1992) (study based on post-verdict interviews with jurors in a single jurisdiction; authors found that many jurors were

quite skeptical of personal injury plaintiffs, their motivations for suing, and their cases).

43. 13 Barb. 2 (N.Y. App. Div. 1852).

44. *Id.* at 15–16.

45. *See generally* Charles Fried, *The Value of Life*, 82 HARV. L. REV. 1415 (1969).

46. *In re* Agent Orange Prod. Liab. Litig., 818 F.2d 145, 151 (2d Cir. 1987), *cert. denied*, 484 U.S. 1004 (1988).

47. Although sometimes other methods were employed to control the problem. Professor Friedman explains how the harsh doctrine of contributory negligence was thought useful as a counterweight to juror sympathy. LAWRENCE FRIEDMAN, A HISTORY OF AMERICAN LAW 470 (New York: Simon & Schuster, 2d ed. 1985).

48. *See, e.g.*, Thomas G. Field, *Scientific Evidence in the Courts (Letter)*, 262 SCI. 1629 (1993).

49. *In re* Richardson-Merrell, Inc. "Bendectin" Products Liability Litigation, 624 F. Supp. 1212, 1271 (S.D. Ohio 1985), *aff'd*, 857 F.2d 290 (6th Cir. 1988).

Chapter 13
The Settlement and Unsettlement of MDL-486

Substantial impediments exist to the settlement of mass toxic substances cases. Numerous plaintiffs represented by a variety of counsel often must contend with dozens, or even hundreds of defendants. Conflict among the lawyers representing plaintiffs and among the defendants over allocational issues is inevitable. Defendants are often insured by a number of successive or layered insurers who have control of or a stake in any settlement. The stakes for single-shot litigants may be quite different from those for the repeat-player defendants.[1] Frequently, provision must be made for future, but as yet unknown, often as yet unharmed, claimants. Uncertainty about the outcome at trial is often an impediment to settlement[2] and may be exacerbated in toxic substances cases because of scientific lacunae on causation questions. Uncertainty about causation also makes the universe of claimants speculative. Most consummated settlements have been reached in bankruptcy court, encouraged by the financial inability of the defendant to meet its anticipated legal liability and the authority and flexibility of the bankruptcy court to approve a reorganization plan.[3] The Agent Orange litigation was settled on a nearly global basis in May 1984, but largely because of the extraordinary efforts and stubborn determination of Judge Jack Weinstein.[4]

The Settlement Negotiations

Stanley Chesley played a major role in the settlement of Agent Orange, and he took on the mantle of chief negotiator on behalf of the PLCC in settlement discussions with Frank Woodside. From the outset Chesley, who has subsequently become the master of mass tort settlement, pursued settlement discussions with Frank Woodside. Settlement of the Bendectin litigation would be easier than in a number of the other mass toxic substances litigations, as there was but one defendant with which to negotiate. But there was one major obstacle: Merrell insisted on a "global" settlement that would resolve all Bendectin claims against it once and for all.[5]

Merrell's position was understandable, even with Bendectin withdrawn from the market. With 18 million pregnant women in the United States and almost twice that many worldwide who had taken Bendectin, a 2 to 3 percent major birth defect rate, and at least 80 percent of the fetuses exposed to Bendectin being born alive, Merrell faced the potential for hundreds of thousands of claims being asserted. Although less than a thousand cases had surfaced by early 1984, a significant nonglobal settlement would trigger an avalanche of additional filings.[6] The statute of limitations, which ordinarily would shield Merrell from liability for claims not raised within two or three years of the injury, provided almost no protection, because most states have Child Savings Acts, which delay the statute of limitations clock for children until they reach the age of majority.[7] Thus Mary Oxendine was 11 years old when she filed suit against Merrell in 1982.

Woodside (based on his marching orders from Merrell) was adamant from the outset about the settlement encompassing all claims. This condition put Chesley and the PLCC in a very difficult and awkward position because the PLCC did not represent many of the plaintiffs whose cases would have to be included in the settlement. The settlement of future claims posed an additional ethical problem for the members of the PLCC: They would be agreeing to a settlement on behalf of individuals they did not represent and who had a conflict with their clients, because any settlement funds allocated to future claimants would diminish the amount available for the present plaintiffs who Chesley did represent.[8]

Chesley, put between the Merrell rock and the plaintiffs-he-didn't-represent hard place, continued to probe Woodside to assess whether Merrell would retreat on its global settlement condition. When Chesley appreciated that Merrell's insistence on a global settlement was nonnegotiable, he ultimately agreed to it. Nevertheless, in the subsequent controversy over the settlement, Chesley claimed that he did so with his fingers crossed. Asserting that the due process clause of the fourteenth amendment bars resolution of future claimants' rights, Chesley argued that later claimants would have the option of eschewing the settlement and pursuing their claim in court. While Chesley's claim is not implausible, a growing body of law tends to suggest that as long as future claimants are afforded adequate representation and reasonable efforts made to provide them notice, their claims can be resolved before they come forward and formally file suit.[9] Moreover, even if Chesley were right, his position on future claimants did not address the problem of existing plaintiffs whose attorneys wanted no part of the settlement that was reached, preferring to pursue their cases outside the MDL-486 structure.[10] Under existing law, Chesley's authority to negotiate a settlement on behalf of plaintiffs he did not represent was in question, but in any case would require the assent of each claimant to any settlement he reached.[11] A related but distinct issue was the propriety of a mandatory class action, which would be the instrument for effectuating a global settlement. That question, addressed later in this chapter, however, determined whether global settlement was possible, not the rights of dissatisfied class members to assert they were not bound by it.

Nevertheless both sides had reasons for finding settlement attractive. From the PLCC's perspective, it had a difficult case to prove. Strong evidence of causation had not emerged or been developed, and the structure of the trial that Judge Rubin had fashioned ruled out trading on Merrell's culpability in exchange for the weakness on causation. The shakiness of the plaintiffs' case was brought home to the PLCC in its preparations for trial, when it conducted six practice trials in early June 1984, before the actual trial was to begin. The practice trials were conducted before mock juries selected to be demographically similar to the actual jury that would be chosen.[12] Each side presented portions of deposition testimony and closing arguments. Doug Peters of the Charfoos firm in Detroit was hired to play the role of defense counsel. The results of the six trials were five defense verdicts and one hung jury. These outcomes were devastating to Tom Bleakley, who had the lead trial role for the plaintiffs, and others on the PLCC. It made Stanley Chesley even more determined to reach a settlement with Merrell.

The weakness of its case on the merits combined with the substantial monetary and labor investment that the PLCC had in the case created strong incentives to settle—even for a deeply discounted amount—so as to avoid taking a complete loss. Since 100 percent of the litigation expenses would be reimbursed in the event of a settlement, the PLCC would fare better than plaintiffs who would receive a substantially discounted proportion of their claim. In a simple two-party case, plaintiff-clients may have some modicum of protection from this conflict between themselves and their attorneys,[13] but in MDL-486 Stanley Chesley was negotiating without any constraints imposed by a client.

Moreover, a settlement would provide a ready source for the award of attorney's fees to the PLCC. Obviously if the case were lost, the PLCC would not receive attorney's fees. Under the "common fund" rationale for awarding attorney's fees, the PLCC could seek an award for its efforts in producing the entire settlement fund. Because of the magnitude of the settlement under discussion, the PLCC would be assured of at least receiving a full hourly rate for its time and perhaps considerably more, if Judge Rubin instead used a percentage-of-recovery method to award fees.[14]

From Merrell's perspective, a global settlement was extremely attractive, despite the strength of its case on the merits of causation. The *Oxendine* verdict had painfully demonstrated to Merrell that despite the power of its evidence on causation, juries could find for plaintiffs. The *McCarrick* case had brought that lesson home to Merrell as well. *McCarrick* was the thalidomide case that Jim Butler had tried successfully against Merrell. It was the only thalidomide case that Merrell did not settle and that was because Merrell was convinced it had a valid defense: Shirley McCarrick had not taken thalidomide during her pregnancy. Despite Merrell's conviction about the merits of its defense, it ended up on the wrong side of a jury verdict in a birth defect case. A global settlement would end, once and for all, the seven years of debilitating litigation over Bendectin, litigation that required the attention and time not only of Merrell's management but its medical and scientific staff and had distracted them from their essential mission. Because of its liability insurance ($1.75 billion) and the reserves that Merrell had itself provided for the Bendectin litigation ($120 million in 1983), even a settlement of several hundred million dollars could be accomplished without significant adverse effect on Merrell's financial condition. Finally, the stakes for Merrell in the MDL-486 trial were far greater than the several hundred cases actually involved. If the jury were to find against Merrell, thousands upon thousands of additional cases loomed on the horizon, cases that might be considerably strengthened both legally and informally by an adverse result for Merrell in MDL-486. The trial in MDL-486 had the potential to be a bet-your-company gamble, a prospect that neither management nor directors are inclined toward. Stanley Chesley's strategy of upping-the-ante by encouraging additional Bendectin filings had the desired effect: it made a risk-averse defendant more interested in settlement.

Although both sides had powerful incentives for settlement, there remained the matter of its magnitude. On that score, the PLCC had an informational problem—a difficulty also faced by the plaintiffs in the Agent Orange settlement negotiations—because little was known about many of the claims that made up MDL-486 and considerably less was known about claims that had not yet been filed. Moreover, there was wide variation among those claims, both in terms of the likelihood of success on the merits and in terms of the expected damage award. An analysis of those cases would require individualistic information about each of the cases, from type of defect to time of the mother's ingestion of Bendectin, to the amount of medical expenses and anticipated future costs, and including the family medical history—an inordinate amount of information about which the PLCC had no systematic data.[15]

Settlement negotiations quickened as the impending trial date approached. Judge Rubin was anxious to effect a settlement and repeatedly brought the parties together to try to facilitate an agreement. However, unlike the aggressive role taken by Judge Weinstein in Agent Orange, Rubin merely attempted to encourage settlement by listening to the lawyers and occasionally offering suggestions that synthesized their views. Rubin believed that the way to encourage settlement was to set early trial dates and make them credible by rarely granting a continuance.

On June 8, 1984 the Friday before the trial was to start, Frank Woodside and Stanley Chesley received a call from Judge Rubin's deputy. She instructed them to appear at a Saturday morning conference and to come with their "last, best, and final offer from which you will not deviate." Woodside called Al Schretter, who had left Davis Polk and was working as in-house counsel for Merrell. Schretter authorized Woodside to transmit an offer of $120 million. Chesley agreed in principle to this amount, convinced that he would be unable to negotiate a larger offer. A variety of details, however, remained for resolution, including when and how the money would be paid, the mechanism for administering claims, and the allocation of the settlement fund among the claimants who would come forward.

Although it was plain after the Saturday meeting that agreement was imminent, Judge Rubin refused to cancel the trial. Holding the parties' noses to the grindstone, he proceeded to select a jury beginning Monday morning to demonstrate his resolve to try the case unless a settlement was concluded.

Effectuating the Settlement: The Mandatory Class

By Wednesday Judge Rubin was satisfied that, although further work remained, the settlement was secure. On Thursday he issued a cryptic order postponing the trial, thereby providing Woodside and Chesley time to work out the many details that remained before the settlement could be reduced to writing. One significant condition—that the settlement include all Bendectin claimants—required the cooperation of Judge Rubin in certifying a mandatory class action. The class would include all present and future Bendectin claimants, whether involved in MDL-486 or not.

On June 18, one week after the trial had begun, Judge Rubin certified a class action in a hastily-drawn order. Judge Rubin employed rule 23(b)(1) of the Federal Rules of Civil Procedure to certify a class consisting of all persons with birth defects exposed to Bendectin in utero and their parents.[16] The class action rule that had typically, although sparingly, been used for mass tort cases in the past was rule 23(b)(3), which permits members of the class the opportunity to opt out of the class and pursue their legal claim on an individual basis outside the class action structure. By contrast, rule 23(b)(1) has no provision for opting out. But if Merrell's insistence on a global settlement was to be accomplished, a rule 23(b)(1) class would be required.

Curiously, Judge Rubin's class certification order was cryptic about the settlement. He made explicit that the class certification was for the purpose of facilitating settlement. Yet the order gave no indication of the parties' agreement and the settlement, which did not become public for another month. The order recognized the conflict between current and future claimants that would occur in dividing any settlement fund. In recognition of that concern the order created two subclasses—one made up of existing claimants who had filed suit by June 18, 1984 and the other of future claimants. Judge Rubin appointed a guardian ad litem to protect the latter subclass's interests.

What the order did not reveal was that there was little legal basis for the certification of a rule 23(b)(1) class and that appointment of a guardian ad litem could not solve the inherent conflict that many attorneys had between clients on whose behalf they had filed suit and those they hadn't. Nor did the order recognize the conflict posed for attorneys had who represented plaintiffs with a variety of different birth defects, for which the merits of the cases varied. Those clients would be competing among themselves in the allocation of the fund to individual claimants.[17]

The class action certification, however, was merely a judicial accommodation of the agreement between Frank Woodside and Stanley Chesley. As such, it was not a product of adversarial proceedings, and as long as no one challenged it, it would stand. Yet beneath the calm of the stipulated class there were roiling waters. The certification of a mandatory class removed from individual plaintiffs and their lawyers the ability to pursue their legal claims individually, an unquestioned freedom that most plaintiff's attorneys view as more sanctified than the Bill of Rights and the moral equivalent of the Ten Commandments. The certification not only destroyed that freedom, but it also meant that the damages recovered by each class member would be determined in an administrative fashion rather than by a jury or an individually negotiated settlement. Perhaps most importantly, it had significant implications for how the attorney's fee pie would be allocated between the PLCC and the attorneys for individual plaintiffs.

The settlement was announced publicly on July 14, 1984, after numerous details were resolved by Woodside and Chesley. The agreement provided for a total payment by Merrell of $120 million over 19 years (with a present value of around $80 to 90 million). Initially, $40 million would be paid, followed by $20 million payments on each of the next two anniversaries of the settlement, $5 million on each of the next two anniversaries, and $2 million a year for each of the following 15 years.

Left unanswered in the agreement were how much would be allocated to future claimants, what mechanism would be utilized for evaluating existing plaintiffs' claims, the evidence that would be required to establish a claim, and most importantly, the amount of money that would be paid to each claimant and how attorney's fees would be handled. Simple mathematics dictated that with over 600 children already involved in MDL-486 (later that would almost double), another hundred or so non-duplicative cases in state courts, perhaps hundreds more in lawyers' offices waiting to be filed, and who knew how many new cases that would emerge, very few, if any, would receive million-dollar awards. The vast majority would receive awards that would not exceed five figures. Yet Barry Nace had already won a $750,000 verdict in *Oxendine.* In a perverse way the settlement convinced other plaintiffs' lawyers that they would fare as well as Nace had in *Oxendine.* If Merrell was willing to settle for $120 million, the thinking went, then surely there was merit to the claims that were being made.

Judge Rubin appointed Sam Porter, a Columbus attorney, as guardian ad litem for future claimants. Porter was assigned to estimate the number of future claims and make a recommendation to the court on how much of the settlement fund would be required for future claimants. Dr. Orley Ashenfelter, a prominent economist at Princeton University, and Dr. Steven Lamm, a health consultant and epidemiologist in Washington, DC, were hired to prepare those estimates. (Lamm's appointment would subsequently have a major impact on the trial of MDL-486, after the Sixth Circuit held that Judge Rubin's settlement class certification was improper.) Judge Rubin scheduled a hearing on October 31, 1984 to evaluate how many future claimants there would be and the appropriate allocation of the $120 million fund between the subclasses.

The Federal Rules of Civil Procedure require that all class action settlements be approved by the court, after holding a hearing in which those affected by the settlement have the opportunity to present their views. Judge Rubin scheduled a hearing to assess the fairness of the settlement for November 30, 1984. But since Judge Rubin had already certified a class to facilitate the settlement, persuading him of the unfairness of the

settlement seemed unlikely. Indeed, given the investment the trial judge
has in the settlement of a class action, fairness might better be served by
requiring another judge, without any vested interest, to preside at the
fairness hearing.

The Controversy over the Settlement

Stanley Chesley knew that a global settlement would engender opposition from attorneys outside the PLCC (it's not clear he appreciated that
it would also run into opposition from lawyers within the PLCC). In May
of 1984, when rumors of the possibility of a global settlement first leaked,
Barry Nace wrote to Chesley, explaining his vehement opposition to any
settlement that would bind his clients and assuring Chesley he would
fight any such settlement.[18] Nace not only felt he could be more successful in individual cases and trials, but was also irked when the PLCC did
not extend an invitation to him to join it after his *Oxendine* verdict.[19]

Stanley Chesley began an immediate public relations campaign to obtain acceptance of the settlement. He was quoted the next day in the
newspapers: "We feel this is a very substantial amount and the largest
per-capita settlement we know for this kind of case."[20] He added that it
was the third largest mass tort settlement ever, the largest drug-products
liability case settlement, and the most money paid to settle a mass toxic
case by a single defendant (both the Agent Orange and MGM Grand
Hotel cases with larger dollar settlements involved multiple defendants).
Chesley scheduled a meeting of lawyers interested in Bendectin litigation at the American Trial Lawyers Association annual meeting in Seattle. Three "road shows" to present and sell the settlement to the
plaintiffs' lawyers were scheduled for early August; Chesley scheduled
those meetings without notifying the dissident members of the PLCC.

The settlement also required a rapid about-face by Chesley in his public evaluation of the merits of the case. Although only three weeks before
he had written to plaintiffs' lawyers assuring them that he was confident
of success at trial, Chesley wrote:

As I am sure you are aware, this is a difficult case from a stand point of causation,
a total of 30,000,0000 women have taken Bendectin and there are currently approximately 700 documented defect cases. In light of the fact that 5 to 7 percent
of the population suffers birth defects naturally, causation is an uphill battle. It
has proven difficult over the last few years for those Plaintiffs whose trials have
preceded the MDL trial.[21]

Despite Chesley's efforts, the opposition mounted and became more organized. Nace received active support from a handful of attorneys around
the country, including Tommy Kline in Philadelphia, Len Schroeter in

Seattle, and Gary Galiher in Hawaii. These lawyers either had a significant interest in Bendectin litigation or were concerned more generally about the principle of protecting their autonomy to pursue cases on behalf of individual clients, unimpeded by committed collective settlers like Stanley Chesley.

In addition to outside opposition, the PLCC itself ruptured over the settlement. Jim Butler was the leader of the opposition. Butler felt that $120 million was a grossly inadequate sum to compensate the number of plaintiffs and the severity of the harms that they had suffered. Butler, who was still deeply affected by his involvement in the thalidomide litigation and the impact of those birth defects on the children, tended to focus on the severe limb defect cases. Earlier discussions among the PLCC about a target settlement amount had been in the range of a quarter to half a billion dollars; individual recoveries from the $120 million would pale in comparison to the injuries suffered.

Tom Bleakley was more conflicted about the settlement. He was disconsolate about the outcome of the practice jury verdicts and their implications for the MDL-486 trial. Bleakley had opted most of his cases out of the consolidated trial, even though he was to be the lead trial lawyer, because of the structure of the trial and Judge Rubin's pretrial rulings. He, along with Jim Butler, were convinced they would fare better outside the MDL-486 trial umbrella. Bleakley had another problem with the settlement: He had not filed suit on behalf of the majority of his Bendectin clients, believing it would be better to wait until the MDL-486 smoke cleared. Those clients were now part of a subclass of future claimants who had a conflict with claimants whose suits had been filed. The future claimant subclass would inevitably bear the risk that the number of future claimants and the severity of their claims would exceed the amount allocated for them out of the settlement proceeds. Bleakley aligned himself with Butler in opposition to the settlement.

George Kokus and Allen Eaton supported Chesley and the settlement. Like Bleakley, they appreciated the difficult task they faced in prevailing at trial, but each had additional reasons to favor the settlement. For Kokus, who had been financially wrung out by the *Mekdeci* case, the settlement was an opportunity to salve, perhaps to pamper, those wounds. Allen Eaton, who was torn by the settlement, consulted with Art Raynes, a friend, mentor, and prominent lawyer in thalidomide litigation. Raynes had decided not to get involved in Bendectin litigation after reviewing the evidence, and his counsel influenced Eaton to support the settlement.

Chesley's efforts to sell the settlement were infected with hyperbole, half-truths, and outright misrepresentations. He claimed, shortly after the settlement was announced: "We did a trial balloon before we went

ahead with this, and we found overwhelming support." [22] But that assertion grossly overstated his support—those plaintiffs' lawyers who were
most knowledgeable and active in Bendectin litigation outside the PLCC
were largely and vehemently opposed to the settlement. At the American Trial Lawyers Association meeting in Seattle in late July 1984, an
angry showdown, lasting six hours, occurred in which Chesley attempted
to defend the settlement and Barry Nace and Len Schroeter attacked it
before 100 plaintiffs' lawyers. Schroeter gave an emotional speech, criticizing the settlement for determining the rights of even the unborn
and thereby denying them their fundamental right to justice. Schroeter characterized the dissidents as "horrified, furious, and feel[ing]
murderous." [23]

Chesley refused to provide the attorneys present with a copy of the
written documentation of the settlement, insisting that the document
was being held in camera by the court. Indeed, Chesley denied there
even was a settlement agreement, characterizing the situation as "nothing more than a means to convey an offer to claimants," [24] which it
plainly was not. The meeting, often degenerating into a shouting match,
ranged over a variety of topics that included the details of the settlement,
case-specific information that the PLCC had (or didn't have), the expected recoveries by plaintiffs with various birth defects, administrative
costs for managing and distributing the settlement fund, the impact of
the settlement and fees for the PLCC on outside attorneys' contingent
fee arrangements with their clients, and the anticipated cost of trying an
individual case. Chesley, with a straight face, estimated that it would cost
$400,000 to $600,000 to try an individual case, even with the common
issues evidence provided by the PLCC. That figure was wildly exaggerated based on previous cases and generated deep skepticism about the
facts Chesley presented. One neutral observer who attended the meeting
and had obtained a confidential copy of the settlement agreement was
"blown away" at the misrepresentations made by Chesley about the settlement. He concluded that "Chesley made bald-faced lies about what
was in the agreement."

There were two aspects of Chesley's role in negotiating the settlement
that also raised touchy ethical questions. Chesley had been the primary
financier of the MDL-486 litigation from the start. He had invested his
own money, $1 million by his own account, to pay the expenses involved
in preparations for trial. [25] That amount does not include the value of the
time spent by lawyers in his office in litigating MDL-486. The expenses
would be reimbursed off the top of the settlement fund, but would go
unreimbursed if the case proceeded to trial and resulted in a defendant's
verdict. At the very least this creates an appearance that Chesley's personal interests were better served by a settlement that was inadequate in

amount, yet certain, and would guarantee both a return of the funds advanced, not to mention a substantial award of attorney's fees. While the contingent fee system necessarily results in plaintiffs' attorneys having a financial stake in the case and sometimes results in a conflict between client and attorney,[26] an investment of the magnitude of Chesley's is highly unusual. Moreover, in the litigation of individual cases, clients retain ultimate control over whether a settlement is accepted.[27]

Second, Chesley's firm was listed as representing Lloyds of London in Martindale-Hubbell, a standard lawyer's directory. Lloyds was an excess insurer for Merrell, and Lloyds would be required to contribute funds if the amount of Bendectin liability verdicts exceeded the primary insurer's coverage limits. Again, regardless of any actual misconduct by Chesley (which seems highly unlikely), this appearance of impropriety fueled suspicion and gave the dissident lawyers more ammunition with which to attack the validity of the settlement.

Even Chesley's authority to negotiate the settlement was called into question. In October Tom Bleakley wrote to Judge Rubin:

[I]t is my understanding that Mr. Chesley represented to the court and Mr. Woodside that he was delegated as a so-called chairman of the subcommittee on settlement. As a member of plaintiffs' Lead Counsel Committee I can represent to this court that no such power has ever been conferred upon Mr. Chesley by plaintiffs' Lead Counsel Committee. In fact it was expressly agreed upon by all members of plaintiffs' Lead Counsel that Mr. Chesley would serve only the administrative function of liaison with the court and would avoid getting involved in the substantive nature of the lawsuit.[28]

The opponents of the settlement probed for weak points to see where it might be vulnerable. Ultimately, they settled on Judge Rubin's class certification order, where they found the weakest link in the global settlement structure.

The Sixth Circuit's Review

Judge Rubin's class certification order began by observing that Bendectin litigation fell within a small class of massive cases that put extraordinary demands on the civil justice system. This observation was buttressed by calculations that demonstrated that trying all of the existing Bendectin cases on an individual basis would require 105 judge-years of time. Judge Rubin's opinion contained two sentences analyzing the propriety of a mandatory class pursuant to rule 23(b)(1):

Continued case by case determinations will inevitably result in varying adjudications which will impose inconsistent standards of conduct upon the defendant, the perquisites of Rule 23(b)(1)(A) have been met. The Court likewise finds that there is a risk that a limited fund may exist from which judgments can be satisfied.[29]

Rubin's reference to the two subsections of rule 23(b)(1) recognized that there are two distinct reasons for certifying such a class. The first addresses the problem of a party who is sued by several plaintiffs, each of whom seeks different and conflicting relief. Thus a rule 23(b)(1)(A) class was certified in *Van Gemert v. Boeing Co.*,[30] in which debenture holders sued the defendant over their right to convert the debentures into common stock. Separate suits by other debenture holders could have resulted in conflicting declarations about how the defendant should provide for the debenture holders' conversion rights. Significantly, the Advisory Committee for the federal rules had made plain in its comments on the class action rules when they were promulgated in 1966 that rule 23(b)(3) was the appropriate class for numerous claimants seeking money damages. If inconsistent outcomes in money damages lawsuits were sufficient to satisfy rule 23(b)(1)(A), then virtually every class action involving money damages could be certified under that rule.[31] A leading case from the Ninth Circuit Court of Appeals had concluded that a rule 23(b)(1)(A) class would rarely be available in suits seeking money damages, despite the risk of inconsistent outcomes: "Certainly the defendants in these proceedings can continue the conduct of which the plaintiffs complain even if the plaintiffs are successful, as the plaintiff [in one case] has been, in their individual actions. Their success by its terms does not fix the rights and duties owed by the defendants to others as, for example, would declaration of the invalidity of [a] bond issue."[32]

This reasoning was particularly applicable to Merrell, as it had already removed Bendectin from the market. Contrary to Judge Rubin's analysis, any plaintiff's success had no implications for Merrell's behavior with regard to Bendectin. Judge Rubin did cite two cases to support his conclusion. One was a 1973 district court decision whose reasoning had been rendered moot by a Supreme Court decision in 1979.[33] The other was a decision by Judge Rubin in the Beverly Hills Supper Club litigation that had not relied on rule 23(b)(1)(A) at all, but instead was based on the second subsection of rule 23(b)(1), the limited fund concern. Finally, the case for a 23(b)(1)(A) class was considerably weaker after a settlement than it was before, a time when Judge Rubin had refused to certify a mandatory class. To put the point in a slightly different way, the mandatory class action provision in rule 23(b)(1)(A) was not written to effectuate global settlements and to thereby prevent individual litigants from pursuing their individual claims.

The second subsection of rule 23(b)(1) authorizes a mandatory class when individual adjudications would have an impact on others with similar claims. The paradigm is multiple claimants to a limited fund, such as an insurance policy, with the claimants seeking more than the available policy limits. This limited-fund concept can be translated into the mass tort context when the available resources of the defendants would be exhausted by individual case adjudications before all claimants came forward.

Assessing the propriety of a limited-fund class in the mass tort context requires consideration of the defendant's financial wherewithal, its liability insurance policies, and other available assets. More difficult is an appraisal of potential claims that will be asserted. This requires an assessment of the number of claims that will be brought, the meritoriousness of the claims, including the impact of different substantive state law applicable to the claims of residents of different states, the severity of the injuries involved in those claims, and the likely recoveries, both in settlements and judgments in those cases. That assessment is both data intensive and fraught with uncertainty, especially early in the life-cycle of a mass toxic substance case.[34]

Judge Rubin made no attempt to assess these matters, instead summarily concluding that the risk of exhausting Merrell's assets "may exist." The Ninth Circuit had already reversed a certification of a limited-fund class in the Dalkon Shield litigation on the ground that the trial judge had failed to make an adequate factual inquiry into the defendant's "actual assets, insurance, settlement experience, and continuing exposure."[35] The court also set the standard for exhausting assets quite high: A limited-fund class would be appropriate only if "separate actions 'inescapably will alter the substance of the rights of others having similar claims.' "[36] Mandatory classes and the courts' treatment of them are addressed in greater detail in chapter 15.

Yet another dubious aspect of the certification order was its failure to come to grips with a federal statute, the Anti-Injunction Act,[37] that prohibits federal judges from issuing orders that enjoin pending state court proceedings. The class definition employed by Judge Rubin included those who had actions pending in state courts, and he also entered an order staying discovery in those state cases. While a vague exception to the Anti-Injunction exists that might be applicable ("except . . . where necessary in aid of its jurisdiction . . . ") the Eighth Circuit had held in the Hyatt Regency Skywalk cases that the Act barred a mandatory class action that had the effect of barring class members from pursuing their state court suits.[38] The certification order neglected to mention the Anti-Injunction Act or its impact on the propriety of the mandatory class.

Finally, although not a basis for reversal, Judge Rubin's "necessity" rationale for certifying the class could not withstand scrutiny. Bendectin was a large congregation of cases, but Judge Rubin had already declined to certify a class *before* the settlement occurred. Surely the imperative for obtaining the efficiencies of a class action were greater then with the trials looming, than they were after the settlement; if a class action could not be justified on efficiency grounds before settlement, it surely could not after one was reached.

Global settlements may or may not be desirable. There is much to be said on that score, and chapter 15 examines the issues implicated in mandatory classes. But the current class action rules are not written to effectuate global settlements on a routine basis; if companies like Merrell are to be afforded a "bill of peace" in exchange for settlement, the class action rules will require modification or some other procedural mechanism must be devised.

Judge Rubin's class certification order was a sitting duck for appellate challenge. The best possibility to protect it was procedural: Because the class certification did not conclude the case (the fairness and apportionment hearings remained, as well as fashioning the scheme for administering the fund), it was not appealable until the case was concluded. The Sixth Circuit so held in dismissing the dissidents' appeal of the certification order.[39] But the challengers also sought a writ of mandamus from the Sixth Circuit, a quite limited procedure that permits appellate review despite the absence of finality. Eight days before the scheduled hearing on the allocation of the settlement fund between the present and future claimants, the Sixth Circuit heard oral argument.

Writs of mandamus (literally, a command) are available only in "exceptional circumstances amounting to a judicial 'usurpation of power.' "[40] Infrequently utilized, it serves as a relief valve for cases in which a trial judge's ruling plainly will not survive appellate review, yet is technically unappealable at the time issued, and substantial efforts or prejudice would occur if appellate review were delayed until the case was concluded.

The most important of the criteria for determining whether the requisite exceptional circumstances exist is a clearly erroneous legal ruling by the lower court. Three days after the argument, an extraordinarily brief period, the court of appeals issued its opinion. The Sixth Circuit easily found that Judge Rubin's reliance on rule 23(b)(1) was clearly erroneous, thereby justifying issuance of a writ of mandamus. Reflecting the prevailing wisdom, the court held that rule 23(b)(1)(A) is not available where a defendant may be subject to inconsistent judgments in money damages suits. The court also found no basis in the record for upholding a limited fund class, the alternative ground relied on by Judge Rubin. The court of appeals returned the case to Judge Rubin with the certification order overturned, hence the key condition for the settlement legally unavailable, and the case in disarray.

How could Chesley, Merrell, and Judge Rubin have miscalculated so badly? Given the legal impediments to a global settlement, why such cursory attention to those obstacles? The best assessment is that neither Merrell nor Judge Rubin appreciated the intensity of opposition the settlement would engender among other plaintiff's attorneys. Without their opposition, the settlement would not have undergone appellate review and could have been effectuated. It is less clear that Stanley Chesley could have been oblivious to this opposition or why he proceeded in the face of it. Perhaps the growing concern with the strength of the case on the merits and concern about an adverse outcome at a consolidated trial led Chesley to attempt a last ditch salvage effort.

The Future Claimants

Despite the Sixth Circuit's decision, Judge Rubin went ahead with the hearing to determine the number of future claimants for the purpose of allocating the $120 million fund between existing and future claimants. The need for such a hearing was moot after the Sixth Circuit ruled the mandatory class could not be maintained, and a number of lawyers involved were perplexed at Judge Rubin's decision nevertheless to proceed with the hearing. However, he appears to have been motivated by a last gasp attempt to salvage the settlement.[41] If the hearing revealed that a manageable number of future claimants could be anticipated, Merrell might be persuaded to settle on a non-mandatory basis. Claimants and known future claimants would have the opportunity to exclude themselves from the settlement and pursue their individual actions. Unknown future claimants might be included or excluded from the settlement, depending on the judgment of the guardian ad litem appointed to represent them. The settlement might include provisions for adjustment or even cancellation in case an excessive number of claimants chose to opt out. Experts had already been hired and paid to estimate the number of future claimants. Judge Rubin felt that something of value might be gained from hearing them out.[42]

The guardian ad litem hired an epidemiologist to assist in estimating the number of future claims. Steven Lamm, an epidemiological consultant from Washington, DC, testified that approximately 15 million live births occurred in which the mother was exposed to Bendectin during pregnancy. From this figure, he calculated that 900,000 congenital malformations would be associated with these births, but only 265,000 of those would involve fetuses exposed to Bendectin during the period of organogenesis of the implicated organ. These defects would implicate between 115,000 and 168,000 children, some suffering multiple birth defects. Lamm had a considerable impact when he testified that after reviewing the Bendectin scientific literature, he found that the relative risk of birth defects was one. Judge Rubin interrupted: "Wait, let me reflect on what you are saying. The literature you consulted does not indicate any greater risk of congenital malformation in those instances when Bendectin was taken?" Lamm responded, "Correct."[43] Although the issue that Lamm was concerned with was the number of potential claimants and not the question of causation, this testimony from an independent expert was quite dramatic.

The range of estimates about the number of future claimants doomed any attempt to salvage the settlement. The PLCC majority hired an expert who concluded that only 1,000 future claimants would emerge. By contrast, the guardian ad litem's experts, working from Dr. Lamm's figures, concluded that between 6,000 and 16,000 claims might be filed in the future. If anywhere near the higher estimates proved correct, the settlement fund would be plainly inadequate. Indeed, if those future claimants were compensated at the same levels contemplated for existing claimants, the settlement would require an additional one billion dollars.

Judge Rubin was visibly disturbed by the variation in estimates. He commented to the final expert: "We have had persons of impeccable credentials, including yourself, testify and the variation is so enormous as to be almost unbelievable."[44] After commending the guardian ad litem, Judge Rubin concluded, "The only conceivable suggestion I could make at this point is maybe we should have conferred with Jimmy the Greek."[45] The hearing persuaded Judge Rubin that settlement would be impossible. Although both Merrell and the PLCC made some cursory attempts to modify and revive the settlement, Judge Rubin brushed them aside; he had concluded that a trial would be the only way to resolve the consolidated Bendectin proceedings.

Notes

1. *See generally* Samuel Gross & Kent Syverud, *Getting to No: A Study of Settlement Negotiations and the Selection of Cases for Trial,* 90 MICH. L. REV. 319 (1991).

2. George L. Priest & Benjamin Klein, *The Selection of Disputes for Settlement,* 13 J. LEG. STUD. 1, 17 (1984).

3. *E.g.,* In the Matter of Johns-Manville Corp., 68 B.R. 618 (Bankr. S.D.N.Y. 1986), *aff'd,* 78 B.R. 407 (S.D.N.Y. 1987), *aff'd sub nom.* Kane v. Johns-Manville Corp., 843 F.2d 636 (2d Cir. 1988); *In re* A. H. Robins Co., 88 B.R. 742 (E.D. Va. 1988). The breast implant settlement appears to be an exception, *In re* Silicone Gel Breast Implant Products Liability Litigation, 1994 WL 114580 (N.D. Al. Apr. 1, 1994), although there remain shoals on which that settlement may yet founder.

4. PETER H. SCHUCK, AGENT ORANGE ON TRIAL: MASS TOXIC DISASTERS IN

THE COURTS 143–67 (Cambridge, MA: Belknap Press of Harvard University Press, enlarged ed. 1987).

5. The account of the settlement negotiations in this chapter is drawn from interviews with Frank Woodside, Alfred Schretter, John Chewning, Tom Bleakley, George Kokus, Stanley Chesley, Allen Eaton, Douglas Peters, and Judge Carl Rubin, correspondence among the members of the PLCC, and court papers filed in MDL-486.

6. In the Agent Orange litigation, estimates of the number of claims just before settlement were 20,000. Less than two years later, over 244,000 claims had been filed to share in the fund created by the settlement. SCHUCK, *supra* note 4, at 162.

7. John H. Derrick, Annotation, *Tolling of Statute of Limitations, on Account of Minority of Injured Child, as Applicable to Parent's or Guardian's Right of Action Arising Out of Same Injury*, 49 A.L.R. 4TH 216 (1993). Most parents' claims, nevertheless, would be barred by the statute of limitations generally two or three years after birth, or in the case of latent birth defects, after the defect was discovered. But the injured child is entitled to the largest share of damages in most cases. In a few jurisdictions, statutes of repose may cut off some of the "long tail" claims.

8. One means to obviate the conflict is to establish a trust mechanism that doles out money to all claimants, regardless of when they come forward with their claims. That structure has been used successfully in the Dalkon Shield proceedings, less successfully in the Manville bankruptcy. Regardless, that was not the way in which the Bendectin settlement was negotiated or concluded: the global settlement fund would be divided, with the largest share divided among current plaintiffs and the remainder to be distributed to future claimants.

9. *See* In the Matter of Johns-Manville Corp., 68 B.R. 618, 626–27 (Bankr. S.D.N.Y. 1986), *aff'd*, 78 B.R. 407 (S.D.N.Y. 1987), *aff'd sub nom.* Kane v. Johns-Manville Corp., 843 F.2d 636 (2d Cir. 1988); *In re* "Agent Orange" Product Liability Litigation, 818 F.2d 145, 167 (2d Cir. 1987), *cert. denied*, 484 U.S. 1004 (1988); Ivy v. Diamond Shamrock Chemicals Co., 996 F.2d 1425 (2d Cir. 1993) (holding members of Agent Orange class bound by judgment in collateral attack), *cert. denied*, 114 S. Ct. 1126 (1994).

10. A year after the settlement, the Supreme Court, in Phillips Petroleum Co. v. Shutts, 472 U.S. 797 (1985), held that class members over whom the court would not have personal jurisdiction could be bound by a judgment provided the class members were afforded notice and the opportunity to opt out of the class. *Phillips* has raised an issue about the validity of mandatory classes where class members with damages claims have insufficient contacts with the forum jurisdiction to support personal jurisdiction. *See* Arthur R. Miller & David Crump, *Jurisdiction and Choice of Law in Multistate Class Actions After* Phillips Petroleum Co. v. Shutts, 96 YALE L.J. 1, 39 (1986); Glen O. Robinson & Kenneth S. Abraham, *Collective Justice in Tort Law*, 78 VA. L. REV. 1481, 1505–07 (1992); Brown v. Ticor Title Ins. Co., 982 F.2d 386, 392 (9th Cir. 1992) (holding mandatory class action could not bind class member over whom it lacked personal jurisdiction with regard to monetary claim), *cert. dismissed*, 114 S. Ct. 1359 (1994); *In re* A.H. Robins Co., 880 F.2d 709, 744–45 (4th Cir.) (avoiding decision on whether mandatory class could bind class members, because all class members had the functional equivalent of a right to opt out), *cert. denied*, 493 U.S. 959 (1989); Ivy v. Diamond Shamrock Co., 996 F.2d 1425, 1435 (2d Cir. 1993) (future claimants can be bound by class action judgment even if they do not receive notice), *cert. denied*, 114 S. Ct. 1126 (1994).

11. *See* Pearson v. Ecological Science Corp., 522 F.2d 171 (5th Cir. 1975), *cert. denied*, 425 U.S. 912 (1976); *In re* Air Crash Disaster at Florida Everglades, 549 F.2d 1006, 1015 (5th Cir. 1977). *But cf.* Mars Steel Corp. v. Continental Illinois Nat'l Bank & Trust Co., 834 F.2d 677, 681 (7th Cir. 1987) (deferring class certification until after settlement is much criticized but not per se prohibited); *In re* Ivan F. Boesky Securities Litigation, 948 F.2d 1358, 1364–66 (2d. Cir. 1991) (lead counsel's authority to negotiate and propose a settlement depends on whether authorized by district court).

12. For a discussion of the use of mock trials, *see* Elliot Cahn, *Winning Big Cases with Trial Simulations*, 69 A.B.A. J. 1073 (1983).

13. *See* MODEL RULES OF PROFESSIONAL CONDUCT, Rule 1.2(a) & Rule 1.4 cmt. 1 (Chicago: ABA, 1983); Geoffrey P. Miller, *Some Agency Problems in Settlement*, 16 J. LEGAL STUD. 189, 213 & n.70 (1987). The lower success rate by plaintiffs in personal injury cases (where lawyers' money is at risk) as opposed to commercial cases (where clients' money is at risk) suggests that personal injury plaintiffs do have some influence with lawyers in determining whether to proceed to trial. *See* Gross & Syverud, *supra* note 1, at 380–81.

14. At the time of the settlement, the Sixth Circuit employed the "lodestar" method of awarding attorneys fees, which was based on an hourly rate for hours worked often adjusted upward for the complexity of the case or the contingencies in succeeding. Northcross v. Bd. of Educ., 611 F.2d 624, 638 (6th Cir. 1979) (statutory fee shifting), *cert. denied*, 447 U.S. 911 (1980); Smillie v. Park Chem. Co., 710 F.2d 271, 274 (6th Cir. 1983) (fees awarded under "common fund" doctrine).

15. The best the PLCC could do as the settlement was being finalized was to group the approximately 725 known claimants into seven rough categories by severity of defect and assign an amount, ranging from $27,000 to $330,000, to which claimants in the category would be entitled. Document entitled "Summary of All Categories 1–6" (June 12, 1984).

16. *In re* "Bendectin" Products Liability Litigation, 102 F.R.D. 239 (S.D. Ohio), *appeal dismissed sub nom.* Schreier v. Merrell Dow Pharmaceutical, Inc., 745 F.2d 58 (6th Cir. 1984), *and mandamus granted*, 749 F.2d 300 (6th Cir. 1984).

17. *See* MODEL CODE OF PROFESSIONAL RESPONSIBILITY DR 5–106 (Chicago: ABA, 1980) (permitting lawyer to make aggregate settlements only if all clients, after being fully informed, consent to such a settlement).

18. Letter from Barry Nace to Plaintiffs Lead Counsel Committee, c/o Stanley Chesley (May 24, 1984).

19. Letter from Barry Nace to Thomas H. Bleakley (Apr. 17, 1984).

20. *Plaintiffs' Lawyer Hails Bendectin Settlement*, UPI, July 15, 1984.

21. Letter from Stanley Chesley to All Co-Counsel and Clients (June 18, 1984).

22. Tamar Lewin, *Proposed Drug Fund a Trade-off for 2 Sides*, N.Y. TIMES, July 17, 1984, at D1.

23. Mary Ann Galante, *ATLA Feud Erupts Over Pact*, NAT'L L.J., Aug. 6, 1984, at 3.

24. *Id.*

25. Ben L. Kaufman & David Lauter, *Bendectin Verdict Doesn't End Suits*, NAT'L L.J., Mar. 25, 1985, at 3.

26. *See* Kevin M. Clermont & John D. Currivan, *Improving on the Contingent Fee*, 63 CORNELL L. REV. 529 (1978); Earl Johnson, Jr., *Lawyers' Choice: A Theoretical Appraisal of Litigation Investment Decision*, 15 L. & SOC. REV. 567 (1980–81); Murray L. Schwartz & Daniel J.B. Mitchell, *An Economic Analysis of the Contingent Fee in Personal-Injury Litigation*, 22 STAN. L. REV. 1125 (1970); Miller, *supra* note 13.

27. *See* Richard Marcus, *Apocalypse Now,* 85 MICH. L. REV. 1267, 1280–86 (1987) (book review).

28. Letter from Thomas Bleakley to Honorable Carl Rubin (Oct. 15, 1984).

29. *In re* "Bendectin" Products Liability Litigation, 102 F.R.D. 239, 241 (S.D. Ohio) (citations omitted), *appeal dismissed sub nom.* Schreier v. Merrell-Dow Pharmaceutical, Inc., 745 F.2d 58 (6th Cir.), *and mandamus granted,* 749 F.2d 300 (6th Cir. 1984).

30. 259 F. Supp. 125 (S.D.N.Y. 1966).

31. *See In re* "Agent Orange" Products Liability Litigation, 100 F.R.D. 718, 725 (E.D.N.Y. 1983).

32. La Mar v. H & B Novelty & Loan Co., 489 F.2d 461, 466 (9th Cir. 1973).

33. Judge Rubin relied on Hernandez v. Motor Vessel Skyward, 61 F.R.D. 558 (S.D. Fla. 1973), *aff'd mem.,* 507 F.2d 1278 (1975). *Hernandez* cited the possibility of non-mutual offensive collateral estoppel being employed after a plaintiff's victory on the common issues, despite a series of defendant victories preceding that. In Parklane Hosiery v. Shore, 439 U.S. 322 (1979), the Supreme Court singled out precisely that situation as a ground not to employ non-mutual estoppel.

34. *See generally* Francis E. McGovern, *Resolving Mature Mass Tort Litigation,* 69 B.U. L. REV. 659 (1989).

35. *In re* Northern District of California Dalkon Shield IUD Products Liability Litigation, 693 F.2d 847, 852 (9th Cir. 1982), *cert. denied,* 459 U.S. 1171 (1983).

36. *Id.* at 851 (quoting McDonnell Douglas Corp. v. U.S. District Court, 523 F.2d 1083, 1086 (9th Cir. 1975), *cert. denied,* 425 U.S. 911 (1976)).

37. 28 U.S.C. § 2283 (1988).

38. *In re* Federal Skywalk Cases, 680 F.2d 1175, 1180–83 (8th Cir.), *cert. denied,* 459 U.S. 988 (1982). *But see In re* Joint Eastern & Southern District Asbestos Litigation, 134 F.R.D. 32, 36 (E. & S.D.N.Y. 1990).

39. Schreier v. Merrell Dow Pharmaceutical, Inc., 745 F.2d 58 (6th Cir. 1984).

40. Will v. United States, 389 U.S. 90, 95 (1967).

41. Transcript of Proceedings at 3, *In re* Richardson-Merrell, Inc. "Bendectin" Products Liability Litigation, MDL-486 (S.D. Ohio Oct. 31, 1984).

42. Letter from Honorable Carl Rubin to author (June 10, 1994).

43. Transcript of Proceedings at 13, *In re* Richardson-Merrell, Inc. "Bendectin" Products Liability Litigation, MDL-486 (S.D. Ohio Oct. 31, 1984).

44. *Id.* at 172; *see also* David Lauter, *Confusion Reigns Over Bendectin,* NAT'L L.J., Nov. 12, 1984, at 3.

45. Transcript of Proceedings at 178, *In re* Richardson-Merrell, Inc. "Bendectin" Products Liability Litigation, MDL-486 (S.D. Ohio Oct. 31, 1984); *see also* Jack B. Weinstein, *Ethical Dilemmas in Mass Tort Litigation,* 88 Nw. U. L. REV. 469, 509–10 (1994) (expressing lack of confidence in ability to predict future claimants).

Chapter 14
The MDL-486 Trial

In the aftermath of the Court of Appeals ruling and the hearing on future claimants, Judge Rubin rescheduled the common issues trial for February 4, 1985. He permitted additional plaintiffs to opt into the trial; by the time the trial began, over 800 cases involving 1,100 children with birth defects and their parents were to have their Bendectin claims resolved in the MDL-486 trial.[1] But all was not as it was before the settlement.

The settlement and unsettlement had a debilitating impact on the PLCC and its ability to coordinate efforts and function cohesively.[2] Jim Butler and Tom Bleakley were angry about Stanley Chesley's overreaching in negotiating the settlement and his aggressive and misleading efforts to market the settlement to other Bendectin plaintiffs' lawyers. Chesley (along with Eaton and Kokus) had seen a multi-million dollar settlement overturned by lawyers who in Chesley's view had unrealistic assessments of the merits of the case. Moreover, Butler and Bleakley had done so by using a variety of materials that were confidential or subject to a protective order (such as Merrell's insurance coverage) and might even harm the underlying case.[3] Chesley tried to obtain a measure of revenge by refusing to provide Butler with evidence gathered during MDL-486 discovery for a Bendectin case Butler was to begin trying in the California state courts in November 1984. Instead, Chesley filed a motion with the court seeking instructions about how to respond to Butler's request, thereby delaying his access to the information. The PLCC remained fractured for the duration of MDL-486.

Another consequence of the enmity created by the settlement schism was conflict over who would assume the lead counsel role at the trial. Tom Bleakley, as the most experienced trial lawyer on the PLCC except for Jim Butler, was the choice for the original trial in 1984. Butler, who had been disqualified from serving on the PLCC by Judge Rubin because of an ethical charge in another case,[4] could not participate in MDL-486 in 1984. Although later reinstated to the PLCC, he was not involved in the second trial, because his California state court case was still being tried in February 1985. But since the conflict over the settlement, Bleakley and Chesley were not talking, and the relationship between Bleakley and the other members of the PLCC was strained. Judge Rubin, upon being informed of the difficulties, appointed Allen Eaton as the chief trial lawyer, although Bleakley was permitted to assist. During the MDL-486 trial, however, Bleakley was denied access to most of the materials gathered by the PLCC during discovery.[5]

The question that the jury had to decide, as Judge Rubin explained at the outset of the trial, was quite, perhaps deceptively, simple: "Does Bendectin cause birth defects, yes or no?"[6] The trial consisted of the testimony of nine experts for plaintiffs and ten experts for Merrell. Ironically, that structure had been forecast by Stanley Chesley when Judge Rubin first proposed a bifurcated trial structure. Chesley complained to Judge Rubin, "it will be a battle of experts, where we put on our ten experts and they put on their ten experts." Judge Rubin reassured him: "Mr. Chesley, there's one thing that I will assure you, as sure as today is Monday [it was], that ain't going to happen. There just aren't going to be twenty experts."[7] There weren't; only nineteen.

At the outset of the trial, Judge Rubin took pains to impress the jury with the significance of the trial they were about to see. Rubin was concerned that, as a result of the bifurcation order and the trial structure, only the scientific evidence on the question of the capacity of Bendectin to cause birth defects would be presented in the first phase. No plaintiffs would testify; no evidence bearing on more familiar concepts like culpability or damages would be presented. Judge Rubin told the jury:

> Let me suggest to you that what you are about to do may be one of the most important things you will ever do in your entire life. . . . It involves not only the plaintiffs, who are individuals; it involves people, scientists, people who have done experiments, people who are employees of the defendant company.[8]

The thrust of the plaintiffs' case, as Allen Eaton explained to the jury in his opening statement, was the combination of results of animal studies, the adverse drug reports, and the impact of chemicals on cells. Once again, as in *Mekdeci,* plaintiffs attacked Merrell's testing of Bendectin, citing the Staples study and the methodological and data deficiencies in the Bunde-Bowles study. The purpose of this critique was to diminish the studies' significance with regard to Bendectin's teratogenicity. Plaintiffs' epidemiologists hammered at the lack of power (ability to detect low-level associations) in the epidemiology studies relied on by Merrell and consequently their inability to prove its safety. They spent considerable time critiquing many of the epidemiological studies, pointing out methodological problems. The other prong of plaintiffs' attack was to downplay the importance of epidemiology in identifying toxic drugs. Eaton pointed out that aspirin was on the market for 60 years before epidemiologists connected it with Reye's syndrome. Of course, epidemiology is a scientific discipline that has become increasingly sophisticated in the last several decades.

Expert witnesses for the plaintiffs also emphasized the similar chemical structure of doxylamine, the antihistamine component of Bendectin, to Benadryl, for which there was evidence of teratogenicity in animals studies.[9] The impact of antihistamines on nerve endings in in vitro tests was also presented. Those tests had been performed in the early 1950s and showed damage to nerve cells. Moreover, plaintiffs stressed, embryo nerve endings are far more sensitive than adult nerve endings. In addition to eliciting this information from its own experts, the plaintiffs repeatedly obtained similar concessions from Merrell's experts on cross-examination.

Dr. William McBride testified as he had in *Mekdeci*, this time by videotape rather than in person. McBride explained the results of his teratology studies of Bendectin with rabbits. Witnesses also discussed the adverse drug reports on Bendectin and especially the large proportion of limb-implicated defects, the same evidence that had been so influential for Betty Mekdeci during her investigation.

As part of their attack on the studies that tended to exonerate Bendectin, the plaintiffs brought out the financial connections between Merrell and many researchers. One particularly revealing episode concerned Dr. Andrew Hendrickx, who performed a primate teratology study that found holes in the hearts of immature fetuses. Merrell then provided a quarter of a million dollars for a subsequent study, which failed to confirm the initial study. Correspondence between Merrell and Hendrickx revealed that the former had considerable influence over the study design and the ultimate written report.

The PLCC made a number of difficult choices in presenting its case. It decided to emphasize the doxylamine component of Bendectin as the culprit rather than dicyclomine. In part, this was because all plaintiffs had been exposed to doxylamine but only those who had taken Bendectin before November 1976 had received dicyclomine. In part, it was because doxylamine was an antihistamine and concerns had been raised about the teratogenicity of another antihistamine, Benadryl. Very little evidence was introduced about the epidemiological studies finding statistically significant associations between heart defects and pyloric stenosis, because the overall strategy was to downplay epidemiology in its significance in identifying teratogens. Far more plaintiffs had limb defects than pyloric stenosis, the latter of which would not justify large damage awards.

Despite the lack of epidemiological evidence, the PLCC managed a persuasive presentation of the teratogenicity of Bendectin during its case in chief. Judge Rubin summarily denied the defendant's motion for a directed verdict at the close of the plaintiff's case; at the time he was of the opinion that the plaintiffs would win the trial. Indeed, he retained that view until the third of Merrell's witnesses testified.

By contrast with the plaintiffs, epidemiology was the centerpiece of Merrell's case. Frank Woodside spent most of his opening statement surveying the many epidemiological studies that had been performed and their outcome. Woodside also confronted the *post hoc, ergo propter hoc* (literally, "after this, therefore because of this") thinking that Merrell worried might lead the jury to conclude that Bendectin was a teratogen. Birth defects exist in many children of mothers who took Bendectin, Woodside conceded. But he then employed a clever analogy to demonstrate why that fact was irrelevant. Most drownings occur in the summer, when the sales of ice cream also are at their height. Despite the association between ice cream sales and drownings, Woodside pointed out, there is no causal connection. Similarly, other causes may be present that explain birth defects and Bendectin's connection is merely casual, not causal. Woodside, like Ed Walsh in *Mekdeci*, also emphasized the importance of statistical significance. Having lost the legal battle with Judge Rubin to exclude any association that was not statistically significant, Merrell took that argument to the jury, vigorously contending that unless a study's results were statistically significant it could not support a causal inference. Finally, Woodside took time to explain to the jury the evolution and development of toxicological and epidemiological methodology, so as to defuse the criticism that he knew would be heaped on the early Bendectin studies.

Dr. Brian MacMahon, head of the Epidemiology Department at the Harvard School of Public Health, was the lead-off witness for Merrell, and he testified about the human studies that had been performed. After pooling the data on specific birth defects and evaluating the overall evidence, MacMahon concluded that there was no basis for believing that Bendectin was teratogenic. The cross-examination of MacMahon was a series of small battles won by Tom Bleakley in obtaining concessions from MacMahon about significant flaws in many of the studies. He admitted the weakness of cohort studies in their ability to identify an association where the effect is rare—the lack of power in that type of study.

He characterized the Bunde-Bowles study, performed by Merrell, as very weak. He acknowledged that a number of studies suffered from a definition of exposure that was too broad, because it included women who took Bendectin outside the period of organogenesis. He explained that some studies suffered from poor identification of birth defects in the cohort and control groups, evidenced by an abnormally low finding of birth defects. He conceded that misclassification may have occurred where Bendectin was available over the counter, and thus a member of the control group might have obtained and taken it. Similarly, using prescriptions as the basis for exposure may result in misclassification because of women who never fill the prescription, or who fill it but never take it. Despite the criticisms of a number of studies, MacMahon remained unflappable about his overall conclusion that Bendectin was not a teratogen.

Dr. James Goddard, a former head of the FDA and the Centers for Disease Control, was Merrell's third witness. Ironically, in light of his assistance to Merrell in its defense of Bendectin, Goddard had been an outspoken administrator who was known as a strict regulator of the industry. Judge Rubin viewed Goddard as the turning point in the trial. The most significant portion of Goddard's testimony was based on the work of Steven Lamm, who had been hired by the guardian ad litem appointed by Judge Rubin in the settlement hearings. At the hearing on how to allocate the settlement fund, Lamm demonstrated the basis for his conclusion that Bendectin did not cause birth defects with powerful graphics. The charts depicted the incidence of birth defects and the number of Bendectin prescriptions over time.

Bendectin sales had fluctuated modestly from 1970 through 1979, when use began to drop off sharply. By 1981 use had dropped by 60 percent, and by 1984 sales ceased altogether. Lamm obtained data on the incidence of birth defects from 1970 to 1984 from the Centers for Disease Control and superimposed birth defect rates for the eight birth defect categories at issue in the trial from 1970 to 1984 on the sales of Bendectin over the same time period. Those charts showed birth defect rates that remained stable or increased while Bendectin sales dropped dramatically. Virtually no correlation could be identified between any of the eight categories of birth defect and Bendectin sales.

Merrell immediately appreciated the power of this evidence. Initially, Merrell sought to persuade Judge Rubin to appoint Lamm as the court's expert, thereby cloaking his testimony with the aura of unbiased expert. When Judge Rubin denied Merrell's request, it nevertheless went ahead and had Dr. Goddard, with his credentials in the public health field, familiarize himself with Lamm's exhibits and testify about them at trial. The exhibits and evidence were a strategical tour de force. Judge Rubin felt that it was Goddard's testimony that turned the tide in the case. In retrospect, he observed: "The most telling single piece of evidence I have ever seen after 23 years on the Federal Bench is the [Lamm] exhibit."[10] His view was shared by a juror who remarked in a post-verdict interview, on the influence of the time-line evidence presented by Goddard and by Tom Bleakley.[11] Bleakley felt that the time-line exhibits played a crucial role and that the PLCC was not well-prepared to handle them in cross-examining Goddard. Although the exhibits had been provided to the PLCC a month earlier, both Allen Eaton and Bleakley were surprised by them at trial.[12] Those crucial time-line charts were available for the MDL-486 trial because of the serendipity of the settlement, which brought Steven Lamm and his time-line exhibits to Bendectin litigation. Those exhibits would not have existed or been introduced if the trial had gone forward when initially scheduled in June 1984.

The weaknesses of time-line studies as evidence of causation deserve mention. Despite their powerful effect on the jury and the judge, several problems prevent time-line analysis from providing conclusive or even particularly probative evidence. The major problem is that by simply comparing two variables, the rate of exposure of the agent and the incidence of the studied effect, time-line studies ignore other causal factors that may also change over time and which are not reflected in a two variable comparison. If those other causal variables are known, they can be accounted for, at least theoretically. However, few of the causes of birth defects are known, leaving Lamm's work to compare only Bendectin sales with birth defects. In addition, the data may contain inaccuracies— as noted above, the number of Bendectin sales is not a perfect measure of the number of fetuses exposed to Bendectin during the period of organogenesis because women may obtain Bendectin after that period or prescriptions may be written for patients who do not take the drug.

Perhaps the primary fallibility of time-line studies is their inability to detect small effects. While a graph of thalidomide usage from 1959 to 1961 against children born with certain birth defect syndromes looks like identical twin peaks with a six month lag, the strength of thalidomide as a teratogen makes it stand out against all other causes.[13] But if an agent has a more modest effect, random variations or other causal factors changing over time might mask a weak effect. Similarly, if the categories of defect employed are too general, an association may be diluted. In short, time-line analyses may be useful for generating hypotheses about causal factors or even providing strong evidence of powerful toxins, but they are not very useful in determining small effects.[14] Because of the structure of MDL-486, without any issue of individual causation, the jury was required in the first phase to answer the question of whether Bendectin had any capacity to cause birth defects, however weak. Plainly, cohort and case-control epidemiological studies are preferable evidence of causation, but the Lamm charts nevertheless played an especially persuasive role both with the jury and Judge Rubin.

After 22 days of testimony over five weeks, the presentations of the parties concluded on March 7, 1985.

In his closing argument to the jury, Allen Eaton first emphasized the importance of the proceedings, explaining that the jury's verdict would affect the lives of thousands of people for many years into the future. Addressing the merits, Eaton cleverly attempted to shift the burden of proof to Merrell: "[Merrell] would say that it's not in our system of justice, say that it's not their burden to prove it's safe. But I ask you, shouldn't that be the starting point, that any drug given to a pregnant woman during the period of organogenesis has to be looked at with a jaundiced eye to be sure that it does not harm this helpless child at the most vulnerable part of its life?" [15]

The closing argument on behalf of the plaintiffs was split between Eaton and Tom Bleakley, who addressed the scientific aspects of the case. Bleakley reiterated the critique of Merrell's epidemiological evidence. In addition to emphasizing the case reports and the abnormal percentage of congenital limb anomalies for Bendectin, Bleakley commented on the identification of German measles and Dilantin as teratogens from case reports—he would have loved to have added thalidomide to that list, but Judge Rubin had forbidden that line of argument.[16]

Frank Woodside asserted in his closing argument that Bendectin was an "innocent bystander" to birth defects that would have occurred anyway. Woodside responded to the plaintiffs' criticism of the epidemiological studies by arguing that, for them to be flawed did not mean that Bendectin causes birth defects, only that there were flaws in the studies. In that regard, Woodside had a valid point: plaintiffs had not taken the next step of showing how the flaws in the studies would have modified the outcome, a considerably more difficult undertaking than merely leveling the criticism. But the burden of proof was on the plaintiffs and without that second step, plaintiffs' evidence was limited to the less salient forms of toxicological evidence such as animal and in vitro studies and chemical structure analysis. In addition, Woodside repeated his arguments about the importance of confidence intervals and statistical significance. If epidemiological evidence were to be employed as evidence in court, he argued, then all of the discipline's methods must be adopted, including statistical analysis and the threshold for accepting a study's results as nonrandom.

Judge Rubin's instructions to the jury explained: "The question you must answer is whether the plaintiffs established by a preponderance of the evidence that the ingestion of Bendectin at therapeutic doses during

the period of fetal organogenesis is a proximate cause of birth defects."
If the jury found that it was, it would then go on and consider eight specific categories of birth defect and determine those for which Bendectin
was a cause.

The jury needed only 4 1/2 hours to reach its verdict in favor of Merrell. While the verdict was an enormous relief for Merrell, it knew that
the outcome would not conclude Bendectin litigation. Barry Nace and
other plaintiffs' lawyers who had eschewed the MDL-486 trial would continue to pursue their cases in a variety of fora. The *Oxendine* verdict and
the unfavorable procedure in MDL-486 persuaded those lawyers that
they could succeed in individual cases. But the trial that could have
spelled devastation for Merrell had concluded with a ringing victory.

As expected, the PLCC filed a post-trial motion seeking to overturn
the jury's verdict. At this point, however, the PLCC was at its lowest organizational ebb. The motion employed a shotgun approach, identifying
44 errors that allegedly justified a new trial, many of which were not
briefed or even clearly articulated. The motion had the flavor of a
cobbled together effort of several uncoordinated attorneys. Despite the
unremarkable and unfocused nature of the motion, Judge Rubin responded with a lengthy (35 pages plus a 25-page appendix) opinion that
was primarily addressed to the court of appeals and designed to persuade
that court why it should not overturn the judgment. The most salient
grounds raised by plaintiffs revolved around the structure of the trial,
which is addressed in chapter 15, and the exclusion of child-plaintiffs
from the courtroom.

The strongest ground for reversal was the exclusion of children under
10 and those with visible birth defects from the trial. In June of 1985,
after the MDL-486 trial was concluded, the Sixth Circuit decided *Helminski v. Ayerst Laboratories*,[17] a case in which the plaintiff's birth defects were
alleged to be the result of his mother's exposure to an anesthetic manufactured by the defendant. The trial judge had excluded the child, by
then a teenager, from the liability phase of the trial. The child was six
feet tall but weighed only 90 pounds, suffered from severe neurological
impairment, was unable to speak, had an extremely low IQ, emitted
frightening sounds at times, and was not toilet trained. Remarkably, despite those characteristics, the Sixth Circuit characterized his physical
appearance as normal.

The Sixth Circuit began with the proposition that a nondisruptive, un-
impaired plaintiff always has the right to be present in the courtroom.
From there, the court recognized the possibility that a party's abnormal
appearance or behavior could prejudice the jury. Nevertheless, the court
recognized three justifications for a party's presence: the evidentiary
value of the injuries with respect to damages, the opportunity for the

party to assist counsel, and the opportunity to be present and to perceive legal proceedings affecting one's rights. Despite potential prejudice, a party could not be excluded where the first ground existed: a plaintiff always has a right to be present at the damages phase of the case. Relying on two earlier decisions, the court also adopted the principle that a plaintiff whose condition, allegedly the result of defendant's conduct, renders her unable to comprehend the proceedings *or* assist counsel could be excluded from the trial. Exclusion, however, required that the trial judge engage in a careful assessment of the plaintiff's condition to determine if her presence at the trial would inevitably be prejudicial.

The child plaintiffs plainly could not have aided their attorneys at the trial. The trial concerned scientific evidence that was well beyond all but the most remarkable plaintiff—a Betty Mekdeci—to comprehend well enough to be of assistance. But surely many of the child plaintiffs, some of whom were adolescents or teenagers, could have readily perceived and understood (to some degree) these proceedings that would determine whether they would recover damages from Merrell. Yet the disjunctive test adopted by the Sixth Circuit in *Helminski* enabled Judge Rubin to conclude in his opinion denying the plaintiffs a new trial that "the children could [not] meaningfully consult with counsel [in the causation] phase of the case." [18]

There was, however, another problem with Judge Rubin's exclusion order. The Sixth Circuit was quite careful in *Helminski* to point out that not every physically impaired plaintiff could be excluded. Only those whose appearance or behavior was so severe that it would intrude upon the jury's unbiased functioning could be barred from the courtroom. The trial judge in *Helminski* had never made any particularized determination about the plaintiff; indeed, the trial judge had never even observed the plaintiff. Without that individualized assessment, the Sixth Circuit held that exclusion was improper, although not reversible error, because the plaintiff could not comprehend nor assist and the jury heard a thorough rendition of his condition.

Judge Rubin had not made any individualized assessment of the child plaintiffs that he excluded, unsurprisingly since *Helminski* was decided after his exclusion decision. Rather, he had excluded all children with visible birth defects, regardless how severe or pitiable they were. In ruling on the plaintiffs' motion for a new trial, he skirted the problem of individual assessment, instead speaking generally about sympathy for children with birth defects, and the adoration for "newborn infants."

Judge Rubin's analysis, however, ignored the fact that some of the excluded plaintiffs were not infants but older children or teenagers. Their birth defects covered a gamut of physical manifestations, some of which were relatively benign, such as a cleft lip. This issue presented the greatest challenge to the validity of the trial and the best opportunity for the PLCC to persuade the court of appeals to order a new trial.

Reversal of a judgment that had consumed enormous private and public resources, however, required a more compelling error than a deprivation of procedural rights to be present and observe the course of proceedings.[19] One will not find the principle that large cases require more severe errors for reversal documented in any appellate decision. Yet it plays a powerful pragmatic role in appellate courts' decision making processes. Because of its concerns about the huge expenditure of resources required for a new trial, the Sixth Circuit, in effect, granted more power to the trial court in the Bendectin consolidated litigation than it would have had in an individual action.[20]

Despite a presumption against nonretroactivity for common-law decisions, a majority of the Sixth Circuit panel held that *Helminski* would not be applied retroactively to cases that were tried before it was decided. The Court of Appeals added that it doubted that any significant change would have resulted even if *Helminski* had been respected because of the need for space management with over a thousand plaintiffs. That justification conflated two distinct problems: first, who was entitled to be present at the trial and second, how available resources would be allocated among those entitled. Addressing the second could hardly obviate ignoring the first.

Judge Jones dissented on the question of retroactivity, arguing persuasively that *Helminski* was not such a break with prior decisions that it should be made nonretroactive. He would have permitted a retrial for the children who were excluded from the trial, although it is difficult to understand why the sub-group whose physical appearance was severe enough to justify exclusion should be afforded that opportunity. By the slim margin of a single judge's vote, the jury's verdict was upheld. The following year, the Supreme Court denied the plaintiffs' last gasp attempt for further review, by denying a petition for certiorari.[21]

Notes

1. *In re Bendectin Litigation*, 857 F.2d 290, 293 (6th Cir. 1988), *cert. denied*, 488 U.S. 1006 (1989). Forty percent of the cases transferred by the multidistrict panel opted into the consolidated trial.

2. *See, e.g.*, Letter from Thomas Bleakley to MDL-486 Lead Counsel (Nov. 29, 1984).

3. Letter from Allen Eaton to James Butler (Aug. 27, 1984).

4. *See* David Lauter, *Bendectin Trial Disintegrates; Allegations of Misconduct in "Perfect Case,"* NAT'L L.J., Feb. 21, 1983, at 1.

5. Letter from Thomas Bleakley to author (July 20, 1994).

6. Transcript of Proceedings at 85, *In re* Richardson-Merrell, Inc. "Bendectin" Products Liability Litigation, MDL-486 (S.D. Ohio Feb. 4, 1985).

7. Transcript of Proceedings at 36, *In re* Richardson-Merrell, Inc. "Bendectin" Products Liability Litigation, MDL-486 (S.D. Ohio Mar. 19, 1984).

8. *In re* Richardson-Merrell, Inc. "Bendectin" Products Liability Litigation, 624 F. Supp. 1212, 1222 (S.D. Ohio 1985), *aff'd*, 857 F.2d 290 (6th Cir. 1988), *cert. denied*, 488 U.S. 1006 (1989).

9. *See* M.C. Shelesnyak & A. Michael Davies, *Disturbance of Pregnancy in Mouse and Rat by Systemic Antihistaminic Treatment*, 89 PROC. SOC. EXP. BIOL. & MED. 629 (1955).

10. Letter from Honorable Carl B. Rubin to author (May 9, 1994).

11. Ben L. Kaufman & David Lauter, *Bendectin Verdict Does Not End Suits*, NAT'L L.J., Mar. 25, 1985, at 3, col. 2.

12. Transcript of Proceedings at 2624, *In re* Richardson-Merrell, Inc. "Bendectin" Products Liability Litigation, MDL-486 (S.D. Ohio Feb. 27, 1985).

13. J. WILSON & E. FRASER, HANDBOOK OF TERATOLOGY 248 (New York: Plenum Press, 1977).

14. S.M. Barlow & F.M. Sullivan, Correspondence, *Debendox and Congenital Malformations in Northern Ireland*, 282 BRIT. MED. J. 148 (1981).

15. Transcript of Proceedings at 3565–66, *In re* Richardson-Merrell, Inc. "Bendectin" Products Liability Litigation, MDL-486 (S.D. Ohio Mar. 11, 1985).

16. *Id.* at 3576.

17. 766 F.2d 208 (6th Cir.), *cert. denied*, 474 U.S. 981 (1985).

18. *In re* Richardson-Merrell, Inc. "Bendectin" Products Liability Litigation, 624 F. Supp. 1212, 1224 (S.D. Ohio 1985), *aff'd*, 857 F.2d 290 (6th Cir. 1988), *cert. denied*, 488 U.S. 1006 (1989).

19. *See* Mark A. Peterson & Molly Selvin, *Mass Justice: The Limited and Unlimited Power of the Courts*, 54 LAW & CONTEMP. PROBS. 227, 242–43 (Summer 1991).

20. *Id.* at 246.

21. 488 U.S. 1006 (1989).

Chapter 15
Aggregative Procedure in Mass Toxic Substances Litigation

Mass torts have emerged as a major portion of the mix of civil litigation and make up a considerable amount of the litigation explosion.[1] A great deal of scholarly, judicial, and reformist attention has been devoted to aggregative procedure in mass torts.[2] The emergence of huge numbers of claimants in the asbestos, Agent Orange, Dalkon Shield, DES, breast implant, and other mass toxic substances litigation has driven this scrutiny. Judges, academics, and lawyers legitimately concerned about the wastefulness, inconsistency, and delay involved in individual adjudications have championed the greater efficiency of aggregate procedure. It is safe to say that no consensus has yet emerged, yet there is an air of openness and willingness to employ a variety of aggregative procedures to accommodate the unusual demands of mass tort litigation. Several reform proposals designed to enhance the potential for aggregative procedure have emerged. The experience with Bendectin provides a number of lessons, some cautionary, about the aggregative movement. There is reason to hesitate before embracing the most radical of the proposals.[3]

By design, this chapter does not attempt a thorough canvassing of all of the proposals, experiments, issues, and conflicts that have surfaced in the cases and literature to date. Thus, for example, two of the more intractable issues of mass tort aggregation under current law, conflict of law and jurisdictional impediments to consolidation of state and federal cases, were not of significance in MDL-486. Similarly, because the MDL-486 trial exonerated Merrell, there was no occasion to confront post-aggregative issues (addressing individual issues, such as individual causation and damages) that have been addressed by several courts and thoughtful commentators. Instead, the focus of this chapter is on several facets of aggregative procedure raised and illuminated by MDL-486. Those matters include the multidistrict consolidation in which common issues discovery was conducted on behalf of all plaintiffs by the PLCC, the common issues trial, and the polyfurcation of the trial that aggregation enabled. Aggregation of mass torts is closely tied with the emergence of competing paradigms of plaintiffs' lawyers, juxtaposing the traditional advocate-agent for an aggrieved victim with the modern entrepreneurial lawyer, who enlists plaintiffs as inventory. That clash of models was starkly presented in the intra-PLCC conflict over the global settlement.

Deterrence is another issue that frequently arises in the aggregative procedure debate. To obtain optimal deterrence, some argue, requires aggregation, especially when the harms suffered by claimants are relatively minor or difficult to prove.[4] This claim may be correct, but our understanding of the role that tort law plays in affecting the behavior of risk producers is quite primitive. Some argue, based on theory or specific example, that tort law over-deters.[5] Bendectin is frequently a favorite of the latter form of proof, a matter taken up in chapter 18. Others argue that the many access barriers to litigation that exist result in far too little deterrence; Professor Sugarman is the leading skeptic about any deterrent effect of the tort system.[6] The search for a correct answer probably requires disaggregating the question and recognizing that the tort system is really many subsystems that affect a wide variety of human behavior and economic activity, ranging from car driving to chemical production to commercial airline travel. So many different deterrent variables exist in those various activities—risk uncertainty, government regulation, length of latency period, time from risk creating activity to lawsuit, and the influence of economic incentives on risk creators, to name a few—that generalizations are probably unhelpful.[7]

The claim for underdeterrence is most plausible for minor injuries in which the damages are too small to incur the expense of litigating. For reasons explained below, the federal courts are quite constrained in providing a forum for these claims,[8] and they carry their own baggage—other low value cases due to weaknesses in liability or causation—that the legal system should not encourage.[9] In any case, the aggregation debate for mass toxic substances focuses on claims that are otherwise viable, and it is those cases that this chapter addresses. I leave to a day of better information the question of the impact of aggregation on optimal deterrence in the mass tort arena.

A reminder-caveat is in order. Chapter 2 explained the benefits and the limitations of categorizations such as mass tort. Bendectin has frequently been referred to as a mass toxic substances litigation, and that refinement recognizes the difference between the single event mass tort such as an airplane crash and those in which the defendants' behavior, the plaintiffs' exposure, and the resulting injuries occur over a period that is typically several decades. But even that powerful dichotomy is an inadequate taxonomy of mass torts. Some mass torts, such as the Beverly Hills Supper Club are modest in their size, amounting to several hundred claimants. Others, such as Bendectin, number in the thousands. The asbestos, Agent Orange, and Dalkon Shield litigation each involved claimants numbering in the hundreds of thousands, although in the latter two cases that was in part because of aggregative procedures that made claiming quite easy. Some mass torts, typically accident cases like the Hyatt Regency Skywalk litigation, are geographically concentrated, while others, including many toxic substance cases, are quite dispersed. Those differences have very important implications for the relative costs and benefits of aggregative procedure. Also crucial in assessing mass tort adjudicative procedure is the legal complexity involved and the nature of the evidence, especially scientific evidence, that will be brought to bear on those issues. As those familiar with the Agent Orange case are aware, the number and complexity of issues presented in that case— including the government contractor defense, the *Feres* doctrine, relative responsibility among multiple defendants, and ascertaining exposure to Agent Orange among those who served in Vietnam—dwarfed the issues confronted in MDL-486.

MDL-486 did not proceed formally as a class action, with the exception of the class certified for settlement and overturned by the Sixth Circuit. Rather MDL-486 comprised a consolidation of several hundred individual cases. In theory, there is a difference: consolidated cases proceed on an individual basis, each represented by counsel, under the unified tent of a single coordinated proceeding.[10] By contrast, a class action is a single case that proceeds on a representational basis to determine the rights of a class of passive individuals. A named plaintiff and class lawyers represent the interests of all members of the class.[11]

MDL-486 much more resembled a class action than a consolidated proceeding. Common issues discovery was conducted by the PLCC without involvement from individual plaintiffs' attorneys. Settlement negotiations on behalf of all claimants were conducted by Stanley Chesley. The trial was conducted by the PLCC; time and space constraints precluded participation by individual counsel.[12] Individual plaintiffs' autonomy in the proceedings was nonexistent. With control of the litigation reposed in the PLCC, and with claimants and their lawyers playing a purely passive role, MDL-486 was a de facto rule 23(b)(3) class action.[13] Thus, a working definition of aggregative procedure for this chapter emerges: the joining together of individual cases for some aspect(s) of adjudication resulting in reduced individual control over the proceedings.[14]

Multidistrict Consolidation

The consolidation of cases for pretrial preparation is far less controversial than class action treatment, even though it is, once invoked,
compulsory.[15] Most have accepted multidistrict consolidation, and it is
common for plaintiffs and defendants to agree on multidistrict consolidation. That agreement is a sure indication that there are significant efficiencies for both sides that outweigh strategical concerns. Even in
the acrimonious controversy over aggregation in the breast implant
litigation, all were agreed that multidistrict consolidation should be
employed.[16] Once again, in theory consolidation does not oust the individual plaintiff or her lawyer from participating, but often, as in MDL-
486, that is the practical effect and a significant contribution to the
efficiency benefit. The consequence of multidistrict consolidation is often to vest in a small cadre of plaintiffs' lawyers the authority and expertise to pursue and litigate that type of claim.

Not surprisingly, the efficiencies derived from consolidated discovery
in MDL-486 appear massive.[17] Comprehensive discovery on liability, punitive damages, and the scientific issues related to causation was conducted. This discovery preempted repetitive and duplicative depositions,
interrogatories, and document production. That prospect prompted
Merrell to seek multidistrict litigation when it glimpsed the costs, distrac-
tions, and general unattractiveness of parallel discovery in the *Koller* and
Cordova cases, following the *Mekdeci* discovery. Although discovery on individual issues and trial remained outside the MDL-486 consolidated
proceedings, it provided an economical means to address a significant
proportion of the resources required to adjudicate Bendectin claims.

The multidistrict consolidation also afforded plaintiff's lawyers a far
more level playing field in terms of stakes and available resources. The
PLCC, which controlled a significant proportion of Bendectin cases either directly or through referrals, had the incentives and resources to
undertake the task of thorough discovery in a large and complex mass
tort case. Indeed, multidistrict consolidation appears to provide the
economies of scale and financial incentives for plaintiffs that Professor
Rosenberg has argued require mandatory class actions. Moreover, the
authority of the multidistrict court to award attorney's fees to the PLCC
from any class or individual recoveries provided additional financial incentive. The contrast with Cohen and Kokus in *Mekdeci*, overwhelmed
with the financial and labor demands of pretrial preparation, is quite
stark.

But all may not be quite what the above suggests. The stark dichotomy between individual and aggregative procedure is misleading. In
reality there are a variety of informal mechanisms that afford plaintiffs'

attorneys significant economies. The accumulation of cases by Kokus and Belli through publicity, solicitation, and referral is one such means. As other attorneys emerged as leaders in Bendectin litigation, including Stanley Chesley, Barry Nace, and Tom Bleakley, they also obtained numerous other cases through referrals by attorneys unwilling or unable to invest the resources required to litigate a Bendectin case.[18] In addition to specialization, information sharing networks are a common phenomenon among plaintiffs' lawyers in multi-claimant case congregations. The first notable example occurred in the MER/29 litigation against Merrell, with the formation of a coordinating group to disseminate information, prepare document forms, and present educational seminars.[19] Specialized seminars for mass disaster cases, such as asbestos and breast implants, litter the continuing legal education landscape. Reporters for a variety of large-scale specialized litigations are prevalent.[20] The American Trial Lawyers Association, an organization of plaintiffs' personal injury lawyers, runs an information exchange, organizes specialized litigation groups, and sponsors meetings that facilitate information sharing. As Professor Marc Galanter observes:

> [N]etworks may provide a solution to the problem of aggregation—i.e., serve as an alternative way to induce lawyer investments, achieve economics of scale, eliminating costly repetitive searches. Transmission of information along litigation networks may be an alternative to the class action or consolidation of cases . . . .[21]

The point is not that multidistrict consolidation is without its efficiencies—it surely is. Rather, more modestly, the advantages of consolidation must be assessed against the alternative—which is not the individual-lawyer-with-separate-client-litigating-independently paradigm that some have employed.[22]

The MDL-486 consolidation does provide several lessons that might improve future toxic substance proceedings. The first concerns the inefficiencies resulting from the lack of precise definition or understanding of the common issues in the case. This uncertainty resulted in wasted discovery efforts and inefficiencies in the production of common issues trial materials, such as videotaped depositions. Yet the prescription to be clearer about defining the common issues at the outset of a toxic substances consolidation is quite unrealistic. As chapters 12 and 14 reveal, the scientific evidence available plays an important role in shaping the factual issues for trial. Beyond causation, liability issues, such as the state of the art, may well be affected by the evidence that is developed during discovery. Thus, a feedback loop operates, with an initial rough common issues formulation guiding discovery, which then requires further refinement of the issues. Indeed, the issues finally tried in MDL-486 might have been better refined to reflect the scientific evidence on specific birth defects, employing categories of birth defects based on common etiological mechanisms.

A related and important issue emerging from the MDL-486 consolidation is the danger of premature consolidation, which might freeze discovery at too early a time.[23] The history of mass toxic substances litigations is replete with the accretive development of information about causation and liability.[24] Multiple lawyers pursuing different approaches and sometimes building on prior work by others is probably best at uncovering the truth. Often causation evidence improves over time, as strikingly occurred in Bendectin litigation and in virtually all other mass toxic litigations.

It would have been unfortunate if consolidation and comprehensive discovery had been conducted in the Bendectin litigation in the late 1970s, when Betty Mekdeci was pursuing the first suit and there was a paucity of evidence about Bendectin's teratogenicity. Consolidations of asbestos, the Dalkon Shield, and perhaps breast implants have avoided this trap, likely because at the outset there existed only a few cases that did not justify multidistrict consolidation. The Agent Orange litigation, which was brought as a class action, may have suffered from this concern, as evidence of its association with a number of specific diseases has emerged subsequently.[25] At the very least, courts should be sensitive to this concern and be open to follow-up discovery after multidistrict consolidated discovery is completed.

Another modest improvement in multidistrict procedure would be to permit the consolidation of issues, rather than requiring that the entire case be transferred for consolidation. Where significant individual issues exist, discovery can be more effectively conducted in the plaintiff's home district. The judge supervising consolidated proceedings is not a convenient or practical overseer of the exchange of medical records, treating physician deposition, or the like. MDL-486 is pockmarked with instances in which Judge Rubin quite understandably resisted exercising control over individual case discovery. Lest there be confusion about authority, the judge overseeing the multidistrict litigation could be vested with the power to remand portions of a case to plaintiffs' home districts for pretrial treatment of individual issues. The Multidistrict Consolidation statute already sensibly provides for the separation of distinct claims; adding the flexibility to separate issues would facilitate the efficiency provided by multidistrict consolidation.

The final suggestion for reform of multidistrict litigation emerges from the difficulties engendered by the appointment of five separate lawyers from five different law firms as co-lead counsel.[26] The lack of hierarchy and absence of an organizational structure resulted in significant inefficiencies in MDL-486, as discussed in chapters 10, 13, and 14. Professor John Coffee has identified the patronage, slacking, inefficiency, and even chaos that attends the dispersal of authority in lead counsel committees.[27] One relatively simple solution is the appointment of a single lead counsel. Lead counsel then would have the authority to contract for additional legal services if required. By placing control over work assignments and compensation in a single lead counsel, an organizational structure would exist that could avoid much of the inefficiencies resulting from dispersed authority.

Appointing a single lead counsel would not come without disadvantages. Because counsel would have to possess the financial wherewithal to fund what might be an enormously expensive piece of litigation, a limited group of attorneys would qualify. Moreover, the attorney best able to fund the litigation may not be the attorney most knowledgeable about the underlying case (Stanley Chesley had little involvement in both Agent Orange and Bendectin when named to the lead counsel committee). Some commentators have also expressed concern about insufficient incentives to investigate and search for valid claims, especially if the attorney who does so is not rewarded with control over subsequent litigation. But as Bendectin and other contemporary mass disaster cases reveal, being involved at the outset provides significant rewards in the form of reputation and future clients. And attorneys who have invested to search, such as Kokus and Cohen in Bendectin, obtain human capital that make it likely they will be hired by lead counsel even if they are not appointed as lead counsel. In essence, that is what happened with the addition of Allen Eaton to the PLCC. In situations in which the individual litigation is at an advanced or mature stage, such as the multidistrict consolidation of asbestos in 1991, providing sole authority to a single lead counsel is probably infeasible.

Class Actionizing

Multidistrict consolidation does not necessarily imply a class action, although the two often accompany each other. Class actions, under current law, have a number of additional effects on class members' claims: a unitary trial on common issues occurs in a single forum determined by class counsel from among the available fora; settlement authority is reposed in class counsel; the legal issues and strategy to pursue are controlled by class counsel; and sometimes participation by claimants is compulsory, denying them an opportunity to opt out and pursue the claim individually.[28]

Several important concepts and procedural values are implicated in the mass tort class action debate: claim effectuation, efficiency, individ-

ual autonomy/dignity, necessity, consistency, and accuracy. A consideration of each of these illuminates the stakes and choices in the movement
toward employing class actions in mass toxic substances litigation.

Claim Effectuation

When the modern class action rules were promulgated in 1966, the
theory justifying them was claim effectuation. Class actions were a device
to permit the aggregation of individual claims that were too small to be
brought separately.[29] Chief Justice Burger reflected this view in *Deposit
Guaranty National Bank v. Roper.* "The use of the class-action procedure
for litigation of individual claims offers substantial advantages for named
plaintiffs; it may motivate them to bring cases that for economic reasons
might not be brought otherwise."[30] Beyond the benefit to individual
class members, the class action offers the social benefit of providing a
means for deterring those whose wrongdoing harms many, but only a
little bit.[31]

The hegemony of claim effectuation in the structure of Fed. R. Civ. P.
23 is evident. Class actions were not to be certified unless there were so
many class members that joinder of the individual cases was not feasible.[32] Rule 23(b)(3) requires notice to class members and the opportunity to exclude oneself from the class. Rule 23(b)(3) also requires that
a class action be superior to other forms of adjudication of the claims,
and expressly recognizes the importance of protecting the interests of
class members in proceeding individually if they so desire.[33]

Few mass personal injury suits fit the claim effectuation model. Moreover, tort actions were thought ill-suited for aggregative resolution because of their personal and discrete nature. Professor Judith Resnik puts
it well: "These individuals . . . have been understood to be complaining
about a personal body-causing wrong, to be addressed in the specific,
concrete circumstances of the events that caused the harm, of the nature
of the bodily injuries, of the extent of the damage, of the diverse legal
principles that governed the claim."[34] The Advisory Committee made
plain its view that large-scale torts were not an appropriate candidate for
class treatment: "a 'mass accident' resulting in injuries to numerous persons is ordinarily not appropriate for a class action . . . ."[35]

In addition to inappropriateness, limits on the federal courts' jurisdiction severely constrain their ability to serve a claim effectuation function for mass torts. That constraint arose in 1973, when the Supreme
Court declared that in class actions in which the claims are based on
state law, federal jurisdiction requires each claim have the statutorily
required amount in controversy (in excess of $50,000; $10,000 until
1988).[36] Claimants without the requisite amount in controversy must be

dismissed. To be sure, there are some cases in which claimants might be able to recover more than $50,000 but which are not viable as individual cases. But the $50,000 threshold surely screens out the vast majority of cases that cannot be feasibly brought as individual actions.[37]

Efficiency

The emergence in the ensuing decades of mass toxic substances litigation, with its extraordinary demands on the civil justice system's resources, has challenged the original presumption. Beginning in the late 1970s, a handful of class actions were certified in mass tort cases, including Agent Orange, asbestos, and the Dalkon Shield.[38] The Dalkon Shield class was reversed on appeal, but ultimately the litigation was resolved on an aggregative basis in bankruptcy court. By the mid- to late 1980s, a widely held opinion had emerged that the Advisory Committee's admonition about class actions for personal injury actions was ill-conceived and anachronistic. A variety of commentators and judges concluded that the time was ripe for aggregating mass tort cases.[39] Indeed, one of the titans of contemporary civil procedure, Professor Charles Alan Wright, has changed his view of the propriety of class treatment of mass torts, believing them appropriate today.[40]

The driving force behind this reappraisal is a shift from the claim effectuation paradigm to an efficiency paradigm.[41] With hundreds, thousands, and, in a few instances, hundreds of thousands of similar cases, the potential savings in public and private resources through aggregative procedure is quite enormous. Rather than repeatedly trying the defectiveness of an asbestos product or the knowledge that a manufacturer had of the dangers in case after case, as has become routine in asbestos litigation, aggregative procedure promised truncating those efforts with a single common hearing. "Class actions could all but eliminate redundant litigation costs," declares Professor David Rosenberg.[42] The shift from claim effectuation to efficiency is quite dramatic: claim effectuation was designed to increase utilization of the courts, while efficiency is designed to reduce consumption of adjudicative resources.

Necessity

Another justification for aggregative procedure present in some mass toxic substances cases is necessity. Necessity is explicitly recognized in Fed. R. Civ. P. 23(b)(1), which permits a mandatory (compulsory) class action when there is a limited fund available, which may be depleted before all claimants can assert their claims. Thus, if the available assets of a defendant are insufficient to satisfy the claims asserted against it, a mandatory class can be certified to provide a means for an equitable division of the available assets among all claimants. The efficiencies of such a procedure also help to preserve assets and increase the recovery of claimants.

Another form of necessity—though rarely characterized as such—is practical necessity: Without aggregative procedure, the number of claims asserted by mass tort plaintiffs is beyond the processing power and resources of the civil justice system. This rationale is most prevalent in asbestos litigation, which Judge Edward Becker has characterized as "the most serious crisis the federal court system has faced in its history."[43] Despite Judge Becker's hyperbole, the number of asbestos cases poses a "great wall" that serves as a practical barrier to the resolution of a large proportion of individual cases. In the Eastern District of Texas, one of the courts with the heaviest concentration of asbestos cases, the ratio of cases filed to cases disposed of was in excess of 2-1 in 1981–82. That ratio soared to over 9-1 during the following three years.[44] The queue was getting longer, and claimants simply could not get their cases resolved through traditional individualistic adjudication.[45] This practical necessity rationale invokes not only efficiency as a justification but elements of claim effectuation in making it possible for claimants frozen out of court by delay to obtain a resolution within a reasonable time frame.[46]

Compulsory Aggregation

Both necessity and efficiency imply compulsory aggregation. With compulsory aggregation, class members are not given the choice to opt out and pursue their individual action—they become captives of the representative suit. Current law limits compulsory class actions to the limited fund situation, but a proposed revision to Fed. R. Civ. P. 23 would provide more flexibility to certify a compulsory class or impose unpalatable conditions on those who choose to opt out. The most ardent champion of compulsory aggregation is Professor David Rosenberg, who argues that the inefficiencies of individual adjudications and free riding by those who choose to proceed individually mandate compulsory classes.[47]

Consistency

Another value implicated in aggregative procedure is one raised by Judge Rubin during the MDL-486 proceedings: consistency of outcome. A fundamental tenet is that similarly situated individuals should be treated equally by the law.[48] Aggregative resolution of common issues avoids the unfairness of differential treatment as well as "lay perceptions of fallibility, arbitrariness, irrationality, or worse"[49] in the legal system. Thus, consistency enhances public respect for judicial process as well as serving fairness through equal treatment. The concern in mass torts extends beyond consistency in liability determinations to avoiding widely disparate awards of damages for similar injuries.[50]

Autonomy

Often invoked in opposition to aggregation, especially compulsory aggregation, are the procedural values of litigant autonomy and dignified treatment.[51] These related non-instrumental concepts are less than crystalline, often difficult to operationalize, and frequently ignored in economic analyses of adjudicatory efficiency. They do reflect, however, deeply felt and long held perceptions regarding adjudicatory fairness that are strong components of the justification for an adversarial system.[52]

Litigant autonomy cedes to the party decisions about the presentation of evidence, settlement, the scope of the case, and similar important decisions in the life-cycle of a lawsuit.[53] Dignified treatment includes the opportunity to appear in an unbiased proceeding, tell a respectful decision maker of one's grievance or story, and have the decision maker take seriously the party's concerns. Litigant autonomy goes hand in hand with dignified treatment—the opportunity to make autonomous choices about framing the issues, presenting evidence and argument, settlement, and similar decisions is central to demonstrating genuine respect and accord for the party. Studies of litigants' attitudes reveal that dignified treatment and control are the variables of greatest concern to parties in their subjective assessments of procedural fairness.[54] Perceptions of procedural fairness, in turn, play a role in legitimating law and legal outcomes, especially outcomes unfavorable to the party.[55] The autonomy/dignity values do not travel comfortably with the aggregation movement.[56]

Aggregation Hesitations: Lessons from MDL-486

The Easy Illusion of Commonality

Central to the aggregation proponents' arguments is the commonality of issues to be resolved within the aggregative proceedings. Understandably, without a careful examination of the evidence and issues, aggregationists readily conclude that issues of causation in toxic substances cases are homogenous; liability questions are identical.[57] Where they recognize variability is in the damages assessment, and some advocate modifying damages law to facilitate the collectivization of the damages determination.[58]

All Bendectin claimants are not the same. Teratogens cause a specific or related group of effects and do not cause all birth defects. While a respectable argument exists that Bendectin is not a teratogen, an examination of the studies would lead one to different assessments of the likelihood that Bendectin causes the variety of birth defects implicated in MDL-486. Even within an apparently similar class of birth defects—limb reductions—bilateral or unilateral status affects the likelihood that the etiology is exogenous. The point can be generalized: toxic agents are specific in their effects; no agent causes all types of disease, and the strength of the effect of an agent may vary dramatically across the diseases that it does cause.[59]

Moreover, Bendectin was not one drug. Before 1976 it consisted of three components; after that time the dicyclomine component was eliminated, creating a different pharmacological entity. An epidemiological or toxicological study of the two-ingredient version has less scientific validity for assessing the teratogenesis of the three-ingredient Bendectin than the subsequent two-ingredient version.

Variance among claimants in the strength of their causation case may exist because of differences in the dose of or the timing of exposure to the agent to which each claimant was exposed.[60] For many toxic agents, the strength of the effect is closely correlated to the dose. Among Bendectin claimants, the timing of exposure affects the assessment of risk. Some women will have taken the drug precisely during the period of organogenesis, some at its periphery, and some beyond the outer bounds. And the evidence bearing on timing may vary from clear to conflicting. This dosage and timing evidence also differentiates the strength of individual claims.[61]

Finally, environmental and genetic factors may be quite heterogeneous among a class of claimants.[62] Betty Mekdeci took several other drugs; some plaintiffs' mothers took none. Exposure to other environmental causes of birth defects will similarly vary. Genetic factors have been associated with some birth defects; the future no doubt will provide additional information about the role of genes in causing birth defects.

It is important to recognize that the extent of commonality on the causal issue is very much a function of the structure of the scientific evidence. Epidemiology, toxicology, and even structure analysis are inherently collective forms of evidence that provide the commonality so alluring to aggregationists. But science evolves, and promising frontiers include genetics and molecular forensics, the latter of which would provide better understanding of the pathological mechanism through which diseases develop. By permitting consideration of the causal steps of the disease in each victim, these new tools might provide means for far more individualistic assessments of causation than are currently attainable.[63]

I should not be understood as claiming that there was no commonality among the 1,100 birth defect children who made up MDL-486. Surely there was. And some of the variance discussed above, for example, timing of exposure, could have been handled in individual hearings after MDL-486 resolved what common issues there were. The point is that there was far less commonality than many might think without carefully examining the state of the scientific record. And the variation among claimants in MDL-486 is quite generalizable to other mass toxic substances cases—it was true in thalidomide, as explained in chapter 5, has been true in asbestos litigation, and continues to be true in the breast implant litigation. Indeed, it may be worse in multi-decade latency situations with the additional time for exposure to alternative causes.[64]

Although MDL-486 never proceeded to address Merrell's liability, similar variances among claimants existed on that issue as well. The duty of a manufacturer to warn is circumscribed by the knowledge that is available at the time of manufacture.[65] The scientific studies, along with case reports and adverse drug reports from the early 1960s until Bendectin production ceased, raised specific concerns, ameliorated them, or reduced the extent of uncertainty about risk generally. A fact finder could reach different conclusions about the scope of the warning obligation along that 20-year time dimension.[66]

The variance among cases in mass torts is exacerbated by the "vacuum cleaner" effect: weak cases are drawn into the class by stronger claims.[67] This legal variant of Gresham's law—bad goods drive out the good ones[68]—is an example of adverse selection. When aggregation is mandatory, the rule might be modified to state that weak cases dilute the strong ones, especially when the class action is settled.

For purposes of discussion, it is important to distinguish two variants of weak cases, though they may tend to merge at the margins. The first class is cases with modest or small damages. The second involves cases that are frivolous or tenuous on liability. Weak cases are not viable on their own and thus only are asserted when they can tag along in an aggregated proceeding. Thus, although intended to promote efficiency, mass tort class actions will inevitably draw in a variety of cases that otherwise would never have been filed. Unfortunately, some of those cases will be ones whose lack of merit makes them unattractive entrants into the judicial tent. That might be tolerable if mechanisms existed to screen them out, but given the ubiquity of settlement and categorical treatment, that prospect is unlikely.

There is every reason to believe that MDL-486 served to draw in numerous cases that would otherwise never have been filed. The array of birth defects involved in Bendectin was quite broad, involving a variety of organs. By contrast, virtually every individual case that was tried involved some form of a limb defect, reflecting the plaintiff's lawyers' assessment that those were the only types of cases that were viable. MDL-486 gave life to hundreds of cases that would never have been asserted if deprived of the comfort and assistance of aggregation.

The vacuum cleaner effect is strongest when a settlement fund has been established for the benefit of a class of claimants, though it exists even without a fund. It happened in the Agent Orange class action; it happened in the Dalkon Shield bankruptcy proceedings, in which the number of claims exceeded expectations by an order of magnitude;[69] it happened in MDL-486 when Stanley Chesley solicited cases from individual plaintiff's lawyers to increase his settlement leverage with Merrell; and it happened in the breast implant settlement. As Professor Ian Ayres trenchantly puts it: "The adverse selection of frivolous claimants represents an important transaction cost . . . that non-frivolous claimants must bear. . . . The general danger of forced pools is that high-damage plaintiffs are forced to accept lower categorical awards of the claims facility pool."[70] Or as a leading plaintiffs' class action lawyer in the securities field recommends: "No one should be in a class action who has a strong individual claim . . . except for a person whose claim is of such small monetary value that it would be economically unfeasible to bring a claim any other way."[71] In essence, aggregated settlements result in wealth redistribution from the claimants with the strongest claims to the claimants with the weaker claims.[72]

Another important implication of this variance in mass toxic claims is the conflicts that it creates among claimants (and consequently for class attorneys), especially in the trial and settlement contexts.[73] In MDL-486, the PLCC was confronted with the question of whether to focus on and emphasize the overall teratogenesis of Bendectin or evidence regarding specific defects, such as pyloric stenosis or cleft palates, for which some epidemiological evidence supported an association. The PLCC faced a similar choice over whether to stress the change in the Bendectin formulation in 1976 or ignore it. Those decisions could have very different impacts on the cases of MDL-486 claimants. In these situations, counsel will make decisions that advantage some claimants while disadvantaging others.

To be sure, the PLCC might, in theory, have pursued alternative arguments and claims. But the dangers of conceding, for argument purposes, that even if Bendectin does not cause limb malformations, it does cause heart defects, made that option unattractive. Similarly, emphasizing in vitro studies as proof of teratogenicity makes it hard to return to epidemiological studies that might support some subgroup of plaintiffs. In short, the MDL-486 trial looked very different from what a trial might have looked like that focused on a more homogeneous subset of Bendectin claimants.

There is nothing inherently wrong with collectivizing mass injuries and diseases, employing scheduling and categories to facilitate administration of a compensation scheme. Attractive arguments can be made on its behalf.[74] Such schemes tend to blur factual differences among claimants, employ broad categories, bright-line tests, and presumptions to reduce administrative costs. Workers' compensation, the black lung compensation act, and the childhood vaccine act are all examples of administrative compensation schemes that, while imperfect, have their advantages. What does seem wrong is for the law to hold out the promise of individualized adjudication of tort claims, and the courts, under the guise of efficiency, to deny that opportunity by employing class actions that function as administrative compensation schemes. Common law courts have traditionally provided and are institutionally best suited to providing individualized adjudications. Legislatures, by contrast, have the appropriate tools to set forth prospective, categorical, and universal rules, the requisites of a compensation system.

Consistency and Accuracy

Variance among claimants also has teachings for the consistency norm. Different outcomes on liability among claimants in a mass toxic substances case may simply reflect differences in those individual cases; sorting out cases based on individual facts is the time-honored function of a jury. Juries may also draw different inferences, albeit reasonable, from the evidence.[75] Uncertainty provides a fertile ground for differing conclusions. Different juries will also reach conflicting results when the governing standard imports normative judgments such as "reasonableness" into the jury domain.[76] As Professor Ken Abraham has pointed out, the consistency norm cannot comfortably coexist with the different-inference concept.[77]

While aggregation provides consistency, it may do so at the cost of inaccuracy. As explained above, all cases may not be the same, though aggregation, unless carefully and sensitively calibrated, may not account for those differences. Aggregation risks outcomes that are 100 percent erroneous, should the court, unfortunately, get it wrong. Individualized case adjudications provide diversification of the overall risk of inaccuracy, which may be most attractive in cases involving significant uncertainty. And uncertainty is likely to be greatest early in the life-cycle of a mass toxic substance litigation.[78]

Others have expressed concern about the variability in damage awards in mass tort cases.[79] However, that same variability exists in routine tort cases, in which equivalently injured claimants routinely receive varying amounts of damages.[80] A number of researchers have developed sensible schemes for providing greater consistency in damage awards, such as recommended ranges for specified injuries, informing juries of the amounts earlier juries had awarded for similar injuries, or enhancing a more aggressive and informed additur and remittitur (court adjustment of the jury damages award) review.[81] These reforms could be usefully employed in all personal injury litigation, aggregated or individual, and if employed, would provide a more finely honed solution to variable damage awards than aggregation.

Attorneys as Primary Stakeholders

Perhaps the most problematical aspect of aggregation is the distortion it has on the respective roles of attorney and client. Contingent fee lawyers routinely acquire a minority stake in the claim of their clients. The conflict thereby created by providing different economic stakes in the same case is tolerated because of the important access function that the contingent fee system provides. But in aggregated cases, the class' lawyers have the largest stake, one that often vastly exceeds the claims of any single plaintiff.[82] Indeed, one of the characteristics that distinguishes the mass disaster lawyers is their ability to make large financial investments in the cases.[83] Stanley Chesley reported that he had invested $3.3 million in attorney time and perhaps $1 million in expenses in MDL-486.[84] The PLCC stood to receive attorney's fees in the range of $20 to $30 million if the settlement had not been overturned. With the enormous investment of the class action lawyer and larger yet potential fee recovery dwarfing any claimants' recovery, control of the case follows the dominant economic interest. This dynamic has long existed in securities and antitrust class actions, in which claimants have relatively modest stakes, but is quite new in the personal injury arena.

The settlement process is where the shift in financial interest from client to attorneys becomes most problematical. With millions of dollars invested in MDL-486, the PLCC would be reimbursed for all of its expenses off of the top of any settlement fund, plus receive attorney's fees that, at a minimum, would provide a handsome hourly rate and likely include a premium based on the amount recovered. (Chesley received five times his hourly rate from another federal judge in the Southern District of Ohio for his work in the Beverly Hills Supper Club litigation.[85]) Often multipliers are used to adjust fees to close to what a contingent fee might have provided; in Beverly Hills the total fee award was approximately 25 percent of the recovery.[86]

By contrast, proceeding to trial risked a complete loss of the PLCC's labor and capital investment and would require the investment of considerable additional attorney efforts. With the amount at stake, and the lack of diversification for attorneys involved in aggregated mass toxics, risk aversion makes settlement yet more attractive to plaintiffs' attorneys.[87] In the event of settlement, the PLCC would be generously paid for its investment, regardless of the discount on claimants' damages reflected in the settlement. The incentives for counsel to settle in mass tort claims, often to the detriment of their clients, are quite significant, perhaps irresistible.[88]

Of course, because of the weakness of the PLCC's evidence on causation, the settlement may well have been in the best interest of claimants. With the benefit of hindsight, it certainly was. But not all mass toxic substances cases will be as weak as MDL-486 was, and the conflict between attorney and client in the settlement decision is a serious problem.[89] By their nature, class action settlements occur without the input or knowledge of class members,[90] quite a contrast from individual litigation, which requires the approval of the client.

At least if the aggregation is voluntary, class members can vote with their feet. If dissatisfied with the settlement, they can opt out and pursue separate actions. But the mandatory settlement entered into by the PLCC barred claimants from voting with their feet: all were required to participate, including even those who had not yet asserted a claim. Moreover, even when the class is voluntary, there is reason to be concerned about the ability of an unrepresented class member to make an informed choice about whether to opt out of a class action. Without some information about the available alternatives (is the class member's claim viable as an individual claim, how likely is defendant to be found liable, what is the range of likely recovery?), the class member is left without the tools to make a considered judgment.[91] That would have been true of the members of the Bendectin settlement class, *had* they been given the opportunity to opt out. In the MDL-486 trial, the opt-in procedure combined with the fact that all eligible to do so already had filed suit and were therefore represented by counsel obviated the concern about informed decision making.

Judicial protection of class members' interests, a significant component of the current class action concept, may not be entirely up to the task. As a number of commentators have pointed out, judicial attitudes toward aggregation may not be entirely neutral.[92] There are strong incentives for judges, facing crowded dockets, demands for greater managerial efficiency, and the grinding boredom of iterative trials of similar cases to find aggregation an attractive alternative. No doubt some of that preference is legitimately a result of concern about economizing on scarce judicial resources or overall societal efficiency; however, some may be the result of self-interested preferences about what kinds of cases present interesting and satisfying challenges.

Judicial oversight and approval of class action settlements exists, in theory, to protect class members' interests. However, once a settlement has been reached by the adversaries and the settlement is presented to the court, "All the dynamics conduce to judicial approval of settlement."[93] Professor Resnik has argued persuasively that aggregative settlement is a particularly appealing resolution for a trial judge faced with the alternative of the burdens of adjudicating a mass case[94] or, even worse, repetitive adjudication of individual cases.[95]

Recognizing these inefficiencies due to placing control of the principals' fate in the hands of their agents, Professor John Coffee argues for a new vision of class actions. Coffee's reform would uncouple class attorneys from their role as agent and representative for client and class members.[96] Instead, Coffee would recognize the class action attorney as entrepreneur and structure class actions so as to avoid agency-cost problems inherent in the attorney-client relationship and to channel the financial self-interests of attorneys in a fashion that furthers the goals of private litigation.

This new model of class action has several virtues: it more accurately conforms to much of contemporary class action practice; it liberates attorneys from ethical requirements that protect clients and class members; it legitimates much of current practice in the seamy world of class actions, and it implies a variety of reforms to enhance the efficiency of aggregation and minimize the agency-costs due to attorneys failing to act in their clients' best interests. In Coffee's reformed class action world, class members' insignificance would be acknowledged, and lawyers would become the principals. Solicitation, along with referral fees, would not only be tolerated, they would be welcomed as enhancing efficiency through diversification and specialization.[97] Attorneys would be authorized to invest in a class action, with the promise of a payoff that would reflect the risk in their investment. At the logical extreme, attorneys would bid for and purchase the class' claims, thereby consolidating the underlying interest and legal representation in a single entity to avoid agency-cost problems.[98]

The model that Professor Coffee describes clashes jarringly with more traditional views of the lawyer's role.[99] Clients' interests are subjugated to societal goals obtained by channeling the attorneys' self-interests. Litigation would be controlled entirely by attorneys, whose decisions would be unencumbered by the views of their clients. It is more than a little ironic that at a time when corporate clients are demanding (and obtaining) more control over their attorneys and the way that those attorneys represent them in litigation,[100] proposals are made to shift greater power to the attorneys for personal injury claimants. Yet Coffee and others with an efficiency approach to mass litigation provide dramatic reform alternatives to the current aggregation muddle. While there is much hard-headed economic sense in their recommendations, they present extreme reforms that require discarding many of the aspirations and idealisms of the legal profession. Indeed, they are inconsistent with the concept of a profession, instead requiring acknowledgement that attorneys are the marketplace equivalent of jewelers.[101] Such a radical change in the self-image of a profession, required to effectuate Coffee's proposals, seems an unlikely occurrence.

The Reality of Client Autonomy

Before concluding any assessment of aggregation, however, a closer look at the reality of individual representation in personal injury litigation is required. One must only recall Betty Mekdeci and her lawsuit to appreciate the ways in which her case was pushed, prodded, and deformed because of her lawyers' interests and the existence of other similar cases. Betty Mekdeci did not get regular reports from her attorneys of developments in her case, and many of her inquiries to counsel went unresponded to for lengthy periods. In the end, her attorneys withheld necessary financial support because she refused to cede to their wishes to delay the second trial. Betty Mekdeci's autonomy was buffeted by two forces: she was a single-case client who did not have the leverage of repeat business with which to control her lawyers; and her freedom was affected by the existence of a much larger congregation of Bendectin cases.

It is no secret to those even modestly familiar with the personal injury system that the ideal of individualized adjudication, with respect for and attention to the details of the claim, faithful attorney-agents reflecting the interests and desires of the clients, and arbiters listening carefully and respectfully to the claims and stories of the parties is a myth.[102] Deborah Hensler dispels the myth with a picture grounded in empiricism rather than romanticism:

The version of legal reality drawn from this research posits a litigation process in which (1) lawyer-client relations are more often perfunctory and superficial than intimate; (2) the locus of control is shifted toward lawyers rather than clients; (3) lawyers educate their clients to a view of the legal process that serves the lawyer's interests as much, if not more than clients' interests; (4) litigants are frequently only names to both lawyers and court personnel; and (5) trial is rarely desired, except perhaps by litigants, or delivered.[103]

Injecting a strong dose of reality should not obscure that there is a continuum of clients' involvement and control in their cases.[104] Betty Mekdeci—to be sure, an extraordinarily motivated individual—played a far more active role in her case than Holly Beth Thomas, Stanley Chesley's first Bendectin client, played in MDL-486. Mekdeci repeatedly prodded her attorneys, reviewed the information obtained during discovery, made numerous suggestions about additional avenues to explore for evidence, consulted with and advised her attorneys about settlement negotiations, and played an active role at the first trial.

Douglas Rosenthal's study of ordinary personal injury litigation reveals a range of client interest and activity, with a small percentage of clients being quite involved in the prosecution of their suit.[105] Subsequent empirical work summarized by Deborah Hensler reveals a half-empty, half-full glass paradox. Hensler's review makes plain that intimate lawyer-client relationships with clients making informed decisions about the course of their cases is not the norm. Yet over 40 percent of personal injury litigants in small stakes cases (up to $50,000) reported that they had "some" or "a lot" of control over their cases. Almost one-half reported that the decision to file suit was either theirs alone or a joint decision with their attorney.[106] Significantly, Rosenthal's study found that the greater the client involvement in the case, the better the outcome.[107]

In sum, there are litigant-autonomy differences between individual and aggregative processing, not as great as the idealized models might suggest, but nevertheless difference there is. Especially where a party prefers individual resolution, we should be cautious about imposing compulsory aggregation.

Aggregation Justified by Necessity

Aggregative adjudication may be unavoidable in two distinct situations identified earlier in this chapter. When the number of claimants in a super-mass case is so large that courts are choking on them, unable to provide any realistic opportunity for timely individualized adjudication, as in asbestos, aggregation may be the best that the courts can provide. For mature super-mass cases, an administrative compensation scheme might be preferable, but to provide one would require overcoming the barriers to legislation.[108]

Bendectin, however, was not one of the super-mass cases that required aggregation to provide plaintiffs their day in court. Judge Rubin threatened the parties with years of continuous individual Bendectin trials if they were unable to agree on a format for an aggregative trial. In his order certifying a mandatory class, Judge Rubin observed that there were 700 identified cases, and that, if each required 30 trial days, 105 judge-years would be needed to resolve the cases.

While Judge Rubin's arithmetic was fine, his analysis was a little less so. First, the class certification was not for the purpose of adjudication, but for the purpose of accommodating the global settlement that Stanley Chesley and Frank Woodside had negotiated. Judge Rubin had already refused to certify a class for trial purposes. It is hard to deny a class action for trial purposes, then justify one for settlement purposes on the grounds of efficiency.

Second, Judge Rubin ignored the prominent role that settlement plays in the resolution of civil suits.[109] Studies of tort cases reveal that somewhat less than 10 percent of cases filed are tried to verdict.[110] Fewer than 4 percent of asbestos cases were tried to verdict in the period before the Johns Manville bankruptcy.[111] Settlements would be especially likely if, after a number of trials, a pattern of outcomes developed that enabled the parties to refine their predictions about the anticipated outcome of pending cases.[112]

Third, even with 700 cases (many of which were not viable as individual actions) that amounts to no more than an average of 7 cases per federal district court, which surely does not approach the paralysis level of, say, asbestos. To be sure, approximately half those cases were concentrated in federal court in Ohio. The vast majority of those cases, however, arose outside Ohio and arrived in Ohio because of referral to or association with Stanley Chesley by attorneys who preferred not to try the case. Yet Judge Rubin, had he been faced with an unmanageable number of Ohio-filed cases that did not voluntarily participate in an aggregated trial, had the simple option of transferring those cases to the federal court where the plaintiff resided, pursuant to the federal forum non conveniens statute, 28 U.S.C. § 1404.

The large proportion of Bendectin claimants who joined the consolidated trial raises the uncomfortable matter of client choice. The structure of the MDL-486 trial, with its polyfurcation, was so unfavorable from a plaintiff's perspective that knowledgeable attorneys like Tom Bleakley and Arthur Tifford chose to keep their clients' cases out of the MDL-486 trial. Those cases that opted in may well have been ones in which it was in their attorney's interest, but not in the client's, to participate in a mass trial conducted by the PLCC rather than opting for an individual proceeding.[113] That concern, however, arising from a conflict between mass tort lawyers and their clients, only counsels more hesitation about aggregation.

Once again, the point is that all mass toxic litigations are not the same.

The modest size of Bendectin (a total of approximately 2,000 individual claims) is quite unlike asbestos with its hundreds of thousands of claimants. While litigations of the magnitude of the latter may require aggregation (and quasi-administrative schemes for individual issues like damages) in the absence of legislative action, the same cannot be said of the more modest several-thousand-claimant toxic litigation.[114] We should be cautious about generalizing from super-mass toxics such as asbestos, in which the pragmatics of necessity require fashioning procedures to accommodate their demands to more modest litigations. We should also appreciate that aggregation, itself, often dramatically increases the number of claimants by lowering the barriers to claiming. That surely has been the case in the Agent Orange, Dalkon Shield, and breast implant litigations.

A second situation in which compulsory aggregation may be required is if the defendant's assets are insufficient to satisfy all claims. In that situation, the due process rights of individual claimants may have to be compromised to protect the rights of later claimants, who otherwise might be foreclosed from recovery because of the exhaustion of a defendant's assets. Once again, the necessity of protecting all claimants justifies aggregation. But if a defendant's assets are truly going to be exhausted, the preferable mechanism for aggregation is a bankruptcy proceeding, not a class action.

The primary reason for preferring bankruptcy as the mechanism for protecting the rights of all claimants is that bankruptcy permits the inclusion of all creditors of the defendant, not just involuntary tort creditors.[115] If a company is insolvent, the burden of insolvency should be borne by all in accordance with the priorities and rules established by bankruptcy law not solely by tort claimants. The Second Circuit made a related point in a recent case reversing the certification of a mandatory class: "[T]he function of the federal courts is not to conduct trials over whether a statutory [bankruptcy] scheme should be ignored because a more efficient mechanism [class action] can be fashioned by judges."[116] In addition, bankruptcy, with its less formally adversarial procedure, is a preferable forum for determining the respective rights of creditors to a mandatory class action and provides greater flexibility for the task of valuing the individual claims.[117]

One of the great difficulties with invoking the limited fund concept is the uncertainty about the value of currently asserted and future claims.[118] Estimating the number of future claims in mass toxic substances litigation is always difficult, and the actual value of currently asserted cases is hard to determine because of the vagaries of compensatory and punitive damages law and uncertainty about the meritoriousness of the cases. Nevertheless, this difficulty is equally present whether the issue is to certify a mandatory class or initiate a bankruptcy proceeding. Whatever the level of certainty required, bankruptcy appears to be the preferred forum. And the threat to corporate management's position in a bankruptcy reorganization suggests that the decision to file for bankruptcy will not be undertaken simply for the convenience of having a forum for universal resolution of tort claims. That is, bankruptcy has its own form of disciplining incentives to avoid mandatory aggregation unless the defendant's financial situation truly requires it.

Mass trials are sure to occur in the future, because of the allure of efficiency, the necessity of providing a forum, or the consent of the parties. MDL-486 provides one additional issue for consideration for the future of mass toxic trials: polyfurcation of the issues bearing on liability.

Polyfurcation

Aggregation is not the only context in which polyfurcation occurs; individual cases can be and are divided for separate hearings on discrete issues. For example, separate trials for punitive damages in individual cases have become quite common. But aggregative procedure often requires polyfurcation, whenever both common and individual issues exist. Aggregation also facilitates polyfurcation; while it makes little sense to separate the general and specific causation questions in an individual case, there is much to be said for that division as occurred in the MDL-486 trial.

Initially employed only with respect to separate claims, bifurcation was authorized when the Federal Rules of Civil Procedure were drafted in 1938 and provided discretion to trial judges to separate claims or issues for trial, if convenience could be furthered or prejudice avoided. In 1966 Fed. R. Civ. P. 42(b) was amended to reiterate the admonition contained in Fed. R. Civ. P. 38: any separation of issues should take full account of the right to a jury trial guaranteed in the United States Constitution.

In *Gasoline Products Co. v. Champlin Refining Co.*,[119] the Supreme Court fleshed out the jury trial concern, albeit in the context of a grant of a new trial limited to the issue of damages. While holding that trials of separate issues did not per se violate the Seventh Amendment jury trial guarantee, the Court limited separate issues trials to those where "it clearly appears that the issue to be retried is so distinct and separable from the others that a trial of it alone may be had without injustice."[120] Although *Gasoline Products* involved a new trial, the standard that emerged has been employed in decisions to separate issues for trial in the first instance.[121]

The concern about routine bifurcation impinging on the jury's function was particularly salient during the reign of contributory negligence, one of the harshest legal rules ever. Bifurcation of liability and damages deprived the jury of the opportunity to employ its own off-line comparative fault scheme, discounting the damages by the plaintiff's fault and thereby nullifying the onerousness of the complete bar of contributory negligence.[122] Hindering the freedom of the jury to "knock the rough edges off" of the harshness or unfairness of the law is a major objection to polyfurcation.[123]

Polyfurcation, however, can improve adjudicatory efficiency and, through limitations on jury freedom, avoid prejudice. In a complicated case, separating the issues for trial may simplify and speed the resolution of the case.[124] More significantly, when the initial issue tried is one that is potentially dispositive and there is a significant probability that it will be decided in the dispositive direction, then efficiency is enhanced by obviating the need to try additional issues.[125] Even when the initially tried issue is decided in a non-dispositive way, efficiency may be enhanced by facilitating settlements.[126] Elimination of the uncertainty associated with the initially adjudicated issue should facilitate compromises.[127] Finally, polyfurcation can avoid prejudice by screening the jury from evidence relevant to another issue that might tend to make the jury decide the issue on legally irrelevant grounds.[128] Those advantages explain the decision of several federal district courts to adopt local rules that create a presumption of bifurcation of liability and damages issues in personal injury cases.[129]

The polyfurcation of the MDL-486 trial had much promise. Plaintiffs cannot win their cases if the defendant's agent does not have the capacity to cause the injuries or diseases from which the plaintiffs suffer. That question, whether Bendectin could cause any of a variety of specific birth defects in any exposed fetus, is a purely scientific question, distinct from the other issues in the case. The plaintiffs had a steep uphill battle on that issue in MDL-486, and, if they were unsuccessful, then liability, damages, and specific causation would be moot. Twenty-two days of trial were sufficient to resolve the case in less time than the average required for the four individual trials that had previously been conducted.[130] Even with Judge Rubin having excluded evidence of thalidomide and Merrell's role in MER/29, there were numerous pieces of embarrassing evidence about Merrell relevant to liability issues that might skew jury decision making through commingling evidence on different issues or make a jury more willing to rule against Merrell simply because it was a deplorable company. Because of the separation of causation from liability, the jury was confronted with a single legal issue and Merrell's culpability could be screened off from the jury while it heard evidence on whether Bendectin caused birth defects. The MDL-486 polyfurcation had both accuracy and efficiency advantages.

Despite those advantages, the Sixth Circuit found Judge Rubin's poly-furcation decision the "most troubling" of all the claims raised on ap-peal. The message delivered by the Sixth Circuit to trial judges would make most quite hesitant to follow in Judge Rubin's footsteps in all but the most complex case—the hat on which the court of appeals hung its decision to affirm. What concerns motivated the Sixth Circuit to raise such a red flag about polyfurcation?

The primary ground expressed by the Sixth Circuit was that trying gen-eral causation created a "sterile laboratory atmosphere." This argument derived from the earlier Beverly Hills Supper Club litigation, in which the Court of Appeals had voiced similar concerns. Of course, the ques-tion whether Bendectin is capable of causing birth defects is a laboratory or, more accurately, a scientific inquiry. The court explained that its con-cern was that the jury, unaware of the importance of the decision, might not give the trial, evidence, and decision-making process adequate atten-tion and effort. That concern seems reasonable: jurors' attentiveness may be piqued and carefulness enhanced by personal confrontation with the human tragedy implicated and the stakes at issue. But the Court of Appeals concern does not speak directly to polyfurcation, rather it im-plicates the decision to exclude visibly deformed children from the courtroom. To put the point in a slightly different way, the general cau-sation issue could have been tried with the plaintiffs, or a representative sample of them, present in the courtroom. Yet there were reasonable grounds, as explained in chapters 12 and 14, for the exclusion of the most seriously injured children. Moreover, as the Court of Appeals rec-ognized, there are alternative means to impress the jury with the gravity of the inquiry with which they are confronted. Judge Rubin and Allen Eaton each stressed the significance and implications of the causation inquiry to the jury, as explained in chapter 14.

Beyond juror ennui, Professor Roger Transgrud, a leading critic of mass tort aggregation, raises another concern about polyfurcation. Trans-grud argues that polyfurcation prevents the jury from discounting weak evidence on one aspect of a case against the damages award, thereby adjusting the damage award to reflect the probability that the plaintiff has a meritorious case.[131] The argument at bottom is to permit the jury to adopt a legal reform that has been proposed by scholars for several decades: toxic substance plaintiffs should be permitted to prove the probability they have been harmed and recover a damage award dis-counted by that probability.

That reform, despite being widely advocated by scholars,[132] has not been accepted by the courts.[133] Should trials be structured so as to pro-vide juries the freedom to engage in this law reform? The well-known experience with jury modification of contributory negligence is the best example of jury lawmaking[134] and finds favor with many. Yet the question remains how much latitude should the jury be permitted. One person's improvement of justice through jury discretion to reflect community values is another person's jury lawlessness and, given the freedom of juries to decline the opportunity, a third person's inconsistent treatment. Few would support completely unshackling the jury by making it the arbiter of both fact and law. On the question of proportionate liability in toxic substances cases, a matter that has had a thorough airing and generated little judicial or legislative acceptance, preserving jury freedom does not seem a powerful or persuasive concern. Moreover, unlike the harshness of contributory negligence which operated exclusively to the detriment of one side in a lawsuit, use of a preponderance standard to award all-or-nothing damages distributes its errors in more egalitarian fashion— sometimes it will benefit plaintiffs; other times defendants. Thus unlike contributory negligence, denying juries the freedom to adopt proportionate liability does not have the same unilateral adverse effect.[135]

In the end, polyfurcation, like other jury control devices, such as the exclusion of evidence on prejudice grounds, trial judge screening of expert witnesses, special interrogatories, and even jury instructions, raises the larger question of confidence in and the authority accorded to the civil jury, a matter of considerable controversy. Appropriate adjustments in the jury's authority are a recurring theme, one that must be responsive to changing demands put before the jury and our understanding about how the jury operates.[136]

What often is neglected in the polyfurcation debate is polyfurcation's contribution to enhancing accuracy by preventing prejudice and focusing jury attention on a single issue. Defendants' culpable acts simply are not relevant to the question of whether a given agent causes disease.[137] The agent causes disease or does not, regardless of whether the defendant is as monstrous as Adolf Hitler or as innocent as Snow White. Polyfurcation permits the jury to focus on the causation question without the distraction and prejudice of the defendant's culpability, especially in cases like MDL-486, in which there was substantial evidence of defendant's culpability. Aside from bias, recent research about juror decision making suggests that jurors do not decide cases in a logical issue-by-issue process, as the law assumes. Rather jurors employ a "story" heuristic to comprehend and organize evidence introduced at a trial.[138] During the course of a trial, jurors will construct one or more stories, consistent with portions of the evidence, to explain it. At the conclusion of the trial, competing stories are compared for plausibility, coherence, and capacity to explain the most evidence. Construction and evaluation of stories are influenced by juror's life experience and world views. The story that emerges victorious from this process is then used to determine the most appropriate verdict. Whether influenced by this research or by experience and intuition, trial lawyers know that they must construct a good "story" from their evidence to tell the jury and to use to organize their presentation.[139]

A critical corollary to this model, for the purpose of evaluating polyfurcation, is that jurors constructing a story may "commingle" evidence on distinct legal elements in constructing their story, so that strong evidence of one element (or an inference based on experience) may substitute for weak evidence of another.[140] Thus jurors may use evidence of Merrell's culpability to fill in the story that its malfeasance in testing, manufacturing, and labeling the drug caused the plaintiff's birth defects. Or a juror may reason: birth defects are caused by something; no other explanation has been presented; drugs are capable of causing birth defects; Bendectin must be responsible for plaintiff's birth defects. This research suggests that polyfurcation and separate consideration of causation, especially with a highly culpable defendant, may contribute to a more accurate jury result. Other experimental work supports this conclusion.

Irwin Horowitz and Kenneth Bordens conducted an experimental study employing eligible jurors who made up 128 six-person juries that heard identical evidence constructed from a toxic substances case.[141] Among the independent variables they employed were unitary as opposed to a bifurcated trial procedure and the order of evidence on issues such as liability and causation. The study examined the impact of those variables on success rates for plaintiffs and damages awarded to plaintiffs.

The study shows a stunning difference in outcome based on whether all evidence (including evidence on liability and punitive damages) was presented in a single proceeding or the general causation issue was tried separately and before evidence of liability was introduced. In the former situation, plaintiffs prevailed in 85.4 percent of the trials conducted; in the latter, they prevailed in only 37.5 percent of the cases.[142] Bordens and Horowitz also found a significant effect on compensatory damages depending on the structure of the trial: unitary trial juries awarded a mean of $274,000 for each plaintiff, while juries in bifurcated cases awarded a mean of $429,000. There was a comparable impact on the damages award based on the order of evidence: $258,000 was awarded to plaintiffs in cases in which liability evidence was presented first, while $402,000 was awarded in cases in which causation was the first issue tried.[143]

The differences in damage awards are susceptible to at least two interpretations. One explanation may be that the unitary juries are engaging in compromises, discounting the damages awards by the probability of liability and causation. Another explanation, proffered by the authors, is that those bifurcated juries that find for plaintiffs on causation do so because they are more sympathetic to plaintiffs and therefore more generous in awarding damages.[144]

The authors of the study, who videotaped the deliberations, suggest that there was substantial commingling of evidence during deliberations by the unitary trial juries: "For example, when deciding general causation, unitary juries appeared to use aspects of the damages evidence."[145] This evidence also tends to refute the Sixth Circuit's concern about a "sterile laboratory atmosphere" creating an inattentive jury. If the Sixth Circuit were correct, one would expect the errors to be randomly distributed. The dramatic difference between unified and causation-first bifurcation suggests that inattention is not a problem. In short, the Horowitz and Bordens study suggests that polyfurcation makes a difference and that the difference is a more accurate result.

The law might be shaped to give primacy to the jury's discretion and protect it as an institution that best reflects community norms. That choice would auger for unitary trials, which present a more complete version of the entire episode for the jury to judge. To do so, however, requires that we be willing to sacrifice a measure of accuracy in legal outcomes. The debate is an old one and reflects the continuing struggle over the allocation of power between judge and jury.[146]

Notes

1. *See* Marc Galanter, *The Day After the Litigation Explosion,* 46 MD. L. REV. 3, 21–25 (1986); GENERAL ACCOUNTING OFFICE, PRODUCT LIABILITY: EXTENT OF "LITIGATION EXPLOSION" IN FEDERAL COURTS QUESTIONED (1988) (3 products responsible for 57 percent of increase in products liability filings from 1974–85).

2. For an extensive bibliography of the literature addressing aggregative procedure for mass torts, see Linda S. Mullenix, *Selected Bibliography on Complex Litigation,* 10 REV. LITIG. 561 (1991).

3. *See, e.g.,* David Rosenberg, *The Causal Connection in Mass Exposure Cases: A "Public Law" Vision of the Tort System,* 97 HARV. L. REV. 849 (1984).

4. Rosenberg, *supra* note 3, at 906–07.

5. *See, e.g.,* Peter W. Huber, *Safety and the Second Best: The Hazards of Public Risk Management in the Courts,* 85 COLUM. L. REV. 277 (1985); Richard J. Mahoney & Stephen E. Littlejohn, *Innovation on Trial: Punitive Damages Versus New Products,* 246 SCI. 1395 (1989) (identifying asbestos-substitute that had been developed but shelved before marketing because of liability concerns).

6. Stephen Sugarman, *Doing Away with Tort Law,* 73 CALIF. L. REV. 555, 587, 590 (1985); *see also* W. L. F. Felstiner & Peter Seigelman, *Neoclassical Difficulties: Tort Deterrence for Latent Injuries,* 11 LAW & POL'Y 309, 309–12 (1989); George L. Priest, *Product Liability Law and the Accident Rate, in* LIABILITY: PERSPECTIVES AND POLICY (Robert E. Litan & Clifford Winston eds., Washington, DC: Brookings Institution, 1988).

7. *See, e.g.,* Robert L. Rabin, *Some Thoughts on the Efficacy of a Mass Toxics Admin-*

istrative Scheme, 52 MD. L. REV. 951 (1993); *cf.* Gary T. Schwartz, *Reality in the Economic Analysis of Tort Law: Does Tort Law Really Deter?*, 42 U.C.L.A. L. REV. 377 (1994) (concluding that tort law has a moderate deterrent effect in different sectors, but that fine tuning is unrealistic); THE LIABILITY MAZE: THE IMPACT OF LIABILITY LAW ON SAFETY AND INNOVATION (Peter W. Huber & Robert E. Litan eds., Washington, DC: Brookings Institution, 1991) (describing very different impact of tort law on innovation in several different industries).

8. *See infra* text accompanying note 36.

9. *See infra* text accompanying notes 67–72.

10. Stephen C. Yeazell, *Collective Litigation as Collective Action,* 1989 U. ILL. L. REV. 43, 44–45.

11. For a thorough cataloguing of the differences between class actions and consolidations, see Charles Silver, *Comparing Class Actions and Consolidations,* 10 REV. LITIG. 495 (1991); Yeazell, *supra* note 10, at 44–45.

12. Transcript of Status Conference at 10–11, *In re* Richardson-Merrell, Inc. "Bendectin" Liability Litigation, MDL-486 (S.D. Ohio Mar. 19, 1984).

13. *See* Silver, *supra* note 11, at 500 ("In short, judges can run consolidations as class actions—that is, as representational suits.")

One exception was the omission of potential claimants who had not yet filed suit. These individuals could have been part of a formal class action, but were not included in the MDL-486 proceedings. *See id.* at 502. Another difference, though relatively insignificant, was that Judge Rubin employed an opt-in procedure for the MDL-486 trial, rather than the opt-out structure of FED. R. CIV. P. 23(b)(3).

14. Other attempts to craft a broader, more-inclusive definition of aggregative or collective procedure can be found in Judith Resnik, *From "Cases" to "Litigation,"* 54 LAW & CONTEMP. PROBS., Summer 1991, at 5, 24–25.

15. Resnik, *supra* note 14, at 46–47.

16. Alison Frankel, *From Pioneers to Profits,* AM. LAW., June 1992, at 82.

17. That generally seems to be the case for multidistrict consolidation. *See* David Lauter, *Mastering MDL,* NAT'L L.J., Nov. 21, 1983, at 1, 24; Roger H. Transgrud, *Joinder Alternatives in Mass Tort Litigation,* 70 CORNELL L. REV. 779, 810 (1986).

18. *See also* Francis McGovern, *Toward a Functional Approach for Managing Complex Litigation,* 53 U. CHI. L. REV. 440, 479 (1986) (reporting on small firms representing 1,000 asbestos clients).

19. *See* Paul D. Rheingold, *The MER/29 Story—An Instance of Successful Mass Litigation,* 56 CALIF. L. REV. 116 (1968); RALPH A. FINE, THE GREAT DRUG DECEPTION: THE SHOCKING STORY OF MER/29 AND THE FOLKS WHO GAVE YOU THALIDOMIDE 156–65 (New York: Stein and Day, 1972).

20. *See* Jack B. Weinstein, *Ethical Dilemmas in Mass Tort Litigation,* 88 Nw. U. L. REV. 469, 480 n.43 (1994).

21. Marc Galanter, Lawyers' Litigation Networks 22 (1985) (unpublished manuscript); *see also* Paul D. Rheingold, *The Development of Litigation Groups,* 6 AM. J. TRIAL ADV. 1 (1982) (noting that litigation groups often do not form when litigation begins gradually and in dispersed locations).

22. *See* Rosenberg, *supra* note 3, at 910–11.

23. *Cf.* Francis E. McGovern, *Resolving Mature Mass Tort Litigation,* 69 B.U. L. REV. 659 (1989) (advocating aggregative resolution after a mass tort has reached maturity, including in development of factual evidence).

24. *See* Michael D. Green, *The Paradox of Statutes of Limitations in Toxic Substances Litigation,* 76 CALIF. L. REV. 965, 993–99 (1988); David Rosenberg, *The Dusting of*

America: A Story of Asbestos—Carnage, Cover-up, and Litigation, 99 HARV. L. REV. 1693 (1986) (book review); DEBORAH R. HENSLER ET AL., ASBESTOS IN THE COURTS: THE CHALLENGE OF MASS TOXIC TORTS 110–11 (Santa Monica, CA: Rand, 1985).

25. *See Is Dioxin a Human Carcinogen?*, 263 SCI. 14 (response by Ann Gibbons).

26. *See generally* Vincent R. Johnson, *The Second Circuit Review—1986-1987 Term: Ethics: Ethical Limitations on Creative Financing of Mass Tort Class Actions*, 54 BROOK. L. REV. 539 (1988).

27. John C. Coffee Jr., *Rethinking the Class Action: A Policy Primer on Reform*, 62 IND. L.J. 625, 640–41 (1987); *see also* PETER H. SCHUCK, AGENT ORANGE ON TRIAL: MASS TOXIC DISASTERS IN THE COURTS (Cambridge, MA: Belknap Press of Harvard University Press, enlarged ed. 1987) (describing numerous failings of, and conflicts among, attorneys who served as class counsel in Agent Orange class litigation).

28. *See* Transgrud, *supra* note 17, at 824.

29. Professor Judith Resnik has done a magnificent job of canvassing the history of the Supreme Court's Advisory Committee that drafted the 1966 revision to Fed. R. Civ. P. 23 and demonstrating its commitment to claim effectuation as the justification for class actions. *See* Resnik, *supra* note 14, at 7–17.

30. 445 U.S. 326, 338 (1980).

31. *See* Andrew Rosenfield, *An Empirical Test of Class Action Settlement*, 5 J. LEGAL STUD. 113 (1976).

32. *See* Swanson v. American Consumer Indus., 415 F.2d 1326, 1333 n.9 (7th Cir. 1969) (small individual stakes make it even more impractical to join all parties); John C. Coffee, Jr., *The Regulation of Entrepreneurial Litigation in the Large Class Action*, 54 U. CHI. L. REV. 877, 906 n.65 (1987).

33. For a careful analysis of Fed. R. Civ. P. 23(b)(3) and its applicability to mass torts, see Transgrud, *supra* note 17, at 785–94.

34. Resnik, *supra* note 14, at 17.

35. *Comments of the Fed. Rules Advisory Comm.*, 39 F.R.D. 69, 103 (1966).

36. The courts have been quite nonchalant in enforcing this limitation in mass tort class actions. *See In re* A.H. Robins Co., 880 F.2d 709, 723–25 (4th Cir.), *cert. denied*, 493 U.S. 959 (1989).

37. *Cf.* Richard L. Marcus, *They Can't Do That, Can They?: Tort Reform Via Rule 23*, 80 CORNELL L. REV. (forthcoming 1995).

38. In addition, class actions were certified in the Beverly Hills Supper Club case by Judge Rubin and in the Hyatt Regency Skywalk case, though the latter was reversed on appeal. *See* Resnik, *supra* note 14, at 18.

39. *See* 3 HERBERT B. NEWBERG, NEWBERG ON CLASS ACTIONS § 17 (Colorado Springs, CO: Shepard's / McGraw-Hill, 2d ed. 1985); Linda Mullenix, *Class Resolution of the Mass-Tort Case: A Proposed Federal Procedure Act*, 64 TEX. L. REV. 1039, 1043, 1060–72 (1986) (advocating a federal statute to facilitate aggregation of geographically and temporally dispersed mass torts); Edward F. Sherman, *Class Actions and Duplicative Litigation*, 62 IND. L. REV. 507 (1987); Coffee, *supra* note 32 (class actions can reduce both public and private costs of litigation); Rosenberg, *supra* note 3 (advocating mandatory class actions and aggregative determination of damages); Spencer Williams, *Mass Torts, Going, Going, Gone?*, 90 F.R.D. 323 (1983) (advocating class actions as best device to handle mass torts); John E. Kennedy, *Class Actions: The Right to Opt Out*, 25 ARIZ. L. REV. 3 (1983) (advocating authority for mandatory class actions to be certified for individual damages actions); *In re* A.H. Robins Co., 880 F.2d 709, 740 (4th Cir.) (certifying a mandatory class and characterizing as "unworkable" and "now increasingly disregarded" the Advisory

Committee comment on the impropriety of mass tort class actions), *cert. denied*, 493 U.S. 959 (1989).

40. *See* Silver, *supra* note 11, at 495 n.2.

41. For an argument that even the claim effectuation function of class actions serves efficiency, see Roger Bernstein, *Judicial Economy and Class Actions*, 7 J. LEGAL STUD. 349 (1978).

42. David Rosenberg, *Toxic Tort Litigation: Crisis or Chrysalis? A Comment on Feinberg's Conceptual Problems and Proposed Solutions*, 24 HOUS. L. REV. 183, 194 (1987).

43. *3d Circuit Hears Three Hours of Arguments on School Class Action Appeals*, ASBESTOS LITIG. REP. (Andrews) 11,480, 11,481 (Jan. 17, 1986).

44. McGovern, *supra* note 23, at 661; *see also* RICHARD H. GASKINS, ENVIRONMENTAL ACCIDENTS: PERSONAL INJURY AND PUBLIC RESPONSIBILITY 169–70 (Philadelphia: Temple University Press, 1989).

45. *See* Resnik, *supra* note 14, at 66 (aggregation efforts borne of "horror" at numbers of claimants and the length of the line to get into court); Samuel Issacharoff, *Administering Damage Awards in Mass-Tort Litigation*, 10 REV. LITIG. 463, 470 (1991) ("Under any theory of the role of tort litigation, a system that delays adjudication to the point of denying it entirely cries out for reform.").

46. *See* Cimino v. Raymark Indus. Inc., 751 F. Supp. 649, 451–52 (E.D. Tex. 1990); Edward F. Sherman, *Aggregate Disposition of Related Cases: The Policy Issues*, 10 REV. LITIG. 231, 236–37 (1991).

47. Rosenberg, *supra* note 3, at 913; David Rosenberg, *Class Actions for Mass Torts: Doing Individual Justice by Collective Means*, 62 IND. L.J. 561 (1986); *see also* Mullenix, *supra* note 39 (advocating the court retain discretion whether to permit opt outs in mass tort class actions).

48. *See, e.g.*, Lawrence C. George, *Sweet Uses of Adversity:* Parklane Hosiery *and the Collateral Class Action*, 32 STAN. L. REV. 655, 675–78 (1980).

49. Michael D. Green, *The Inability of Offensive Collateral Estoppel to Fulfill Its Promise: An Examination of Estoppel in Asbestos Litigation*, 70 IOWA L. REV. 141, 212 (1984).

50. Kenneth S. Abraham & Glen O. Robinson, *Aggregative Valuation of Mass Tort Claims*, 53 LAW & CONTEMP. PROBS., Autumn 1990, at 137, 147.

51. *See* Jerry Mashaw, *The Supreme Court's Due Process Calculus for Administrative Adjudication in* Mathews v. Eldridge: *Three Factors in Search of a Theory of Value*, 44 U. CHI. L. REV. 28, 48–52 (1976).

52. *See* Frank Michelman, *The Supreme Court and Litigation Access Fees: The Right to Protect One's Rights*, 1973 DUKE L.J. 1153, 1173; E. ALLAN LIND & TOM R. TYLER, THE SOCIAL PSYCHOLOGY OF PROCEDURAL JUSTICE 110–17 (New York: Plenum Press, 1988) (greater inaccuracy of adversarial system might be justified by its improved fairness); Laurens Walker et al., *The Relation Between Procedural and Distributive Justice*, 65 VA. L. REV. 1401 (1979); John Thibault & Laurens Walker, *A Theory of Procedure*, 66 CALIF. L. REV. 541 (1978).

53. Edward Brunet, *The Triumph of Efficiency and Discretion over Competing Complex Litigation Policies*, 10 REV. LITIG. 273, 284 (1991).

54. *See* Tom R. Tyler, *A Psychological Perspective on the Settlement of Mass Tort Claims*, 53 LAW & CONTEMP. PROBS., Autumn 1990, at 199; LIND & TYLER, *supra* note 52, at 93–106. *But cf.* E. ALLAN LIND ET AL., THE PERCEPTION OF JUSTICE: TORT LITIGANTS' VIEWS OF TRIAL, COURT-ANNEXED ARBITRATION AND JUDICIAL SETTLEMENT CONFERENCES 62–63 (Santa Monica, CA: Rand, 1989) (finding that dignity but not participation correlated with perceptions of procedural justice among parties in settlement hearings, arbitration, and traditional trials).

55. *See* LIND & TYLER, *supra* note 52, at 64, 76–82.

56. *See* Robert G. Bone, *Personal and Impersonal Litigative Forms: Reconceiving the History of Adjudicative Representation*, 70 B.U. L. REV. 213, 214–16 (1990).

57. *See, e.g.*, Rosenberg, *supra* note 3, at 909 ("The inherently probabilistic character of proof of causation in mass exposure cases belies the notion that, in a separate action, the victim can personalize the case by presenting 'particularistic' evidence"); Mullenix, *supra* note 39, at 1071 ("the facts establishing causation and injury do not differ meaningfully among claimants in the typical mass tort action").

58. For efforts to reform damages law to reduce or eliminate the variability that is currently recognized, see Rosenberg, *supra* note 3, at 916; Cimino v. Raymark Indus. Inc., 751 F. Supp. 649 (E.D. Tex. 1990).

59. Thus, while asbestos is responsible for virtually all cases of asbestosis and mesothelioma, its relative risk for lung cancer is about 5, and under 2.0 for colon cancer.

60. *Cf.* Philip M. Boffey, *Lack of Military Data Halts Agent Orange Study*, N.Y. TIMES, Sept. 1, 1987, at A1 (study of Agent Orange's toxicity among Vietnam veterans suspended because of inadequate information about exposure).

61. *See* Daniel A. Farber, *Toxic Causation*, 71 MINN. L. REV. 1219, 1243–44 (1987).

62. *See* James Robins & Sander Greenland, *The Probability of Causation Under a Stochastic Model for Individual Risk*, 45 BIOMETRICS 1125 (1989).

63. *See, e.g.*, Kenneth S. Kosik, *Alzheimer's Disease: A Cell Biological Perspective*, 256 SCI. 780 (1992).

64. *See* E. Donald Elliott, *Why Courts?*, 14 J. LEGAL STUD. 799, 803 (1985).

65. *See, e.g.*, Feldman v. Lederle Lab., 479 A.2d 374 (N.J. 1984); RESTATEMENT (THIRD) OF TORTS: PRODUCTS LIABILITY § 2 cmt. l (Philadelphia: American Law Institute, Tentative Draft No. 2 Mar. 13, 1995).

66. *Cf.* Green, *supra* note 49, at 190–94 (explaining the impact of time in creating different issues about the duty to warn in asbestos litigation).

67. *See In re* "Agent Orange" Product Liability Litig., 818 F.2d 145, 166 (2d Cir. 1987), *cert. denied*, 484 U.S. 1004 (1988); *In re* Joint Eastern & Southern District Asbestos Litig., 129 B.R. 710, 745–55 (Bankr. E. & S.D.N.Y. 1991), *vacated*, 982 F.2d 721 (2d Cir. 1992); Coffee, *supra* note 32, at 906.

68. *See* ARMEN A. ALCHIEN & WILLIAM R. ALLEN, EXCHANGE & PRODUCTION 285 n.1 (Belmont, CA: Wadsworth Publishing, 3d ed. 1983).

69. *See* McGovern, *supra* note 23, at 677; *see also* Ian Ayres, *Optimal Pooling in Claims Resolution Facilities*, 53 LAW & CONTEMP. PROBS., Autumn 1990, at 159, 160, 169.

70. Ayres, *supra* note 69, at 160, 169.

71. Kurt Eichenwald, *Millions for Us, Pennies for You*, N.Y. TIMES, Dec. 19, 1993, § 3, p. 1.

72. *See* Coffee, *supra* note 32, at 878.

73. *See generally* Deborah L. Rhode, *Class Conflicts in Class Actions*, 34 STAN. L. REV. 1183 (1982) (noting the ethical rules do not address lawyers' role in representing classes with conflicting claims); Weinstein, *supra* note 20, at 506–07.

74. II AMERICAN LAW INSTITUTE REPORTERS' STUDY, ENTERPRISE RESPONSIBILITY FOR PERSONAL INJURY 441–83 (Philadelphia: American Law Institute, 1991).

75. *See* Roger H. Transgrud, *Mass Trials in Mass Tort Cases: A Dissent*, 1989 U. ILL. L. REV. 70, 77.

76. Green, *supra* note 49, at 214–15.

77. *See* Kenneth S. Abraham, *Individual Action and Collective Responsibility: The Dilemma of Mass Tort Reform*, 73 VA. L. REV. 845, 871 (1987).

78. *See* McGovern, *supra* note 23.

79. *See* Kenneth R. Feinberg, *The Toxic Tort Crisis: Conceptual Problems and Proposed Solutions*, 24 HOUS. L. REV. 155 (1987); Edith Greene, *On Juries and Damage Awards: The Process of Decisionmaking*, 52 LAW & CONTEMP. PROBS., Autumn 1989, at 225; HENSLER ET AL., *supra* note 24, at 42 (identifying two similarly injured asbestos plaintiffs, one of whom was awarded $15,000 and the other $1.2 million; the judge who tried the cases remarked that: "These results make this litigation more like roulette than jurisprudence"); Abraham & Robinson, *supra* note 50, at 147. *But see* Ralph K. Winter, Comment, *Aggregating Litigation*, 54 LAW & CONTEMP. PROBS., Summer 1991, at 69, 70 (recognizing range of variables that bear on determination of damages).

80. *See* MARK PETERSON, COMPENSATION OF INJURIES 29–37 (Santa Monica: Rand, 1984); Randall R. Bovbjerg et al., *Valuing Life and Limb in Tort: Scheduling "Pain and Suffering"*, 83 NW. U. L. REV. 908 (1989) (finding huge variations in awards for comparable injuries).

81. *See, e.g.*, Bovbjerg et al., *supra* note 80; 1 DAVID BALDUS ET AL., IMPROVING JUDICIAL OVERSIGHT OF JURY DAMAGE ASSESSMENTS: A PROPOSAL FOR THE COMPARATIVE ADDITUR/REMITTITUR REVIEW OF AWARDS FOR NONPECUNIARY HARMS AND PUNITIVE DAMAGES (Report to State Justice Institute 1994) (forthcoming in Iowa Law Review).

82. *See* Johnson, *supra* note 26, at 567–70.

83. *See* John C. Coffee, Jr., *Understanding the Plaintiff's Attorney: The Implications of Economic Theory for Private Enforcement of Law Through Class and Derivative Actions*, 86 COLUM. L. REV. 669, 669–70 n.1 (1986).

84. Ben Kaufman, *Bendectin Attorneys Don't Regret Their Gamble*, CINCINNATI ENQUIRER, Mar. 14, 1985, at A1, col. 1.

85. *In re* Beverly Hills Fire Litigation, 639 F. Supp. 915 (E.D.Ky. 1986).

86. *Id.*; *In re* Activision Securities Litigation, 723 F. Supp. 1373, 1377 (N.D.Cal. 1989) (nearly all common fund lodestar fee awards end up around 30 percent of the fund recovered).

87. *See* Mark A. Peterson & Molly Selvin, *Mass Justice: The Limited and Unlimited Power of Courts*, 54 LAW & CONT. PROBS., Summer 1991, at 227, 239; *cf.* Samuel R. Gross & Kent D. Syverud, *Getting to No: A Study of Settlement Negotiations and the Selection of Cases for Trial*, 90 MICH. L. REV. 319, 332 (1991).

88. *See generally* Coffee, *supra* note 83, at 714–20; Weinstein, *supra* note 20, at 502–04; Richard L. Marcus, *Apocalypse Now?*, 85 MICH. L. REV. 1267, 1285–86 (1987) (book review); Sylvia R. Lazos, Note, *Abuse in Plaintiff Class Action Settlements: The Need for a Guardian During Pretrial Settlement Negotiations*, 84 MICH. L. REV. 308 (1985).

89. John C. Coffee, *The Corruption of the Class Action*, WALL ST. J., Sept. 7, 1994, at A13 (decrying use of collusive settlements in mass tort class actions).

90. *See* Yeazell, *supra* note 10, at 45.

91. *See* Marcus, *supra* note 37.

92. *See* Resnik, *supra* note 14, at 48–49; Peterson & Selvin, *supra* note 87, at 231; Marcus, *supra* note 37 (hypothesizing that because judges have preferences about the substantive outcome of settlements, they may be less than careful arbiters of the fairness of a class action settlement). *But see* Lea Brilmayer, *Comment on Peterson and Selvin*, 54 LAW & CONT. PROBS., Summer 1991, at 249 (questioning whether judicial self-interest preferring aggregation is a universal phenomenon).

93. Alleghany Corp. v. Kirby, 333 F.2d 327, 347 (2d Cir. 1964) (Friendly, J., dissenting), *aff'd by equally divided court*, 340 F.2d 311 (2d Cir. 1965), *cert. dismissed*, 384 U.S. 28 (1966).

94. Resnik, *supra* note 14, at 60.

95. *See* Peterson & Selvin, *supra* note 87, at 231.

96. *See* Coffee, *supra* note 32; Coffee, *supra* note 83.

97. *See* JACK B. WEINSTEIN, INDIVIDUAL JUSTICE IN MASS TORT LITIGATION: THE EFFECT OF CLASS ACTIONS, CONSOLIDATIONS, AND OTHER MULTIPARTY DEVICES 44 (Evanston, IL: Northwestern University Press, 1995) (musing about whether ethical rules need to be modified to permit processing mass tort cases).

98. Jonathan R. Macey & Geoffrey P. Miller, *The Plaintiffs' Attorney's Role in Class Action and Derivative Litigation: Economic Analysis and Recommendation for Reform*, 58 U. CHI. L. REV. 1 (1991); Randall S. Thomas & Robert G. Hansen, *Auctioning Class Action and Derivative Lawsuits: A Critical Analysis*, 87 NW. U. L. REV. 423 (1993); *see also In re* Oracle Securities Litigation, 132 F.R.D. 538 (N.D. Cal. 1990) (selecting class counsel based on bids for providing legal services to the class).

99. *Cf.* Marcus, *supra* note 88, at 1274; Coffee, *supra* note 32, at 896 ("Today, private, entrepreneurial law enforcement is a fact of life that we sometimes accept and sometimes repress.").

100. *See* Carl D. Liggio, *Clients in Control*, LITIG., Fall 1993, at 20; *see also* DOUGLAS E. ROSENTHAL, LAWYER AND CLIENT: WHO'S IN CHARGE? 147 (New York: Russell Sage Foundation, 1974).

101. *Cf.* Weinstein, *supra* note 20, at 527 (rejecting use of auctions to finance and appoint counsel to represent plaintiff classes in mass torts).

102. *See* Resnik, *supra* note 14, at 66; ROSENTHAL, *supra* note 100, at 111–25.

103. Deborah R. Hensler, *Resolving Mass Toxic Torts: Myths and Realities*, 1989 U. ILL. L. REV. 89, 92.

104. Coffee, *supra* note 27, at 631. *But see* Rosenberg, *supra* note 47, at 583 n.86 ("Generally, there is no reality to the notion that claimants have significant personal influence or involvement").

105. ROSENTHAL, *supra* note 100, at 30–31.

106. Hensler, *supra* note 103, at 94–95; *cf.* Gross & Syverud, *supra* note 87, at 351 (plaintiffs' personal injury lawyers reporting that they sometimes try cases that they would personally prefer to drop).

107. ROSENTHAL, *supra* note 100, at 3.

108. *See* Rabin, *supra* note 7; GASKINS, *supra* note 44, at 169. *But see* Abraham, *supra* note 77, at 885–98 (identifying difficulties in fashioning a mass tort compensation scheme).

109. *See* Transgrud, *supra* note 75, at 78.

110. *See* Hensler, *supra* note 103, at 97–98.

111. *See* JAMES S. KAKALIK ET AL., VARIATION IN ASBESTOS COMPENSATION AND EXPENSES 19 (Santa Monica, CA: Rand, 1984).

112. *See* John J. Donohue, III, *The Effects of Fee Shifting on the Settlement Rate: Theoretical Observations on Costs, Conflicts and Contingency Fees*, 54 LAW & CONTEMP. PROBS., Summer 1991, at 195, 217; *cf.* Francis McGovern, *Toward a Functional Approach for Managing Complex Litigation*, 53 U. CHI. L. REV. 440, 483 (1986) (explaining incentives for defendants to delay settlement, even where substantial information exists).

113. *See* Transgrud, *supra* note 75, at 74.

114. *See* Abraham & Robinson, *supra* note 50, at 138; *see also In re* "Agent Orange" Product Liability Litigation, 100 F.R.D. 718, 720 (E.D.N.Y. 1983).

115. *See* Kane v. Johns-Manville Corp., 843 F.2d 636 (2d Cir. 1988); *In re* A.H. Robins, 88 B.R. 742 (E.D. Va. 1988), *aff'd*, 880 F.2d 694 (4th Cir. 1989); *cf.* Abraham, *supra* note 77, at 868–69 ("The longer the period between the actions that produce mass injuries and the final resolution of all claims that result, the greater the opportunity for the commercial creditors and owners of the responsible enterprise to divert their assets and thereby to preclude tort claimants from recovering their losses"); Mark J. Roe, *Bankruptcy and Mass Tort*, 84 COLUM. L. REV. 846 (1984) (advocating bankruptcy so as to preserve firm value and protect future claimants). For an argument that the claims of those whose injuries have not yet occurred cannot be discharged in bankruptcy, see Gregory A. Bibler, *The Status of Unaccrued Tort Claims in Chapter 11 Bankruptcy Proceedings*, 61 AM. BANKR. L.J. 145 (1987).

116. *In re* Joint E. & S. Dist. Asbestos Litig., 14 F.3d 726, 733 (2d Cir. 1994); *see also* Marcus, *supra* note 37.

117. *See* Yeazell, *supra* note 10, at 65. *But see* RICHARD B. SOBOL, BENDING THE LAW: THE STORY OF THE DALKON SHIELD BANKRUPTCY (Chicago: University of Chicago Press, 1991).

118. *See, e.g., In re* N. Dist. of California Dalkon Shield IUD Prods. Liability Litig., 693 F.2d 847 (9th Cir. 1982) (reversing certification of mandatory class because of insufficient evidence that class members' individual suits would exhaust defendant's assets), *cert. denied*, 459 U.S. 1171 (1983).

119. 283 U.S. 494 (1931).

120. *Id.* at 500.

121. Transgrud, *supra* note 17, at 829 & n.282.

122. *See, e.g.,* John Makdisi, *Proportional Liability: A Comprehensive Rule to Apportion Tort Damages Based on Probability*, 67 N.C. L. REV. 1063 (1970); Rosenberg, *supra* note 3.

123. Jack B. Weinstein, *Routine Bifurcation of Jury Negligence Trials: An Example of the Questionable Use of Rule Making Power*, 14 VAND. L. REV. 831 (1961).

124. For a discussion of the efficiencies of polyfurcation and the impact on the litigants' incentives, see William M. Landes, *Sequential v. Unitary Trials: An Economic Analysis*, 22 J. Legal Stud. 99 (1993).

125. Hans Zeisel & Thomas Callahan, *Split Trials and Time Saving: A Statistical Analysis*, 76 HARV. L. REV. 1606, 1624–25 (1963) (20 percent saving through use of routine bifurcation of liability and damages in personal injury actions); Julius H. Miner, *Court Congestion: A New Approach*, 45 A.B.A. J. 1265 (1959); Note, *Separation of Issues of Liability and Damages in Personal Injury Cases: An Attempt to Combat Congestion by Rule of Court*, 46 IOWA L. REV. 815 (1961).

126. *See* Zeisel & Callahan, *supra* note 125, at 1617–18.

127. *See* George Priest & Benjamin Klein, *The Selection of Disputes for Settlement*, 13 J. LEG. STUD. 1, 17 (1984); *see also* Gross & Syverud, *supra* note 87, at 373.

128. *See, e.g.,* Utilities Natural Gas Corp. v. Hill, 239 S.W.2d 431, 434 (Tex. Civ. App. 1951) (fraud claim separated from breach of contract claim because of concern about prejudice).

129. Albert P. Bedecarre, Comment, *Rule 42(b) Bifurcation at an Extreme: Polyfurcation of Liability Issues in Environmental Tort Cases*, 17 B.C. ENV. AFF. L. REV. 123, 135 & n.93 (1989).

130. *See In re* Richardson-Merrell, Inc. "Bendectin" Products Liability Litigation, 624 F. Supp. 1212, 1221 n.5 (S.D. Ohio 1985), *aff'd*, 857 F.2d 290 (6th Cir. 1988), *cert. denied*, 488 U.S. 1006 (1989).

131. Transgrud, *supra* note 75, at 80.

132. *See, e.g.*, II AMERICAN LAW INSTITUTE REPORTERS' STUDY, ENTERPRISE LI-ABILITY FOR PERSONAL INJURY 369–73 (Philadelphia: American Law Institute, 1991).

133. *See* Glen O. Robinson, *Probabalistic Causation and Compensation for Tortious Risk*, 14 J. LEGAL STUD. 779, 781 (1985).

134. *See* Weinstein, *supra* note 123, at 833–34; JOSEPH N. ULMAN, A JUDGE TAKES THE STAND 31–32 (New York: A.A. Knopf, 1933).

135. *But see* Landes, *supra* note 124, at 121 (bifurcation of liability and damages in a contributory negligence regime does not always favor defendants).

136. *See generally* AMERICAN BAR ASSOCIATION/BROOKINGS INSTITUTION, CHARTING A FUTURE FOR THE CIVIL JURY SYSTEM (Washington, DC: Brookings Institution, 1992).

137. To be sure, there are special cases in which the defendant's behavior or other factors may result in modifying the substance or procedure of the causation requirement. *See, e.g.*, Haft v. Lone Palm Hotel, 478 P.2d 465 (Cal. 1970); Summers v. Tice, 199 P.2d 1 (Cal. 1948); Hymowitz v. Eli Lilly & Co., 539 N.E.2d 1069 (N.Y.), *cert. denied*, 493 U.S. 944 (1989).

138. *See* Nancy Pennington & Reid Hastie, *A Cognitive Theory of Juror Decision Making: The Story Model*, 13 CARDOZO L. REV. 519 (1991).

139. *See, e.g.*, THOMAS A. MAUET, FUNDAMENTALS OF TRIAL TECHNIQUES 43–44 (Boston: Little, Brown, 3d ed. 1992); *see also* Richard Lempert, *Telling Tales in Court: Trial Procedure and the Story Model*, 13 CARDOZO L. REV. 559, 561 (1991).

140. *See* Joseph Sanders, *From Science to Evidence: The Testimony on Causation in the Bendectin Cases*, 46 STAN. L. REV. 1, 52–53 (1993).

141. Irving A. Horowitz & Kenneth S. Bordens, *An Experimental Investigation of Procedural Issues in Complex Tort Trials*, 14 LAW & HUM. BEHAVIOR 269 (1990).

142. *Id.* at 277 (Table 2).

143. *Id.* at 278–79.

144. *Id.* at 283.

145. *Id.* at 282.

146. *See* Joseph Sanders, *The Bendectin Litigation: A Case Study in the Life Cycle of Mass Torts*, 43 HASTINGS L.J. 301, 388–90 (1992).

Chapter 16
The Third Phase of Bendectin Litigation: *Oxendine, Richardson,* and the Individual Trials

On June 10, 1985 Judge Rubin returned some 300 MDL-486 cases to their home courts. The Judicial Panel on Multidistrict Litigation had initially transferred those cases to Judge Rubin over a three year period from 1982 to 1985. A number were filed in the aftermath of the unsettlement: Merrell's willingness to pay $120 million convinced many plaintiffs' lawyers that it was worthwhile to file suit on behalf of clients. All plaintiffs in those 300 cases had declined to opt into the MDL-486 trial, thereby preserving their right to proceed individually. Many were ready for trial or nearly so; others still had individual discovery to complete. Thus began the third phase of Bendectin litigation—the resolution of individual cases—approximately two dozen of which have been tried, in courts across the country.[1]

The *Oxendine* and *Richardson* cases are illustrative of the third phase of Bendectin litigation and played an important role in its development.[2] Although the verdict in *Oxendine* occurred before the MDL-486 trial, it was the first unequivocal plaintiff's verdict in a Bendectin case. As such, it greatly influenced the post-MDL-486 individual trials. *Oxendine* was also Barry Nace's first Bendectin case; Nace and Tom Bleakley were the primary plaintiffs' lawyers pursuing Bendectin cases after MDL-486. It was in *Oxendine* that Dr. Alan Done developed his four-factor basis for concluding that Bendectin is a teratogen, a theory that he testified to in many of the subsequent individual Bendectin cases and trials.[3] *Oxendine* remains as one of only three judgments favorable to a Bendectin plaintiff that has not been overturned.

By contrast, *Richardson* is important for the role that the trial and appellate courts played in overturning the jury verdict for the plaintiff. *Richardson* supplied the precedent for overturning two other District of

Columbia jury verdicts for plaintiffs in Bendectin cases. Even more importantly, *Richardson* played a critical role in the development of law that gave greater authority to courts to control expert witness abuse in toxic substances cases, the subject of chapter 17.

In addition to the District of Columbia cases, there were a number of other individual trials across the country. Merrell won the vast majority of those other trials; only in two cases in Texas and one in Pennsylvania did juries find for plaintiffs in the individual Bendectin cases.[4] Many other cases were resolved without trials by judges granting summary judgment in favor of Merrell.

One sorry event that came to light in the third phase of the Bendectin litigation was the disgrace of Dr. William McBride, the Australian physician whose co-discovery of thalidomide's teratogenicity made him a hero in Australia. McBride had testified in *Mekdeci*, MDL-486, and a few post-MDL-486 trials on behalf of plaintiffs and had published a study in 1984 identifying birth defects in the kits of rabbits fed doxylamine. Although it was not revealed publicly until 1987, McBride had been under a cloud for five years, accused of scientific misconduct by collaborators in a study he conducted at the research institute he founded, Foundation 41. An investigation prompted by the complaints of two co-authors found that McBride deliberately falsified data and several other aspects of a study published in 1982 that examined the teratogenicity of scopolamine in rabbits.[5] Later, McBride was stripped of his medical license by the Medical Tribunal in Australia.[6] Once the information about Dr. McBride became known in the United States (Merrell had been aware of the allegations since 1984, when one of its lawyers stumbled on the information while interviewing a witness in Tasmania), he no longer testified in Bendectin cases.

Both Carita Richardson and Mary Oxendine were born in the 1970s with severe birth defects involving their limbs. Both were daughters of mothers who took three-part Bendectin. Both sued Merrell in Washington, DC. Both were represented by Barry Nace, and both were successful in persuading a jury that their birth defects were caused by Bendectin. Ultimately, however, the Richardsons and Oxendines were treated very differently by the legal system. Difference in outcomes, often blamed on the caprice of juries, was instead a result of appellate courts with very different views about expert witnesses, the appropriate deference to be afforded to them, the respective role of judge and jury, and the teratogenicity of Bendectin.

In October 1989 Nace received word that the Supreme Court had refused to review the court of appeals decision in *Richardson*. At that point the *Oxendine* jury verdict had been reinstated, and the Supreme Court's refusal to review *Richardson* meant the end of that case. Nace wrote a poignant letter to the Richardsons, informing them of the Court's decision and remarking on the inconsistent outcomes:

It would appear at this point, that therefore, Mary Oxendine is going to be able to collect her judgment and go back to the court for punitive damages. Do not ask me to explain how this is possible, other than the fact that her case was left in the court system of the District of Columbia by the defendant, while your case was transferred to the federal court, and our court system in the United States does provide for different results in similar cases. That is not a good explanation, especially when one considers in your case, we had eight times as many experts saying that Bendectin was a drug that causes birth defects as we had in the Oxendine case. I have of course previously explained to you my thoughts as to why you cannot win in the federal courts and there really is nothing that I can add to it. There was no way of keeping the case out of the federal courts unfortunately.

Mary Oxendine was born in 1971 with a shortened right forearm, two missing fingers on her right hand, and webbing between the remaining three. Her mother read the *National Enquirer* article about Bendectin and began investigating legal action by contacting the District of Columbia Bar Association lawyer referral service. There, she and her husband found the name of Barry Nace and contacted him because they noted that he had a degree in chemistry, and they thought that expertise would be helpful in a drug case.

Nace is a large, physically imposing man. He is tough, determined, blunt, stubborn, and a superb trial lawyer. His success as a trial lawyer is a product of thinking quickly on his feet, getting directly to the heart of the matter, appreciating the importance of thorough preparation, having a keen awareness of and sensitivity to juries, and possessing an uncanny sense of when to take risks in questioning or cross-examining a witness. One juror in a Bendectin case compared Nace with Perry Mason in a post-verdict interview.[7] Nace is aggressive, outspoken, and sometimes those qualities lead to intemperate attacks, especially toward adversaries and judges who he feels have wronged him. His written briefs, at least in his Bendectin cases, tend to include rhetoric, conclusions, and ineffective ad hominem attacks.

Oxendine avoided being swept up in the MDL-486 litigation because Mary's mother, Joan, had also taken the drug Provera, manufactured by Upjohn, during her pregnancy. Both Upjohn and Merrell Dow were sued in the District of Columbia Superior Court, the local trial court for the District of Columbia (the District of Columbia has a dual court system similar to the states; both court systems are a product of the federal government, although one is comparable to federal courts throughout the country and the other comparable to a state court). Merrell could not remove the case to federal court, because removal to federal court requires that all defendants agree to request it, and Upjohn refused.

At the time, Merrell was routinely removing all Bendectin cases filed in state court to federal court. Federal law permits defendants to remove cases filed in state court to federal court if the case could have originally been filed in federal court. In almost every state (except for Delaware and Ohio, because Merrell was deemed a citizen of those states) federal jurisdiction based on diversity of citizenship existed, providing a basis for federal court jurisdiction and therefore removal.[8] Thus, *Oxendine* was one of a very few individual cases in state courts that proceeded simultaneously with MDL-486. Had Joan Oxendine not taken Provera, thereby not implicating Upjohn, the case would have been transferred to Cincinnati and become part of MDL-486. Not only would it have been resolved in the opposite way (either as part of the MDL-486 trial or upon being returned to federal court in Washington, DC), but its absence would have had a significant, perhaps critical, impact on the course of post-MDL-486 Bendectin litigation.

Oxendine proceeded much more rapidly than MDL-486 and other individual cases, such as *Mekdeci* and *Koller*. Filed on February 1, 1982, it was tried just 15 months later. Even for routine products liability litigation, 15 months is an exceedingly short period of time to prepare for trial. In a case with the scientific and factual complexity present in Bendectin cases, it is extraordinary. This headlong rush to trial would often favor defendants. They have a natural advantage over plaintiffs because of superior knowledge about the product and the technical issues implicated in a case. Even when plaintiffs engage experts, those experts rarely have the in-depth knowledge about the specific product that the manufacturer has. Barry Nace, on reflection, concedes that he had little idea about the complex causation issues involved in the *Oxendine* case at its outset, and because of the pace at which it proceeded to trial it wasn't until after the case was concluded that he felt he understood the science and evidence bearing on causation.

Merrell was not without difficulties in responding to the expedited scheduling for trial. Frank Woodside and Dinsmore Shohl were defending in MDL-486, and Davis, Polk was defending *Koller*, which was shaping up as the Waterloo of Bendectin litigation, with trial anticipated in 1982. As with the decision to hire Woodside to defend MDL-486, Merrell was unwilling to pay the premium rate charged by Davis, Polk to defend the *Oxendine* case. Sid Leech, a Baltimore lawyer, was hired to represent Merrell in *Oxendine*. Mark Austrian, who as an associate at Davis, Polk had worked on the *Mekdeci* case and later moved to a Washington, DC firm, was hired to assist Leech. With *Cordova* on the west coast, MDL-486 beginning to grind into serious discovery activity, and *Koller* looking like it was on the verge of trial, Merrell-Dow officials were also stretched thin in responding to the demands of firm-threatening litigation. Uncharacteristically, Merrell, which had pushed so hard to have the *Mekdeci* case tried and retried promptly, sought an extension of the original *Oxendine* trial date, which grudgingly was granted, but only for an additional three months.

The trial began early in May 1983 and required only three weeks, in comparison to *Mekdeci*, which took two months at each of the two trials. Upjohn settled with the Oxendines a few weeks before the trial began; hence, Merrell was the only defendant at trial. The trial was limited to liability and compensatory damages; the Oxendines' claim for punitive damages was bifurcated and would be addressed at a later hearing if they prevailed in the initial proceeding.[9]

The only expert witness that Barry Nace called during his case-in-chief was Dr. Done. Done had previously testified as an expert witness in a number of drug cases, including *Mekdeci* and a pharmaceutical case that Allen Eaton tried successfully just before he joined the *Mekdeci* trial team. Nace had previously hired an associate of Eaton's, and the associate recommended Done to Nace. With Nace, Done developed his four-factors-proving-teratogenicity testimony.

Done testified that Bendectin was a teratogen because of the epidemiological studies, the animal toxicology studies, chemical structure analysis, and in vivo studies. None of the four components was sufficient by itself to prove Bendectin's teratogenicity, but considered together, they did so, according to Done.[10] That basis for his opinion was considerably more refined than the testimony he provided in *Mekdeci*, in which he relied on the pattern of defects in the drug experience reports and the Staples rabbit study. Nevertheless, it required that Done reanalyze the Bunde-Bowles study, correcting for methodological errors that he identified, because the original study found no association between Bendectin and birth defects. Shanna Swan testified in rebuttal on behalf of the Oxendines; the thrust of her testimony was to refute Merrell's claim that a statistically significant association was required to support a finding of causation.

By contrast, Merrell had 11 expert witnesses testify, and continuing its strategy in *Mekdeci*, five of the experts were authors of studies about Bendectin. Brian MacMahon, who also served as the primary expert on causation at the MDL-486 trial, was the leadoff expert for Merrell in *Oxendine*. In addition, Merrell had two pediatrician-geneticists testify, an animal toxicologist, a chemist (who addressed chemical-structure similarities raised by Dr. Done), an orthopedic surgeon, and Dr. Bunde, one of the co-authors of the in-house Bunde-Bowles study of Bendectin.[11]

The jury awarded the Oxendines $750,000 in compensatory damages, and on May 27, 1983 Judge Joseph G. Hannon entered judgment in favor of the Oxendines and against Merrell. The judgment was for $450,000, reduced to reflect the earlier settlement with Upjohn.

There were two peculiarities in the way the case was tried for Merrell that raise suspicions that had they been treated differently, the outcome might have been changed. First, because Upjohn was a co-defendant, Merrell decided that it would not assist the Oxendines by asserting that Upjohn's drug, Provera, was responsible for the birth defects. As a result, Merrell conceded during discovery that it had no explanation for Mary Oxendine's birth defect. After Upjohn settled with the Oxendines, Judge Hannon held Merrell to that concession and would not permit argument that there was another explanation for the birth defect (despite the fact that Provera was a more likely target than Bendectin).[12] Thus Merrell was left to argue only that Bendectin did not cause the birth defect, but was foreclosed from presenting to the jury an alternative explanation for the defect.[13]

The second oddity about Merrell's strategy in *Oxendine* is that it failed to make any argument on specific causation. In essence, Merrell implicitly conceded, that if the jury found that Bendectin increased the risk of birth defects at all, the Oxendines should recover. While Merrell's lawyers did make the argument that no study should be considered valid unless it was statistically significant at the .95 level, its concession left Barry Nace to argue that relative risks of even 1.15 found in one of the epidemiology studies would justify a plaintiff's verdict.[14]

Merrell filed a motion for judgment notwithstanding the verdict and for a new trial, asserting a number of grounds in support of its motion. In a two-page order, Judge Hannon granted Merrell's motion for judgment n.o.v. (as a matter of law, the Oxendines could not recover) and conditionally for a new trial (if the judgment n.o.v. were reversed by the appellate court, the new trial order would then become effective). Even before Judge Weinstein's pathbreaking decision expressing his skepticism about the plaintiffs' experts in *Agent Orange* (addressed in the next chapter), Judge Hannon indicated in his terse order that the plaintiff's evidence of causation was inadequate to present a factual question for the jury. Hannon's decision constituted an unequivocal rejection of Dr. Done and his testimony.

Done, who later emerged as the leading expert witness for individual plaintiffs in Bendectin litigation, had quite a respectable career and resume, although subsequent events cast a shadow over his credibility and integrity. Done obtained a medical degree from the University of Utah, had specialized training in pediatrics, and had taken graduate courses in the biomedical sciences. He had held appointments in academic medicine after his graduation from medical school, including stints at Stanford University, the University of Utah, the Food and Drug Administration, and with his then-current institution, Wayne State University. Done's research work focused on endocrinology and childhood drug poisoning. Thus he had a grounding in pharmacology, toxicology, and epidemiology, although not in teratology.[15]

Despite Judge Hannon's grant of judgment as a matter of law for Merrell, Barry Nace and indeed all the Bendectin plaintiffs' attorneys were encouraged by the *Oxendine* verdict. The announcement of the withdrawal of Bendectin three weeks after the verdict did nothing to diminish that optimism. In the publicity following the *Oxendine* verdict, numerous potential plaintiffs and their lawyers contacted Nace. In October 1983 Nace filed three additional cases against Merrell in the District of Columbia Superior Court. Merrell promptly removed all of them to federal court, and they were sent off to Cincinnati for consolidation in MDL-486. Nace, however, who was a vigorous opponent of the MDL-486 settlement, refused to have his clients remain in the consolidated trial. The three cases that Nace filed in 1983 were returned to federal court in Washington, DC in 1985.

Before any of Nace's three pending District of Columbia Bendectin cases went to trial, the Court of Appeals for the District of Columbia reversed Judge Hannon and reinstated the jury's verdict in *Oxendine*. Characterizing the trial as a classic "battle of the experts" between Dr. Done and Dr. MacMahon, the lead expert for Merrell, the Court of Appeals quoted from its sister court, the Circuit Court of Appeals for the District of Columbia, in another toxic substances case, *Ferebee v. Chevron Oil Co.*[16] The *Ferebee* opinion reflected the traditional court response to conflicting expert testimony:

Judges, both trial and appellate, have no special competence to resolve the complex and refractory causal issues raised by the attempt to link low level exposure to toxic chemicals with human disease. On questions such as these, which stand at the frontier of current medical and epidemiological inquiry, if experts are willing to testify that such a link exists, it is for the jury to decide whether to credit such testimony.[17]

While the reversal of the judgment notwithstanding the verdict was understandable, the reversal of Judge Hannon's alternative granting of a new trial to Merrell bordered on the bizarre. Appellate courts, which only have the benefit of a cold written record, and who, even at that, rarely slog through all of the transcript, give great deference to trial judges. Trial judges, after all, have had the opportunity to observe the proceedings at trial. When a judge feels that a new trial should be granted, appellate courts are loath to interpose their contrary judgments.[18] The court of appeals explanation for reversing was unconvincing: because Merrell had not had any witness explicitly contradict Dr. Done's four-factor analysis, the jury verdict was not against the weight of the evidence, the standard for awarding a new trial. But Merrell had presented solid expert testimony on each of the factors relied on by Done, and, given the dearth of positive epidemiological evidence, especially for limb reduction defects, it surely was a reasonable call for Judge Hannon to order a new trial. Nevertheless, the court of appeals finding that Judge Hannon abused his discretion in awarding a new trial meant reversal of the judgment he had entered, and a remand of the case for a hearing on punitive damages.

The court of appeals decision, however, was not to be the final word in *Oxendine*, which became a battle not only between plaintiff and defendant, but also between the trial court and the appellate court. Even before the court of appeals reversed, Merrell sought to reopen the case because of alleged perjury by Dr. Done at trial. After the court of appeals ruling, the Done perjury matter became Merrell's last chance to escape from the first final judgment for a plaintiff in Bendectin litigation.

The gist of Merrell's claim of perjury was that Dr. Done had misrepresented his position at Wayne State University when he testified at trial. There were a number of specific facets to Merrell's claims, but they revolved around Done's testimony that he was a Professor of Pediatrics, Pharmacology, and Toxicology at Wayne State University.[19] Done had resigned his position at Wayne State effective May 1, 1983 in a letter dated April 24, 1983. Also, there was no such position as Professor of Toxicology at Wayne State.

Thus was launched satellite litigation that took on all of the characteristics of a litigated case. Depositions were taken of Henry Nadler, Done's Dean at Wayne State, as well as several of Done's colleagues who had submitted affidavits in support of Merrell's motion. Nadler reported that he had requested Done's resignation because he had been derelict in fulfilling his academic duties at Wayne State and that he was devoting a "large percentage" of his time to testifying as an expert in lawsuits. Perhaps most significantly, Nadler asserted that Done's testifying had brought "discredit" on Wayne State Medical School, thereby vaguely implying that his testimony in *Oxendine* was scientifically embarrassing. Merrell's attorneys, with considerable effort, put together an itinerary of Done's expert testifying over the period before his resignation, which demonstrated a great deal of time spent traveling to testify at trials or depositions. The bottom line was clear: Dr. Done had a lucrative consulting operation as an expert witness, he had neglected his academic obligations to pursue his consulting, and his extensive consulting for private litigants called into question his scientific judgment.

Ultimately, however, Done's exaggerations of his credentials before the *Oxendine* jury are hardly the stuff of which cases are overturned after judgment. As Barry Nace demonstrated, Done had remained on the Wayne State personnel rolls until May 26, 1983, thereby technically justifying Dr. Done's testimony on May 9, 1983 in *Oxendine* that "I am a full professor in pediatrics,"[20] even though Done had submitted his written resignation to Dean Nadler in April suggesting his termination "be effective at the end of this month."[21] His false claims of being Professor of Toxicology and of being the sole teacher of a course that was team taught could be explained as misunderstandings. Even if not, his statements were well within the range of what many experts do in hyping their credentials. The alleged perjury did not address Done's expertise, nor did it implicate any of his substantive testimony. The proposition that Merrell's evidence of Done's misstatements, had they been brought to the jury's attention, would have had an effect on the outcome of the trial seems most improbable. The *reasons* for Done's resignation, which might have influenced a fact-finder, would, in all likelihood, have been inadmissible.

Yet Judge Peter H. Wolf, to whom the *Oxendine* case was assigned on remand after Judge Hannon recused himself, found that Dr. Done had committed perjury in several respects at trial. In an opinion that openly expressed contempt for Dr. Done, Judge Wolf overturned the judgment and ordered a new trial:

> The court has found that Dr. Done lied in several respects. . . . The court finds that his testimony was so deliberately false that *all* his testimony on behalf of plaintiff is suspect. His lies went so much toward enhancing his status as a witness that he reeks of the hired gun who will say anything that money can buy so long as it is glibly consistent with his prior testimony in other cases. In a proverbial spiral his professional witness status led him to shirk his duties at the Wayne State Medical School. That got him fired (gently, by a forced resignation). The true circumstances of that resignation detracted from his professional witness status, and so he covered it up with lies to maintain his purported status.[22]

Judge Wolf only hinted at the true reason for overturning the verdict with the comment about Dr. Done being a hired gun. The *Oxendine* verdict was overturned the second time not because of Done's enhancing his credentials, but because the trial court did not believe Done and thought that his causation testimony was unreliable.[23] Yet the court of appeals had already declared that Done's testimony was sufficient for the jury to find that Mary Oxendine's birth defects were caused by Bendectin and that the trial judge was not to substitute his disagreement with the jury in evaluating Done's testimony.

Not surprisingly, the court of appeals once again overturned the trial court, reinstating the *Oxendine* jury verdict.[24] Thus, almost three years of litigation over Dr. Done's positions at Wayne State concluded with the same outcome that had previously been reached. But the litigation revealed the determination and tenacity of Merrell in defending Bendectin, regardless of the litigation costs involved. Indeed, at the time this book was published, over six years after the court of appeals decision, thirteen years after the case was filed, Mary Oxendine, age 24, has still not recovered any money from Merrell due to further delays and appeals in that case.[25]

Merrell's strategy was a sound one in the early and mid 1980s: one successful case might open the floodgates for an outpouring of individual cases—cases that attorneys would seriously pursue. But by April 1989, when the court of appeals reinstated the *Oxendine* verdict, the plaintiffs' Bendectin efforts were flagging. That was in large part because of the appellate decision in *Richardson* and in two other courts of appeals that revealed judicial impatience with expert witness abuse, the filing of weak or marginal toxic substances cases, and a profound desire to tighten the law so that such cases would not be so readily pursued.

Richardson was the first of Barry Nace's three District of Columbia federal court Bendectin cases filed in the wake of the *Oxendine* verdict to go to trial. Even at that point, the summer of 1986, the plaintiffs' attorneys were quite discouraged, and the end of Bendectin litigation appeared near. Jim Butler had lost *Cordova* in California, MDL-486 had been lost, another case tried by Barry Nace in 1985 in Georgia, *Will v. Richardson-Merrell, Inc.,*[26] resulted in a verdict for Merrell, and the attack on the *Oxendine* verdict was in full swing.

Judge Thomas Penfield Jackson presided over the *Richardson* trial. Jackson, the son of a prominent Washington lawyer, spent three years in the Navy before attending Harvard Law School. Upon graduation, he joined his father's firm, and spent much of his career defending medical malpractice cases. Jackson practiced during the transition from the "conspiracy of silence" when physicians would refuse to identify or testify about another doctor's misadventures to the proliferation of medical expert witnesses, including those who, Jackson has observed, are "utterly irresponsible, purely result-oriented."[27]

Jackson has a reputation for being businesslike and no-nonsense while presiding at trial, although he is not humorless. Appointed as a federal trial judge by President Ronald Reagan in 1982 at the age of 45, Jackson has presided over some notable cases, including the prosecution of Marion Barry, the mayor of Washington, DC, in 1990 for drug offenses and perjury, and the prosecution of Michael Deaver, the former Reagan aide who was convicted of perjury for his denials about improper lobbying after he left government service.

Carita Richardson suffered far more serious birth defects than Mary Oxendine. Carita was missing her right leg and other bones, and had a shortened left leg and left arm. Her father, Sam, testified to his thoughts upon seeing his daughter for the first time as she was emerging from her mother's womb: "I saw one of the legs, her right leg, right leg sticking out. A foot was sticking out of her hip, didn't have no leg at all, and the left arm didn't have no hand on it at all." Judge Jackson recalls Carita, who sat through the entire trial, as a sweet, darling ten-year-old girl who evoked enormous sympathy.[28]

By the summer of 1986 when the *Richardson* trial began, Barry Nace had put together a more sophisticated team of experts to testify on causation than he had in *Oxendine*. In part, this was due to the experts identified and developed during MDL-486. The team was anchored by Dr. Done, who was forced by the growth of epidemiological studies that tended to exonerate Bendectin as a teratogen to insist that epidemiology was not a trump over other forms of evidence. Dr. Stuart Newman, a developmental biologist whose specialty was cell development in the fetus and embryo, was another key witness. He testified about in vitro studies with Bendectin and their implications. Nace also called Adrian Gross, a veterinarian and toxicologist, as an expert. Gross explained the animal studies of Bendectin and concluded based on them that Bendectin was a teratogen.

Nace also used testimony from three experts that had been developed by the PLCC during MDL-486. Nace had the deposition of Frederick Crescitelli, who performed studies in the 1950s examining the effect of antihistamines on frog nerve cells, read to the jury during the trial. Dr. John Thiersch, the teratologist who had testified for Jim Butler in his thalidomide case and whose testimony was videotaped by the PLCC during pretrial proceedings in MDL-486, was presented to the jury via videotape. Dr. Thiersch concluded in that testimony that Bendectin was a generic teratogen based on in vitro and in vivo test results. Another witness whose testimony had been videotaped by the PLCC in MDL-486 was presented to testify about structural activity similarities between doxylamine and other antihistamines.

As in *Oxendine* and MDL-486, Shanna Swan testified as a rebuttal witness. The gist of her testimony was to deflate the significance of Merrell's epidemiological evidence. She criticized aspects of several of the studies, pointing out biases that may have skewed the results. Swan explained that while a given epidemiological study may not have found a statistically significant association, it should not be understood as proving the safety of Bendectin. She explained that the study was as consistent with the upper confidence interval boundary as with the lower one. Taking on her role as a public health official, she explained that the upper bound of the confidence interval is the one of primary concern: "[I]f you want to protect the public health and you want to know how bad can the situation be and still be calling something safe and I think to do that you need to look at the upper confidence levels. . . . "[29] Of course, public health regulation and the requisite showing in a private tort suit are two quite different matters, but no objection was raised to this testimony, and no cross-examination was conducted to educate the jury about the differences.

Swan also presented the results of her reanalysis of a Bendectin case-control study performed by Godfrey Oakley and Jose Cordero at the Centers for Disease Control.[30] Her reanalysis, Swan testified, was performed at the behest of, and paid for by, plaintiff's lawyers. The original study had used children who were born with birth defects other than the one being studied as the control group. In reanalyzing the risk of limb reduction defects, Swan changed the control group from children born with birth defects other than limb reduction defects to children born with only Down's syndrome, a genetic birth defect. The reason, she explained, was to avoid diluting the results if Bendectin caused birth defects other than limb reductions. Swan's reasoning was sound: if Bendectin caused both limb reduction and other birth defects, the controls would have a higher exposure to Bendectin than true non-case controls would.

However, Mark Austrian pointed out on cross-examination, it would be very easy for someone with the published study to determine that the Down's syndrome group, which had a very low rate of Bendectin exposure, would result in a significantly higher odds ratio than the authors of the study had found using the entire birth defect group as controls.[31] Dr. Swan, however, denied that she had "looked behind the curtain" in setting the parameters for her reanalysis. Austrian also emphasized that Swan's reanalysis had not been published nor had it been peer reviewed. Later, during closing statements, Austrian argued to the jury that all of the epidemiological studies upon which Merrell's experts relied had been published and peer reviewed, in an attempt to discredit Swan's work and Done's earlier testimony.[32] The issue of publication and peer review would later play a major role in many of the Bendectin appellate cases, including the Supreme Court's opinion in *Daubert v. Merrell Dow Pharmaceuticals, Inc.*[33]

A telling example of Barry Nace's trial skills occurred during surrebuttal, when Merrell called an epidemiologist from Johns Hopkins University, Allen Gittelsohn, to critique Swan's reanalysis. Gittelsohn testified that it was ludicrous to use a sample of 168 Down's syndrome children to serve as a control group for a study that encompassed 28,000 live births. "[N]o one, at least in the United States would have chosen Down's syndrome to be the reference population,"[34] Gittlsohn insisted. Had such a paper been submitted to any of the journals for which he was a peer reviewer, it would have been summarily rejected because of the control group choice. Gittelsohn implied that the very choice of such an odd control group, with its low Bendectin exposure, suggested that Swan had peeked behind the curtain before performing her reanalysis.

Nace cross-examined Gittelsohn, a cross-examination that was without the benefit of a pretrial deposition, because Gittelsohn was a rebuttal witness. First, Nace had Gittelsohn reaffirm his direct testimony; then Nace introduced and showed Gittelsohn a study performed by Godfrey Oakley, a co-author of the study Swan reanalyzed and head of the section at the Centers for Disease Control responsible for identifying the causes of birth defects. The study examined the relationship between prenatal exposure to Valium and cleft lip and was published in the *Lancet*, the leading British medical journal. Oakley's control group, as Nace pointed out to an embarrassed Gittelsohn, was children with Down's syndrome.[35]

Merrell replaced Brian MacMahon as its primary expert on epidemiology with Raymond Seltser, Dean of the School of Public Health at the University of Pittsburgh. Seltser played the same role as MacMahon, reviewing the epidemiological studies of Bendectin, explaining the role of statistical significance, and concluding that there was no association between Bendectin and birth defects generally or limb reduction defects specifically. Dr. James Goddard testified to the same time line data that had played such a powerful role in MDL-486. Raymond Harbison, a toxicologist and pharmacologist who had conducted teratology studies in animals, testified about the Bendectin animal studies. In addition, Merrell called Carita Richardson's treating orthopedist, a prominent Washington DC pediatrician and geneticist, and a local obstetrician who had frequently prescribed Bendectin for his patients, all of whom expressed the view that Bendectin was not the cause of Carita's birth defects.

Consistent with his approach in *Oxendine*, Mark Austrian did not present the jury with an alternative explanation of the cause of Carita Richardson's birth defects. As he candidly told the jury, "We cannot prove to you what in fact caused Carita Richardson's birth defects because we simply don't know."[36] Austrian explained that the majority of birth defects are of unknown origin, but insisted that Bendectin was not the source of the defects. Austrian also presented no argument on specific causation based on relative risks that were less than 2.0. Instead, once again, statistical significance was the basis of Austrian's claim that the epidemiology presented showed that Bendectin was not a teratogen. Austrian argued that, even though a study might find an association greater than 1.0, it should not be considered proof of teratogenicity unless the association was statistically significant. None of the epidemiological studies found a statistically significant association between Bendectin exposure and limb reduction defects.

The trial continued for seven weeks. To prevent a compromise verdict by the jury, Jackson required the jury to deliberate and deliver an initial verdict on whether Bendectin caused Carita's birth defects. In doing so, Judge Jackson kept the jury from awarding a discounted amount of damages to the plaintiff if it had reservations about causation. After the jury responded affirmatively on causation, Judge Jackson sent the jury to deliberate on liability and compensatory damages. On September 18, 1986 the jury returned a verdict finding that Merrell had failed adequately to warn of the risks of taking Bendectin and awarding $1,000,000 to Carita and $160,000 to her parents.

Judge Jackson, however, granted Merrell's motion for judgment notwithstanding the verdict and, in the event that judgment was reversed on appeal, he ordered that a new trial be held. Jackson was convinced that the Richardsons won in spite of the merits and because of Barry Nace's superior trial abilities. Thus, while Nace triumphed over Leech and Austrian at trial, Leech and Austrian were successful in developing a record that persuaded Judge Jackson, as well as the court of appeals.

Jackson also believed that the expert witness business has become corrupted and that the courts were too lax in policing abuses. Cases in which courts abdicate review with the explanation that a "battle of the experts" is for the jury to decide are "terribly dangerous." Opinions such as Judge Jackson's and the perception of widespread expert witness abuse led a number of judges in the latter half of the 1980s and the early 1990s to develop a variety of legal weapons to combat the abuse, a matter explained in chapter 17.

The District of Columbia Circuit Court of Appeals affirmed Judge Jackson's decision, albeit on somewhat different grounds than those on which he relied. The impact of the *Richardson* case, which may constitute the most lasting influence of Bendectin litigation on the legal landscape, is treated in the next chapter. But before the court of appeals ruled, Barry Nace won two more jury verdicts in the other two cases that were filed the same day as *Richardson, Ealy v. Richardson-Merrell, Inc.* and *Raynor v. Richardson-Merrell, Inc. Raynor* and *Ealy* completed a string of four successful jury trials for Barry Nace in Bendectin cases in Washington, DC. *Ealy* resulted in a stupendous jury verdict: $20 million in compensatory damages for Sekou Ealy, an eight-year-old with severe arm and hand deformities, and $75 million in punitive damages.[37]

Reflecting the frustration and concern that the *Ealy* verdict must have caused, Frank Popoff, Dow Chemical Company's President and Chief Operating Officer, commented to reporters that the judge, jury, and plaintiff in the case were all black. Popoff might have added (though he did not) that the plaintiffs and the vast majority of jurors in all three of the other Washington, DC cases were black. Pressed by reporters who smelled an opportunity to develop a racial angle or at least a sore loser's claim of racial bias, Popoff realized his improvidence and immediately retreated, stating he was sure that the jury's verdict was the result of sympathy for the plaintiff rather than racial bias.

Popoff's comments about race raise an interesting issue. To what extent does the jury composition affect the outcome of a case? Lawyers think about that question all the time. Increasingly, researchers are examining the issue with a wide variety of methodologies. Can the conflicting outcomes of jury trials in Bendectin litigation be attributed to jury composition?

Two patterns of interest emerge in the outcomes of Bendectin jury trials. One is the overall success rate of plaintiffs. The plaintiffs' success rate in Bendectin trials is roughly comparable to the rate of success found in several studies of products liability trials. That is a higher success rate than one would expect, based on the scientific record that exists on Bendectin.[38] Moreover, as the scientific record has grown over time, reducing uncertainty, the plaintiffs' success rate has not changed. The second aspect is the geographic, racial, and socioeconomic pattern to the outcomes. Major urban areas and Texas account for all plaintiff victories, while jury verdicts for defendants are scattered across the country. Might demographic aspects of jury composition account for the difference in outcomes?

Virtually all research into jury decision making indicates that the strongest predictor of outcome is the evidence that is introduced at trial.[39] Professor Joseph Sanders, in an insightful and illuminating article, identifies a number of factors that go a long way to explaining why the evidence presented in Bendectin trial was a skewed version of the scientific record.[40] Sanders starts by recognizing that the scientific deck is stacked against plaintiffs with regard to Bendectin's teratogenicity and proceeds to consider what might explain the success of plaintiffs in jury trials. After reviewing the transcripts of a representative group of Bendectin trials, Sanders explains a variety of structural and other factors that impeded the jury's ability to obtain an accurate understanding of the scientific record.

To begin with, one must appreciate that virtually all the scientific evidence is introduced through expert witnesses.[41] The selection process for expert witnesses, forged in the crucible of the adversarial system, tends to produce experts who are polished and persuasive but not necessarily the most committed to accuracy or the most knowledgeable in their field. The experts who testify at trial are unlikely to reflect a random sample of scientific opinion or provide the jury the most accurate assessment of it.

In MDL-486 and a number of the individual Bendectin trials, equal numbers of expert witnesses testified for each side. This equalization tends to convey to the jury that scientific opinion on the issue is split, when in reality there may be a strong consensus on the matter, as is the case for Bendectin.

As mentioned earlier, Merrell retreated from using authors of published studies as experts, instead relying on a small cadre of experts to testify repeatedly and summarize the studies. This reliance on repeat experts provides opportunity for cross-examiners to paint an appearance of a "hired gun," that results in a tendency to discount the summary expert's testimony.[42] Although the same charge was made of plaintiffs' experts, this merely results in leveling the experts (and science) in the jury's eyes. The use of summary experts may also tend to diminish the jury's ability to discern the strength of the evidence, as only one witness is presenting it. Sanders observes: "It proved very difficult for Merrell to translate the very large body of epidemiological science into a body of evidence that reflected the quality and quantity of the science."[43]

Another impediment to juror comprehension is the difficulty of assessing the relative importance of the various types of scientific evidence. As the epidemiological record on Bendectin matured in the early and mid-1980s, Merrell attempted to emphasize its greater importance in assessing teratogenicity. At the same time, plaintiffs were deemphasizing epidemiology and devoting more effort to animal studies and in vitro evidence. Merrell's efforts to explain the greater salience of epidemiology were unsuccessful in at least some instances; Professor Sanders interviewed several jurors after the conclusion of a Texas Bendectin case that resulted in a verdict for the plaintiff. The jurors reported that they did not believe epidemiology to be of primary importance in assessing teratogenicity. That lack of understanding may not be entirely the jury's fault; the adversarial system encourages parties to take extreme positions that often are unhelpful to the jury in sorting out the truth.

An illuminating example of this phenomenon occurred in a multi-plaintiff asbestos case tried in Texas in 1984. Each of the four plaintiffs claimed to suffer from asbestosis, a progressive respiratory disease. The defendants' experts testified that three of the plaintiffs did not have asbestosis, while conceding that the fourth, who was seriously ill, did. In awarding damages to the three whose disease was contested, the jury incorrectly assumed that each would progress to the same stage as the most severe case. The defendants, choosing to deny the existence of asbestosis, never provided the jury with information about individual variability in the progression of asbestosis.[44]

The structure of the respective parties' evidentiary presentations also favored plaintiffs in the individual trials. As explained in the previous chapter, "commingling" of evidence occurs when the jury uses evidence of one element of a legal claim to substitute for proof of another element for which the evidence is not legally relevant. If the story presented by a party is persuasive and includes all the elements necessary for that party to prevail, the jury may, in effect, trade evidence in support of one of the legal elements for another element. The plaintiffs presented a plausible story of Merrell's malfeasance in testing and marketing Bendectin, which caused plaintiff's birth defects. The jury, confronted with a credible account, may have conflated the two independent legal issues—fault and cause—thereby bolstering a weak causation case with stronger evidence of fault and the existence of a birth defect.[45] By contrast, Merrell's case tended increasingly to focus only on the question of whether Bendectin was a teratogen, and in many individual cases presented no alternative explanation for the plaintiff's birth defects, leaving them to unknown causes. Of course, given the large percentage of birth defects for which there is no known cause, Merrell had little choice in most cases. Nevertheless, Merrell's focus on the general causation element in its defense provided a less appealing story for the jury, since it did not account for the true cause of plaintiff's birth defect.

Professor Sanders surveyed a variety of reform measures that might be employed in an attempt to assist the jury better to understand scientific evidence and employ it so as to enhance the accuracy of their verdicts.[46] One of the structural changes he endorses is polyfurcation in mass trials, a subject addressed in chapter 15. A second promising suggestion is designed to overcome the blinders imposed on the jury by the adversarial system. Professor E. Donald Elliott proposes that courts appoint their own experts in those instances in which substantial doubt about the validity of an expert's methodology is established by an opposing party. Elliott's proposal and the difficulties in implementing any court-appointed expert scheme are discussed in chapter 17.

With the structural, adversarial, and psychological limitations identified by Sanders balancing the scientific evidence, the possibility of other, nonevidentiary factors playing a role in the outcome becomes more plausible. Harry Kalven and Hans Zeisel, in their pioneering study of jury decision making, identified the "liberation" hypothesis to explain differences between judge and jury outcomes.[47] When the evidence in a case is closely balanced, juries are most likely to employ their own sympathies and values in deciding a case.

The outcomes of Bendectin trials and their variance based on fora/ geography surely contribute to the suspicion that demographic aspects of the jury have an impact on outcome. As noted above, all 4 cases tried in Washington, DC resulted in plaintiff's verdicts. The outcome of individual Bendectin trials outside Washington, DC was distinctly different. Of 18 post-MDL-486 Bendectin jury trials, the jury found for Merrell in 12 of them and for plaintiff in 4; 2 resulted in hung juries. The 4 plaintiff's verdicts occurred in Philadelphia and Texas (2 each).[48] However, 2 of the defendant verdicts were based on statute of limitations grounds, so Merrell only prevailed in 10 of 16 jury trials on the merits, although plaintiffs only won 4 of 16.[49] Barry Nace's record for Bendectin jury trials outside Washington, DC is 1 win and 4 losses.

Nace's record in Bendectin jury trials reflects the impact of geography and demography on trial outcome. Nace tried a total of 9 cases to jury verdict, winning 5 and losing 4. Each one involved a plaintiff with limb reduction birth defects. His success rate in the District of Columbia was 100 percent; the juries were residents of the District of Columbia, predominantly African-American in 2 of the cases, and exclusively so in the other 2. Because of the ease with which prospective jurors were able to avoid serving in the lengthy Bendectin trials in Washington, DC, the jurors who served were of a significantly lower socioeconomic class than average.[50] In his 5 cases outside Washington, DC, he lost 4 jury verdicts in federal courts, while winning but 1 trial in state court in Corpus Christi, Texas. The juries in the 5 non-Washington, DC cases included jurors both from mid-sized cities and surrounding suburban and rural areas, and were exclusively white or predominantly so, except for the Texas case. The jury in the Texas case was split between white and Hispanic jurors. The outcomes, locations, and juries' racial (socioeconomic status was not available) make-up of Nace's Bendectin cases is set forth in Table 1.[51]

The evidence Nace presented in the individual cases varied only modestly from case to case. In the later cases, Jay Glasser was added as an epidemiologist, John Palmer took the place of Dr. Done, some of the videotaped depositions from MDL-486 were dropped, and as, Nace puts it, "I got smarter," by which he means that he understood the science better and was therefore a more effective cross-examiner. From the 1987 *Ealy* trial on, there was virtually no difference in the evidence Nace employed to prove causation. After *Ealy*, Nace lost two jury trials outside Washington, DC and won one, in Texas. The numbers are small, to be sure, and other variables no doubt are at work, including the opposing counsel, individual characteristics of the plaintiffs, and the defense evidence, but an intriguing pattern exists.

TABLE 1

	Trial Order	Case and Verdict	Date of Trial	Trial Court and Location	Jury Makeup
DC Cases	1	Oxendine, Plaintiff	1983	DC local	all African-American
	3	Richardson Plaintiff	1986	DC federal	12-person jury 1 or 2 white
	5	Raynor Plaintiff	1987	DC federal	6-person jury mixed
	6	Ealy Plaintiff	1987	DC federal	all African-American
Other Cases	2	Will Defendant	1986	Savannah, GA federal	2 African-American 4 white
	4	Wilson Defendant	1986	Tulsa, OK federal	all white
	7	Rudell Defendant	1987	Kansas City, MO federal	1 African-American 7 white
	8	Hill Defendant	1988	Tacoma, WA federal	all white
	9	Havner Plaintiff	1991	Corpus Christi, TX state	7 white 5 Hispanic

The demographic variables that appear most significant are those associated with socioeconomic status: education, income, employment status, and occupation. Race may play a role, but it is strongly correlated with socioeconomic factors, especially in the inner-city juries involved in Bendectin trials. Thus it is difficult to separate race from socioeconomic variables,[52] for which there is better evidence. Indeed, socioeconomic status alone may not account for differences within the underclass between those who are resentful of their situation, blame others for it, and disdain authority, and others, who while similarly situated, accept their status, not perceiving it as imposed on them by an unjust and illegitimate system.[53]

There are three sources of evidence that bear on the role of demographic factors in jury outcomes: lawyers' views, social psychology research into jury decision making, and comparisons of jury outcomes or perceptions in different jurisdictions. None of these sources of evidence is entirely satisfactory, for a variety of methodological reasons, explained below. However, the cumulative evidence, while less than overpowering, points toward a socioeconomic effect that supports the hypothesis that jury composition helps explain the conflicting Bendectin jury verdict outcomes.

Lawyers certainly believe that demographic factors play an important role in jury outcomes. The most important aspect of this perception is the difference between rural or suburban jurors on the one hand and inner-city jurors, on the other. One jury researcher explains the reasoning is that "the general affluence and conservatism of those who live outside big cities makes them sympathetic toward defendants, especially when they are businesses, while big-city jurors, who are much less well-to-do on the average, are likely to sympathize with the small individual who is taking on the 'system' (big business, insurance companies) through his or her suits."[54] Lawyers not only believe this, they vote their perceptions with their clients' feet: A survey of attorneys' forum selection efforts found approximately 50 percent of responders citing differences between the jury composition in federal court and state court as a reason for their choice. Both plaintiff and defendant attorneys agreed that state court juries tend to favor plaintiffs and federal court juries favor defendants, especially in large urban areas.[55]

There is a substantial body of experimental (using surrogate jurors and trial recreations) and observational research (examining real jurors and trial outcomes) into jury decision making, albeit primarily in the criminal trial context. Much of the research tends to focus on the jury selection process and the identification of attributes that might predict a juror's inclinations or "pre-deliberation bias" in a case.[56] That research unfortunately omits a significant consideration: the effect of group deliberations on outcome.[57] Little research exists that compares differently composed juries and the impact of composition on outcome. Those that do are observational, and they may suffer from selection biases—cases in different courts or regions may not be equivalent.[58]

For the most part, researchers debunk much of the advice provided to lawyers about selecting a jury based on knowledge of individual characteristics, especially personality characteristics such as arrogance or humility.[59] A number of threads, however, suggest that socioeconomic status (including employment status, education, residence, occupation, and income) have a measurable impact on juror attitudes and their decision making.

The strongest evidence of a socioeconomic and racial effect on outcome emerges from a recent experimental study by Brian Bornstein and Michelle Rajki.[60] Bornstein and Rajki showed jury-eligible subjects a toxic substance hypothetical case with conflicting evidence on causation, the only issue in dispute. Bornstein and Rajki found a significant effect on liability judgments based on education, income, and race (all of which were correlated; the authors did not attempt to analyze the role of each variable independent of the others). Those subjects who had post-college education were only one-half as likely to find liability as those with no more than a high school diploma ($p < .02$). Similarly, those in the high income category rendered a verdict for the plaintiff 36 percent of the time, compared to a 57 percent rate among those in the low income group ($p < .02$). The difference in outcome between the white subjects and minority subjects, while not quite as large (41 percent for white; 52 percent for minority) was still notable and statistically significant ($p < .025$).

Another experimental study showed a filmed reenactment of a criminal trial to eligible jurors in Massachusetts. The single most influential characteristic in explaining verdict differences was whether a juror was employed, with those employed more likely to convict. (Favoring conviction in a criminal case is often thought to correlate with a pro-defendant bias in civil cases.) In a subset of participants who were questioned more thoroughly, residence in a wealthy suburb emerged as the most significant variable explaining differences in outcome. Juror education was also found to have a correlation with pre-deliberation verdict preferences and with outcome.[61] Another experiment found that the more education a juror had, the lower the damage award.[62] In the Chicago Jury Project, conducted by Professors Kalven and Zeisel, an experimental study found that occupational status correlated with the amount of damages awarded, with unskilled laborers awarding 50 percent more than those in the professional proprietary class.[63]

The Chicago Jury Project also found a significant geographic influence on the amount of damages awarded in personal injury cases:

The size of damage awards given by juries for comparable personal injuries was strongly related to the jury's domicile. The larger the community from which the jury came, the larger the award; in addition, juries in the states along the two seacoasts proved to be more generous than juries from the Midwest and the South. City size and region cumulated so that there was a maximum spread between awards from juries from large eastern or western cities and those from small midwestern towns.[64]

The Rand Institute conducted an observational study of verdicts by urban juries in Chicago, Los Angeles, and San Francisco and by juries in smaller cities or rural locations. Consistent with the evidence above, Rand found that plaintiffs succeeded at a higher rate in products liability cases in the large city jurisdictions as opposed to the smaller city or rural jurisdictions. The median and average damage awards in the larger cities was roughly twice what it was in smaller jurisdictions.[65] A study of jurors in state courts in Philadelphia, suburban counties, and federal court (which combines jurors from suburban counties and the city) found several differences between the inner city jurors and the federal and suburban jurors. Inner city jurors were more likely after opening statements by the attorneys to express an inclination to vote for the plaintiff than federal and suburban jurors (36 percent to 25 percent). Only 3 percent of inner city jurors favored the defendant after opening statements, compared to 16 percent of suburban and federal court jurors. A difference, albeit smaller, existed between the jurors after the verdict. Inner city jurors were more likely to believe that the plaintiff's testimony had helped his or her case after hearing it than federal and suburban jurors. Conversely, the latter group gave more credence to defendant's testimony than did the former.[66]

Skeptics will protest that the evidence does not prove much of anything. The cautious will believe the evidence interesting, even provocative, but desire additional evidence. Partisans will reach their preferred conclusions. Swashbucklers will follow the lead of Professor Mashaw and conclude that, in sidestepping accurate causal assessments; "We seem to . . . have a lot of potential revolutionaries (plaintiffs and jurors) who are throwing bombs (litigation) and who aren't too interested in what shape the rubble (the civil liability system) takes after the litigation is over." [67]

Better evidence in the form of more inner city jury trials might have developed. But the story to this point omits the role of the trial and appellate judges in the Bendectin litigation. A fair assessment of the impact of Bendectin cases on the civil justice system requires consideration of the judicial reaction to these jury verdicts, the subject of chapter 17.

Notes

1. And in Europe as well. Two cases were tried in Germany in 1986 and one case in Italy in 1990. All resulted in a verdict for Merrell. *See* Joseph Sanders, *From Science to Evidence: The Testimony on Causation in the Bendectin Cases*, 46 STAN. L. REV. 1, 6 (1993) (Table 1).

2. The descriptions of the *Oxendine* and *Richardson* proceedings in this chapter (unless otherwise footnoted) are based on interviews with Mark Austrian, Judge Thomas Penfield Jackson, Barry Nace, and Alfred Schretter, the reported opinions in the two cases, Richardson v. Richardson-Merrell, Inc., 649 F. Supp. 799 (D.D.C. 1986), *aff'd*, 857 F.2d 823 (D.C. Cir. 1988), *cert. denied*, 493 U.S. 882 (1989); Oxendine v. Merrell Dow Pharmaceuticals Inc., 563 A.2d 330 (D.C. 1989), *cert. denied*, 493 U.S. 1074 (1990); Oxendine v. Merrell Dow Pharmaceuticals Inc., 506 A.2d 1100 (D.C. 1986), and trial transcripts and documents that were filed in the two proceedings.

3. *See* Ealy v. Richardson-Merrell, Inc., 897 F.2d 1159 (D.C. Cir.), *cert. denied*, 498 U.S. 950 (1990); Blum v. Merrell Dow Pharmaceuticals Inc., 560 A.2d 212 (Pa. Super. Ct. 1989), *aff'd*, 626 A.2d 537 (Pa. 1993). Dr. Done was replaced by Dr. John Palmer, but Palmer's testimony was quite similar to Done's. *See* Merrell Dow Pharmaceuticals, Inc. v. Havner, 1994 Tex. App. LEXIS 572, at *31–33 (Tex. Ct. App. Mar. 17, 1994).

4. *See* Sanders, *supra* note 1, at 6 (Table 1). The Pennsylvania case resulted in a second plaintiff's verdict, after the first was overturned on appeal.

5. The study was published as: William G. McBride, *Effects of Scopolamine Hydrobromide on the Development of the Chick and Rabbit Embryo*, 35 AUSTR. J. BIOL. SCI. 173 (1982). The Committee's report was: Sir Harry Gibbs et al., Report of Committee of Inquiry Concerning Dr. McBride (unpublished 1988).

6. Graeme O'Neill, *The Fall and Fall of William McBride*, THE AGE (Melbourne), Feb. 20, 1993, at 13.

7. JOSEPH SANDERS, BENDECTIN ON TRIAL (Ann Arbor: University of Michigan Press, forthcoming 1996).

8. Two of the foreign-plaintiff cases filed initially in Ohio state courts went to the United States Supreme Court on the question of removal. Because Merrell was deemed a citizen of Ohio, it could not remove cases filed in the Ohio state courts based on diversity. It removed anyway, asserting that plaintiff's claim that violation of the federal Food, Drug, and Cosmetic Act was prima facie negligence created a federal question, making the case removable. The Supreme Court, in a 5–4 decision, held that where the federal statute does not provide an implied cause of action for its violation, no federal question sufficient to support subject matter jurisdiction exists. Merrell Dow Pharmaceuticals Inc. v. Thompson, 478 U.S. 804 (1986).

9. Oxendine v. Merrell Dow Pharmaceuticals, Inc., 506 A.2d 1100, 1103 n.1 (D.C. 1986).

10. *See* Sanders, *supra* note 1, at 44 n.208.

11. Transcript of Trial at 2277–351, Oxendine v. Merrell Dow Pharmaceuticals Inc., Civ. No. 1245-82 (D.C. Super. Ct. 1983).

12. Dr. Done testified during pretrial proceedings in *Oxendine*, before Upjohn settled, that Provera was a more potent teratogen than Bendectin. Trial Transcript at 1071, Oxendine v. Merrell Dow Pharmaceuticals Inc., Civ. No. 1245-82 (D.C. Super. Ct. 1983).

13. *Id.* at 2332–33.

14. Trial Transcript at 2365–66, Oxendine v. Merrell Dow Pharmaceuticals Inc., Civ. No. 1245-82 (D.C. Super. Ct. 1983). Thus, it should not be surprising that the District of Columbia Court of Appeals, when it reviewed the lower court's granting of judgment n.o.v., ignored the specific causation question. Oxendine v. Merrell Dow Pharmaceuticals Inc., 506 A.2d 1100, 1107–09 (D.C. 1986); *see* Sanders, *supra* note 1, at 29 n.139.

15. Ironically, the District of Columbia Court of Appeals, when it reinstated the jury's verdict, observed that "Dr. Done testified as an expert in the field of teratology. . . ." Oxendine v. Merrell Dow Pharmaceuticals Inc., 506 A.2d 1100, 1104 n.3 (D.C. 1986).

16. 736 F.2d 1529, 1535 (D.C. Cir.), *cert. denied*, 469 U.S. 1062 (1984).

17. Oxendine v. Merrell Dow Pharmaceuticals Inc., 506 A.2d 1100, 1104 (D.C. 1986) (quoting Ferebee v. Chevron Chemical Co., 736 F.2d 1529, 1535 (D.C. Cir.), *cert. denied*, 469 U.S. 1062 (1984)).

18. *See* Lind v. Schenley Indus., Inc., 278 F.2d 79, 88 (3d Cir.), *cert. denied*, 364 U.S. 835 (1960).

19. A complete account of Dr. Done's misstatements is contained in Oxendine v. Merrell Dow Pharmaceuticals, Inc., 563 A.2d 330 (D.C. 1989), *cert. denied*, 493 U.S. 1074 (1990).

20. Transcript of Trial at 536, Oxendine v. Richardson-Merrell Co., Civ. No. 1245-82 (May 9, 1983).

21. Letter from Dr. Alan K. Done to Dean Henry Nadler, Wayne State Medical School (Apr. 24, 1983).

22. Memorandum Order at 4, Oxendine v. Merrell Dow Pharmaceuticals, Inc., Civ. No. 1245-82 (D.C. Super. Ct. Feb. 11, 1988).

23. Judge Wolf wrote:

> These problems are only exacerbated by the crucial, yet weak, nature of Dr. Done's testimony in this case. As aforesaid, he was plaintiff's only causation witness directly linking Bendectin to the minor child's deformities. But even more important, his substantive testimony herein may be described as creating a preponderance of more than 50 percent by aggregating parts that added up to less than 50 percent.

Id.

24. Oxendine v. Merrell Dow Pharmaceuticals, Inc., 563 A.2d 330 (D.C. 1989), *cert. denied*, 493 U.S. 1074 (1990).

25. *See* Merrell Dow Pharmaceuticals Inc. v. Oxendine, 649 A.2d 825 (D.C. 1994) (granting Merrell limited opportunity to demonstrate that new scientific studies persuasively indicate that a new trial would result in a different outcome).

26. 647 F. Supp. 544 (S.D. Ga. 1986).

27. Interview with Judge Thomas Penfield Jackson (May 8, 1990).

28. *Id.*

29. Transcript of Trial at 3913, Richardson v. Richardson-Merrell, Inc., Civ. No. 83-3505 (Sept. 5, 1986).

30. Jose Cordero et al., *Is Bendectin a Teratogen?*, 245 JAMA 2307 (1981).

31. Transcript of Trial at 3937–39, Richardson v. Richardson-Merrell, Inc., Civ. No. 83-3505 (Sept. 5, 1986).

32. *Id.* at 4265, 4273 (Sept. 11, 1986).

33. 113 S. Ct. 2786 (1993).

34. Transcript of Trial at 4096, Richardson v. Richardson-Merrell, Inc., Civ. No. 83-3505 (Sept. 9, 1986).

35. *Id.* at 4100–01.

36. Transcript of Trial at 4307, Richardson v. Richardson-Merrell, Inc., Civ. No. 83-3505 (Sept. 11, 1986).

37. Ealy v. Richardson-Merrell, Inc., 897 F.2d 1159 (D.C. Cir.), *cert. denied*, 498 U.S. 950 (1990).

38. Sanders, *supra* note 1.

39. *See, e.g.*, REID HASTIE ET AL., INSIDE THE JURY 130 (Cambridge, MA: Harvard University Press, 1983); Martha A. Myers, *Rule Departures and Making Law: Juries and Their Verdicts*, 13 LAW & SOC'Y REV. 781 (1979); Christy A. Visher, *Jury Decision Making: The Importance of Evidence*, 11 LAW & HUM. BEHAV. 1 (1987).

40. Sanders, *supra* note 1.

41. *See* Edward J. Imwinkelreid, *A Comparatavist Critique of the Interface Between Hearsay and Expert Opinion in American Evidence Law*, 33 B.C. L. REV. 1, 4 (1991).

42. *See generally* Stephen A. Saltzburg, Frye *and Alternatives*, 99 F.R.D. 208 (1983).

43. Sanders, *supra* note 1, at 46–47.

44. *See* MOLLY SELVIN & LARRY PICUS, THE DEBATE OVER JURY PERFORMANCE: OBSERVATIONS FROM A RECENT ASBESTOS CASE (Santa Monica, CA: Rand, 1987).

45. Of course, more overt bias against a highly culpable party or sympathy for a seriously injured party might also affect the jury's outcome.

46. Sanders, *supra* note 1, at 62–85.

47. HARRY KALVEN, JR. & HANS ZEISEL, THE AMERICAN JURY 164–66 (Chicago: University of Chicago Press, Phoenix ed. 1971).

48. The Texas cases were tried in state court in Corpus Christi and in federal court in Tyler. The jury in the latter case was all white. Letter from Tom Bleakley, attorney for plaintiff, to author (Sept. 21, 1994).

49. The data were drawn from Sanders, *supra* note 1, at 5–9. Omitted are three cases that were decided on statute of limitations grounds, the two *Mekdeci* verdicts, and MDL-486. Included is a plaintiff's jury verdict that occurred in 1994, after the Sanders article was published.

50. Motion for Judgment Notwithstanding the Verdict or, in the Alternative, for a New Trial on Issues of Causation and Liability, at 67–70, Richardson v. Richardson-Merrell Inc., Civ. No. 83-3505 (Sept. 29, 1986) (30 of 32 professionals excused from the venire; 27 of 33 executives or managers excused from the venire); Letter from Al Schretter, former litigation counsel for Merrell, to author (Sept. 2, 1994). For a review of studies finding that jury selection systematically discriminates on the basis of socioeconomic status, see Cookie Stephan, *Selective Characteristics of Jurors and Litigants: Their Influences on Juries' Verdicts, in* THE JURY SYSTEM IN AMERICA 97, 114 (Rita J. Simon ed., Beverly Hills, CA: Sage Publications, 1975).

51. The information about jury make-up in Table 1 was supplied by Barry Nace. Telephone interview with Barry Nace, attorney for plaintiffs (May 11, 1994). Glenn Forrester, Corporate Counsel—Litigation at Merrell, confirmed that the jury information was accurate to the best of his recollection. Telephone interview with Glenn Forrester (Nov. 8, 1994).

52. African-Americans have been found less likely to convict than Caucasians in criminal cases. The Chicago Jury Project found a race effect in the amount of damages, with awards by African-Americans 50 percent higher than "third generation Americans [presumably caucasians]." Harry Kalven, Jr., *Juries in Personal Injury Cases: Their Functions and Methods, in* TRAUMA AND THE AUTOMOBILE 346, 347 (William J. Curran & Neil L. Chayet eds., Cincinnati: W.H. Anderson, 1966).

53. *See* ARNE WERCHICK, CIVIL JURY SELECTION 77 (New York: Wiley Law Publications, 2d ed. 1993); *see also* David M. Engel, *The Oven Bird's Song: Insiders, Outsiders, and Personal Injuries in an American Community,* 18 L. & SOC'Y REV. 551 (1984) (study identifying contrasting attitudes between long-time residents and newcomers toward personal injury litigation and its propriety).

54. JOHN GUINTHER, THE JURY IN AMERICA 89–90 (New York: Facts on File Publications, 1988).

55. *See* Neal Miller, *An Empirical Study of Forum Choices in Removal Cases Under Diversity and Federal Question Jurisdiction,* 41 AM. U. L. REV. 369, 420–21 (1992); *see also* GUINTHER, *supra* note 54, at 89–90; Clinton H. Coddington & Randolph J. Hicks, *The Arena: Defendant's Choice of Forum,* 46 J. AIR L. & COM. 941, 945 (1981).

56. ROBERT J. MACCOUN, GETTING INSIDE THE BLACK BOX: TOWARD A BETTER UNDERSTANDING OF JUROR BEHAVIOR 19 (Santa Monica, CA: Rand, 1987).

57. *See* Tracy L. Treger, Note, *One Jury Indivisible: A Group Dynamics Approach to Voir Dire,* 68 CHI.-KENT L. REV. 549 (1992). For a discussion of research that has addressed the jury deliberation process, see Joan B. Kessler, *The Social Psychology of Jury Deliberations, in* Simon, *supra* note 50, at 69.

58. *See, e.g.,* Neil Vidmar, *Making Inferences About Jury Behavior from Jury Verdict Statistics,* 18 L. & HUM. BEHAV. 599, 601–04 (1994).

59. *See, e.g.,* VALERIE HANS & NEIL VIDMAR, JUDGING THE JURY 76 (New

York: Plenum Press, 1986); HASTIE ET AL., *supra* note 39, at 127. Justice Scalia recently expressed an interesting view on the relative validity of lawyers' opinions and social science: "Personally, I am less inclined to demand statistics, and more inclined to credit the perceptions of experienced litigators who have had money on the line." J.E.B. v. Alabama, 114 S. Ct. 1419, 1436 (1994) (Scalia, J., dissenting).

60. Brian H. Bornstein & Michelle Rajki, *Extra-Legal Factors and Product Liability: The Influence of Mock Jurors' Demographic Characteristics and Intuitions About the Cause of an Injury,* 12 BEHAV. SCI. & LAW 127–47 (1994).

61. HASTIE ET AL., *supra* note 39, at 128–29, 133.

62. Neil Vidmar, *Empirical Evidence on the Deep Pockets Hypothesis: Jury Awards for Pain and Suffering in Medical Malpractice Cases,* 43 DUKE L.J. 217 (1993). *But see* Neil Vidmar & Jeffrey J. Rice, *Assessments of Noneconomic Damage Awards in Medical Negligence: A Comparison of Jurors With Legal Professionals,* 78 IOWA L. REV. 883, 895 (1993) (modest correlation between size of damage award in medical malpractice experiments and both education and income).

63. Kalven, *supra* note 52.

64. KALVEN & ZEISEL, *supra* note 47, at 466; *see also* Dale W. Broeder, *The Chicago Jury Project,* 38 NEB. L. REV. 744, 749 (1959).

65. MARK A. PETERSON, CIVIL JURIES IN THE 1980s 43, 46 (Santa Monica, CA: Rand, 1987).

66. GUINTHER, *supra* note 54, at 62, 90, 297, 299, 315.

67. Jerry L. Mashaw, *A Comment on Causation, Law Reform, and Guerilla Warfare,* 73 GEO. L.J. 1393, 1395 (1985).

Chapter 17
The Legacy of Bendectin
for Toxic Causation Law

The appellate courts' confrontation with the causal issues in Bendectin occurred at a time of increasing concern about the treatment of science and expert witnesses by the legal system. At roughly the same time that the Bendectin litigation was peaking, Judge Jack Weinstein, a highly-regarded federal judge in New York, addressed similar issues in the *Agent Orange* litigation. The combination of Judge Weinstein's pioneering decision in *Agent Orange* and the appellate decisions in Bendectin fueled a reform movement in the treatment of proof of causation in the toxic arena that transcends those cases. Punctuated by the Supreme Court's prominent decision in *Daubert v. Merrell Dow Pharmaceuticals, Inc.*,[1] another Bendectin case, controversy continues to reign over the appropriate role of the courts in overseeing the admissibility of expert witness testimony and the adequacy of proof in toxic substances cases. The impact of the Bendectin litigation on toxic causation law is considerable, although it is premature to draw any final conclusions. This chapter begins with Judge Weinstein's opinion in *Agent Orange*. It then proceeds to the Bendectin appellate decisions, their impact on subsequent cases, and a cautionary note about their generalizability to other toxic substances litigation.

The *Agent Orange* Decision

Many of the scientific and evidentiary questions about toxic causation came to the forefront in the massive post-Vietnam War lawsuit captioned In re *"Agent Orange" Product Liability Litigation*.[2] Dioxin, a contaminant formed in the manufacture of the herbicide Agent Orange, had long been thought to be one of the most toxic substances known. When veterans of the Vietnam War developed cancers, neurological disorders, and other insidious diseases and their children were born with birth defects, suspicion was cast on Agent Orange. Yet epidemiological evidence to demonstrate Agent Orange's toxicity was lacking, especially at the doses to which veterans were thought to have been exposed.

After masterminding a settlement of $180 million on behalf of the *Agent Orange* class,[3] Judge Weinstein confronted the claims of several hundred plaintiffs who had opted-out of the class to pursue their individual claims. Defendants sought summary judgment based on a lack of proof of a causal connection between exposure to Agent Orange and the plaintiffs' diseases.

In the course of Judge Weinstein's lengthy opinion granting the defendants' motion, he canvassed a variety of expert evidentiary issues and reviewed the methodology of epidemiology, toxicology, and the science of determining the cause of disease. The influence of Judge Weinstein's opinion no doubt stems from his prominence as a trial judge, teacher, and scholar in the evidence field and his active participation on the lecture and seminar circuit. It also derives from the comprehensiveness and authority with which he wrote the *Agent Orange* opinion.

Although there are many notable features of the *Agent Orange* opinion,[4] its influence on future cases centers around three key aspects. The most striking aspect of the opinion is its emphasis on epidemiology as the critical source of evidence of toxic causation: "A number of sound epidemiological studies have been conducted on the health effects of exposure to Agent Orange. These are the only useful studies having any bearing on causation."[5]

A corollary of Judge Weinstein's endorsement of epidemiology was his dismissal of animal studies (and industrial accident-high dose studies) of exposure to dioxin. Ultimately, Judge Weinstein sounded the death knell for animal studies: "[They] are not helpful in the instant case because they involve different biological species. They are of so little probative force and are so potentially misleading as to be inadmissible. They cannot be an acceptable predicate for an opinion under Rule 703."[6]

The second significant aspect of the *Agent Orange* decision was Judge Weinstein's skepticism about expert evidence in toxic substances litigation generally:

Such careful scrutiny of proposed evidence is especially appropriate in the toxic tort area. The uncertainty of the evidence in such cases, dependent as it is upon speculative scientific hypotheses and epidemiological studies, creates a special need for robust screening of experts and gatekeeping under Rules 403 and 703 by the court.[7]

Judge Weinstein followed through on his "careful scrutiny" prescription, conducting a rigorous and penetrating critique of the expert witness affidavits presented by plaintiffs. At virtually every turn, Judge Weinstein pointed out the weaknesses and inadequacies in the expert affidavits submitted by plaintiffs. At one point, Judge Weinstein impeached one expert's affidavit with a book authored by that expert, of which Judge Weinstein took judicial notice.[8]

Third, Judge Weinstein resurrected the concerns raised in *Frye v. United States*[9] over 60 years ago and expanded the scope of these concerns beyond the original treatment of novel scientific principles or methodology to encompass novel opinions, even when based on conventional methods and principles. *Frye* concerned the admissibility in a criminal case of the results of a lie detector test, which were not recognized as valid by the scientific community. The court held that because the test had not received general acceptance by the relevant scientific community, the results of the test administered to defendant were inadmissible. *Frye* has been recognized as establishing this "general acceptance" standard for admissibility. In a larger sense, however, *Frye* reflects a critical matter relevant to the toxic substances causation debate: Are courts capable of independently assessing the validity of science when brought into the courtroom? The answer to that question implies the extent to which courts should rely on a variety of surrogate measures, including the *Frye* test.[10]

While acknowledging the debate over whether *Frye* survived the adoption of the Federal Rules of Evidence, Judge Weinstein nevertheless concluded that *Frye* concerns justify more careful scrutiny when an expert's opinion is not consistent with mainstream scientific thought. After concluding that plaintiffs' experts' testimony was not admissible, the dismissal of the plaintiffs' cases based on the absence of a genuine dispute over causation was inevitable.

The Bendectin Decisions

Although the earliest Bendectin cases preceded the Agent Orange litigation, the two proceeded largely on a parallel track. The year after Judge Weinstein's opt-out decision in *Agent Orange*, the *Richardson* jury returned its $1.2 million verdict.

Unlike Judge Weinstein, Judge Jackson denied Merrell's motion for summary judgment and presided over a trial in which both sides presented expert testimony on causation. Nevertheless, Judge Jackson's decision granting judgment notwithstanding the verdict relied on the epidemiological evidence introduced by Merrell. None of the published epidemiological studies found a statistically significant risk of limb reduction defects.[11] Although evidence was introduced of Bendectin's teratogenicity based on animal studies, in vitro studies, and chemical structure similarity, Judge Jackson focused on the epidemiological evidence:

The ominous hypothesis of two decades ago, namely, that Bendectin might be another Thalidomide, has been reduced to the status of a perdurable superstition by the worldwide epidemiological investigations it provoked . . . . [12]

Referring to the published studies introduced by the defendant, Judge Jackson concluded that "the literature on Bendectin, individually and in the aggregate, fails to demonstrate Bendectin's teratogenicity to a scientifically acceptable degree of accuracy." [13] Judge Jackson added another important slant to the evaluation of scientific evidence, influenced by his experience as a litigator specializing in medical malpractice. During that time, Jackson was educated about the extent to which medical professionals rely on the "literature"—peer-reviewed, scientific journal articles—as their bible. [14] Dr. Alan Done and Shanna Swan, experts who, in testifying for plaintiffs in Bendectin cases, criticized some studies and conducted a reanalysis of another, were discounted because of their failure to publish their work. This failure to publish would be adopted by the court of appeals and later by other courts—including the Supreme Court in *Daubert*—as a factor in scrutinizing the admissibility of expert witness opinions.

While plainly dubious about Done, [15] Judge Jackson did not follow Judge Weinstein's course in *Agent Orange* precisely, although Jackson did cite the *Agent Orange* opinion in support of his decision. Rather than following Weinstein and holding the expert testimony inadmissible, Jackson found that, after all the evidence had been introduced, a reasonable jury could not conclude that Bendectin caused limb reduction birth defects. Significantly, the trial afforded plaintiffs the opportunity to critique the epidemiology studies relied on by the defendant.

On appeal, the court of appeals was faced with a troubling conflict between one of its recent decisions, *Ferebee v. Chevron Chemical Co.*[16] and the lower court's *Richardson* decision. In *Ferebee* the court had ruled that epidemiological evidence was not necessary for a toxic substance (paraquat, a herbicide) plaintiff to meet the burden of production on cause in fact. Rather, the court set forth what has been characterized as the traditional laissez faire treatment of expert witnesses—passive acceptance of scientific testimony, leaving to the jury resolution of conflicting expert opinion. Thus the *Ferebee* court concluded that the plaintiff's experts, two treating pulmonary specialists who testified that the fatal lung disease was a result of exposure to paraquat, provided sufficient evidence to support a jury verdict for plaintiff. As long as "experts are willing to testify" about complex and technical matters at the boundaries of scientific knowledge, then the questions are for the jury, ruled the *Ferebee* court. In support of its decision, the court commented on its view of the relative expertise of judge and jury: "Judges, both trial and appellate, have no special competence" to review and decide complex causal questions.[17]

Perhaps because of *Ferebee*'s admonition that battles of experts are to be left to the jury, the court of appeals in *Richardson* adopted a different tack in affirming the lower court. The court ruled that the plaintiffs' experts' testimony was inadmissible. After devoting almost three pages of its opinion to a review of Dr. Done and his testimony, the court concluded that the opinion lacked an adequate foundation. The lower court was affirmed, but the court of appeals tilted its approach in the direction of Judge Weinstein in *Agent Orange*,[18] focusing on the admissibility of expert testimony that ran contrary to mainstream scientific thinking and extant epidemiological evidence, rather than a comparative assessment of the strength of the respective parties' case.[19] The inadmissibility of plaintiffs' expert's testimony both affirmed the lower court decision and made summary judgment more available in toxic substances cases, an effect the court noted with approval.[20]

By contrast, *Ferebee* had permitted experts to testify about causation who didn't even purport to rely on traditional toxicological methods. Rather, the plaintiff's experts were treating physicians who relied on their clinical examination of the patient and three similar cases.[21] In what sounded very much like Merrell's claims in *Richardson*, the defendant argued that the plaintiff's experts' opinions were outside the mainstream of scientific thought and therefore inadmissible. Nevertheless, the *Ferebee* court held that neither epidemiological nor animal studies were required to support an expert opinion in a toxic substance case: "As long as the basic methodology employed to reach such a conclusion is sound, . . . products liability law does not preclude recovery until a 'statistically significant' number of people have been injured or until science has had the time and resources to complete sophisticated laboratory studies of the chemical."[22] The *Richardson* court distinguished *Ferebee* on the ground that Bendectin involved a drug for which the scientific evidence was mature, unlike paraquat, about which there had been little scientific study.[23]

The court of appeals also found succor in a First Circuit Bendectin opinion. In *Lynch v. Merrell-National Laboratories Division of Richardson-Merrell, Inc.*,[24] the court affirmed the trial court's grant of summary judgment for defendant on the same ground as the court of appeals in *Richardson*. The *Lynch* court similarly began with a survey of the extensive epidemiological record on Bendectin. The court relied on *Agent Orange* to reject out of hand all non-epidemiological evidence relied on by

Dr. Done: "Studies of this sort, singly or in combination, do not have the capability of proving causation in human beings in the absence of any confirmatory epidemiological data,"[25] thereby implying that epidemiological evidence would be required for a plaintiff to present a case sufficient for submission to a jury.

The *Lynch* court confronted perhaps the strongest evidence (especially in light of the court's emphasis on epidemiology) on behalf of the plaintiff—Dr. Shanna Swan's reanalysis of the CDC study. Dr. Swan had testified both in *Richardson* and MDL-486 that Bendectin was capable of causing birth defects, based on her reanalysis. Although the jury in the MDL-486 trial had rejected her testimony, it appeared sufficient to meet the plaintiff's burden of production and to require a jury to resolve the cause-in-fact issue. Nevertheless, the court rejected Dr. Swan's work, concluding that it could not be employed as the basis for an expert opinion. The court gave two grounds: first, it criticized her methodology in failing to take into account that the control group she employed (those with Down's syndrome) might have been subject to a negative confounder (i.e., genetic birth defects exert a protective effect for other birth defects) that would reduce the incidence of limb reduction defects; second, echoing Judge Jackson in *Richardson*, the court observed that the study had never been published or subjected to peer review.[26]

Thus, as in *Richardson*, the First Circuit concluded that plaintiff's experts' opinions were not admissible. Without that testimony, the trial court's summary judgment for defendant was affirmed. A recurring theme through all four of the *Richardson* and *Lynch* opinions is skepticism about Dr. Done, his methodology, biases, and ultimate opinions.[27]

Potentially the most far-reaching and influential of the Bendectin cases is the third court of appeals decision, *Brock v. Merrell Dow Pharmaceuticals, Inc.*[28] Unlike *Richardson, Brock* involved a plaintiff's jury verdict that the trial judge declined to overturn. Moreover, unlike *Richardson* and *Lynch*, Dr. Done, about whom there was a fair degree of judicial skepticism, did not testify about causation as part of plaintiff's case-in-chief (evidence presented initially to prove elements of the claim) in *Brock*. Finally, unlike *Richardson* and *Lynch*, the Fifth Circuit did not cast its decision in terms of control of expert witness testimony, instead analyzing the case on sufficiency-of-the-evidence grounds.

Acknowledging the traditional deference afforded medical experts, the court, echoing Judge Weinstein in *Agent Orange*, contended that toxic substances litigation is different and requires a more critical analysis of expert witnesses. By relying on *Agent Orange* and broadly addressing toxic substances, the court expanded the potential scope of its decision beyond the prior Bendectin opinions, which at times had appeared limited to Bendectin.

Turning to the causation evidence introduced at trial, the court began by recognizing the superiority of epidemiological studies. The court went on to acknowledge, as Judge Weinstein did not in *Agent Orange*, the methodological flaws and difficulties that may infect an epidemiological study. The court adverted to several of these methodological problems, including some that Bendectin plaintiffs had asserted for years: too few subjects in a study, confounders (both of these matters are addressed later in this chapter), and recall bias (those with the disease better recalling exposure to agents than those without the disease), as well as the role that chance plays whenever sampling techniques are used. Employing the concept of statistical significance and the related idea of a confidence interval, the court triumphantly observed that it need not concern itself with any methodological problems in the Bendectin studies:

Fortunately, we do not have to resolve any of the above questions, since the studies presented to us incorporate the possibility of these factors by use of a *confidence interval*. The purpose of our mentioning these sources of error is to provide some background regarding the importance of confidence intervals.[29]

Although the reanalysis of an epidemiological study relied on by plaintiffs found a relative risk of 1.49 (indicating a 50 percent increase over the background rate) for limb reduction defects, the finding was not statistically significant. Thus, the *Brock* court concluded that a Bendectin plaintiff must have a statistically significant epidemiological study to satisfy her burden of production on causation. Because of its view that statistical significance provided a panacea for scientific error, the court concluded that "the lack of *conclusive* epidemiological proof [is] fatal to the Brocks' case." [30]

The *Brock* court was flat wrong in its notion that statistical significance or confidence intervals reflect anything about possible sources of error in an epidemiological study other than sampling error. Even requiring statistical significance as a screening device to avoid sampling error is a terribly overbroad rule that courts should not adhere to once they become comfortable with the concept and its meaning.

Curiously, *Brock* did not emphasize the epidemiological record on Bendectin to support its view that judgment notwithstanding the verdict was required. The only mention of the epidemiological record on Bendectin was in the context of the court pointing out that the plaintiffs could not meet their burden of proof because there were no other studies introduced or available that found a statistically significant association between Bendectin and limb reduction defects.[31] Instead, the court looked only to the plaintiffs' evidence and held that it was inadequate to make out a jury question on causation. That omission implied there was nothing particularly special about Bendectin, making *Brock* far more potent than the prior Bendectin decisions, all of which emphasized the state of the epidemiological record on Bendectin. But the *Brock* court, anticipating the logical extension of its opinion, equivocated: "[w]hile we do not hold that epidemiologic proof is a necessary element in all toxic tort cases, it is certainly a very important element."[32] Yet, in the very next sentence, the court denigrated animal studies, the primary alternative source of evidence of causation. If epidemiology is not required, what would be adequate to take its place?

Creation of a Causation Threshold

General Concerns: The Tort Crisis, Case Management, and Skepticism About Expert Testimony.

In addition to the *Agent Orange* and Bendectin decisions, other factors no doubt have played a role in the expert-witness-testimony reform movement. Before assessing and critiquing the impact of these decisions on future toxic substances litigation, it is prudent to recognize the other related forces that have contributed to the reformist movement.

The expansion of liability theories over the past twenty-five years, especially in the products liability and environmental tort areas, raises increasingly frequent and complex scientific questions.[33] The tort crisis of the mid-1980s contributed to the perception that the courts had gone too far in advantaging plaintiffs.[34] Procedurally, case management and docket control have become the buzzwords for a judiciary that finds itself chronically overwhelmed with its caseload. The Supreme Court, in a trilogy of recent decisions,[35] has revived and encouraged employment of summary judgment to truncate cases without the time-consuming need for jury trial.[36] Summary judgment has proved a potent weapon to combat the perceived abuse of science in the courts.

By the mid-1980s the courts also were confronting the impact of the liberalization of expert witness testimony reflected in the Federal Rules of Evidence.[37] This liberalization, in conjunction with the expansion of liability, brought more experts into court with more marginal credentials and more tenuous theories and opinions.[38] The liberalization of expert witness testimony inevitably created its own backlash.[39] The perception that the expert witness business[40] has simply gone too far—in misleading juries rather than assisting them in resolving a broad range of cases—has become quite prevalent.[41] Perhaps most saliently, even members of the plaintiffs' bar have added their concurrence. Paul Rheingold, a well respected plaintiffs' attorney and the organizer of the successful mass litigation over MER/29 in the 1960s, has written of the abuse of expert witnesses and singled out his colleagues in Bendectin litigation for using questionable experts who were long on speculation and short on substance.[42]

The Impact of the *Agent Orange* and Bendectin Litigation

With the backdrop of skepticism about expert witnesses generally, the question of interest is how influential the *Agent Orange* and Bendectin decisions will be in future cases. More importantly, the issue is whether those decisions are specific to the toxic agent involved or whether the skepticism about expert testimony and insistence on epidemiological proof will be exported beyond *Agent Orange* and Bendectin. The preliminary returns are in, and they are mixed. However, a significant proportion of the cases accept *Agent Orange* and the Bendectin decisions as having tightened the evidentiary screws in toxic cases generally.

Courts have read the lessons of *Agent Orange, Richardson, Lynch,* and *Brock* at varying levels of generality, including 1) as a matter of stare decisis, plaintiffs' expert witnesses cannot opine on causation in Bendectin cases, effectively foreclosing plaintiffs from submitting their cases to the jury;[43] 2) plaintiffs' expert witnesses' opinions should be carefully scrutinized and the bases for the experts' opinions critically reviewed in toxic substances cases;[44] 3) an expert may not rely on a study that has not been published and undergone peer review;[45] 4) plaintiffs cannot make out a submissible toxic substances case without statistically significant epidemiological evidence;[46] 5) an expert may not testify that causation exists if there are contrary epidemiological studies;[47] and 6) expert witness abuse is a serious and pandemic phenomenon.[48]

The influence of the Bendectin decisions in toxic substances cases is most notable in two post-*Brock* decisions. In *Thomas v. Hoffman-La Roche, Inc.,*[49] the plaintiff, who suffered from a severe neurological disorder, sued the manufacturer of an acne drug she had taken, Accutane. The plaintiff introduced the testimony of two neurologists who stated that her neurological condition was the result of her ingestion of Accutane. After a jury verdict of one million dollars, the defendant moved for judgment notwithstanding the verdict on the ground that the plaintiff's expert witnesses' opinions were inadmissible. Without any discussion of the state of the scientific record on the toxicity of Accutane, the court invoked *Brock* and granted the motion for judgment as a matter of law:

The court notes that there is a total absence of any statistically significant study to assist the jury in its determination of the issue of causation. . . . In taking into account the total absence of any epidemiological proof from the plaintiff, the court is of the opinion in applying Brock to the case sub judice that the motion for judgment notwithstanding the verdict should be granted.[50]

Similarly, in *Christophersen v. Allied-Signal, Corp.*,[51] the trial judge ruled the plaintiff's expert's opinion on causation inadmissible because "it was not based on epidemiological, animal, or in vitro studies showing a 'statistically significant link between colon cancer and exposure to nickel and/or cadmium.' "[52] Without the expert's testimony, plaintiff could not satisfy her burden of proof on causation, which resulted in summary judgment for the defendant.

To be sure, there are significant exceptions to the above interpretations of the *Agent Orange* and Bendectin litigation—Judge Rubin, the trial judge in MDL-486, ruled that causation would be submitted to the jury in a group of recent Bendectin cases over which he presided.[53] Other courts, albeit a minority, have followed Judge Rubin's lead in relying on the jury to determine whether the scientific evidence on causation is adequate.[54]

To a large extent, the conflicting treatment appears premised on the intractable conflict regarding the jury and its role. The civil jury is probably the single most controversial contemporary procedural device, and differences in views about the quality of its decision making have spilled over into the toxic substances causation debate.[55] Those comfortable with juries and their decision making do not find judicial screening the imperative that those who are distrustful of juries do. If means to assist juries in their evaluation of scientific evidence could be found, that should relieve some of the pressure for more intrusive judicial screening.

Before pursuing the debate, two other recent Bendectin decisions require mention. Plainly influenced by the earlier Bendectin decisions, two additional federal courts of appeals ruled against Bendectin plaintiffs. Expressing concern about biased experts, the Sixth Circuit in *Turpin v. Merrell Dow Pharmaceuticals, Inc.*,[56] concluded that "close judicial analysis" was required in toxic substances cases. But the court analyzed the evidence on which the parties relied, rather than the admissibility of expert testimony. The court concluded that Merrell's epidemiological evidence was not as powerful as it claimed: "An analysis of this evidence demonstrates that it is possible Bendectin causes birth defects even though these studies do not detect a significant association."[57] Nevertheless, the court concluded that the plaintiff's evidence of Bendectin's teratogenicity simply could not suffice to permit a reasonable jury to conclude that Bendectin more likely than not caused the plaintiff's birth defects. The *Turpin* court upheld judgment for Merrell on grounds that Merrell had not presented to juries in the individual post-MDL-486 trials: Even if Bendectin is a weak teratogen, it was not likely the cause of the plaintiff's birth defects. In ruling on sufficiency of the evidence grounds, the *Turpin* court's approach resembled that of Judge Jackson in *Richardson*. Remarkably, the *Turpin* court was able to engage in its extensive analysis without the benefit of a trial record—the district court had granted summary judgment to Merrell.

The second court of appeals decision ultimately produced the Supreme Court's decision in *Daubert v. Merrell Dow Pharmaceuticals, Inc.*[58] Arising quite late in the Bendectin litigation life-cycle, both the district court and the court of appeals decisions were heavily influenced by the earlier trilogy of Bendectin decisions—*Lynch, Richardson,* and *Brock.* Indeed, what is unusual was the casualness of the court of appeals.[59] In a disdainful two-page decision, the court invoked *Frye,* then dismissed the plaintiffs' expert witnesses' reanalyses because they had not been subjected to peer review or published, which the court concluded were necessary components of generally accepted scientific methodology as required by *Frye.*

The court of appeals invocation of *Frye* as the appropriate law by which to judge the admissibility of expert witness testimony provided precisely the straw person that Barry Nace needed to attract the Supreme Court's attention: whether the *Frye* rule survived the adoption of the federal rules of evidence. The Supreme Court had previously refused to review *Brock, Richardson,* and another case based on *Richardson.* The Court declined to grant certiorari on two other Bendectin decisions after it agreed to review *Daubert;* the Court plainly was uninterested in the science, methodology, and proof problems raised by the Bendectin cases. Had the Ninth Circuit written an evidentiary threshold opinion or even an expert witness inadmissibility opinion like the court of appeals in *Richardson, Daubert* would not have made it to the Supreme Court.

Thus, it is unsurprising that the Court spoke broadly about judicial screening of expert witness testimony in *Daubert,* unencumbered by the disputes over epidemiology, relative risk, statistical significance, scientific bias, the role of animal toxicology, and other forms of testing that were so controversial in Bendectin litigation and which arise regularly in toxic substances litigation. Justice Blackmun's opinion contained but three prosaic paragraphs about the facts before proceeding to explain and address the Ninth Circuit's use of the *Frye* general acceptance test.[60]

The Court declined to revive *Frye* as the governing test for determining the admissibility of expert testimony, yet at the same time made clear that judges must examine expert testimony when it is challenged and determine its admissibility. Relying on the language in Federal Rule of Evidence 702, which permits an expert to testify to an opinion based on "scientific . . . knowledge," the Court held that valid scientific methodology and reasoning is the key to admissibility. The Court commented that trial courts should review the expert's methodology and reasoning, but not the conclusions drawn therefrom.[61]

Elaborating on the requirement of scientific validity, the Court provided a non-exclusive list of factors to be employed by federal judges in assessing the validity of an expert's methodology. Three of those factors had been employed in Bendectin litigation: Judge Jackson's peer review and publication, acceptance in the scientific community, and the known or potential error rate. The fourth factor identified by the Court is more central to what is distinctive about the the scientific method: constructing and testing hypotheses for falsity.

While *Daubert* plainly buried *Frye* as the standard for determining the admissibility of expert testimony, the *Daubert* decision leaves much to be resolved about the new regime.[62] There are several reasons for this conclusion. The Court's opinion contains something for everyone: rejecting *Frye*, which the plaintiffs had argued, yet requiring that judges exercise a "gatekeeping" role, as advocated by defendant. Yet the court tempered the screening function by rejecting the "junk science" criticism and observing that the time-worn methods for finding truth in the adversary system are "vigorous cross-examination, presentation of contrary evidence, and careful instruction on the burden of proof."[63] *Daubert* provides courts with a non-exclusive list of four general, sometimes inapplicable, and unweighted factors, which are intended to be applied across all scientific disciplines. This leaves much discretion in the hands of the trial judge applying the *Daubert* criteria, determining whether additional factors should be employed, and weighing the outcomes to determine the validity of the expert's methodology.[64] The Court's failure to recognize that scientific validity, unlike pregnancy, is not a dichotomous condition, but rather a question of degree leaves for the future the question of how valid an expert's methods must be.[65] In addition, how to deal with the methodologically legitimate expert who reaches illogical conclusions, given the *Daubert* Court's statement that methods but not conclusions are to be examined, is yet another difficulty to be resolved.[66] That difficulty is a significant one, however, as most scientific inquiry is of a general nature (e.g., epidemiology examines disease in populations), while toxic substances lawsuits are concerned with the particular. Reaching illogical conclusions about the particular from valid scientific studies can induce as much error as poor science. Both because of its importance in contemporary litigation and because of its incomplete resolution, commentators have been busy analyzing and explaining *Daubert*.[67]

An assessment of the real impact of *Daubert* will require considerably more experience with it in the lower courts. One suspects that having jumped into the expert witness admissibility quagmire in *Daubert*, the

Court will feel some obligation to revisit the gaps left by its opinion, especially as conflicts emerge in the lower courts. But science is a multifaceted discipline, the potential for error or abuse quite variegated, and its application in litigation quite diverse. Broad standards, such as those provided in *Daubert*, will inevitably require substantial amplification with more specific and contextual principles.

Thus there is reason to believe that many of the legal issues raised by the Bendectin decisions will continue to be controverted in the post-*Daubert* world. The Supreme Court's opinion would appear to require much from federal judges confronted with a challenge to the admissibility of a scientific witness: to identify both the methods and reasoning upon which experts base their testimony, to educate themselves about the relevant scientific discipline, and to make considered judgments about the validity of experts' methodology and reasoning.[68]

The temptation to rely on easier surrogates for assessing scientific validity, such as statistical significance or peer review, or to dismiss evidence that is difficult to assess, such as animal toxicology, will surely be great. Indeed, at least some post-*Daubert* toxic substances decisions look very much like those that were decided before it, save for empty obeisance to *Daubert*.[69] It may be fair to say that *Daubert* captured the expert witness windstorm reflected in the Bendectin decisions, cut off some of the more extreme eddies, but largely served as a conduit, releasing the airstream to be further processed, as future cases arise. The next section of this chapter makes the argument that the threshold decisions employed in the Bendectin and *Agent Orange* decisions should not be routinely adapted to other toxic substances cases.

A Critique of the Adoption of an Epidemiological Threshold

The *Agent Orange* and Bendectin decisions are best understood as adopting an epidemiological threshold, or more restrictively, a statistically significant epidemiological threshold, for plaintiffs. Courts can employ evidentiary thresholds alternatively to grant summary judgment (or judgment as a matter of law) or to preclude an expert from testifying that the agent at issue caused plaintiff's disease. The effect is the same—an evidentiary barrier is erected that the plaintiff must overcome or lose. Whether this threshold requirement is enforced by excluding expert testimony on toxic causation unless it has an epidemiological foundation, or by requiring the plaintiffs to produce epidemiological evidence to satisfy their burden of production, is largely immaterial.[70]

Imposing an epidemiological threshold on plaintiffs to satisfy their burden of production on causation would be an unfortunate generalization from litigation over two toxic substances, each of which represents a special case. In short, the *Agent Orange* and Bendectin decisions should not be generalized to other toxic agents. The *Agent Orange* and Bendectin cases are different, and the *Brock* court's insistence on statistically significant epidemiological studies is inconsistent with legal standards of proof.

The Non-Generalizability of the *Agent Orange* and Bendectin Cases.

The *Agent Orange* opt-out plaintiffs were doomed to failure in their attempt to avoid the settlement so relentlessly pursued, managed, and shaped by Judge Weinstein. Right from the beginning of his assignment to the *Agent Orange* case, Judge Weinstein's every step was made with the aim of crafting a settlement of this enormously complicated and emotion-charged class action brought for a variety of disparate reasons by Vietnam veterans.[71] The ultimate $180 million settlement, although the largest personal injury settlement at the time, represented a comparatively small per capita recovery given the 600,000 veterans exposed to Agent Orange and their family members, all of whom were included in the class.[72] Nevertheless, that figure represented the value that Judge Weinstein put on the case and on which he ultimately insisted in the eleventh hour of settlement negotiations, even though the defendants were prepared to pay more.

Since the *Agent Orange* class action had been certified pursuant to rule 23(b)(3) of the Federal Rules of Civil Procedure, the possibility of numerous opt-outs proceeding in individual cases, potentially subjecting defendants to additional liability, complicated the settlement discussions. David Shapiro, a special master appointed by Judge Weinstein to facilitate settlement, assured defendants that Judge Weinstein had both the inclination and ample means to ensure that the number of opt-outs would be minimized.[73]

By the time of the settlement, there were 2,500 opt-out plaintiffs. Presumably, these plaintiffs had stronger cases, such that pursuing their claims individually was more feasible and attractive than it was for those plaintiffs suffering only minor problems. If only half of the opt-outs obtained low six-figure recoveries, the total would match or exceed the amount paid by defendants in settling the class action. Recovery of even a small percentage of that amount by such a small fraction of the class would raise grave doubts about the fairness of the settlement that Judge Weinstein had crafted.

After the settlement, Judge Weinstein made good on Shapiro's implicit promise. First, although the period for deciding on whether to opt-out had expired, Judge Weinstein permitted those plaintiffs who had chosen to opt-out to return to the class. Indeed, one plaintiffs' counsel asserted in a recusal motion that Judge Weinstein coerced the opt-out plaintiffs back into the fold.[74] Ultimately, fewer than 300 of the opt-out plaintiffs pursued their individual claims.

After defendants moved for summary judgment, Judge Weinstein put virtually impossible deadlines on the opt-out plaintiffs' attorneys to submit affidavits about individual causation. That aspect had not been part of the class action trial preparations, which were concerned with proving the general toxicity of Agent Orange, rather than its effect on any specific member of the class. Finally, Judge Weinstein did what he had virtually cornered himself into doing; in order to uphold the settlement as fair, he granted the defendants' motion for summary judgment against the opt-out plaintiffs in an opinion that is likely the most significant emerging from all of the *Agent Orange* decisions.[75]

Curiously, the Second Circuit skirted Judge Weinstein's treatment of the plaintiffs' experts in affirming his decision. Instead, the court relied on the military contractor defense to affirm, a matter that occupied only three paragraphs of Judge Weinstein's 44-page opinion. In the course of its opinion, the Second Circuit acknowledged the absence of any epidemiological studies demonstrating hazards to Vietnam veterans, but only in the context of determining whether the defendant-manufacturers had satisfied the third element of the military contractor defense—that the manufacturer had notified the government of any risks in the design of the product of which the manufacturer was aware.[76]

Beyond Judge Weinstein's manipulation of the opt-out cases, one must consider the validity of his opt-out opinion on its own terms. In large measure, Judge Weinstein's insistence on a modest settlement resulted from his dim view of the plaintiffs' causation evidence. Thus the treatment of the opt-out plaintiffs might be justified if there were no basis for a finding of causation in their cases.

Professor Peter Schuck, in his account of the *Agent Orange* case, extensively critiques Judge Weinstein's opt-out opinion. The most important criticism is Judge Weinstein's unquestioning acceptance of three epidemiological studies that failed to find an association between exposure and disease in veterans. Judge Weinstein did not breathe a hint of the possibility of methodological flaws that might have compromised these findings, nor did he entertain any doubts about the correctness of the studies' conclusions. While Judge Weinstein recognized the possibility that a lack of association might be due to prematurity—the studies were completed before the lengthy latency period required for the development of some diseases—he nevertheless refused to discount the studies' value.[77]

The causation question in *Agent Orange* becomes very different if the studies on which Judge Weinstein relied are viewed as inconclusive.[78] To be sure, the studies do not provide plaintiffs the evidence required to meet their burden of production on causation. But the probity of other forms of toxicological evidence, most significantly animal studies, varies inversely to the state of the epidemiological record. Once one discounts the epidemiological evidence, animal toxicology becomes more significant. Yet this is precisely where Judge Weinstein cast off his methodological-error blinders and rejected a variety of animal and industrial accident studies brought forth by plaintiffs to justify submission of the case to the jury.

The point of this discussion is not that the opt-out plaintiffs in *Agent Orange* should have won their cases. For example, evidence of exposure and the dioxin dose to which veterans were exposed would be exceedingly difficult to establish—samples of Agent Orange from different supplier's differed by two orders of magnitude in the percentage of dioxin contamination.[79] Furthermore, extrapolating to causation for the opt-out plaintiffs from studies of dioxin's toxicity in different species and in contexts involving different diseases would entail much analyzing and hypothesizing, including assessment of the similarity of diseases and the biological plausibility of similar mechanisms of disease between the study subjects and any given opt-out plaintiff. Yet one is left with the nagging feeling that Judge Weinstein's treatment of the plaintiffs' experts and causation evidence was driven more by concerns about upholding the fairness of a settlement that was essential to making the *Agent Orange* class action manageable than by a detached assessment of the causation record. In the end, before concluding that a jury should not have heard and resolved the evidence on causation, fairness required an even more rigorous scrutiny of the toxicological record than Judge Weinstein provided.

Similarly, there are a number of reasons why Bendectin is distinctive and should not be analogized to other toxic substance cases. First, the scientific record on Bendectin's teratogenicity by the mid- to late 1980s had become unusually rich, in contrast to the situation when Betty Mekdeci began her quest in 1976.[80] By 1985 there were 21 epidemiological studies that focused on Bendectin and 14 other studies that included Bendectin (or one of its components) among the agents studied. These numbers are somewhat misleading in evaluating the epidemiological record on Bendectin with regard to limb reduction defects. Many of the Bendectin studies did not differentiate the type of birth defect or studied specific birth defects other than limb reductions. There were four cohort (one unpublished) and four case control studies of limb reduction defects, the primary birth defect in the individual Bendectin trials.[81] Even that number, however, constitutes an unusually large body of epidemiological evidence for any given drug or chemical.

Moreover, Bendectin was a drug whose toxicity was more readily investigated than that of many other suspected toxic substances. The vast majority of birth defects are apparent at birth, which means that the latency period from exposure to disease is less than nine months. Hospital records document birth defects, and a number of data bases involving births had been developed for research purposes. Information about exposure to prescription drugs is almost always more readily available than exposure to environmental or occupational toxins. Many carcinogens have latency periods of decades, which greatly delay (and make more expensive) epidemiological study to identify them. Thus the first study addressing the connection between Bendectin and childhood leukemia, with its longer latency period, was not published until 1989.[82] By contrast, the short latency period for the disease of focus in the Bendectin cases—limb reduction defects—and the greater availability of relevant data made the development of a significant epidemiological record much more feasible than for other toxic substances.[83]

Indeed, we might better view the Bendectin causation cases as an instance of the courts making a finding of legislative fact [84] that Bendectin does not cause birth defects.[85] After the pioneering opinions of *Lynch, Richardson,* and *Brock,* many subsequent courts' opinions have relied substantially on these prior decisions as the basis for concluding that plaintiffs cannot prevail because of a dearth of causation evidence.[86] On this view, the *Lynch, Richardson,* and *Brock* decisions would be limited to other Bendectin cases. Bendectin might safely be generalized to the relatively few agents for which an established and mature body of epidemiological evidence exists. Tobacco and asbestos are other such agents that come to mind, albeit ones for which the epidemiological record demonstrates causation. The likelihood of a similarly extensive body of negative evidence developing in the future for another suspected toxic substance is quite low; researchers do not explore, agencies do not fund grants, and journals do not publish studies about agents that result in negative findings. In that respect, Bendectin may truly be unique.

The additional confidence provided the courts by the Food and Drug Administration's regulatory authority over Bendectin and its continuing approval of it is yet another reason why the Bendectin decisions are not generalizable. The FDA focused a great deal of attention on Bendectin once allegations of its teratogenicity emerged, not only at the time of its Advisory Committee Hearing in 1980, but subsequently as well in response to the political and legal attention that Bendectin attracted. The

FDA's continuing stance behind the safety of Bendectin no doubt emboldened the courts that were confronted with the validity of those experts' opinions that Bendectin was teratogenic.

Implications for Future Toxic Substances Litigation: Employing an Epidemiological Threshold

For most potentially toxic substances, there will not be a solid body of epidemiological evidence on which to rely. Epidemiology is expensive and time consuming, and, as for most scientific research, there is limited funding available. Thousands upon thousands of synthetic agents being used in the United States might pose toxic risks,[87] yet only a tiny fraction have been the subject of any epidemiological inquiry.[88] As of 1982, among 75 chemicals found to be carcinogens in animals, only 13 had been the subject of epidemiological study.[89] Imposing a burden of production that includes an epidemiological threshold will screen out all of these cases, but at a cost of precluding more refined attempts to assess whether causal relationships exist based on animal studies, structure analysis, available knowledge about biological mechanisms and related evidence.[90]

Toxic causation should be assessed with due regard for the available evidence.[91] When the epidemiological record is substantial, reliable, and consistent, the saliency of animal studies or other evidence of toxicity is quite low. However, if epidemiological evidence is lacking, thin, of questionable validity, and ultimately inconclusive, other toxicological evidence should be given consideration. Plaintiffs should be required to prove causation by a preponderance of the available evidence, not by some predetermined standard that may require nonexistent studies. This means that in every case involving an alleged toxic agent for which a mature epidemiological record does not exist, analysis of the sufficiency of plaintiff's evidence (or the admissibility of plaintiff's expert's testimony) would begin by considering the universe of available evidence of toxicity. Evaluating the likelihood that the agent was truly toxic (and ultimately whether, even if it was toxic, it caused the plaintiff's injury) would require the assessment of experts schooled in that scientific area. Even more difficult, if some evidence exists in a variety of scientific areas, scientists whose expertise spanned all fields would be required to make a considered assessment of the weight of the available evidence. No doubt, opening the courthouse doors to plaintiffs with relatively thin and attenuated evidence and rendering a decision on such a record is discomfiting and unfortunate. But the reality is that stronger and better evidence is unavailable (through no fault of anyone) and a decision based on the preponderance of the available evidence, rather than imposing an evidentiary threshold, would seem closest in keeping with the role of the civil justice system.[92]

The desire for simple, bright-line tests to determine admissibility poses a risk that courts will follow decisions like *Brock* that employ statistical significance as a talisman for admissibility. Recall that statistical significance is a heuristic employed to assess the likelihood that any study outcome could have occurred due to random error even if there is no association between disease and agent. Contrary to the *Brock* court, statistical significance addresses only random error due to the sampling inherent in any epidemiological study. It cannot and does not speak to systematic error, which requires an informed review of the methodology employed in conducting the study. Moreover, statistical significance is merely an instrument for assisting in evaluating a study, not a truth serum that can be simplistically prescribed.

The argument is complicated and has been more thoroughly articulated elsewhere.[93] Nevertheless, it is important to appreciate that a lack of statistical significance does not mean that there is no association—only that the association found could have occurred due to random chance even if there is truly no association. Moreover, statistical significance only protects against false positive error—concluding an association exists when there is no association. The more protection against false positive error provided by significance testing, the greater the risk of another kind of error—false negative—concluding that no association exists when there is one.

Peremptorily rejecting all studies that are not statistically significant would be an unfortunate decision, particularly if there are multiple studies tending to show a consistent effect. Similarly, blindly accepting statistically significant studies as sufficient would be comparably foolhardy. A methodologically sound study that finds a strong association but at a signficance level somewhat below the arbitrary .05 standard is quite probative and should be admitted in a toxic substances case. The legal system can reach more accurate outcomes with a considered assessment of the possibility of random error (as well as methodological error) in an epidemiological study rather than relying on a bright-line statistical significance test.

Conclusion

There are two important points to be drawn from this discussion. First, it would be unwise to generalize from the evidentiary threshold lessons of *Agent Orange* and Bendectin to other toxic substances cases. Second, if courts avoid the easy allure of imposing evidentiary thresholds, they (and juries) will be confronted with the complicated task of assessing the methodologies and reasoning of expert witnesses based on epidemiology, animal toxicology, and other relevant evidence. That is not an enviable assignment, but it is the challenge posed by *Daubert*.

To begin with the latter point first, several proposals to assist courts and juries confronted with these tasks have emerged. One of the most prominent proposals for reform would employ science panels to advise the courts on sticky toxic causation questions. Troy Brennan has convincingly demonstrated that such panels are only realistic options in instances of large or mass litigation over a given agent.[94] Such panels, though, pose little practical promise for a sole case or handful of cases over an agent for which there is a scant toxicological record. Moreover, the opinion of a science panel at any given time may become stale as the scientific record marches on and matures. Another concern with the use of science panels—albeit not an insuperable one—is the difference in the concept of proof in the scientific world and the legal realm. This difference is illustrated in medical journals when scientists bemoan "worrying trends" that the courts are imposing different standards of proof than the scientific community from which the author comes.[95] Of course they are, and necessarily so. Scientists are much more cautious about declaring a proposition "proved" than the law is when resolving a civil case.[96] The luxury of reserving judgment and advocating further investigation to resolve an uncertainty is not one available to the legal system, yet is frequently invoked by scientists.[97] Courts must resolve disputes based on their best estimate of the truth, regardless of the uncertainty that infects that assessment.

A solution lies in plainly and frankly explaining to experts who provide advice to the civil justice system that legal standards of "proof" are not the same as the scientific standards with which they are familiar. The question of interest in the civil justice system is which of two alternatives is more probable: causation or not? Once that difference is understood, claims that one testifying expert is operating outside scientific methodology—say, by relying on a single positive epidemiology study, rather than insisting on a second confirmatory study before making a judgment—can be recognized as erroneously equating the civil justice system's standards of proof with the scientific community's standards of proof.[98]

Beyond science panels in mass toxic substance litigations, a proposal by Professor E. Donald Elliott takes on added attractiveness in light of the *Daubert* requirement of scientific validity and the impediments to juries receiving an accurate account of the state of the scientific record, discussed in chapter 16.[99] Professor Elliott advocates the appointment of expert witnesses, but not to address the relative merits of the parties' respective positions. Rather the court-appointed expert would testify about whether the methodology and reasoning[100] by a party's expert is recognized and accepted by other scientists who are expert in the implicated discipline. The court would appoint such an expert when a party makes a showing that there is substantial doubt in the relevant peer group community about an opposing expert's methods or reasoning. One purpose of this proposal would be to provide incentives to tame the more far-fetched testimony of experts hired by the parties. The other function would be to provide the jury with what the adversarial system may not: an unbiased explanation of the relevant scientific discipline, identification of the assumptions and inferences implicit in the respective experts' opinions, and a neutral account of the weight of scientific opinion on the methods and reasoning of the contending experts. The expert's views would not be binding on the jury and would be subject to cross-examination by both sides. But the court-appointed expert would not be clothed in the hired-gun shroud of party-employed experts. The reform is not without its difficulties: identifying scientists with the willingness and expertise to testify, screening those experts with financial, social, or other connections with any of the parties,[101] avoiding experts who have significant biases that might affect their judgment,[102] and the historical reluctance of judges to appoint neutral experts. Nevertheless, the promise of such an effort is evident in light of the skewed view of scientific evidence provided to juries that was identified by Professor Sanders's research and discussed in chapter 16.

The confluence of the *Agent Orange* and Bendectin cases is one of those historical contingencies that may have a major impact on the toxic substances landscape. The legal environment was quite receptive to the lessons those cases purported to teach: increasing concern about expert witness abuse has been expressed across a wide variety of scientific areas with which the courts are grappling.

On the other hand, there is hope that the courts will recognize the wisdom of Professor Daniel Farber's observation:

Perhaps the most striking characteristic of toxic causation cases is their diversity. In some, the defendant's responsibility for the plaintiff's injury is nearly indisputable; in others, defendants may be clearly innocent of causal responsibility. Some cases involve individual plaintiffs who were exposed to rare chemicals; others involve thousands of plaintiffs and imperil the financial stability of entire industries. It is the beginning of wisdom to realize that no one approach can do justice under such diverse circumstances.[103]

The peculiar constraints of the massive *Agent Orange* litigation and Bendectin's unusually rich epidemiological record should not be generalized across the toxic substances spectrum to impose causal thresholds. Epidemiological studies are merely a tool, not a panacea, for finding toxic causation. If studies are well-planned methodologically and carefully carried out, they are the best of the available evidence on causation, even if far from the final word. Methodological flaws, however, bedevil epidemiological work, including limited samples, chance, confounding, and systematic biases that can compromise the validity of the study. Moreover, epidemiological studies are expensive and enormously time-consuming, especially where the diseases of interest are long-latency ones like cancer.

Unfortunately, the *Agent Orange* and Bendectin cases have created a veneer of infallibility and conclusiveness to epidemiology studies, as well as the implication that they are necessary for a plaintiff to satisfy his burden of proof. One hopes that the law will have the wisdom to recognize the danger of generalizing the causal threshold lessons of the *Agent Orange* and Bendectin litigations to other toxic substances cases.[104]

Notes

1. 113 S. Ct. 2786 (1993).
2. Numerous opinions were issued by both the district court and the court of appeals in the course of the *Agent Orange* litigation. The opinion of interest is *In re* "Agent Orange" Prod. Liab. Litig., 611 F. Supp. 1223 (E.D.N.Y. 1985).
3. For elaboration on Judge Weinstein's role in the settlement, see PETER H. SCHUCK, AGENT ORANGE ON TRIAL: MASS TOXIC DISASTERS IN THE COURTS (Cambridge, MA: Belknap Press of Harvard University Press, enlarged ed. 1987).
4. Professor Schuck catalogues and critiques them in SCHUCK, *supra* note 3, at 226–44.
5. *In re* "Agent Orange" Prod. Liab. Litig., 611 F. Supp. 1223, 1231 (E.D.N.Y. 1985).
6. *Id.* at 1241 (citations omitted).
7. *Id.* at 1260.
8. *Id.* at 1252.
9. 293 F. 1013 (D.C. Cir. 1923).
10. For an argument that courts should not rely on surrogates, but directly assess the validity of scientific propositions brought into court, see Bert Black et al., *Science and the Law in the Wake of* Daubert: *A New Search for Scientific Knowledge*, 72 TEX. L. REV. 715 (1994).
11. Richardson v. Richardson-Merrell, Inc., 649 F. Supp. 799, 802 n.9 (D.D.C. 1986), *aff'd*, 857 F.2d 823 (D.C. Cir. 1988), *cert. denied*, 493 U.S. 882 (1989).
12. *Id.* at 803.
13. *Id.* at 802.
14. Interview with Judge Thomas Jackson (May 8, 1990).
15. *See Richardson*, 649 F. Supp. at 801 n.6, 803.
16. 736 F.2d 1529 (D.C. Cir.), *cert. denied*, 469 U.S. 1062 (1984).
17. *Id.* at 1534–35.
18. As with the lower court, the court of appeals cited Judge Weinstein's *Agent Orange* opinion and drew from it the proposition that expert witness testimony that runs counter to the views of the scientific community should be carefully

scrutinized and that in toxic substances cases, "epidemiologic studies are of critical significance." Richardson v. Richardson-Merrell, Inc., 857 F.2d 823, 831 n.59 (D.C. Cir. 1988), *cert. denied*, 493 U.S. 882 (1989).

19. The court of appeals attempted to minimize the difference by stating that the lower court concluded that Dr. Done lacked an adequate foundation for his opinion. *Id.* at 826. That revisionist characterization ignored the lower court's opinion, which never invoked any of the federal rules of evidence and relied simply on the view that the overwhelming weight of the scientific evidence was contrary to plaintiffs' claims.

20. *Id.* at 827.

21. Ferebee v. Chevron Chemical Co., 736 F.2d 1529, 1535 (D.C. Cir.), *cert. denied*, 469 U.S. 1062 (1984).

22. *Id.* at 1535–36.

23. Doubt has been expressed about *Richardson*'s distinction of *Ferebee*. Rather, it has been suggested, *Richardson* evinces a rejection of or retreat from *Ferebee. See, e.g.*, Rubanick v. Witco Chemical Corp., 576 A.2d 4, 21 (N.J. Super. 1990), *modified*, 593 A.2d 733 (N.J. 1991).

24. 830 F.2d 1190 (1st Cir. 1987). The record in *Lynch* appears to have been carefully constructed by the defendant to present both its evidence about the epidemiological record as well as a rebuttal of the evidence the plaintiff *might have employed*; the plaintiff submitted no affidavits or other evidentiary material in opposition to the motion. The defendant's submissions included pieces of transcripts from several of the Bendectin cases that had previously been tried. Lynch v. Merrell National Laboratories, Division of Richardson-Merrell, Inc., 646 F. Supp. 856, 857, 865–67 (D. Mass. 1986), *aff'd*, 830 F.2d 1190 (1st Cir. 1987).

25. *Lynch*, 830 F.2d at 1194.

26. *Id.* at 1195. The first criticism surely goes to the weight to be given the study, not its admissibility. Many of the studies admitted in the Bendectin litigation have more serious flaws than the one identified by the *Lynch* court. Moreover, Dr. Swan articulated a reasonable basis for her selection of the control group: if Bendectin caused other birth defects, using all other children with birth defects would result in underestimating Bendectin's association with limb defects. *See* chapter 16.

27. The Done perjury episode initially surfaced in the *Oxendine* case in June 1986, several months before the first of these opinions was issued. *See* chapter 16.

28. 874 F.2d 307 (5th Cir.), *modified*, 884 F.2d 166 (5th Cir. 1989), *cert. denied*, 494 U.S. 1046 (1990).

29. *Brock*, 874 F.2d at 312.

30. *Id.* at 313 (emphasis added). The court later modified its opinion, substituting "statistically significant" for "conclusive." Brock v. Merrell Dow Pharmaceuticals, Inc., 884 F.2d 166, 167 (5th Cir. 1989), *cert. denied*, 494 U.S. 1046 (1990).

31. *Brock*, 874 F.2d at 312 & n.14.

32. *Id.* at 313.

33. Sheila Jasanoff, *Science and the Courts: Advice for a Troubled Marriage*, 2 NAT. RESOURCES & ENV'T 3, 3 (1986).

34. *See generally* W. Kip Viscusi, *The Dimensions of the Product Liability Crisis*, 20 J. LEGAL STUD. 147 (1991).

35. Celotex Corp. v. Catrett, 477 U.S. 317 (1986); Anderson v. Liberty Lobby, Inc., 477 U.S. 242 (1986); Matsushita Elec. Indus. Co. v. Zenith Radio Corp., 475 U.S. 574 (1986).

36. *See generally* Samuel Issacharoff & George Loewenstein, *Second Thoughts*

About Summary Judgment, 100 YALE L.J. 73 (1990); Jeffrey W. Stempel, *A Distorted Mirror: The Supreme Court's Shimmering View of Summary Judgment, Directed Verdict and the Adjudication Process,* 49 OHIO ST. L.J. 95 (1988).

37. Common law treatment of experts and the restrictions that impeded the usefulness of experts are described in Jack B. Weinstein, *Improving Expert Testimony,* 20 U. RICH. L. REV. 473, 475–76 (1986).

38. Some indication of the growth in expert witnesses is that in the fifteen-year span from 1974, just before the Federal Rules of Evidence were adopted, to 1989, the number of regularly testifying experts in Cook County increased 1540 percent, from 188 to 3,100. *See* Andrew Blum, *Experts: How Good are They?,* NAT'L L.J., Aug. 24, 1989, at 1, col. 4; *see also* Samuel R. Gross, *Expert Evidence,* 1991 WIS L. REV. 1113, 1119.

39. To be sure, testimony of expert witnesses employed by the parties has long been the subject of criticism. Professor Wigmore observed, "It [the rule permitting expert testimony] has done more than any one rule of procedure to reduce our litigation to a state of legalized gambling." 7 JOHN H. WIGMORE, EVIDENCE IN TRIALS AT COMMON LAW § 1929, at 39 (Boston: Little, Brown, James H. Chadbourn rev. 1978). *See also* Barry M. Epstein & Marc S. Klein, *The Use and Abuse of Expert Testimony in Products Liability Actions,* 17 SETON HALL L. REV. 656, 660 n.13 (1987) (citing nineteenth century opinions critical of expert witnesses); Learned Hand, *Historical and Practical Considerations Regarding Expert Testimony,* 15 HARV. L. REV. 40, 54–55 (1901) (asserting that the jury has no rational basis upon which to determine truth of conflicting expert witnesses' opinions).

40. Anyone who doubts that the expert witness business has long outgrown its cottage industry roots should simply peruse the classified advertisements in a recent issue of *Trial* magazine. The June 1994 issue contained over 160 advertisements by would-be experts covering esoterica from equine consultants to college campus security. *See also* PETER W. HUBER, LIABILITY: THE LEGAL REVOLUTION AND ITS CONSEQUENCES 44 (New York: Basic Books, 1988); National Center for State Courts, *Study to Investigate Use of Scientific Evidence, in* NAT'L CENTER FOR STATE COURTS REPORT (Williamsburg, VA: National Center for State Courts, 1988).

41. *See* Peter W. Huber, *Safety and the Second Best: The Hazards of Public Risk Management in the Courts,* 85 COLUM. L. REV. 277, 333 (1985) ("a Ph.D. can be found to swear to almost any 'expert' proposition, no matter how false or foolish"); *see also* Chaulk v. Volkswagen of America, Inc., 808 F.2d 639, 644 (7th Cir. 1986) (Posner, J.); E. Donald Elliott, *Toward Incentive Based Procedure: Three Approaches for Regulating Scientific Evidence,* 69 B.U. L. REV. 487 (1989); Epstein & Klein, *supra* note 39, at 656 (cataloging criticism, both ancient and modern, of expert witnesses); Peter W. Huber, *Junk Science and the Jury,* 1990 U. CHI. LEGAL F. 273; Walter Olson, *The Case Against Expert Witnesses,* FORTUNE, Sept. 25, 1989, at 133; President's Council on Competitiveness, *Agenda for Civil Justice Reform in America, in* PROD. SAFETY & LIAB. REP. (BNA) 926 (1991) (decrying "expert witnesses and 'Junk Science' ").

42. Paul Rheingold, *It's Time to Change the System On Junk-Science, Quack-Expert Issues,* MANHATTAN LAWYER, Nov. 1–7, 1988, at 13.

43. *See* Bernhardt v. Richardson-Merrell, Inc., 892 F.2d 440 (5th Cir. 1990); DeLuca v. Merrell Dow Pharmaceuticals, 131 F.R.D. 71 (D.N.J.), *rev'd,* 911 F.2d 941 (3d Cir. 1990); Ambrosini v. Richardson-Merrell, 1989 U.S. Dist. LEXIS 7568 (D.D.C. June 30, 1989), *amended,* 1989 U.S. Dist. LEXIS 8036 (D.D.C. July 12, 1989).

Ealy v. Richardson-Merrell, Inc., 897 F.2d 1159 (D.C. Cir.), *cert. denied,* 498 U.S. 950 (1990), resoundingly affirmed this lesson in the District of Columbia Circuit. Written by Judge Mikva, the author of *Ferebee, Ealy* reiterated *Richardson's* distinction of *Ferebee* and concluded that without a new study demonstrating causation, *Richardson* precluded any experts from opining that Bendectin was a teratogen. *Id.* at 1162.

44. This reading is often accompanied with the conclusion that FRE 703 requires something—data, methodology, or opinion—that has general acceptance in the scientific arena. *See* Daubert v. Merrell Dow Pharmaceuticals, Inc., 727 F. Supp. 570 (S.D. Cal. 1989) (both "principle" and "facts or data"), *aff'd,* 951 F.2d 1128 (9th Cir. 1991), *vacated,* 113 S. Ct. 2786 (1993); Turpin v. Merrell Dow Pharmaceuticals, Inc., 736 F. Supp. 737 (E.D. Ky. 1990), *aff'd,* 959 F.2d 1349 (6th Cir.), *cert. denied,* 113 S. Ct. 84 (1992); DeLuca v. Merrell Dow Pharmaceuticals, 131 F.R.D. 71, 74 (D.N.J.) (both "information" and opinion with which the "scientific community generally agrees"), *rev'd,* 911 F.2d 941 (3d Cir. 1990); Felgenhauer v. Texaco, Inc., 1987 U.S. Dist. LEXIS 11258 (E.D. Pa. Dec. 1, 1987); Landrigan v. Celotex Corp., 579 A.2d 1268 (N.J. Super. Ct. App. Div. 1990), *rev'd,* 605 A.2d 1079 (N.J. 1992); Rubanick v. Witco Chemical Corp., 542 A.2d 975 (N.J. Super. Ct. App. Div. 1988) (opinion of expert on causation must be accepted by at least a significant minority of the scientific community to be admissible), *rev'd,* 576 A.2d 4 (N.J. Super. Ct. App. Div. 1990), *modified,* 593 A.2d 733 (N.J. 1991).

45. Daubert v. Merrell Dow Pharmaceuticals, Inc., 727 F.2d 570, 575–76 (S.D. Cal. 1989), *aff'd,* 951 F.2d 1128 (9th Cir. 1991), *vacated,* 113 S. Ct. 2786 (1993); Turpin v. Merrell Dow Pharmaceuticals, Inc., 736 F. Supp. 737 (E.D. Ky. 1990), *aff'd,* 959 F.2d 1349 (6th Cir.), *cert. denied,* 113 S. Ct. 84 (1992).

46. Sometimes this position is limited to Bendectin cases, Daubert v. Merrell Dow Pharmaceuticals Inc., 727 F. Supp. 570, 572 (S.D. Cal. 1989), *aff'd,* 951 F.2d 1128 (9th Cir. 1991), *vacated,* 113 S. Ct. 2786 (1993), sometimes it is not. Renaud v. Martin Marietta Corp., 749 F. Supp. 1545 (D. Colo. 1990), *aff'd,* 972 F.2d 304 (10th Cir. 1992); Carroll v. Litton Systems, Inc., 1990 U.S. Dist. LEXIS 16,833, at *138 (W.D.N.C. 1990); Thomas v. Hoffman-La Roche, Inc., 731 F. Supp. 224 (N.D. Miss. 1989), *aff'd on other grounds,* 949 F.2d 806 (5th Cir.), *cert. denied,* 112 S. Ct. 2304 (1992). Sometimes it is expressed in terms that animal studies are inadequate to prove causation in humans. Rubanick v. Witco Chemical Corp., 576 A.2d 4, 23 (N.J. Super. Ct. App. Div. 1990), *modified,* 593 A.2d 733 (N.J. 1991); *In re* Paoli R.R. Yard PCB Litig., 706 F. Supp. 358, 368 (E.D. Pa. 1988) ("relying on the reasoning of *Agent Orange* and Richardson v. Richardson-Merrell, Inc., I find that the expert opinions based on animal studies are inadmissible"), *rev'd,* 916 F.2d 829 (3d Cir. 1990), *cert. denied,* 499 U.S. 961 (1991); Viterbo v. Dow Chemical Co., 826 F.2d 420, 421 (5th Cir. 1987) ("In this case today we consider the question whether it is so if an expert says it is so. . . . We uphold the district court because the plaintiff's expert brought to court little more than his credentials and a subjective opinion").

47. Lee v. Richardson-Merrell, Inc., Civ. No. 84-2228 (W.D. Tenn. Jan. 30, 1991), *aff'd,* 961 F.2d 1577 (6th Cir.), *cert. denied,* 113 S. Ct. 197 (1992); *In re* Paoli R.R. Yard PCB Litig., 706 F. Supp. 358, 369 (E.D. Pa. 1988), *rev'd,* 916 F.2d 829 (3d Cir. 1990).

48. Longmore v. Merrell Dow Pharmaceuticals, Inc., 737 F. Supp. 1117, 1121 (D. Idaho 1990) ("When the three circuit decisions are read carefully, they evidence a profound frustration with hired-gun experts. This Court shares those frustrations.").

49. 731 F. Supp. 224 (N.D. Miss. 1989), *aff'd on other grounds*, 949 F.2d 806 (5th Cir.), *cert. denied*, 112 S. Ct. 2304 (1992).

50. *Id.* at 228.

51. CA-W-88-98 (W.D. Tex.), *rev'd*, 902 F.2d 362 (5th Cir. 1990) (three-judge panel), *rev'd en banc*, 939 F.2d 1106 (5th Cir. 1991), *cert. denied*, 112 S. Ct. 1280 (1992).

52. 902 F.2d 362, 366 (5th Cir. 1990) (quoting the district court's unreported opinion), *rev'd en banc*, 939 F.2d 1106 (5th Cir. 1991), *cert. denied*, 112 S. Ct. 1280 (1992).

53. *In re* Bendectin Prods. Liab. Litig., 732 F. Supp. 744 (E.D. Mich. 1990).

Rubanick v. Witco Chemical Corp., 593 A.2d 733 (N.J. 1991), is a recent opinion of this genre reflecting an appreciation for the range of evidence that may be available regarding toxic causation and, consequently, the flexibility that must be employed in judging acceptable evidence and expert's opinions. The *Rubanick* court, cognizant of the difference between scientific and legal proof, also declined to defer to scientific standards for acceptable proof of causation.

54. *See, e.g.*, Weilein v. United States, 746 F. Supp. 887 (D. Minn. 1990); Villari v. Terminix, Inc., 692 F. Supp. 568 (E.D. Pa. 1988). *See generally* Kimberly Moore, Note, *Exploring the Inconsistencies of Scrutinizing Expert Testimony Under the Federal Rules of Evidence*, 22 TEX. TECH. L. REV. 885 (1991).

55. *Compare* Huber, *Junk Science and the Jury, supra* note 41, *with* Robert L. Schwartz, *There is No Archbishop of Science—A Comment on Elliott's Toward Incentive-Based Procedure: Three Approaches for Regulating Scientific Evidence*, 69 B.U. L. REV. 517 (1989).

56. 959 F.2d 1349 (6th Cir.), *cert. denied*, 113 S. Ct. 84 (1992).

57. *Id.* at 1357.

58. 113 S. Ct. 2786 (1993).

59. Daubert v. Merrell Dow Pharmaceuticals, Inc., 951 F.2d 1128 (9th Cir. 1991), *vacated*, 113 S. Ct. 2786 (1993).

60. Moreover, the Court's opinion, after explaining that plaintiff had responded to defendant's motion for summary judgment with the testimony of eight experts, omitted any mention of what those experts' testimony was. Daubert v. Merrell Dow Pharmaceuticals, Inc. 113 S. Ct. 2786, 2791 (1993).

61. For a cogent discussion of social science methodology, see Laurens Walker & John Monahan, *Social Facts: Scientific Methodology as Legal Precedent*, 76 CALIF. L. REV. 877 (1988).

62. *See* Joseph Sanders, *Scientific Validity, Admissibility, and Mass Torts After* Daubert, 78 MINN. L. REV. 1387, 1395–99 (1994).

The Federal Judicial Center conducted two programs for federal judges that were designed to explain a variety of scientific areas and assist judges in their handling of challenges to scientific evidence. The programs were held in December 1994 and January 1995, with over 100 federal judges attending each of the programs. The author, who was present at both, was impressed with the variation in views expressed by the judges present about the requirements of *Daubert*, especially with regard to the degree to which those judges would have to educate themselves in the relevant scientific discipline in order to rule on admissibility.

63. *Daubert*, 113 S. Ct. at 2798.

64. For a discussion of several other factors that might be appropriate, see *In re* Paoli R.R. Yard PCB Litigation, 35 F.3d 717, 742 (3d Cir. 1994); Bert Black et al., *Science and the Law in the Wake of* Daubert: *A New Search for Scientific Knowledge*, 72 TEX. L. REV. 716, 783–85 (1994).

65. *See* Sanders, *supra* note 62, at 1391.

66. An example used by Justice Blackmun illustrates just this problem. Blackmun referred to an expert astronomer who used the phases of the moon to conclude that an individual acted irrationally at a given time, as an example of testimony that would not be permitted. Yet the proponent of that evidence (though perhaps in a less obvious and absurd context) would no doubt argue that since the methodology was valid, the court should not examine the expert's conclusions, consistent with *Daubert's* methodology-conclusion distinction. The answer may be the one provided by Judge Becker in *In re* Paoli R.R. Yard PCB Litigation, 35 F.3d 717, 746 (3d Cir. 1994), that *Daubert* requires scrutiny of the reasoning process of the expert from the scientific test, study, or principle to the conclusion. Thus, the *Daubert* Court's statement that judges were not to evaluate the correctness of the expert's conclusion was not meant to insulate from judicial examination the reasoning process that leads to that conclusion.

67. *See, e.g.,* Symposium, *Scientific Evidence After the Death of* Frye, 15 CARDOZO L. REV. 1745 (1994); Margaret A. Berger, *Procedural Paradigms for Applying the* Daubert *Test,* 78 MINN. L. REV. 1345 (1994); Susan R. Poulter, Daubert *and Scientific Evidence: Assessing Evidentiary Reliability in Toxic Tort Litigation,* 1993 UTAH L. REV. 1307.

68. *See* Daubert v. Merrell Dow Pharmaceuticals, Inc., 43 F.3d 1311, 1316 (9th Cir. 1995).

69. *See* Wade-Greaux v. Whitehall Laboratories, Inc., 1994 U.S. Dist. LEXIS 7649 (D.V.I. Mar. 1, 1994) (in absence of statistically significant epidemiological studies to support expert's conclusion, it lacked valid scientific methodology).

70. *See* Wade-Greaux v. Whitehall Laboratories, Inc., 1994 U.S. Dist. LEXIS 7649 (D.V.I. Mar. 1, 1994) (employing *Daubert* as a surrogate for an evidentiary threshold; court concluded that employing animal studies to infer causation in humans is scientifically invalid and that without statistically significant epidemiological evidence an expert's opinion on causation is not admissible).

71. The account of Judge Weinstein's handling of the *Agent Orange* case is drawn from SCHUCK, *supra* note 3, at 143–69, 226–44; *see also* Charles Nesson, *Agent Orange Meets the Blue Bus: Factfinding at the Frontiers of Knowledge,* 66 B.U. L. REV. 521, 536 (1986).

72. *See In re* "Agent Orange" Prod. Liab. Litig., 597 F. Supp. 740, 756 (E.D.N.Y. 1984).

73. SCHUCK, *supra* note 3, at 151–52.

74. *Id.* at 232.

75. *Id.* at 234.

76. *See In re* "Agent Orange" Prod. Liab. Litig., 818 F.2d 187, 193–94 (2d Cir. 1987), *cert. denied,* 487 U.S. 1234 (1988).

77. A later epidemiological study of dioxin found a relative risk of 1.5 of mortality due to cancer among chemical workers exposed to high doses of dioxin and a relative risk of 9 for death due to soft tissue sarcoma. Martin A. Fingerhut et al., *Cancer Mortality in Workers Exposed to 2, 3, 7, 8-Tetra-Chlorodibenzo-p-Dioxin,* 324 NEW ENG. J. MED. 212 (1991).

78. This is precisely what one prominent epidemiologist familiar with the studies has suggested. SCHUCK, *supra* note 3, at 341 n.41; *see also* Nesson, *supra* note 71, at 538.

79. *In re* "Agent Orange" Prod. Liab. Litig., 565 F. Supp. 1263, 1276–77 (E.D.N.Y. 1983).

80. The information on Bendectin studies set out in the text is derived from

Joseph Sanders, *The Bendectin Litigation: A Case Study in the Life Cycle of Mass Torts,* 43 HAST. L.J. 301 (1992).

81. *See* Defendant's Exhibits C-90, 91, Richardson v. Richardson-Merrell, Civ. No. 83–3505 (D.D.C. 1986).

82. *See* Leslie Robison et al., *Maternal Drug Use and Risk of Childhood Nonlymphoblastic Leukemia Among Offspring,* 63 CANCER 1904 (1989).

83. JOSEPH GASTWIRTH, STATISTICAL REASONING IN LAW AND PUBLIC POLICY 839 (Boston: Academic Press, 1988).

84. *See* Kenneth Davis, *An Approach to Problems of Evidence in the Administrative Process,* 55 HARV. L. REV. 364 (1942).

85. To be more precise, the current record would justify a conclusion that no Bendectin-exposed child with a limb reduction birth defect could prove that the birth defect was more likely than not caused by Bendectin. *See* chapter 18.

86. *See, e.g.,* Turpin v. Merrell Dow Pharmaceuticals, 736 F. Supp. 737, 743 (E.D. Ky. 1990) ("the Court is persuaded that the prevailing school of thought governing expert testimony in Bendectin cases is best exemplified by Brock"), *aff'd,* 959 F.2d 1349 (6th Cir.), *cert. denied,* 113 S. Ct. 84 (1992); DeLuca v. Merrell Dow Pharmaceuticals, 131 F.R.D. 71 (D.N.J.), *rev'd,* 911 F.2d 941 (3d Cir. 1990); Daubert v. Merrell Dow Pharmaceuticals, Inc., 727 F. Supp. 570 (S.D. Cal. 1989), *aff'd,* 951 F.2d 1128 (9th Cir. 1991), *vacated,* 113 S. Ct. 2786 (1993).

87. The ten millionth chemical was synthesized in 1990. However, only 100,000 or so of these chemicals are (or have been) in common enough use to be of interest. *See* James Huff et al., *Scientific Concepts, Value and Significance of Chemical Carcinogenesis Studies,* 21 ANN. REV. PHARMACOL. & TOXICOL. 621, 622 (1991).

88. "The general scarcity of epidemiological studies . . . must be stressed." Lorenzo Tomatis et al., *Evaluation of the Carcinogenicity of Chemicals: A Review of the Monograph Program of the International Agency for Research on Cancer,* 38 CANCER RES. 877, 881 (1978). *See also* FRANK B. CROSS, ENVIRONMENTALLY INDUCED CANCER AND THE LAW: RISKS, REGULATION, AND VICTIM COMPENSATION 51–52 (New York: Quorum Books, 1989) (far more new agents introduced each year than studies conducted); NATIONAL RESEARCH COUNCIL, TOXICITY TESTING: STRATEGIES TO DETERMINE NEEDS AND PRIORITIES (Washington, DC: National Academy Press, 1984); Troyen Brennan, *Helping Courts With Toxic Torts: Some Proposals Regarding Alternative Methods for Presenting and Assessing Scientific Evidence in Common Law Courts,* 51 U. PITT L. REV. 1, 47 n.197 (1989).

89. *See* Myra Karstadt & Renee Bobal, *Availability of Epidemiologic Data on Humans Exposed to Animal Carcinogens,* 2 TERATOGENESIS, CARCINOGENESIS & MUTAGENESIS 151 (1982).

90. *See generally* Ellen Silbergeld, *The Role of Toxicology in Causation,* 1 COURTS, HEALTH SCI. & LAW 374 (1991) (toxicologist arguing for use of animal studies in making causal determinations in tort litigation).

91. *See* SCHUCK, *supra* note 3.

92. *See* Michael D. Green, *Expert Witness and Sufficiency of Evidence in Toxic Substances Litigation: The Legacy of Agent Orange and Bendectin Litigation,* 88 NW. U. L. REV. 643, 687 (1992).

93. *See* Green, *supra* note 92, at 682–94; Linda A. Bailey et al., *Reference Guide on Epidemiology, in* FEDERAL JUDICIAL CENTER, REFERENCE GUIDE ON SCIENTIFIC EVIDENCE 121, 151–56 (1994).

94. Brennan, *supra* note 88.

95. *See, e.g.,* Denis R. Miller, *Courtroom Science and Standards of Proof,* 2 LANCET 1283, 1283 (1987).

96. *See* Stephen G. Breyer, REGULATION AND ITS REFORM 144–45 (Cambridge, MA: Harvard University Press, 1982). *But see* Bert Black, *The Supreme Court's View of Science: Has* Daubert *Exorcised the Certainty Demon?,* 15 CARDOZO L. REV. 2129 (1994). For an essay on the clash of values, incentives, and biases between science and law, see Peter H. Schuck, *Multi-Culturalism Redux: Science, Law, and Politics,* 11 YALE L. & POL. REV. 1 (1993).

97. *See* Earl v. Cryovac Division of W.R. Grace Co., 772 P.2d 725 (Idaho 1989) (recognizing the differences between the quality and degree of evidence sufficient for a scientific judgment of causation and a legal judgment of causation); Howard Latin, *Good Science, Bad Regulation and Toxic Risk Assessment,* 5 YALE J. REG. 89, 92–93 (1987).

98. *See* Rubanick v. Witco Chemical Corp., 593 A.2d 733 (N.J. 1991) (opposing experts accused expert of operating outside the scientific method because there was insufficient evidence to conclude that PCBs cause cancer).

99. E. Donald Elliott, *Toward Incentive-Based Procedure: Three Approaches for Regulating Scientific Evidence* 69 B.U. L. REV. 487 (1989).

100. Elliott would have permitted the court-appointed expert to address the testifying experts' conclusions as well. That avenue would appear foreclosed, at least for the admissibility determination, in light of *Daubert's* admonition that the court is not to consider the expert's conclusions.

101. In many specialized scientific disciplines there is but a small group of individuals with expertise. Where the discipline has utility for commercial interests, many of those individuals may have ties to the commercial entities that might be parties in a lawsuit. Thus, in the pharmaceutical arena, many researchers in specific fields have conducted research, acted as consultants, served as expert witnesses, or developed social relationships at sponsored conferences for or with private pharmaceutical companies.

102. *See, e.g.,* Breyer, *supra* note 96, at 145 (experts' philosophy affects their objectivity, especially when the evidence is weak).

103. Daniel Farber, *Toxic Causation,* 71 MINN. L. REV. 1219, 1259 (1987).

104. Two recent toxic substances cases in the Court of Appeals for the District of Columbia are heartening in their recognition that *Richardson* and the other Bendectin decisions are not universally generalizable. *See* Mendes-Silva v. United States, 980 F.2d 1482 (D.C. Cir. 1993); Ambrosini v. Labarraque, 966 F.2d 1464 (D.C. Cir. 1992).

Chapter 18
The Lessons and Non-Lessons of Bendectin Litigation

If nothing else, Bendectin litigation demonstrates that the tort system can go awry. As explained later in this chapter, it seems reasonably clear that no plaintiff should be able to satisfy the burden of proof on causation in a Bendectin case. Yet, approximately 40 percent of all juries found for plaintiffs. The Bendectin litigation dragged on for almost twenty years, exacting substantial direct costs from the parties (and in the case of plaintiffs, from their lawyers as well). It also imposed substantial indirect social costs. Perhaps that is why critics of the tort system promote it so tirelessly. Bendectin is the taj mahal of horror stories about the tort system: the single most criticized piece of large-scale litigation of all time.[1] Like most other horror stories, however, the situation is considerably more complicated than the simplified public pronouncements.

This chapter begins with a consideration of what we do know about the teratogenicity of Bendectin. It then proceeds to consider how Bendectin litigation could have begun, continued, and flourished in light of the scientific evidence on causation. The chapter then identifies the considerable social costs imposed by the Bendectin litigation and inquires whether Bendectin is in the middle of the bell curve of tort cases, or whether it should be located well to one extreme of the curve. The chapter closes with consideration of several reform measures that might be considered for future mass toxic substances congregations that will no doubt arise.

What can we safely say about the teratogenicity of Bendectin? Today the range of uncertainty has been considerably narrowed, due to the extraordinary number of studies that have been performed.[2] While the studies are dotted with occasional findings of an association between Bendectin and a specific type of birth defect, none of those associations appears consistently, and the number are quite consistent with random error and noise due to methodological errors. Despite the extensive research that exists, current scientific methods are incapable of eliminating all uncertainty—we simply don't have a magnifying lens powerful enough to eliminate the possibility of any risk. Moreover, methodological concerns exist for many of the studies, leaving room for the skeptics to remain doubtful. For example, some studies define exposure to Bendectin as use during the first trimester (or even more broadly, during pregnancy).[3] That definition is overinclusive and tends to dilute any association that might exist. The best that we can say is that if Bendectin causes any birth defects, it does so extremely infrequently.[4] The residual doubt is unlikely to be resolved. Bendectin has attracted an extraordinary amount of scientific attention, it is no longer on the market, and the relevant scientific community has moved on in its interests.

Perhaps most significantly, given the substantial background rate of birth defects and the power of the Bendectin studies, no plaintiff should be able to succeed in demonstrating that her birth defects were more likely than not caused by Bendectin. That is, even if Bendectin is a very weak teratogen, its effect is dwarfed by other causes and science is incapable of identifying such a weak effect. For strategic reasons, Merrell never presented that argument to a jury. Perhaps that was a wise judgment; perhaps it was not. Regardless, that is the strongest reason why Merrell should prevail before a fact finder, not because we can say that Bendectin has no teratogenic capacity, the claim that Merrell did make to juries.

How could Bendectin litigation have begun and flourished with scientific evidence that is about as conclusive as it gets? We must remember that Bendectin litigation did not begin today. It had its genesis in 1975, when Betty Mekdeci undertook her investigation to find the cause of her son's birth defects. At that time and for the two decades before, the scientific record on Bendectin was quite different from what it is today. Contrary to the claims of the critics,[5] Bendectin did not begin as a case of avaricious lawyers pursuing suits against a deep-pocket defendant over a drug whose safety was well established over a long period of time by numerous solid scientific studies.

When Bendectin was first marketed in 1957, the three ingredients that it included had been sold separately for a number of years. Testing of those individual drugs for efficacy and acute toxicity failed to reveal significant concerns. No reproductive studies were performed on any of the individual components, nor did the efficacy studies report on congenital effects.[6]

Although Bendectin was marketed exclusively for pregnant women, no reproductive testing of the combined ingredients was performed until the Staples rabbit study in 1963. Although only a handful of pharmaceutical companies were performing reproductive testing during that time, as explained in chapter 5, Bendectin was the first drug designed and approved solely for use during the critical stages of organ formation in the fetus.

It is probably an overstatement to say that Bendectin's lack of terato-genicity is entirely serendipitous, given the lack of investigation before it was marketed and the paucity of studies for twenty years thereafter. How-ever, it is considerably less of an exaggeration than many have made in trumpeting Bendectin's absolute safety. Peter Huber claims: "A large vol-ume of published epidemiological data has previously revealed no statis-tically significant association between Bendectin and birth defects."[7] If Huber means that pooling all studies of all birth defects does not reveal a statistically significant association between birth defects generally and exposure to Bendectin, he is technically correct, but quite misleading. Since agents tend to cause a specific or related group of harms, pooling all birth defects is a sure way to mask any association that may exist be-tween Bendectin and a specific birth defect. If Huber means that no studies have found a statistically significant association between Bendec-tin and a birth defect, there is no other way to put it than to say that that claim is false.[8] Whether those associations are causal is a different ques-tion, but several statistically significant epidemiological studies do exist.

Another commentator, echoing several others, wrote: "Despite over-whelming scientific evidence that Bendectin is safe for both the mother and the unborn child . . . ."[9] If the author means that scientific evidence exists that proves that Bendectin does not have adverse effects on the fetus, once again it is wrong. The range of risk that is consistent with the scientific evidence is small, but it still exists. Paul R. Orrefice, Chairman of Dow Chemical Company, Merrell's parent, made another one of those claims in a speech, referring to Bendectin as "proven safe throughout the decades."[10]

Even after thalidomide revealed the vulnerability of the fetus to exoge-nous insult, the only useful epidemiological studies of Bendectin until the late 1970s were the Bunde-Bowles study and a very small study that had little power to reveal much of anything.[11] The animal studies per-formed by Merrell during that period, including the controversial Staples study, contained suggestions of problems and would not have led one to confidence in Bendectin's safety. The Bunde-Bowles study has been severely criticized for shoddy methodology, even by Merrell's ex-perts.[12] Merrell ultimately abandoned any effort to defend its validity, merely explaining that it was a product of the methods of its time. In-deed, the Bunde-Bowles study, which was not peer-reviewed and was pub-lished in an obscure journal, is precisely the sort of study that the junk science critics would excoriate, at least if the outcome had been contrary to their political leanings.[13] Yet Bunde-Bowles remained for years as the basis for assuring physicians and pregnant women of Bendectin's safety. It was also the basis for Bendectin's labeling, which provided no hint of risk or uncertainty about birth defects, until 1981.[14]

In 1980, 23 years after Bendectin's emergence on the market and three years after Betty Mekdeci's suit began, Dr. Franz Rosa, a specialist in birth defects employed at the National Institutes of Health, testified at the FDA Advisory Committee hearing on Bendectin:

> There are those who feel that there is no substantial evidence of risk from Bendectin use in early pregnancy. There are those who feel that there may be a substantial risk with Bendectin which could have gone undetected, despite the fact that there have been more human studies on Bendectin than on any other drug experience with pregnancy.
>
> It is quite possible that both points of view are correct. There is a lot we don't know, but we do know that about three percent of pregnancies end up with serious congenital malformations.[15]

Rosa's comments reflected the ambiguity, scarcity, and uncertainty of the scientific evidence on Bendectin's teratogenicity. Methodological error, preliminary and crude studies, and judgments about data interpretation often provide a wide range of judgments by scientists examining the same information. Scientific consensus may occur, but usually only after a substantial shakedown period, in which increasingly refined and valid studies add to the accumulated evidence.[16]

At the conclusion of a day of hearings on Bendectin and birth defects, Rosa summarized the evidence by observing that the most recent studies had reduced the range of uncertainty from a possibility of a five-fold risk of specific birth defects such as cleft palate and limb defects due to Bendectin to a two-fold risk.[17] To put Rosa's point another way, existing studies were insufficiently powerful to rule out the possibility that Bendectin doubled the risk of limb defects. It may or may not have; the evidence simply wasn't available. This was in 1980, 23 years after Bendectin had first been marketed and after millions of pregnant women had taken the drug.

How many women with morning sickness in the 1970s would have taken Bendectin if they had been told that scientific studies could not rule out a five-fold increase for a given type of birth defect? How many women in the early 1980s would have declined Bendectin and attempted to manage their morning sickness by more conservative means if aware that a doubling of birth defects had not been ruled out? What advice would physicians have given their patients if aware of the degree of risk that might exist? Would Betty Mekdeci have received a prescription for Bendectin based on a telephone call to a doctor's office where she had yet to be examined? No doubt different choices would have been made by the millions of women confronting it, but until 1981 nothing appeared in the labeling for Bendectin that mentioned anything about the risk of birth defects.

The growth of scientific evidence about Bendectin's teratogenicity and its status as the best studied drug available for morning sickness is due in significant part to the lawsuits that were brought by Betty Mekdeci and her successors. One of the published epidemiology studies in 1977 of the teratogenicity of drugs used in pregnancy did not address Bendectin exposure, only assessing exposure to the separate components of Bendectin.[18] Merrell, which was defending itself in the *Mekdeci* case, paid one of the authors to reanalyze the data for Bendectin exposure. The pattern of scientific inquiry of Bendectin in the late 1970s and into the 1980s was driven by the litigation, the consequent concerns raised about Bendectin, making it a "hot topic" for researchers,[19] and by the FDA, which received not-so-subtle prompting by two Congressmen who were sympathetic to those pursuing Bendectin litigation.[20] As Professor Sanders has concluded: "There was a substantial mobilization of resources devoted to the study of Bendectin, much of it apparently in response to the litigation and concomitant political pressure."[21]

To understand the Bendectin litigation thus requires an appreciation for the uncertainty about Bendectin that existed when Betty Mekdeci began searching for the cause of David's birth defects. If the scientific record of ten years later had existed at the time of his birth, it is inconceivable that Betty Mekdeci would have seized on Bendectin as the cause of David's birth defects. It is equally inconceivable that any plaintiff's lawyer would have been willing to represent her, especially given the investment of the lawyer's time and money required to pursue such a case. Toxic substances litigation simply couldn't breed in the scientific record that ultimately developed on Bendectin. We should also recognize the critical role of contingency and fortuity in the inception and course of the litigation. Thousands upon thousands of women had taken Bendectin and borne children with birth defects before David Mekdeci was born in 1975 and his mother decided to investigate what caused his birth defects. Only with her extraordinary determination and stamina, along with encouragement from disaffected anonymous sources at the FDA, was Bendectin litigation initiated. It seems a reasonable hypothesis that had David Mekdeci not been born with birth defects, Bendectin litigation would never have occurred or would have existed only as a minuscule blip on the tort scene. The unusual proportion of limb defects among the birth defects reported in DERs that Betty Mekdeci unearthed and which persuaded her that Bendectin was the candidate to be held responsible cannot be discounted in the chain of events that led to Bendectin litigation. Better evidence has since demonstrated that the DERs did not reflect a teratogenic effect, but they surely raised suspicions (even at Merrell) and the explanations that were proffered were not entirely convincing.

If the *National Enquirer* had not picked up on the *Mekdeci* suit (at Melvin Belli's prompting) with its sensational report, providing dozens of additional potential clients, Kokus, Cohen, and Belli might not have been as avid in pursuing Bendectin and Merrell. Grover Ashcraft's presence on the first *Mekdeci* jury, and his stubbornness in forcing a compromise verdict, provided a modicum of encouragement not only for the lawyers in *Mekdeci*, but for others as well. In the midst of asbestos litigation, the ongoing Agent Orange class action, and DES and the Dalkon Shield IUD, Bendectin looked to be yet another mass toxic litigation that would provide a large number of clients with sympathetic cases.

The plaintiff's verdict in *Oxendine* in Washington, DC in 1983 was critical to the third phase of Bendectin litigation, after MDL-486 was tried. The Oxendines might have found a lesser trial lawyer than Barry Nace; or he might have turned down their case because he knew nothing about Bendectin, or Mrs. Oxendine might not have taken an Upjohn drug, thereby permitting removal of the *Oxendine* case to federal court and transfer as part of MDL-486. Had any of those events occurred, the plaintiff's verdict that demonstrated that individual Bendectin cases were winnable would not have existed. MDL-486, with its broad discovery, newly published epidemiological studies, and failure to develop significant evidence of causation might otherwise have been the terminus of Bendectin litigation.

But the success in *Oxendine* and the structure of the MDL-486 trial persuaded plaintiff's lawyers that individual cases could be pursued more successfully. Ironically, the polyfurcation and the exclusion of impaired children contributed to an accurate outcome—a verdict for Merrell—but at the same time convinced several plaintiffs' lawyers that the outcome was unrepresentative of what might occur in individual cases, without a separate hearing on causation.

Yet it should be remembered that only three plaintiff's lawyers seriously pursued Bendectin cases after MDL-486 and at a point where the scientific evidence tending to exonerate Bendectin as a teratogen mounted. Barry Nace, the successful lawyer in *Oxendine*, Tom Bleakley, who was so frustrated with the structure of the MDL-486 trial that he kept his clients out of the trial, and Tom Kline were the only lawyers who pursued Bendectin seriously after MDL-486. Many lawyers settled with Merrell for a few thousand dollars per case, a sum that for most didn't even cover the costs for preliminary investigation. A number of plaintiffs' lawyers, including some very prominent ones, declined to undertake representation of Bendectin claimants after examining the scientific evidence that existed.

The *Richardson* verdict in 1986 came at a time when plaintiff's lawyers were quite discouraged with Bendectin litigation. Followed quickly by two more victories, including the spectacular $95 million verdict in *Ealy*, *Richardson* and its progeny dragged Bendectin litigation out by several years after it would have died a more natural death.

But it was not just fortuity that fed Bendectin litigation and convinced plaintiff's lawyers to continue to pursue Merrell. The course of Bendectin litigation is littered with actions by Merrell that raise serious questions about its good faith and corporate character that plaintiffs' lawyers latched onto like barnacles to a ship hull. The story begins with Merrell's blatantly culpable conduct in MER/29 and continues with its insistent lobbying and aggressive preapproval marketing of thalidomide. Though those episodes did not bear on Bendectin's teratogenicity, they persuaded Melvin Belli, George Kokus, and Arthur Cohen that Merrell would make a highly culpable defendant. The story continues with the indulgent reclassifications of the Staples study, the delay in providing the Staples study to the FDA, ghost-written medical articles, the sloppiness and casualness of the Bunde-Bowles study, and the behind-the-scenes manipulation of medical and public attitudes reflected in the Tommy B. Evans letter to *60 Minutes*.

Merrell's cozy relationship with and financial support of many of the researchers involved in studying Bendectin's teratogenicity also plays a critical explanatory role. Richard Smithells' letter seeking more money based on the assistance his research results would provide to Merrell in lawsuits against it, payments to support research by a number of others, and the undisclosed hiring of Dr. Flowers to express the consequences of Bendectin's withdrawal contributed to skepticism about the research that emerged and fed suspicions that Merrell was manipulative, unscrupulous, and untrustworthy. The five juries that awarded punitive damages against Merrell did not concoct out of thin air their findings of recklessness or wanton disregard, required for awarding punitive damages.

For many of these episodes and incidents Merrell has explanations, some convincing. It is true that toxicological and epidemiological research costs money and that firms that stand to benefit from the sale of an agent or drug are in the most logical position to sponsor research into its safety. It is also inconceivable that an independent researcher would consciously manipulate a study to obscure an evident teratogenic effect. The professional, personal, and psychic rewards of identifying a teratogen are far too great to believe that someone would engage in a deliberate cover-up. Of course, subconscious biases do exist, and especially when judgments and appropriate inferences are implicated, the course of sponsorship may affect the outcome. Even if no biases existed, the cozy relationship between industry and researchers creates unfortunate, yet very real, perceptions about the credibility of the work of researchers with industry ties. Those perceptions permitted a discounting of the force of the evidence that emerged that exonerated Bendectin, evidence that contradicted the impressions formed at an earlier and scientifically less certain time.

At least with pharmaceuticals, the possibility of having the FDA administer clinical safety testing, including selection of the researchers, is one that deserves further consideration.[22] The interested company could be charged the costs of the study, but the FDA would be interposed between sponsor and investigator, so as to ensure both independence and perceptions of independence.

Before consideration of other possible reforms, let us consider and acknowledge the costs of the Bendectin litigation. Merrell resolutely declines to reveal what it spent defending itself, but an estimate in the range of $100 million appears reasonable, especially in light of reports that *Mekdeci* cost over $1 million and *Koller* in excess of $7 million. The opportunity costs to Merrell of its employees' time devoted to the litigation and distracted from the work of developing and producing drugs should be added to that total. Plaintiffs' expenses and their lawyers' expenses and time seem likely to be in the tens of millions of dollars, although probably not as high as Merrell's costs.

The high transaction costs of the tort system have been widely criticized.[23] This concept reflects the "tax" that the tort system imposes on every dollar paid by defendants in order to transfer money to successful plaintiffs. Most estimates put the percentage at from 50 to 70 percent, depending on the type of tort action and its complexity. Bendectin surely represents the worst case of transaction costs: no plaintiffs have recovered money pursuant to a judgment, and only a handful of trivial nuisance settlements have resulted in any transfers, most of which was probably used to pay costs rather than compensate plaintiffs. The transaction costs of Bendectin litigation are awfully close to 100 percent.

Merrell's willingness to settle the litigation for $120 million reveals that high transactions costs and small risks of devastating adverse outcomes can extract substantial sums from defendants regardless of the merits of their position. Given the subsequent jury verdicts against it and their magnitude (*Ealy* alone was for $95 million), that settlement appears quite rational, particularly without the hindsight that the appellate courts would uniformly overturn the plaintiffs' verdicts.

Beyond the huge direct transaction costs, critics have identified a variety of significant indirect social costs that both deserve mention and critical consideration. These include the withdrawal of Bendectin from the market and its consequences for pregnant women and the health of their fetuses. More generally, the experience with Bendectin is cited as deterring research and innovation in the pharmaceutical industry, an industry that has the capacity to improve greatly public health and welfare.[24] Let's take a closer look at these claims and consequences.

The withdrawal of Bendectin from the United States market has no doubt deprived some pregnant women of relief from the nausea and vomiting of pregnancy. It appears that it has also resulted in an increase in hospitalizations for hyperemesis gravidarum, a severe form of morning sickness that requires medical intervention, often by intravenous rehydration. But the loss of Bendectin is not nearly as tragic as some of the critics' semi-hysterical claims have made it out to be, most notably the claim that its withdrawal has *increased* the incidence of birth defects.

First, Bendectin's efficacy in treating morning sickness was quite modest. A study performed in the mid-1970s as part of the DESI review by the FDA found that Bendectin relieved morning sickness in only 10 percent more women than obtained relief from a placebo. Bendectin fared somewhat better in providing relief for nausea alone, providing benefit to 23 percent more of those receiving Bendectin than those who were given a placebo. For vomiting, on the other hand, there was only a 7 percent difference in relief between the Bendectin treatment and placebo groups. While some women truly benefited from Bendectin, many who took it would have been just as well off with a sugar cube. Subsequent, albeit smaller, studies found accupressure and vitamin B6 (pyridoxine) to be more efficacious in treating morning sickness than the DESI study found for Bendectin.[25]

The absence of Bendectin from the market and the publicity and litigation that led to its withdrawal has also avoided the significant overuse of the drug that occurred in the 1970s, when it was routinely prescribed for pregnant women with even mild or modest morning sickness. Betty Mekdeci, who obtained a prescription over the telephone from a nurse at an obstetrics practice where she had not yet had an initial appointment, may be an extreme example, but it is symptomatic of the indiscriminate use of Bendectin. This overprescribing flew in the face of the thalidomide experience, which demonstrated the horror that drugs could wreak on the developing fetus. It also flew in the face of the advice of cautious and prudent experts who counseled conservative measures to attempt to control morning sickness, which in the vast majority of cases resolves itself by the end of the first trimester of pregnancy and causes no lasting harm to mother or fetus.[26]

In 1975 Dr. H. Tuchmann-Duplessis, a prominent French teratologist, explained the basis for this concern:

In no other field of medicine is the therapeutic risk higher than in the treat-ment of pregnant women. While in the adult most of the unexpected side-effects of drugs are reversible, they are irreversible in the embryo and can lead to abnor-malities in the newborn . . . . *Corner* (1944), in a brilliant series of lectures "Our-selves Unborn" stressed the importance of the prenatal life in the destiny of the adult:

> The months before birth are the most eventful part of life and we spend them at a rapid pace. At the beginning the body consists of one cell: by the time of birth it has two hundred billion cells. Some time in the third week of life your heart began to beat, you had the beginning of a brain before you had hands, and of arms before legs, you developed muscles and nerves and began your struggle: in the darkness you faced strange perils and you came at last to the threshold of the world.[27]

Even though Bendectin is no longer available, there are a variety of substitute drugs that are employed to treat morning sickness.[28] None is approved by the FDA for treatment of morning sickness, although that does not prevent doctors from legally prescribing or recommending the drugs for that purpose. None of the alternative drugs has been subjected to as extensive testing as was Bendectin, which poses a greater possible risk than existed with Bendectin. Yet, it also seems clear that morning sickness is being treated more conservatively, with drug therapy being reserved for more serious cases that cannot be resolved by diet change or other benign treatments. Smaller and less well designed studies than the Bendectin DESI study indicate that Meclizine is as (or more) effec-tive as Bendectin in treating morning sickness,[29] although no interdrug efficacy studies have been conducted.[30] And while Bendectin cannot be obtained, its active ingredients can be, as most obstetricians and phar-macists are aware.[31] A Bendectin cocktail can be concocted with readily available over-the-counter ingredients.[32]

The most serious and troubling claim (and an equally ironic one), is that the absence of Bendectin has *increased* the incidence of birth de-fects. Dr. Charles Flowers, then Vice-President of the American College of Obstetricians and Gynecologists, first predicted this consequence when the cessation of Bendectin's production was announced on June 9, 1983. It has since been repeated in a variety of sources, including the Journal of the American Medical Association,[33] and briefs filed in the Supreme Court in the *Daubert* case, that make it appear more as fait ac-compli than prognostication.[34]

The reasoning behind this claim is that nausea and vomiting of preg-nancy results in a nutritional deficit that affects the normal development of the fetus. The most severe form of morning sickness, hyperemesis gravidarum, involves persistent vomiting, dehydration, undernourish-ment, and electrolyte imbalance that, in the worst cases, pose serious risks to the mother. With Bendectin unavailable to treat the most severe cases of nausea and vomiting, more women suffer this condition un-abated, resulting in an increase of birth defects in their children.

There are several difficulties with this claim. First, the connection be-tween morning sickness and *better* pregnancy outcomes in terms of mis-carriages, stillbirths, low birthweight, and birth defects is generally positive.[35] As one researcher concluded: "The present data are consis-tent with previous reports indicating that the presence of nausea and vomiting is a favorable risk factor for pregnancy outcome . . . . "[36]

Second, the vast majority of women with morning sickness do not suf-fer nutritional deficits. Even for those that do, there is little concern about the impact on the fetus. One expert on birth defects has com-mented: "The epidemiology on diet and pregnancy, which is very extensive, indicates that acute food restriction does not influence fetal nutrition in previously well-nourished women."[37]

Finally, there is little evidence to demonstrate Bendectin's efficacy in treating hyperemesis. In theory, it might do so in either of two different ways: 1) by preventing morning sickness from progressing to hypereme-sis; or 2) by providing relief for women who suddenly present with hyperemesis. For the latter class of women, severe vomiting requires treatment with other than oral medication, the only form in which Ben-dectin was available. For the former, as mentioned above, there is no clinical study of the efficacy of Bendectin in treating morning sickness that later progresses to hyperemesis. The DESI study of Bendectin did not distinguish the degree of morning sickness of the participants. More-over, the significant placebo effect found in the DESI study (81 percent) suggests that most of the participants had mild or modest cases of morn-ing sickness.

Another claim about the consequences of the withdrawal of Bendectin and the concerns raised about teratogenicity of drugs for morning sick-ness appears better grounded than the increased birth defects assertion. Dr. Steven Lamm is a consulting epidemiologist who first became in-volved in Bendectin litigation when he was hired by the guardian ad li-tem for future claimants in MDL-486. Dr. Lamm, who has since testified as an expert witness for Merrell in a number of Bendectin cases, has iden-tified, in an abstract, a doubling of hospitalizations for hyperemesis since Bendectin became unavailable. Lamm found a decrease in the use of antiemetic drugs (including Bendectin) that correlates with this increase in hospitalizations. Thus Lamm concludes that the attempt to treat morning sickness with more conservative non-drug therapy has resulted in an increase of hyperemesis that requires hospitalization. Lamm's data appear correct and it is implausible that there is some other change dur-ing the 1980 to 1984 period when Bendectin use was dropping and ultimately ended that is responsible for the increased hospitalizations. Thus it seems reasonable to conclude that an indirect cost of the Bendectin litigation and its impact on obstetricians' treatment of morning sickness is an increase in hospitalizations for hyperemesis. Of course, this conclusion assumes that Bendectin truly was effective in reducing the incidence of severe cases of hyperemesis, a proposition for which none of the efficacy studies of Bendectin provides proof.

Perhaps most important is the claim that the tort system is a giant social drag. In this account, Bendectin is emblematic of a tort system that drives good products off of the market, deters innovation and new technology, and causes greater social costs through lost or never-developed drugs and medical devices than it provides in social benefits by way of improved safety.

The short answer to these claims is that we simply don't know. There simply is no way to identify or measure the foregone research efforts of companies or to identify systematically those drugs that never made it to market or that were withdrawn from the market because of liability concerns. Moreover, there is good reason to be skeptical that Bendectin signals much of anything about the net social impact of tort law on the pharmaceutical industry.

A thorough and careful study of the impact of liability on the pharmaceutical industry by Rand's Institute for Civil Justice observes that liability effects on innovation "cannot be observed or quantified." [38] Nor can we systematically identify and measure dangerous drugs never brought to market or withdrawn from the market because of liability concerns. [39] The additional warnings or safety information due to liability concerns are also unmeasurable. "The difficulty of attributing observed behavior to liability and the possibility of unobserved responses imply that a reliable . . . judgment about the net social benefits of liability-induced changes in product availability is far out of reach." [40] Another commentator examining the same question concurs on the inability to draw any conclusion on the matter. [41]

By contrast, withdrawals (or supply limitations) of popular drugs in which liability concerns play a role are likely to be well publicized. The drugs with substantial support—Bendectin, several vaccines, the Copper-7 IUD, and orphan drugs—are paradigmatic. On the other side are drugs and medical devices like DES and the Dalkon Shield IUD, which are seen as triumphs of the tort system. These highly publicized episodes are employed as ammunition by both sides in the debate over the tort system. Ironically, the extensive publicity about the impact of liability in producing shortages of vaccines and the withdrawal of Bendectin have a life of their own in creating exaggerated perceptions of the impact of liability rules among decision makers in the pharmaceutical industry. Thus, the publicity itself may affect behavior by creating greater concerns about liability risk than is objectively justified.[42]

Yet liability and perceptions about it probably play a relatively minor role in the mix of factors that ultimately determine the areas in which pharmaceutical firms focus their research, decide which compounds to pursue in early testing, and ultimately undertake clinical trials. Potential profits, consistency with a company's market niche and strategic goals, and federal regulation probably weigh much more heavily than potential tort liability in determining those drugs that make it to market. The vast majority of drugs do not have significant liability concerns, and even among those that do, some, such as Accutane, a known teratogen that is quite useful in treating severe acne, remain on the market despite substantial risks of liability.[43]

Steven Garber, the author of the Rand Study, concludes that liability is unlikely to deter efforts to develop a drug that offers a major breakthrough and the promise of huge profits. Liability concerns may deter efforts to develop more modest drugs. That effect, however, is likely to shift pharmaceutical research dollars from one area to another, rather than reduce the resources devoted to research in an industry that is highly dependent on product innovation for its success.[44]

Thus, the most significant effect of tort law on research in the pharmaceutical industry is likely to be in areas that are associated with grave adverse events. The extent of uncertainty about the scope of the risks will also play a role, as most assume that decision makers are risk averse. Whether actors breach a tort duty or not, those who are in proximity to tragedies or huge losses are more likely to be sued and, where uncertainty exists, held liable for the losses. Obstetricians have discovered this phenomenon: They are exposed to substantial medical malpractice risks because of their proximity to devastating injuries that emerge during the birthing process.[45]

The single greatest area of risk and uncertainty in the pharmaceutical context is in the field of drugs for pregnant women.[46] A significant background rate of birth defects exists with the potential for harm to infants that may endure for a lifetime. If those cases get to court, recent research suggests that a number of circumstances unite to make it particularly difficult for the defendant to exonerate itself. Juries are more likely to hold a corporate defendant liable if the plaintiff's injuries are severe. Both the economics of litigation and severity-of-injury effects filter the cases that are filed: the vast majority of individual Bendectin cases involved limb reduction defects. Tort defendants often benefit because jurors are often quite careful and critical in evaluating the responsibility of the plaintiff in causing the injury and excessive appeals for sympathy.

But, the child plaintiffs in Bendectin litigation were genuinely sympathetic innocents who played no role in their injuries and who could not be faulted for seeking to play on jurors' emotions.[47] Rather than being emblematic, Bendectin may be idiosyncratic in assessing the role of the tort system's impact on pharmaceutical technology and innovation.[48]

Even if it is aberrational, rather than exemplary, Bendectin must be added to the debit side of the mass toxic tort system ledger. We should be cautious, however, about overemphasizing its impact. More successful mass toxic substances litigations, such as the Dalkon Shield IUD and asbestos litigations, in which plaintiffs' lawyers, spurred by the financial incentives of the tort system, uncovered corporate wrongdoing that caused massive harm to the public health. Tobacco litigation, while unsuccessful to date, has provided a glimpse of the industry and its venal and seamy efforts to keep the enormous risks of cigarette smoking from the public.[49]

Even with "successes" like asbestos, Dalkon Shield, MER/29, and other smaller toxic litigation, the transaction costs are so high that they make one look longingly at alternatives—compensation schemes that use simplified criteria for recovery or expanded social welfare schemes in conjunction with greater regulation to replace the tort system. The difficulties of a general toxic harm compensation fund are less visible, but have been convincingly demonstrated by Professor Ken Abraham.[50] Most notably, the difficulties and costs of ascertaining causation would remain. Expanded governmental regulation to fill the deterrence gap that would be created by replacing the tort system with improved social welfare benefits is antithetical to the current political climate. More specific compensation schemes for individual toxic substances, imposed after they have emerged and relatively good evidence is available about causation, might be the most attractive means to reduce transactions costs.[51] Yet, as is demonstrated by Congress's unfortunate failure to enact an asbestos compensation scheme, once a mass toxic litigation matures, there are many with enormous investments in the status quo, and even compelling public policy is inadequate to overcome those encrusted interests.

Whether desirable when viewed with a larger lens or not, it seems inevitable that we will have more mass toxic substances litigation in the future. Perhaps not the number of victims involved in asbestos, or the malevolence of some in the A.H. Robins Company, but future congregations of cases implicating a toxic substance seem inevitable. The plaintiffs' bar has transformed itself over the past quarter century; many law firms are organized and capitalized to deal with the demands of large-scale tort litigation. A number of lawyers have developed the entrepreneurial and technical expertise to pursue these suits. Galloping strides in the chemical, biotechnological, pharmaceutical, and other scientific are-nas seem likely to accommodate those poised to embark on the next mass toxic substance case.

What might the Bendectin experience contribute by way of improv-ing our handling of those future cases? Before addressing several sug-gestions that might make a marginal improvement, the question of a regulatory compliance defense, at least in those areas, such as the pharmaceutical industry, in which a strong regulatory presence exists, deserves consideration. The FDA, after all, possesses expertise that sur-passes what a private lawsuit can muster—for the scientific questions like causation—and a nonadversarial context in which to resolve the compli-cated scientific questions that are posed. Why pay the price for a brief ride in the tort system, one that is quite expensive and which we aren't sure is backwards or forward?

There are a number of variations of a regulatory standards defense that might be crafted. The first would simply exempt any drug approved by the FDA from tort liability.[52] The effect would be quite similar to em-ploying federal preemption, as for example exists for cigarette advertis-ing.[53] At least in this regard, the best answer for rejecting this alternative is the contribution of the tort system to encouraging compliance with FDA regulatory requirements. While the FDA is quite protective of con-sumer safety, it is, as detailed in chapter 4, quite dependent on industry members for information and cooperation in compliance with a variety of regulatory requirements. The FDA does not have the resources to monitor and ensure universal compliance of a large, technologically complex, and informationally massive industry. (The budget for the en-tire human drug division of the FDA totaled an estimated $233 million in 1994.[54]) Nor can it bring suit for every violation of which it may become aware. Much informal negotiating between the FDA and phar-maceutical companies exists, especially when the situation falls in a regu-latory gray area. Given the generality of many regulatory requirements (e.g., "efficacy" and "safety") and the vagaries of cost-benefit analyses, those instances are not uncommon. There is reason—reinforced by the opinion of FDA administrators—to believe that the threat of tort liability assists considerably in effective enforcement of the nation's drug laws by the FDA, both by encouraging voluntary compliance and in providing additional leverage for the FDA in informal negotiations.

Tort law's role in effectuating regulation would seem most significant in encouraging drug manufacturers to provide accurate and thorough information to the FDA in NDAs, in the reporting of adverse drug reac-tions after the drug is marketed, and in assuring accurate and timely updating of the drug's labeling in light of the experience with the drug after marketing. While the FDA can perform a thorough review of an

NDA (assuming that it is provided with reliable information), there is no scheduled review of drugs after marketing, and the manufacturer plays a critical role in the identification of those adverse effects that inevitably are not identified in pre-marketing tests.

Another alternative might be a regulatory compliance defense, only available to a manufacturer for drugs that were not only approved by the FDA, but for which the manufacturer had complied with all aspects of FDA standards, including the NDA process, reporting adverse drug reactions, and similar requirements. Rand's study of the impact of liability on the pharmaceutical industry observed that a regulatory compliance defense, in which companies that meet FDA standards would be shielded from liability, while any companies that violate the standards would be held liable for any harm caused by the violation, would promote economic efficiency. Others concur.[55] Such a reform has the attractiveness of placing responsibility for risk assessment and management in the hands of experts who can make considered decisions based on the scientific evidence available.

Adopting FDA standards as conclusive tort standards would be unlikely to provide the simplicity that might be expected. FDA regulation of the pharmaceutical industry is quite extensive, from the Investigational New Drug application, through standards for conducting the IND testing, drug marketing, through to post-marketing monitoring and reporting of adverse drug reports. A compliance-with-FDA-standards defense would likely shift the focus of drug litigation to those standards and the manufacturer's role in meeting them, rather than avoid litigation. Longer and more uncertain causal chains would be litigated, as questions arise about whether a violation of an FDA standard would have made any difference in the chain of events that led to the plaintiff's injury. Thus in Bendectin litigation the question whether the Staples study was provided in timely fashion to the FDA, the legitimacy of the reclassifications of the animal abnormalities, and what effect earlier or more complete explanations of the data generated by the study would have had on Bendectin's approval would still have to be litigated with a regulatory compliance defense. In short, a regulatory compliance defense is unlikely to short-circuit a substantial amount of pharmaceutical litigation, and in some instances may make it yet more expensive by adding another layer of inquiry.

If the greater technical expertise of the FDA is not used to truncate tort litigation, what alternative mechanisms might be employed? From the Bendectin perspective, two proposals might assist juries to better assess the science that exists and employ it to make a more accurate determination. First, polyfurcation provided a means to try the pure general causation issue separately. This procedure enabled the jury to attend

without distraction to the question of whether Bendectin has any teratogenic potential. Merrell's derelictions were irrelevant and thus could neither prejudice the jury nor permit it to shore up the weakness of the
evidence on causation with the stronger evidence of culpability. Polyfurcation may even provide the opportunity to keep a particularly sympathetic and badly injured plaintiff from the jury while it addresses whether
the agent is capable of causing the disease or harm in question. The vast
majority of federal and state judges polled about separate-issue trials expressed the view that it contributed to the fairness of the outcome.[56] Nevertheless, separating general causation for trial only seems realistic when
a large number of cases have been consolidated or in a class action proceeding, but it certainly contains promise for those situations. Even in
individual cases, the entire causal question could be tried separately, especially if there are concerns about other aspects of the case affecting
the jury's consideration of the causation issue. In addition to the enhanced accuracy this procedural measure would provide, there is evidence to suggest that it would also reduce the costs of resolving these
cases.

The second reform that appears quite attractive after the Bendectin
litigation is examined is to encourage greater consideration and use of
court appointed experts.[57] The experts need not testify about the ultimate issue of causation; indeed, they might be more valuable in educat-
ing the jury on the science, the issues in dispute, the assumptions and
inferences drawn by the contending experts, and the reasonableness of
those assumptions. Proposals to employ court appointed experts are not
new, and historically have faced considerable resistance from portions of
the judiciary and the bar. However, the increasing need to deal with complex scientific and technological matters in courts, the mandate of *Daubert* that federal judges examine the methodology of scientific experts'
testimony, and the experience with Bendectin all suggest that there is
increased motivation as well as reason to further explore this method to
assist the jury. It is not, as mentioned in chapter 17, without serious obstacles, but making a serious attempt at identifying and overcoming
those obstacles may well be worth the effort.

In the end, it was the judiciary that got Bendectin right. The path was
not smooth, there were some embarrassing way stations, succor was provided by the FDA's treatment of Bendectin, and the journey was far too
costly. Providing the courts with the tools to continue to backstop those
juries that go awry should be a high priority. The Federal Judicial Center
has recently completed an impressive science manual that is designed to
provide some of the basics of a variety of scientific fields, including epidemiology and toxicology, to the judiciary.[58] Enhancing judges' understanding of science, the questions science is capable of answering (albeit

with some risk of error) and the questions it is not capable of answering, and the assumptions, inferences, and conventions that influence scientific work but often result in the conflicts and disagreements that show up in court, can only improve the judiciary's ability to correct the inevitable mistakes that juries will occasionally make.

Beyond the question of improving the accuracy of the system, the experience with Bendectin litigation supports the resistance of the courts to move to a regime that many commentators have advocated. Instead of making the question of causation a dichotomous decision, some have proposed that juries be instructed to discount the award based on the likelihood that the agent caused the plaintiff's disease. Especially with weak effects, the argument goes, defendants whose agents do not double the background risk will not pay for any of the damage that they caused.[59] The difficulty with these proposals is that they fail to recognize the reality of epidemiological and toxicological evidence. Those instruments, because of methodological biases, confounding, and sampling error, are simply not able to detect small effects. The Bendectin epidemiology landscape is littered with studies finding relative risks such as 1.05, 1.40, or 1.17. To assume that those associations reflect a causal association and should be the basis for the law to award proportionate damages is not much different from using a yardstick to measure the diameter of an atom. It should also be pointed out that the Bendectin record is littered with relative risks of .85 and .95, yet no informed observer would think those studies justify believing that Bendectin has a protective effect. And there is no opportunity for a manufacturer to make a claim for a protective effect, comparable to the claim by a plaintiff based on very small relative risks. Relying on a threshold (it need not be 2.0 in all cases)[60] avoids using what are almost surely spurious results to generate litigation.

While the Bendectin litigation is not the tort system's finest hour, the many who have used it as a whipping post have overstated the criticisms and overgeneralized to make it an exemplar of what exists in the tort system today. Bendectin litigation is not in the middle of the bell curve; indeed it is really quite far under the tail. It is not surprising that certain factions in the current debate over the tort system would find it useful to employ. That is not a reason to ignore that which it can tell us, but we should be cautious about interpreting all the claims. Some of what the Bendectin experience does teach has already begun its inevitable impact on the law. The *Daubert* decision, while quite moderate, nevertheless unmistakably identifies a role for the court in attempting to minimize error due to science and those experts who testify about it who are unreliable. Momentum is building for assisting juries confronted with complicated scientific evidence; completing that task is a long-term project, but it has begun. We should not forget that Bendectin and the other toxic substances litigation are newcomers to the legal landscape.

As might be expected, there are even indications that some may have overreacted, imposing requirements that overshoot the accuracy and justice mark for which the law aims. In the end, overreacting to the Bendectin litigation may be a greater danger than ignoring its lessons.

Notes

1. *See, e.g.*, Dennis P. Hays, *Bendectin: A Case of Mourning Sickness*, 17 DRUG INTELLIGENCE PHARMACY 826 (1983); Raymond G. Mullady, Jr., *Considerations in the Management and Defence of Pharmaceutical Litigation in the United States, in* PRODUCT LIABILITY, INSURANCE AND THE PHARMACEUTICAL INDUSTRY: AN ANGLO-AMERICAN COMPARISON 123–24 (Geraint G. Howells, ed., New York: Manchester University Press, 1991); PETER W. HUBER, GALILEO'S REVENGE: JUNK SCIENCE IN THE COURTROOM 111–29 (New York: Basic Books, 1991).

The most prominent of the critics is Peter Huber, who devotes a chapter in *Galileo's Revenge* to Bendectin. Huber's writings are so filled with errors, inaccuracies, and distortions that it is difficult to take him seriously. For example, in the first paragraph of his chapter critiquing the experts and science employed by plaintiffs in Bendectin, he states that it was an "over-the-counter" drug. It wasn't. In the next paragraph he equates hyperemesis gravidarum (the name of which he gets wrong) with morning sickness—also incorrect, as hyperemesis affects a very tiny subset of those with morning sickness. He suggests that Bendectin was approved as a therapy for hyperemesis by the FDA, but that is at best misleading. Bendectin was approved for nausea and vomiting of pregnancy; as explained later in this chapter, there is no scientific evidence of its efficacy in treating hyperemesis. And in his third paragraph, Huber is wrong about the name of the company that first marketed Bendectin. The remainder of Huber's chapter on Bendectin is filled with similar misstatements, exaggerations, and disinformation.

Huber has created something of a cottage industry of critics. Those critics have detailed the sloppiness, exaggerations, undocumented claims, polemical style, and poor methodology employed by Huber. Many have been unable to resist the temptation to turn Huber's allegations of junkiness on his work. *See* Joseph A. Page, *Deforming Tort Reform*, 78 GEO. L.J. 649 (1990); Jeff L. Lewin, *Calabresi's Revenge? Junk Science in the Work of Peter Huber*, 21 HOFSTRA L. REV. 183 (1992); Ken Chesebro, *Galileo's Retort: Peter Huber's Junk Scholarship*, 42 AM. U. L. REV. 1637 (1993); Mark M. Hager, *Civil Compensation and Its Discontents: A Response to Huber*, 42 STAN. L. REV. 539 (1990); Mark Galanter, *Pick a Number, Any Number*, AM. LAW., Apr. 1992, at 82.

2. A list and bibliography of the epidemiological and toxicological studies on Bendectin through 1991 can be found in Joseph Sanders, *The Bendectin Litigation: A Case Study in the Life Cycle of Mass Torts*, 43 HAST. L.J. 301, 394–95, 403–06 (1992). A subsequent meta-analysis of Bendectin's teratogenicity identifies a few other unpublished studies. Paul M. McKeigue et al., *Bendectin and Birth Defects: I. A Meta-Analysis of the Epidemiologic Studies* 50 TERATOLOGY 27 (1994). *See also* Jon T. Powell, Comment, *How to* Tell the Truth *With Statistics: A New Statistical Approach to Analyzing the Bendectin Epidemiological Data in the Aftermath of* Daubert v.

Merrell Dow Pharmaceuticals, Inc., 31 Hous. L. Rev 1241 (1994) (meta-analysis of Bendectin limb reduction studies).

3. *See* McKeigue, *supra* note 2, at Tables 1 & 2.

4. *See* Louis Lasagna & Sheila R. Shulman, *Bendectin and the Language of Causation, in* Phantom Risk: Scientific Inference and the Law 101, 109 (Kenneth R. Foster et al. eds., Cambridge, MA: MIT Press, 1993) ("The possibility that [Bendectin] might cause undetectably small increases in the rate of birth defects cannot be ruled out by scientific data."); *see also* Joseph Sanders, *From Science to Evidence: The Testimony on Causation in the Bendectin Cases,* 46 Stan. L. Rev. 1, 9, 18–27 (1993).

5. *See The Cause And Defect of Orange Mail,* N.Y. Times, March 24, 1985, §4, p. 22; C.I. Barash & Louis Lasagna, *The Bendectin Saga: "Voluntary" Discontinuation,* 1 J. Clin. Res. & Drug Develop. 277, 289 (1987); Howard Denemark, *Improving Litigation Against Drug Manufacturers for Failure to Warn Against Possible Side Effects: Keeping Dubious Lawsuits from Driving Good Drugs Off the Market,* 40 Case W. Res. L. Rev. 413, 427–28 (1989–90); Walter Olson, The Litigation Explosion 164 (New York: Dutton, 1991); *see generally* Stephen Daniels, *The Question of Jury Competence and the Politics of Civil Justice Reform: Symbols, Rhetoric, and Agenda-Building,* 52 Law & Contemp. Probs., Autumn 1989, at 269, 280.

6. Three studies of pyridoxine's efficacy were published between 1942 and 1944. None mentioned any adverse reactions or indicated that toxicity testing had been performed. Four toxicological and one human clinical study of doxylamine were published in 1948. None of the studies examined reproductive effects. Four published human studies and one animal study of dicyclomine in the early 1950s do not reveal a single pregnant female on whom the drug was tested.

7. Huber, *supra* note 1, at 113.

8. *See* chapter 10.

9. Denemark, *supra* note 5, at 414; *see also* W. Kip Viscusi et al., *Deterring Inefficient Pharmaceutical Litigation: An Economic Rationale for the FDA Regulatory Compliance Defense,* 24 Seton Hall L. Rev. 1437, 1473–74 & n.133 (1994) (FDA and scientific community have judged Bendectin "safe to the unborn child"); Note, *A Question of Competence: The Judicial Role in Regulation of Pharmaceuticals* 103 Harv. L. Rev. 773, 774 (1990) ("studies have consistently concluded that [Bendectin] is safe").

10. The Recorder, Jan. 1988, at 4 (quoting an Orrefice speech).

11. General Practitioner Research Group, *General Practitioner Clinical Trials: Drugs in Pregnancy Survey,* 191 Practitioner 775 (1963).

12. *See, e.g.,* Letter from R.W. Smithells, consultant to Merrell, to Dr. Mark Hoekenga, Vice-President, Research, Medical and Regulation Affairs, Merrell (Aug. 29, 1973) ("the results [of the Bunde-Bowles Study] raise a number of problems").

13. *See* Peter Huber, *Junk Science in the Courtroom,* Forbes, July, 1991, at 68, 70 (criticizing a study that tentatively suggested a causal relationship between spermicides and birth defects and that was relied on in the notorious *Wells v. Ortho Pharmaceutical* case).

14. Even then, the labeling reported that both animal and epidemiological studies had found no association, although it concluded that as with all drugs taken during pregnancy "Bendectin should be used only when clearly needed."

15. Transcript of FDA Fertility and Maternal Health Drugs Advisory Committee Hearing at Vol. I, p. 151 (Sept. 15, 1980).

16. *See* Phantom Risk, *supra* note 4, at 1–7.

17. Transcript of FDA Fertility and Maternal Health Drugs Advisory Committee Hearing at Vol. I, p. 258 (Sept. 15, 1980).

18. OLLI P. HEINONEN ET AL., BIRTH DEFECTS AND DRUGS IN PREGNANCY (Littleton, MA: Publishing Sciences Group, 1977).

19. *See* Brenda Eskenazi & Michael B. Bracken, *Bendectin (Debendox) as a Risk Factor for Pyloric Stenosis,* 144 AM. J. OBSTET. GYNECOL. 919 (1982) ("The possible association between Bendectin . . . and an increased risk of congenital malformation . . . has received considerable attention in the scientific literature as well as the lay press"). Jean Golding, the author of another Bendectin study, explained that "If nothing had been happening over the drug [Bendectin], I doubt even whether I would have written it up." Transcript of FDA Fertility and Maternal Health Drugs Advisory Committee Hearing at Vol. I, p. 223 (Sept. 15, 1980).

20. *See* Louis Lasagna, *The Chilling Effect of Product Liability on New Drug Development, in* THE LIABILITY MAZE 340 (Peter W. Huber & Robert E. Litan eds., Washington, DC: Brookings Institution, 1991).

21. Sanders, *supra* note 2, at 347.

22. Sidney A. Shapiro, *Divorcing Profit Motivation from New Drug Research: A Consideration of Proposals to Provide the FDA with Reliable Test Data,* 1978 DUKE L.J. 155.

23. *See, e.g.,* Robert Rabin, *Tort System on Trial: The Burden of Mass Toxics Litigation,* 98 YALE L.J. 813, 820–21 (1989) (book review); David Rosenberg, *Class Actions for Mass Torts: Doing Individual Justice by Collective Means,* 62 IND. L.J. 561, 564 (1986); Stephen D. Sugarman, *Doing Away with Tort Law,* 73 CALIF. L. REV. 558 (1985).

For empirical studies of the amount of transaction costs the tort system exacts, *see* DEBORAH HENSLER ET AL., TRENDS IN TORT LITIGATION: THE STORY BEHIND THE STATISTICS 26 (Santa Monica, CA: Rand, 1987) (transaction costs in the range of 44 to 66 percent); JAMES S. KAKALIK & NICHOLAS M. PACE, COSTS AND COMPENSATION PAID IN TORT LITIGATION (Santa Monica, CA: Rand 1986); DEBORAH HENSLER ET AL., ASBESTOS IN THE COURTS: THE CHALLENGE OF MASS TOXIC TORTS (Santa Monica, CA: Rand, 1985).

24. Peter Huber has been the most vocal and widely-published of the "deterring technology" critics. *See, e.g.,* Peter W. Huber, *Safety and the Second Best: The Hazards of Public Risk Management in the Courts,* 85 COLUM. L. REV. 277 (1985); HUBER, *supra* note 1; *see also* Denemark, *supra* note 5; W. KIP VISCUSI, REFORMING PRODUCTS LIABILITY 66–67 (Cambridge, MA: Harvard University Press, 1991); OLSON, *supra* note 5, at 165–66.

25. *See* D. De Aloysio & P. Penacchioni, *Morning Sickness Control in Early Pregnancy by Neiguan Point Accupressure,* 80 OBSTET. & GYNECOL. 852 (1992); Vicken Sahakian et al., *Vitamin B6 is Effective Therapy for Nausea and Vomiting of Pregnancy: A Randomized Double-Blind Placebo Controlled Study,* 78 OBSTET. & GYNECOL. 33 (1991).

26. *See, e.g.,* Transcript of FDA Fertility and Maternal Health Drugs Advisory Committee Hearing at Vol. I, p. 151 (Sept. 15, 1980) (statement by Dr. Franz Rosa, Director of the Congenital Malformation Program, National Institute of Child Health and Human Development: "[I]t is a foolhardy professional who would advise a mother to take any drug in early pregnancy without serious consideration").

27. HERBERT TUCHMANN-DUPLESSIS, DRUG EFFECTS ON THE FETUS 249 (Sydney: ADIS, 1975).

28. *See* GERARD N. BURROW & THOMAS N. FERRIS, MEDICAL COMPLICATIONS DURING PREGNANCY (Philadelphia: Saunders, 1988) (listing 11 drugs prescribed

for morning sickness); Anne M. Leathem, *Safety and Efficacy of Antiemetics Used to Treat Nausea and Vomiting*, 5 CLIN. PHARM. 660 (1986) (indicating that a number of epidemiological studies of Meclizine were conducted that found no association with birth defects; as a result the FDA removed its restriction on the use of the drug by pregnant women).

29. In a controlled study, Meclizine provided good to fair relief of morning sickness in 98 percent of those who took it compared to 47 percent with a placebo, a substantially better showing than for Bendectin in the DESI study. P. L. C. Diggory & J. S. Tomkinson, *Nausea and Vomiting in Pregnancy*, 2 LANCET 370, 371 (1962). One uncontrolled study found that Meclizine provided excellent or good relief of morning sickness for 90 percent of women with morning sickness and 100 percent of 11 cases of hyperemesis. T. B. Lebherz & J. H. Harris, *Bonamine: An Effective New Therapy in Nausea and Vomiting of Pregnancy*, 6 OBSTET. & GYNECOL. 606 (1955). That corresponds with another uncontrolled study (of the same vintage) which found that Bendectin relieved morning sickness for 91 percent of women. G. Warnecke, *The Treatment of Vomiting in Pregnancy with Lenotan*, 17 MED. MSCHR. 691 (1963).

30. Leatham, *supra* note 28, at 666.

31. *See* Dwight P. Cruikshank, *Disease of the Alimentary Tract, in* OBSTETRICS & GYNECOLOGY (David N. Danforth et al. eds., Philadelphia: Lippincott, 5th ed. 1986) (explaining the components of Bendectin and their availability over the counter).

32. One prominent California obstetrician estimates that 25–33 percent of obstetricians recommend a Bendectin cocktail for patients suffering from severe morning sickness. Mike McKee, *Thumbing Their Noses at the Plaintiffs Bar*, THE RECORDER, Apr. 26, 1993, at 1.

33. Andrew Skolnick, *Key Witness Against Morning Sickness Drug Faces Scientific Fraud Charges*, 263 JAMA 1468, 1468 (1990).

34. *See* Brief of the Pharmaceutical Manufacturers Association as Amicus Curiae, Daubert v. Merrell Dow Pharmaceuticals, Inc., No. 92–102 (U.S. 1993); HUBER, *supra* note 1, at 129 ("Excessive vomiting starves the pregnant mother's body of normal nourishment, and the body begins to metabolize its own carbohydrates, fats, and proteins to nourish the unborn child. Toxic chemical by-products of this self-digestion are known to cause birth defects"); *see also* David A. Williams, *How Nader Campaign Killed a Beneficial Drug*, HUM. EVENTS, Jan. 14, 1984, at 10 ("In essence, it is entirely possible and even probable that denial of Bendectin will lead to more infant deformities, not less"); Christopher Downey, *Courts Should Conduct Pre-Trial Qualification Hearings for Expert Witnesses in Products Liability Cases*, 16 J. PRODS. & TOXICS LIAB. 45, 46 (1994) ("With no effective drug on the market to combat chronic morning sickness, many pregnant women will suffer from malnutrition, depriving their fetuses of food and causing birth defects as a result."); Denmark, *supra* note 5, at 426 (explaining that severe morning sickness can require a choice between therapeutic abortion and maternal death, then observing that Bendectin can make pregnancy "safer").

35. Ronald M. Weigel & M. Margaret Weigel, *Nausea and Vomiting of Early Pregnancy and Pregnancy Outcome: An Epidemiological Study*, 96 BRIT. J. OBSTET. & GYNECOL. 1304 (1989); Ronald M. Weigel & M. Margaret Weigel, *Nausea and Vomiting of Early Pregnancy and Pregnancy Outcome: A Meta-analytical Review*, 96 BRIT. J. OBSTET. & GYNECOL. 1312 (1989); Mark A. Klebanoff & James L. Mills, *Is Vomiting During Pregnancy Teratogenic?*, 292 BRIT. MED. J. 724 (1986) (vomiting not associated significantly with any specific malformation).

One case-control study found an increased risk of limb reduction defects associated with morning sickness (OR = 2.3), although it has not been replicated in other studies. Anne Kricker et al., *Congenital Limb Deficiencies: Maternal Factors in Pregnancy*, 26 AUST. N.Z. J. OBSTET. & GYNECOL. 272 (1986).

For the explication of a theory that morning sickness is a trait developed during the evolutionary process to protect the sensitive fetus from toxins, especially food toxins that might harm it, see Margie Profet, *Pregnancy Sickness as Adaptation: A Deterrent to Maternal Ingestion of Teratogens, in* THE ADAPTED MIND (Jerome H. Barkow et al. eds., New York: Oxford University Press, 1992).

36. Mark A. Klebanoff et al., *Epidemiology of Vomiting in Early Pregnancy*, 66 OB-STET. & GYNECOL. 612, 615 (1985).

37. Transcript of FDA Fertility and Maternal Health Drugs Advisory Committee Hearing at Vol. I, p. 139 (Sept. 15, 1980) (statement of Franz Rosa).

A few studies that examined severe malnutrition in the Netherlands during blockades imposed during World War II identified a relationship between folic acid deficiencies and neural tube defects. *See* Robert L. Brent, *Maternal Nutrition and Congenital Malformations*, 21 BIRTH DEFECTS: ORIGINAL ARTICLE SERIES 1 (1985); Martha M. Werler et al., *Periconceptional Folic Acid Exposure and Risk of Occurrent Neural Tube Defects*, 269 JAMA 1257 (1993). Generally studies of women with hyperemesis indicate that they are much like women with morning sickness in terms of adverse birth outcomes. *See* Klebanoff et al., *supra* note 36, at 613; Robert H. Depue et al., *Hyperemesis Gravidarum in Relation to Estradiol Levels, Pregnancy Outcome, and Other Maternal Factors: A Seroepidemiologic Study*, 156 AM. J. OB-STET. GYNECOL. 1137, 1139 (1987); *cf.* Raleigh K. Godsey & Roger B. Newman, *Hyperemesis Gravidarum: A Comparison of Single and Multiple Admissions*, 36 J. RE-PROD. MED. 287 (1991) (finding no change in incidence of birth defects based on severity of hyperemesis). Data from the Centers for Disease Control show that the overall incidence of central nervous system defects declined from 1979–80, the apex of Bendectin use, to 1986–87, when Bendectin use was zero, thus suggesting that Bendectin and its prevention of severe malnutrition played little role in preventing central nervous system birth defects. CENTERS FOR DISEASE CON-TROL, MORBIDITY & MORTALITY WEEKLY REPORT 22 (Dec. 1990).

38. STEVEN GARBER, PRODUCT LIABILITY AND THE ECONOMICS OF PHARMA-CEUTICAL AND MEDICAL DEVICES 2 (Santa Monica, CA: Rand, 1993).

39. *Id.* at 95–97.

40. *Id.* at 103–04.

41. Judith P. Swazey, *Prescription Drug Safety and Product Liability, in* THE LIABIL-ITY MAZE 291 (Peter W. Huber & Robert E. Litan eds., Washington, DC: Brook-ings Institution, 1991).

42. GARBER, *supra* note 38, at 60, 72–73, 91.

43. *Id.* at 103; Swazey, *supra* note 41, at 327–28.

44. GARBER, *supra* note 38, at 166, 174.

45. *See* FRANK SLOAN ET AL., SUING FOR MEDICAL MALPRACTICE 6–7, 32 (Chicago: University of Chicago Press, 1993); 1 INSTITUTE OF MEDICINE, MEDICAL PROFESSIONAL LIABILITY AND THE DELIVERY OF OBSTETRICAL CARE 2 (Washington, DC: National Academy Press, 1989) (malpractice claims frequency against obstetricians two to three times the average for all physicians); Roger Bulger & Victoria P. Rostow, *Medical Professional Liability and the Delivery of Obstetrical Care*, 6 J. CONTEMP. HEALTH LAW & POL. 81, 82–84 (1990) (citing study that found that obstetricians are subject to a greater number and higher severity of malpractice claims than other specialists).

46. *See* GARBER, *supra* note 38, at 166, 174; Elyse Tenouye, *Suits Involving De-*

funct Bendectin Chill Development of Pregnancy Medications, WALL ST. J., June 22, 1993, at B1 (attributing unwillingness of pharmaceutical companies to develop new drugs for use during pregnancy to Bendectin litigation).

47. On juries being swayed by the severity of injury, *see* AUDREY CHIN & MOLLY PETERSON, DEEP POCKETS, EMPTY POCKETS: WHO WINS IN COOK COUNTY JURY TRIALS 42, 45, Tables 4.4, 4.5 & Figure 4.1 (Santa Monica, CA: Rand, 1985); JOHN GUINTHER, THE JURY IN AMERICA 89 (New York: Facts on File Publications, 1988). On jurors evaluating the responsibility of plaintiffs, *see* Valerie P. Hans, *The Jury's Response to Business and Corporate Wrongdoing,* 52 LAW & CONTEMP. PROBS., Autumn 1989, at 177, 199–200; Valerie P. Hans & William S. Lofquist, *Jurors' Judgments of Business Liability in Tort Cases: Implications for the Litigation Explosion,* 26 LAW & SOC'Y REV. 85 (1992); Neil Vidmar, *Empirical Evidence on the Deep Pockets Hypothesis: Jury Awards for Pain and Suffering in Medical Malpractice Cases,* 43 DUKE L.J. 217, 250–51 (1993). On juror sympathy for children, albeit in the criminal context, *see* Martha A. Myers, *Rule Departures and Making Law: Juries and Their Verdicts,* 13 LAW & SOC'Y REV. 781 (1979).

48. *See* GARBER, *supra* note 38, at 147 (suggesting that drugs for conditions peculiar to pregnancy is the one area where innovation might be "stifled" because of liability concerns, regardless of the potential for profits).

49. *See, e.g.,* Haines v. Liggett Group, Inc., 140 F.R.D. 124 (D.N.J.), *vacated,* 975 F.2d 81 (3d Cir. 1992).

50. Kenneth Abraham, *Individual Action and Collective Responsibility: The Dilemma of Mass Tort Responsibility,* 73 VA. L. REV. 845, 883–907 (1987).

51. For a discussion of legislation to adopt a compensation system for asbestos, see Louis Treiger, *Relief for Asbestos Victims: A Legislative Analysis,* 20 HARV. J. LEGIS. 179 (1983).

52. A variation on this defense was part of the federal products liability bill that was defeated in 1994. The Product Liability Fairness Act (S-687) barred punitive damages from being awarded for any drugs that had received pre-market approval from the FDA. *See U.S. Senate Kills Consumer Product Liability Bill,* Pharm. Litig. Rep. (Andrews) 9679 (Sept. 1994).

53. *See* Cipollone v. Liggett Group, Inc., 112 S. Ct. 2608 (1992).

54. *Hearings on Appropriations for 1994 Before the Subcomm. on Agriculture, Rural Development, Food and Drug Administration, and Related Agencies of the House Comm. on Appropriations,* 103rd Cong., 1st Sess. 204 (1994).

55. *See, e.g.,* W. Kip Viscusi, *Product Liability and Regulation: Establishing the Appropriate Institutional Division of Labor,* 78 AM. ECON. REV. 300 (1988).

56. *Judges' Opinions on Procedural Issues: A Survey of State and Federal Trial Judges Who Spend at Least Half Their Time on General Civil Cases,* 69 B.U. L. REV. 731, 733–34 (1989).

57. *See generally* Joe S. Cecil & Thomas E. Willging, *Court-Appointed Experts, in* FEDERAL JUDICIAL CENTER, REFERENCE MANUAL ON SCIENTIFIC EVIDENCE 525 (Washington, DC: Federal Judicial Center, 1994).

58. FEDERAL JUDICIAL CENTER, *supra* note 57.

59. *See, e.g.,* David Rosenberg, *The Causal Connection in Mass Exposure Cases: A "Public Law" Vision of the Tort System,* 97 HARV. L. REV. 849 (1984); II AMERICAN LAW INSTITUTE REPORTERS' STUDY, ENTERPRISE LIABILITY FOR PERSONAL INJURY 369 (Philadelphia: American Law Institute, 1991).

60. The quality, quantity, and consistency of the epidemiological record, along with how much is known about other causes of the disease (which might thereby be ruled out for a given plaintiff) would all affect this determination.

Selected Bibliography

Kenneth S. Abraham, *Individual Action and Collective Responsibility: The Dilemma of Mass Tort Reform*, 73 VA. L. REV. 845 (1987).

AMERICAN BAR ASSOCIATION/BROOKINGS INSTITUTION, CHARTING A FUTURE FOR THE CIVIL JURY SYSTEM (Washington, DC: Brookings Institution, 1992).

AMERICAN LAW INSTITUTE REPORTERS' STUDY, ENTERPRISE RESPONSIBILITY FOR PERSONAL INJURY (Philadelphia: American Law Institute, 1991).

ROBERTA J. APFEL & SUSAN M. FISHER, TO DO NO HARM: DES AND THE DILEMMAS OF MODERN MEDICINE (New Haven, CT: Yale University Press, 1984).

Barbara Atwood, *The Choice-of-Law Dilemma in Mass Tort Litigation: Kicking Around Erie, Klaxon, and Van Dusen*, 19 CONN. L. REV. 9 (1986).

RONALD J. BACIGAL, THE LIMITS OF LITIGATION: THE DALKON SHIELD CONTROVERSY (Durham, NC: Carolina Academic Press, 1990).

Linda A. Bailey et al., *Reference Guide on Epidemiology, in* FEDERAL JUDICIAL CENTER, REFERENCE MANUAL ON SCIENTIFIC EVIDENCE (Washington, DC: Federal Judicial Center, 1994).

DAVID W. BARNES, STATISTICS AS PROOF: FUNDAMENTALS OF QUANTITATIVE EVIDENCE (Boston: Little, Brown, 1983).

Joan E. Bertin & Mary S. Henifin, *Science, Law and the Search for Truth in the Courtroom: Lessons from Daubert v. Merrell Dow*, 22 J.L. MED. & ETHICS 6 (Spring 1994).

Bert Black & David E. Lilienfeld, *Epidemiological Proof in Toxic Tort Litigation*, 52 FORDHAM L. REV. 732 (1984).

Robert G. Bone, *Statistical Adjudication: Rights, Justice, and Utility in a World of Process Scarcity*, 46 VAND. L. REV. 561 (1993).

Troyen A. Brennan, *Causal Chains and Statistical Links: The Role of Scientific Uncertainty in Hazardous Substance Litigation*, 73 CORNELL L. REV. 469 (1988).

STEPHEN G. BREYER, REGULATION AND ITS REFORM (Cambridge, MA: Harvard University Press, 1982).

PAUL BRODEUR, OUTRAGEOUS MISCONDUCT: THE ASBESTOS INDUSTRY ON TRIAL (New York: Pantheon Books, 1985).

R. Brodie, *Idiosyncrasy and Intolerance, in* DRUG RESPONSES IN MAN, CIBA Foundation Symposium (Gordon E.W. Wolstenholme & Ruth Porter eds., London: Churchill, 1967).

Nigel Brown & Sergio Fabro, *The In Vitro Approach to Teratogenicity Testing, in* DEVELOPMENTAL TOXICOLOGY (Keith Snell ed., New York: Praeger, 1982).

Edward Brunet, *The Triumph of Efficiency and Discretion over Competing Complex Litigation Policies*, 10 REV. LITIG. 273 (1991).

EDWARD J. CALABRESE, PRINCIPLES OF ANIMAL EXTRAPOLATION (New York: Wiley, 1983).

Gary P. Carlson, *Factors Modifying Toxicity, in* TOXIC SUBSTANCES AND HUMAN RISK: PRINCIPLES OF DATA INTERPRETATION (Robert G. Tardiff & Joseph V. Rodricks eds., New York: Plenum Press, 1987).

DAN CASSIDY, LIABILITY EXPOSURES (London: Witherby, 1989).

Ruth Clayton & Ahment Zamir, *The Use of Cell Culture Methods for Exploring Teratogenic Susceptibility, in* DEVELOPMENTAL TOXICOLOGY (Keith Snell ed., New York: Praeger, 1982).

John C. Coffee Jr., *Rethinking the Class Action: A Policy Primer on Reform*, 62 IND. L.J. 625 (1987).

John C. Coffee, Jr., *Understanding the Plaintiff's Attorney: The Implications of Economic Theory for Private Enforcement of Law Through Class and Derivative Actions*, 86 COLUM. L. REV. 669 (1986).

FRANK B. CROSS, ENVIRONMENTALLY INDUCED CANCER AND THE LAW: RISKS, REGULATION, AND VICTIM COMPENSATION (New York: Quorum Books, 1989).

FRED DAVIS, PASSAGE THROUGH CRISIS: POLIO VICTIMS AND THEIR FAMILIES (Indianapolis: Bobbs Merrill, 1963).

MARY DOUGLAS & AARON WILDAVSKY, RISK AND CULTURE: AN ESSAY ON THE SELECTION OF TECHNICAL AND ENVIRONMENTAL DANGERS (Berkeley: Univeristy of California Press, 1982).

HARRY F. DOWLING, MEDICINES FOR MAN: THE DEVELOPMENT, REGULATION, AND USE OF PRESCRIPTION DRUGS (New York: Knopf, 1970).

Barry M. Epstein & Marc S. Klein, *The Use and Abuse of Expert Testimony in Products Liability Actions*, 17 SETON HALL L. REV. 656 (1987).

FDA, NEW DRUG DEVELOPMENT IN THE UNITED STATES (1990).

RALPH A. FINE, THE GREAT DRUG DECEPTION: THE SHOCKING STORY OF MER/29 AND THE FOLKS WHO GAVE YOU THALIDOMIDE (New York: Stein and Day, 1972).

O.P. Flint, *An In Vitro Test for Teratogens Using Cultures of Rat Embryo Cells, in* IN VITRO METHODS IN TOXICOLOGY (C.R. Atterwill & C.E. Steele eds., New York: Cambridge University Press, 1987).

DAVID FREEDMAN ET AL., STATISTICS (New York: Norton, 2d ed. 1991).

LAWRENCE M. FRIEDMAN, A HISTORY OF AMERICAN LAW (New York: Simon & Shuster, 2d ed. 1985).

Marc Galanter, *The Day After the Litigation Explosion*, 46 MD. L. REV. 3 (1986).

GENERAL ACCOUNTING OFFICE, BRIEFING REPORT TO THE CHAIRMAN, SUBCOMMITTEE ON COMMERCE, CONSUMER PROTECTION AND COMPETITIVENESS, COMMITTEE ON ENERGY AND COMMERCE, HOUSE OF REPRESENTATIVES: PRODUCTS LIABILITY, EXTENT OF "LITIGATION EXPLOSION" IN FEDERAL COURTS QUESTIONED (1988).

STEVEN GARBER, PRODUCT LIABILITY AND THE ECONOMICS OF PHARMACEUTICAL AND MEDICAL DEVICES (Santa Monica, CA: Rand, 1993).

RICHARD H. GASKINS, ENVIRONMENTAL ACCIDENTS: PERSONAL INJURY AND PUBLIC RESPONSIBILITY (Philadelphia: Temple University Press, 1989).

JOSEPH GASTWIRTH, STATISTICAL REASONING IN LAW AND PUBLIC POLICY (Boston: Academic Press, 1988).

JERRY T. GIBSON, MEDICATION, LAW AND BEHAVIOR (New York: Wiley, 1976).

HENRY G. GRABOWSKI & JOHN M. VERNON, THE REGULATION OF PHARMACEUTICALS: BALANCING THE BENEFITS AND RISKS (Washington, DC: American Enterprise Institute, 1983).

Michael D. Green, *Expert Witnesses and Sufficiency of Evidence in Toxic Substances Litigation: The Legacy of Agent Orange and Bendectin Litigation*, 86 Nw. U. L. Rev. 643 (1992).

Michael D. Green, *The Paradox of Statutes of Limitations in Toxic Substances Litigation*, 76 Calif. L. Rev. 965 (1988).

Michael D. Green, *The Inability of Offensive Collateral Estoppel to Fulfill Its Promise: An Examination of Estoppel in Asbestos Litigation*, 70 Iowa L. Rev. 141 (1984).

Samuel Gross & Kent Syverud, *Getting to No: A Study of Settlement Negotiations and the Selection of Cases for Trial*, 90 Mich. L. Rev. 319 (1991).

John Guinther, The Jury in America (New York: Facts on File, 1988).

Learned Hand, *Historical and Practical Considerations Regarding Expert Testimony*, 15 Harv. L. Rev. 40 (1901).

Valerie P. Hans & William S. Lofquist, *Jurors' Judgments of Business Liability in Tort Cases: Implications for the Litigation Explosion*, 26 Law & Soc'y Rev. 85 (1992).

Valerie Hans & Neil Vidmar, Judging the Jury (New York: Plenum Press, 1986).

Ronald W. Hansen, *The Pharmaceutical Development Process: Estimates of Development Costs and Times and the Effects of Proposed Regulatory Changes, in* Issues in Pharmaceutical Economics (R. Chien ed. Lexington, MA: Lexington Books, 1979).

Richard Harris, The Real Voice (New York: Macmillan, 1964).

Reid Hastie et al., Inside the Jury (Cambridge, MA: Harvard University Press, 1983).

Ollie Heinonen et al., Birth Defects and Drugs in Pregnancy (Littleton, MA: Publishing Sciences Group, 1977).

Deborah R. Hensler, *Resolving Mass Toxic Torts: Myths and Realities*, 1989 U. Ill. L. Rev. 89.

Deborah R. Hensler et al., Asbestos in the Courts: The Challenge of Mass Toxic Torts (Santa Monica, CA: Rand, 1985).

Ernest Hodgson, *Measurement of Toxicity, in* Modern Toxicology (Ernest Hodgson & Patricia Levi eds., New York: Elsevier, 1987).

Michael D. Hogan & David G. Hoel, *Extrapolation to Man, in* Principles and Methods of Toxicology (A. Wallace Hayes ed., New York: Raven Press, 1982).

Morton Horwitz, The Transformation of American Law, 1780–1860 (Cambridge, MA: Harvard University Press, 1977).

Peter W. Huber, Galileo's Revenge: Junk Science in the Courtroom (New York: Basic Books, 1991).

Peter W. Huber, *Junk Science and the Jury*, 1990 U. Chi. Legal F. 273.

Peter W. Huber, Liability: The Legal Revolution and Its Consequences (New York: Basic Books, 1988).

Peter W. Huber, *Safety and the Second Best: The Hazards of Public Risk Management in the Courts*, 85 Colum. L. Rev. 277 (1985).

The Liability Maze: The Impact of Liability Law on Safety and Innovation (Peter W. Huber & Robert E. Litan eds., Washington, DC: Brookings Institution, 1991).

Peter B. Hutt & Richard A. Merrill, Food and Drug Law: Cases and Materials (Westbury, NY: Foundation Press, 2d ed. 1991).

The Insight Team of the Sunday Times, Suffer the Children: The Story of Thalidomide (London: Andre Deutsch, 1979).

JOHN A. JENKINS, THE LITIGATORS: INSIDE THE POWERFUL WORLD OF AMERICA'S HIGH-STAKES TRIAL LAWYERS (New York: Doubleday, 1989).

Friedrich K. Juenger, *Mass Disasters and the Conflict of Laws*, 1989 U. ILL. L. REV. 105 (1989).

Harold A. Kahn & Christopher T. Sempos, STATISTICAL METHODS IN EPIDEMIOLOGY (New York: Oxford University Press, 1989).

JAMES S. KAKALIK ET AL., COSTS OF ASBESTOS LITIGATION (Santa Monica, CA: Rand, 1983).

HARRY KALVEN, JR. & HANS ZEISEL, THE AMERICAN JURY (Chicago: University of Chicago Press, 1971).

MICHAEL A. KAMRIN, TOXICOLOGY: A PRIMER ON TOXICOLOGY PRINCIPLES AND APPLICATION (Chelsea, MI: Lewis Publishers, 1988).

Joan B. Kessler, *The Social Psychology of Jury Deliberations, in* THE JURY SYSTEM IN AMERICA: A CRITICAL OVERVIEW (Rita J. Simon ed., Beverly Hills, CA: Sage Publications, 1975).

Milan Korcok, *The Bendectin Debate*, 123 CAN. MED. ASS'N J. 922 (1980).

Jack L. Landau & Hugh O'Riordan, *Of Mice and Men: The Admissibility of Animal Studies to Prove Causation in Toxic Torts*, 25 IDAHO L. REV. 521 (1988).

Louis Lasagna & Sheila Shulman, *Bendectin and the Language of Causation, in* PHANTOM RISK: SCIENTIFIC INFERENCE AND THE LAW (Kenneth R. Foster et al. eds., Cambridge, MA: MIT Press, 1993).

Louis Lasagna, *The Chilling Effect of Product Liability on New Drug Development, in* THE LIABILITY MAZE: THE IMPACT OF LIABILITY LAW ON SAFETY AND INNOVATOR (Peter W. Huber & Robert E. Litan eds., Washington, DC: Brookings Institution, 1991).

E. ALLAN LIND & TOM R. TYLER, THE SOCIAL PSYCHOLOGY OF PROCEDURAL JUSTICE (New York: Plenum Press, 1988).

E. ALLAN LIND ET AL., THE PERCEPTION OF JUSTICE: TORT LITIGANTS' VIEWS OF TRIAL, COURT-ANNEXED ARBITRATION AND JUDICIAL SETTLEMENT CONFERENCES (Santa Monica, CA: Rand, 1989).

ROBERT LITAN & WILLIAM D. NORDHAUS, REFORMING FEDERAL REGULATION (New Haven, CT: Yale University Press, 1983).

ROBERT J. MacCOUN, GETTING INSIDE THE BLACK BOX: TOWARD A BETTER UNDERSTANDING OF JUROR BEHAVIOR (Santa Monica, CA: Rand, 1987).

FREDERICK B. MacKINNON, CONTINGENT FEES FOR LEGAL SERVICES (Chicago: Aldine Publishing, 1964).

John Makdisi, *Proportional Liability: A Comprehensive Rule to Apportion Tort Damages Based on Probability*, 67 N.C. L. REV. 1063 (1970).

DAVID MASON, THALIDOMIDE: MY FIGHT (London: Allen & Unwin, 1978).

Frank M. McClellan et al., *Strict Liability for Prescription Drug Injuries: The Improper Marketing Theory*, 26 ST. LOUIS U. L.J. 1 (1981).

Francis McGovern, *Toward a Functional Approach for Managing Complex Litigation*, 53 U. CHI. L. REV. 440 (1986).

Arthur R. Miller & David Crump, *Jurisdiction and Choice of Law in Multistate Class Actions After* Phillips Petroleum Co. v. Shutts, 96 YALE L.J. 1 (1986).

MORTON MINTZ, AT ANY COST: CORPORATE GREED, WOMEN AND THE DALKON SHIELD (New York: Pantheon Books, 1985).

MORTON MINTZ, BY PRESCRIPTION ONLY: A REPORT ON THE ROLE OF THE UNITED STATES FOOD AND DRUG ADMINISTRATION, PHARMACEUTICAL MANUFACTURERS, AND OTHERS IN CONNECTION WITH THE IRRATIONAL AND MASSIVE USE OF PRESCRIPTION DRUGS THAT MAY BE WORTHLESS, INJURIOUS, OR EVEN LETHAL (Boston: Houghton Mifflin, 1967).

EDMOND A. MURPHY, THE LOGIC OF MEDICINE (Baltimore: Johns Hopkins University Press, 1976).

Martha A. Myers, *Rule Departures and Making Law: Juries and Their Verdicts*, 13 LAW & SOC'Y REV. 781 (1979).

NATIONAL RESEARCH COUNCIL, NATIONAL ACADEMY OF SCIENCES, RISK ASSESSMENT IN THE FEDERAL GOVERNMENT: MANAGING THE PROCESS (Washington, DC: National Academy Press, 1983).

RICHARD NEELY, THE PRODUCT LIABILITY MESS: HOW BUSINESS CAN BE RESCUED FROM THE POLITICS OF STATE COURTS (New York: Free Press, 1988).

HERBERT B. NEWBERG, NEWBERG ON CLASS ACTIONS (Colorado Springs, CO: Shepard's/McGraw Hill, 2d ed. 1985).

IAN C.T. NISBET & NATHAN J. KARCH, CHEMICAL HAZARDS TO HUMAN REPRODUCTION (Park Ridge, NJ: Noyes Data, 1983).

Note, *A Question of Competence: The Judicial Role in the Regulation of Pharmaceuticals*, 103 HARV. L. REV. 773 (1990).

Note, *Class Certification in Mass Accident Cases Under Rule 23(b)(1)*, 96 HARV. L. REV. 1143 (1983).

SAM PELTZMAN, REGULATION OF PHARMACEUTICAL INNOVATION: THE 1962 AMENDMENTS (Washington, DC: American Enterprise Institute, 1974).

SUSAN PERRY & JAMES L. DAWSON, NIGHTMARE: WOMEN AND THE DALKON SHIELD (New York: MacMillan, 1985).

MARK A. PETERSON, CIVIL JURIES IN THE 1980s (Santa Monica, CA: Rand, 1987).

MARK A. PETERSON, COMPENSATION OF INJURIES (Santa Monica, CA: Rand, 1984).

George L. Priest, *The Invention of Enterprise Liability: A Critical History of the Intellectual Foundations of Modern Tort Law*, 14 J. LEGAL STUD. 461 (1985).

George L. Priest & Benjamin Klein, *The Selection of Disputes for Settlement*, 13 J. LEG. STUD. 1 (1984).

William Prosser, *The Assault upon the Citadel (Strict Liability to the Consumer)*, 69 YALE L.J. 1099 (1960).

William Prosser, *The Fall of the Citadel (Strict Liability to the Consumer)*, 50 MINN. L. REV. 791 (1950).

Robert L. Rabin, *Some Thoughts on the Efficacy of a Mass Toxics Administrative Scheme*, 52 MD. L. REV. 951 (1993).

REFERENCE MANUAL ON SCIENTIFIC EVIDENCE (Washington, DC: Federal Judicial Center, 1994).

RESTATEMENT (THIRD) OF TORTS: PRODUCTS LIABILITY (Philadelphia: American Law Institute, Tentative Draft No. 2, 1995).

Paul D. Rheingold, *The MER/29 Story—An Instance of Successful Mass Disaster Litigation*, 56 CALIF. L. REV. 116 (1968).

Deborah L. Rhode, *Class Conflicts in Class Actions*, 34 STAN. L. REV. 1183 (1982).

Glen O. Robinson & Kenneth S. Abraham, *Collective Justice in Tort Law*, 78 VA. L. REV. 1481 (1992).

JOSEPH V. RODRICKS ET AL., ELEMENTS OF TOXICOLOGY AND CHEMICAL RISK ASSESSMENT (Washington, DC: Environ, 1986).

David Rosenberg, *Class Actions for Mass Torts: Doing Individual Justice by Collective Means*, 62 IND. L.J. 561 (1986).

David Rosenberg, *The Causal Connection in Mass Exposure Cases: A "Public Law" Vision of the Tort System*, 97 HARV. L. REV. 849 (1984).

DOUGLAS E. ROSENTHAL, LAWYER AND CLIENT, WHO'S IN CHARGE? (New York: Russell Sage Foundation, 1974).

ETHEL ROSKIES, ABNORMALITY AND NORMALITY: THE MOTHERING OF THALIDO-MIDE CHILDREN (Ithaca, NY: Cornell University Press, 1972).

KENNETH J. ROTHMAN, MODERN EPIDEMIOLOGY (Boston: Little, Brown, 1986).

Michael J. Saks & Peter D. Blanck, *Justice Improved: The Unrecognized Benefits of Aggregation and Sampling in the Trial of Mass Torts*, 44 STAN. L. REV. 815 (1992).

Joseph Sanders, *From Science to Evidence: The Testimony on Causation in the Bendectin Cases*, 46 STAN. L. REV. 1 (1993).

Joseph Sanders, *The Bendectin Litigation: A Case Study in the Life Cycle of Mass Torts*, 43 HASTINGS L.J. 301 (1992).

Joseph Sanders & Craig Joyce, *"Off to the Races": The 1980s Tort Crisis and the Law Reform Process*, 27 HOUS. L. REV. 207 (1990).

PETER H. SCHUCK, AGENT ORANGE ON TRIAL: MASS TOXIC DISASTERS IN THE COURTS (Cambridge, MA: Belknap Press of Harvard University Press, enlarged ed. 1987).

MOLLY SELVIN & LARRY PICUS, THE DEBATE OVER JURY PERFORMANCE: OBSER-VATIONS FROM A RECENT ASBESTOS CASE (Santa Monica, CA: Rand, 1987).

SIDNEY A. SHAPIRO, *Limiting Physician Freedom to Prescribe a Drug for any Purpose: The Need for FDA Regulation*, 73 NW. U. L. REV. 801 (1979).

MARSHALL S. SHAPO, A.B.A, SPECIAL COMMITTEE ON THE TORT LIABILITY SYS-TEM, TOWARDS A JURISPRUDENCE OF INJURY: THE CONTINUING CREATION OF A SYSTEM OF SUBSTANTIVE JUSTICE IN AMERICAN TORT LAW (Chicago: ABA, 1984).

Ellen Silbergeld, *The Role of Toxicology in Causation*, 1 COURTS, HEALTH SCI. & LAW 374 (1991).

MILTON M. SILVERMAN & PHILIP R. LEE, PILLS, PROFITS, AND POLITICS (Berkeley: University of California Press, 1974).

HENNING SJÖSTRÖM & ROBERT NILSSON, THALIDOMIDE AND THE POWER OF THE DRUG COMPANIES (Harmondsworth: Penguin, 1972).

Andrew Skolnick, *Key Witness Against Morning Sickness Drug Faces Scientific Fraud Charges*, 263 JAMA 1468 (1990).

RICHARD B. SOBOL, BENDING THE LAW: THE STORY OF THE DALKON SHIELD BANKRUPTCY (Chicago: University of Chicago Press, 1991).

HARVEY TEFF & COLIN MUNRO, THALIDOMIDE: THE LEGAL AFTERMATH (Farn-borough, England: Saxon House, 1976).

Randall S. Thomas & Robert G. Hansen, *Auctioning Class Action and Derivative Lawsuits: A Critical Analysis*, 87 NW. U. L. REV. 423 (1993).

SUSAN TOLCHIN & MARTIN TOLCHIN, DISMANTLING AMERICA: THE RUSH TO DEREGULATE (Boston: Houghton Mifflin, 1983).

William D. Torchiana, Comment, *Choice of Law and the Multistate Class: Forum Interests in Matters Distant*, 134 U. PA. L. REV. 913 (1986).

Roger H. Transgrud, *Mass Trials in Mass Tort Cases: A Dissent*, 1989 U. ILL. L. REV. 70.

Roger H. Transgrud, *Joinder Alternatives in Mass Tort Litigation*, 70 CORNELL L. REV. 779 (1986).

HERBERT TUCHMANN-DUPLESSIS, DRUG EFFECTS ON THE FETUS (Sydney: ADIS, 1975).

JOSEPH N. ULMAN, A JUDGE TAKES THE STAND (New York: Knopf, 1933).

Sanford J. Ungar, *Get Away With What You Can*, in IN THE NAME OF PROFIT 106 (R. Heilbroner et al. eds., Garden City, NY: Doubleday, 1972).

U.S. ATT'Y GEN.'S TORT POLICY WORKING GROUP, REPORT OF THE TORT POLICY WORKING GROUP ON THE CAUSES, EXTENT AND POLICY IMPLICATIONS OF THE CURRENT CRISIS IN INSURANCE AVAILABILITY AND AFFORDABILITY (1986).

Neil Vidmar, *Empirical Evidence on the Deep Pockets Hypothesis: Jury Awards for Pain and Suffering in Medical Malpractice Cases*, 43 DUKE L.J. 217 (1993).

W. Kip Viscusi, *The Dimensions of the Product Liability Crisis*, 20 J. LEGAL STUD. 147 (1991).

Christy A. Visher, *Jury Decision Making: The Importance of Evidence*, 11 LAW & HUM. BEHAV. 1 (1987).

WILLIAM W. WARDELL & LOUIS LASAGNA, REGULATION AND DRUG DEVELOPMENT (Washington, DC: American Enterprise Institute, 1975).

Josef Warkany, *History of Teratology, in* HANDBOOK OF TERATOLOGY (James Wilson & F. Clarke Fraser eds., New York: Plenum Press, 1977).

JOSEF WARKANY, CONGENITAL MALFORMATIONS, NOTES AND COMMENTS (Chicago: Yeat Book Medical, 1971).

Jack B. Weinstein, *Improving Expert Testimony*, 20 U. RICH. L. REV. 473 (1986).

JACK B. WEINSTEIN, INDIVIDUAL JUSTICE IN MASS TORT LITIGATION: THE EFFECT OF CLASS ACTIONS, CONSOLIDATIONS, AND OTHER MULTIPARTY DEVICES (Evanston, IL: Northwestern University Press, 1995).

Jack B. Weinstein, *The Role of the Court in Toxic Tort Litigation*, 73 GEO. L.J. 1389 (1985).

Jack B. Weinstein, *Routine Bifurcation of Jury Negligence Trials: An Example of the Questionable Use of Rule Making Power*, 14 VAND. L. REV. 831 (1961).

G. EDWARD WHITE, TORT LAW IN AMERICA: AN INTELLECTUAL HISTORY (New York: Oxford University Press, 1980).

THOMAS E. WILLGING, TRENDS IN ASBESTOS LITIGATION (Washington, DC: Federal Judicial Center, 1987).

Stephen C. Yeazell, *Collective Litigation as Collective Action*, 1989 U. ILL. L. REV. 43.

JAMES H. YOUNG, THE TOADSTOOL MILLIONAIRES: A SOCIAL HISTORY OF PATENT MEDICINES IN AMERICA BEFORE FEDERAL REGULATION (Princeton, NJ: Princeton Univeristy Press, 1972).

Index